In the Beginning

Salleys Kitchen

A novel

by

Bruce Wise Weeks

IN THE BEGINNING

SALLEYS KITCHEN

by Bruce Wise Weeks

ISBN-13: 978-0-692-05991-3

ISBN-10: 0-692-05991-1

Cover Design: Jacob Hunt Chambers
               JC Photography & Design
               Townville, South Carolina

First Edition

Printed in the United States of America

A Note to the Reader

Please understand my story is a work of fiction. While the tale may vaguely mention a few of the events that occurred during my boyhood, the story, as a whole, is fiction. Any names or characters thought to represent any persons in particular are just coincidental and they do not have reference to any specific individual, family, or community. Those acquainted with me are well aware of my impulsive obsession to spin yarns and those unfamiliar with me soon find all knowledge gleaned may become part of an eclectic hodgepodge of bits and pieces molded and shaped into a story. Never is there any intent to offend or disrespect anyone, any place or anything, in any way. However, I do not apologize for any emotions the historical facts may evoke.

I find great pleasure and understanding in placing imaginary characters among the historical facts and then allowing their voices and actions to play out a story of how the events may have occurred.

Also, I must offer an explanation for the title being Salleys Kitchen as opposed to Salley's Kitchen. I grew up in the cotton fields with African Americans and loved them with all of my heart. They had a colloquial language that was heavily influenced by the Gullah people from the coast. In a layman's way I have tried to illustrate their actual voice and dialect. Putting an 's' on the end of names of places was part of their voice. They would not say, "That boy is from Salley" - rather, they would say, "Dat bo bez fom Salleys." It was a distinct part of their everyday language, as well as mine, for a time. To honor and remember my friends of the field, I choose to use Salleys Kitchen as the title of my book. I offer my sincere apologies to all teachers of English grammar.

Dedication

This book is dedicated to Debbie Weeks in great appreciation for the immeasurable amount of time she contributed in bringing this story to publication. Debbie is my cousin, my editor and my confidante in all matters concerning this book and without her continuing support, this book would still be a tale stored on my computer. She is my corrector, my motivator and my inspirer. I may have been the sailboat, but she was the wind. For those of you who will enjoy this book, it is Debbie that you must thank for getting it to you.

Introduction

In the Beginning - Salleys Kitchen is the second in a series of stories that make up the epic tale of Salleys Kitchen. With these words, the history of this imaginary community, set among the sand hills of western South Carolina, is told in unrelenting detail. The history of every generation of the venerable Sullivan family, for better or worse, is laid bare for all to see. From the arrival of an Irish immigrant named James Anthony Sullivan just before the birth of our nation, through the early 1990s, each ancestor of this stalwart family is showcased and his or her contributions and misdeeds are observed. All of their actions and reactions mirror and commingle with the events that actually occurred in this region of our nation during that same time period. Much like the story of the United States of America, the story of the Sullivan family is a plethora of growing pains, mistakes and recoveries, laden with exhilarating highs and gut-wrenching lows, a mosaic of resiliency, determination and independence.

It is my intention to seamlessly intertwine the historical facts within the lives of the characters in this story. I hope this approach offers you an unobstructed and realistic view of the past. It must be remembered, however, this is a work of fiction and for that reason, it is incumbent upon each reader to determine where the truth ends and fiction begins. As an old educator, I believe within that task lies the immense joy of this tale.

Prologue

In my mind's eye, I can clearly see the community and the people of Salleys Kitchen. It is a mostly unheralded community situated at a sandy crossroad along the banks of the South Edisto River. Through the lives of the imaginary Sullivan family, this story will reveal the history of that community as it parallels the history of our nation. From its inception in the late1700s, we will follow the people of this sand hill community through the wars and turbulent times that threatened their very existence. I hope to open wide a window through which all can see the true and astonishing events that have shaped this region and our nation. Though part of the original fabric of our nation, the first Europeans that settled in this backcountry region have been largely forgotten through time. Their contributions and sacrifices, however, played a large role in the creation of our nation. Without their efforts, the dreams of freedom and independence for all living in this land could have been deferred for quite a long time.

Many of the people now living among the sand hills and longleaf pines of this region feel their home is situated in the middle of nowhere and offers only an immaterial past of no great consequence. Nothing could be further from the truth! The amazing and world-changing events that occurred in and around this unique region were crucial in forming the United States of America. This remarkable story must be shared with all people, but most especially, it must be shared with those who have long made this area home, for many are unknowingly descendants of those strong and determined people who sacrificed so much to create this country. For untold generations, the descendants of these irrepressible people have baptized their children in the tannin colored waters of the region and ingrained in them the steeped traditions and strong beliefs that are its hallmark. Many of the family names that now permeate this area are the family names of the pioneers and founders of this very region and have long been associated with the area's rich history and culture. There is much to tell and much more to learn.

In the Beginning

Salleys Kitchen

(continued from Salleys Kitchen)

Chapter One

From the moment she sat down in her brother's truck, Salley was deluged with reasons why she should never return to Salleys Kitchen. Having no more tears to cry, she sat next to the passenger window like a department store mannequin as the wind danced through her long ebony hair. The most hurtful of the things her brother was saying was she should never see James again. The shock of that statement hit Salley like a knife to the heart. She almost choked at the thought of never seeing James again. Salley knew it would be impossible for her to reply to her brother's tirade without getting physical, so she sat silent, like a pressure cooker building steam. Being separated from James made Salley feel as if her world was falling apart. She felt vulnerable and weak without him in her life. Each time she was forced to think of never seeing him again, another block was torn from the foundation of her soul. The tragic occurrences of the previous night were still simmering in her brain like a surreal nightmare and the thought of Sully lying in that hissing and pumping machine made her sick to her stomach. As her brother's bombardment continued, she tuned him out and stared into oblivion, thinking of her father and the boy she loved.

Once they arrived at Dr. Carr's office and Salley's brother explained the circumstances, the vet was more than willing to accommodate her horse, Spot. Though she was gentle with him and talked softly to him as she backed him out of the trailer, he was a bundle of nerves, jerking the lead rope and shying away from everything and everyone. When he was finally in a nice clean stable next to a mare that was about to foal, he seemed baffled at what all had occurred and what was about to occur. He didn't kick the walls or stomp and paw the ground as he usually did, but nickered soft and low, as if crying. When Salley left him alone, he began to belt out his protest in a long mournful moan that the old vet said he had never heard from a horse. Her beloved Appaloosa continued his mournful cries as they pulled her brother's truck around back and unhooked the trailer. It was all Salley could do to keep from running to comfort the grieving horse. With her insides being torn apart, the only thing she had on her mind was getting to the hospital and Sully. Spot would, regretfully, have to wait for her attention.

Once back in the truck, her brother, Andy, renewed his lecture, this time wagging his finger at her and telling her she was never to go back to Salleys Kitchen again. He placed particular emphasis on telling her she was to never see James again. Having not been around his sister as she had grown into a woman, he was foolishly unaware of her volatility and propensity to suddenly attack those who goaded her. He was about to receive an education on how not to treat Salley Sullivan.

Suddenly, something snapped in Salley's mind. In a flash of rage, she grabbed her brother's throat and shoved his head against the driver's window. Just as quickly, she used her other hand to open the driver's door and as it flung open, she kicked her nagging brother from the truck. Quickly shoving the shifter into reverse as James had taught her, she popped the clutch while flooring the accelerator and the pickup lurched backwards as her brother rolled into the ditch. Stomping the brakes to stop the truck's backwards motion, she forgot to depress the clutch and in a fit of anger, snatched the shifter down into first gear. The grinding gears finally meshed together as she floored the accelerator and sped down the narrow street toward the hospital. Having only driven a few times with James, her driving was suspect and she swerved from shoulder to shoulder on the road. Struggling to keep the vehicle on her side of the white lines, the novice driver made no attempt to shift the gears as she made her way to the hospital. The few cars that met her knew immediately that they should just pull over and allow her to use both lanes.

Entering the hospital parking lot, she made her way to the front entrance and slammed on the brakes. Screeching to a halt, everyone was watching as she hopped out. Seeing the parking offender, a security guard yelled and ran toward her.

"Hey, young lady! You can't park there! You'll have to move that truck to a regular parking spot!"

As she turned to face him, intense anger shot from her eyes like summer lightening. The guard stopped in his tracks, recoiling. Cautiously, he said, "That truck has got to be moved! It can't stay in that spot." Keeping his distance, he recognized the concentrated wrath she was focusing in his direction. His attitude waned somewhat as she turned and threw something at him. Seeing her actions, he instinctively raised his forearm to protect his head. The truck keys hit his arm, then jingled to the ground.

"Here, you can have it! I damn sure can't drive it - do what you want with it!" With that pronouncement, she bounded up the steps and into the huge brick building.

Trying to compose herself, she combed her hair away from her eyes with her fingers as she walked down the hospital corridor to the big room that housed Sully and that awful machine. Pushing the door open to the ward, she saw Sully buried up to his neck in a gurgling and humming iron coffin. She painted a smile on her face as she walked into Sully's view. Her mother rose from the chair where she had been sitting next to Sully's head. Without a word, Salley stroked her father's unruly hair and kissed him on the forehead. Sully beamed as if he were seeing the sun after three dreary days.

"Bonjour, mademoiselle - and what mischief have you created so early on this bright and blissful day?"

"Sully, why do you always think I have been causing trouble? And what makes you think it's a blissful day? That sounds kind of weird coming from a man buried up to his neck in a machine!"

Sully's laughter could be heard in every corner of the ward as he cackled loudly and said, "Come - sit here beside me and tell me what you have done. Any day that I am fortunate enough to see that 'devil may care' look on your face is, of course, my dear, a blissful day!"

Looking at her mother, Salley said, "Well, your son might disagree with you at the moment."

Again, the roar of laughter filled the room and Sully demanded to know every detail of her encounter with her brother. As she told him, verbatim, what she had done to Andy, Sully was laughing so much, she had to wipe the spit from his lips, but she did not tell him about Blackie or James or Boot Cutter. Sully knew she was not telling him everything and he told her to lean close to his face as he whispered, "When your mother leaves, you can tell me everything that happened." He looked into her eyes and as she had always known, he could read her like a book!

Dr. Baughman's face appeared around the corner and he asked, "What have I missed? I heard brakes screeching outside and then as I approached this ward, I could hear laughter. My guess is the two sounds are related and involve Sully and his beautiful daughter. I so want to join the jocularity of this rowdy bunch! Fill me in Sully - what's so funny?"

Still smiling, Sully answered his doctor. "My daughter may become a teacher. She just taught my son, Andy, an invaluable lesson on the decorum demanded while in her presence. Upon his delayed arrival you may notice, per chance, a difference in my son's attitude toward his sister, Salley, along with a little road rash."

Looking to Salley, the medicine man inquired further, "Did he have an accident?"

Salley unabashedly looked at him and said, "No, he lectured me all the way from Salleys Kitchen to Aiken. I got tired of him trying to boss me around, so I shoved him out of his truck!"

Quickly and with a smile on his face, the doc probed further, "I hope his truck was at a stop when you ejected him."

Unable to control herself any longer, she smiled as she said, "Well, we weren't going too fast and besides, he rolled into the ditch pretty quickly. I don't think he hurt anything seriously except his pride and he'll get over that!"

At this point, Sully and his doctor were both roaring with laughter and Salley was again wiping the spittle from the corners of Sully's mouth. As the two calmed down, the doctor asked how he was feeling and Sully delighted in saying, "I'm always exuberant when my Salley is near. Her presence has always been the best tonic for my melancholy mood!"

The doctor turned for the door while offering a parting shot. "There's no doubt about that! Just the mention of her name makes me sit up and pay attention, too. Your Salley is quite a girl. I will try to never anger her." Sully was laughing as the doctor left with Salley's mother following him out of the room.

Pulling her chair close to Sully's head, Salley leaned down and kissed him again on the cheek as she asked how he was faring. He dismissed her question and demanded she tell him the truth of the events of the night. Through tears and moments when she was overcome, she told him the complete and gut-wrenching truth about Blackie's death and Boot Cutter's involvement. Her worst news for Sully was that she had no idea where James was at present.

Sully was very concerned about his young neighbor's whereabouts and feared for his safety. His heart was broken at the news that Blackie had been poisoned and that James had to be the one to put him down. Lying helplessly in the machine, he could see the grief draped across his precious daughter's face as she told him about James. Sully was quick to remind Salley that her James was now a lost soul with no home and no one to call his friend. This reminder further ripped at Salley's heart and she was, again, momentarily overcome. *What could she do? Who could she get to check on him? Was he still alive?* As wave after wave of emotions crashed upon her heart, she did something she promised herself she would not do: she cried in Sully's presence.

The iron lung had Sully trapped and left him feverishly wanting to free his arms and hold his daughter close to him once again. Sully had been told that moving his head was a risky proposition. Even so, the sight of Salley crying tore at his heart and he began to turn his head from side to side and moan in frustration. Seeing and hearing her father so distraught made Salley quickly regain her composure and press her cheek on his face to stop him from moving his head. He calmed down and they stayed in that position until her brother and mother entered the room.

There was an awkward silence with brother and mother staring at Salley. With his equanimity restored, Sully spoke, "I presume, Andy, that you have been enlightened as to what your younger sibling is willing to tolerate. Let's use this experience as an example of the volatility our emotions can evoke and try to move forward. The recent events perpetrated by those hoodlums in Salleys Kitchen have placed a tremendous strain on our family. If we are to remain a family, we must always remember to treat each other with dignity and respect."

After he spoke, a deafening silence filled the room while Salley's brother and mother glared at her. In a manner she had perfected as a little girl, she moved close to Sully and smiled back at them. When the silence was too much to endure, Sully said, "I see you have much to learn, my son." After those words from his father, Andy moved to sit in a chair away from Sully. He folded his arms tightly across his chest.

Finally, Polly spoke up and told everyone that the doctor gave Sully a good report and besides his spinal injury, everything appeared OK. It was not a glowing report, however, and it was taken by all with a grain of salt. The doctor had explained earlier that the x-ray had clearly shown the reason for his paralysis. Sully had sustained severe trauma to the Atlas and the Axis, or in layman's terms, the C-1 and C-2 vertebra in his spine. The doctor warned that in his weakened condition, Sully would be susceptible to any germ and even a cold could cause his death.

A nurse stuck her head in the room and told Salley that there was someone in the waiting room who wanted to speak with her. She looked at Sully and he nodded yes to her, thinking it would be James. He didn't say it out loud, but she knew what he was thinking. As soon as she left the room, Sully spoke to his son and his wife in a most serious manner.

"Salley and James are very much in love and I will not have anything or anyone coming between them. That boy risked his life to save me and his act of bravery has put him in constant peril. There are people in Salleys Kitchen who would like to see his demise. I want you to take the two of them home with you to the mountains. I will make arrangements to pay for whatever they need to be together. I hope this morning's experience has illustrated the need for Salley to be somewhat independent and not told what to do. James is a smart boy and Salley is a very smart girl and I believe they will make good decisions as to how they will proceed with their lives." No words were spoken as mother and son stared at the floor.

With Salley out of the room, Polly decided to break the news to Sully that they had to go back to their lives in the mountains and if James and Salley were to go with them it would have to be soon. They would be spending only one more day with him and then would be leaving. With promises to return as soon as possible, they were going to leave the hospital soon to pack up for their trip home. Sully seemed somewhat relieved at the news.

Chapter 2

With a little spring in her step at the possibility of James being in the waiting room, Salley managed a little smile as she turned the corner and entered the waiting room. Quickly jumping to his feet as she entered the room, Jon Chesterfield, Jr. moved toward her and embraced her.

Salley was taken aback by Jon's appearance and she stood like a statue as he wrapped his arms around her shoulders. She was even more shocked when he kissed her on the cheek. "I am so sorry to hear of your father's accident. I want you to know I'm here to help in any way I can." Stepping back from him, she offered him a fake smile and asked him what he was doing at the hospital. He told her that one of his father's friends saw Spot in Dr. Carr's stable and asked why he was being boarded at his facility. Dr. Carr told the person the entire story, as much as he knew, and Jonathan Chesterfield, Sr. had asked around to complete the saga. He told her he was so sorry she had been terrified so needlessly and again told her he was there to help her in any way he could.

Overwhelmed, Salley didn't know what to say. In a flash, as if he had practiced, Jon, Jr. offered to move Spot to the paddocks where his father's polo ponies were kept and trained. He knew just what to say. "Spot doesn't need to be shut up in a stable with all of those sick horses. Let me take him to the polo meadows where he can run and have some room. My father's people will take excellent care of him. It would be a small way I could help."

Still shocked at his presence, Salley was dumbfounded as she stumbled to give him an answer. Hastily trying to decide if it was a good move or not, she knew she did not want Spot to be shut up with a bunch of horses in a sick bay and she knew he would have excellent care at the Chesterfield compound. He certainly could not go back to Salleys Kitchen. In the heat of the moment, she consented to let Jon, Jr. take charge of Spot and told him she would call Dr. Carr and tell him of the move. Again, he embraced her and kissed her on the cheek, then hurried off to see that her horse had the best care available.

Stunned, Salley walked back to Sully's room with a perplexed look on her face.

Taking her seat beside Sully, Salley touched his face with her hand and he knew immediately James was not the visitor in the waiting room. In despair, she held his head with her hands and placed her cheek next to her father's. As the two communed, Salley's mother said, "From the look on your face, I take it your James was not in the waiting room? From what I hear, there are a lot of people who want to see him." Just before they left the room, Salley's brother looked at her and put a folded newspaper on the table near the door. Then mother and son walked out of the room.

Telling Sully about Jon Chesterfield, Jr. and his offer to board Spot at his father's facility, Salley was apprehensive about his generosity and Sully told her straight up, "My dear darling, that boy wants you as his wife!"

Salley hooted at that announcement and dismissed it as something that would never, ever happen. She felt in her heart that James was somewhere waiting on her and he would soon come and join her beside Sully. She told Sully that James was her soulmate and she would never want any other man except him. The mention of his name out loud made her shiver and her heart panged for his touch.

Salley walked over to get the folded newspaper so she could read it to her father. She wondered why her brother had left it. Opening it, she read aloud the blaring headlines across the top: **4 Presumed Dead – 3 Severely Burned in Store Explosion**. As she continued to read aloud, she gasped after she read the words below the headlines. Roy Asholee's store had exploded in multiple fireballs, killing him and his wife, along with Boot Cutter and Wesley Staley. Three other men sitting near the front of the store were able to escape, but were severely burned. It went on to say James Williams, Sr. was sitting in a pickup truck near the store at the time of the explosion, but was unharmed. He told the newspaper reporter that his son, James Williams, Jr., was the last person to enter the store before it exploded. It went on to say Williams, Jr. was out of town attending the Agriculture College and was unavailable for comment. Salley was horrified at the news and a million thoughts flashed through her head. *Did James blow up Roy Asholee's store? How did he do it? Maybe it was just a coincidence that he was there. It's good that he left Salleys Kitchen and is using the scholarship he won to attend college. He's gone - he's safe, but will I ever see him again? Oh God - please no! What will I do without him? Oh God - why, why, why?*

Hearing what Salley read out loud, Sully immediately recognized the pain his daughter was experiencing because of her separation from James. He was extremely limited in his ability to soothe her, but as was his hallmark, he launched into one of his unorthodox problem-solving methods in a desperate attempt to placate his daughter for a while.

"Salley, he's safe and I know he will come back! I don't know when, but I know he will come back to you. I know it will be hard, but you must be strong and patient while he's away. I know in the end, things will work out. You two are meant for each other. I don't know how long it will be, but I do know you two will be together again.

"Sweetheart, you are my North Star. You are the one person who always gave me a sense of direction. Having you in my life makes me a better person. I love you with all of my heart."

After those profound words, Salley's tears began to cease. She snubbed a few times, then walked over and held Sully's head with both of her hands. Kissing him on the forehead, she said, "I love you with all of my heart, too, Daddy!" A quiet calm enveloped the room as Salley sat down beside Sully and stared into his eyes. With a nearby napkin, Salley wiped the tears that were forming in his eyes and said, "We are two peas in a pod, Sully. How did we get in such a mess? Why is so much evil being heaped upon us?"

Without missing a beat, Sully launched into his story. "That is precisely what I want you to know… who you are and how you got here. Sweetheart, within your blood runs the goodness of the Sullivan family. My great-great-grandfather, the first Sullivan to live on this land, was a driven community builder. He had an inner longing to create a society of like-mined people who cared about their neighbors. His greatest desire was to live and work among people who wanted to improve their lives, improve the lives of their children and improve the lives of those around them. That desire was in his blood. It was part of his makeup, but unfortunately, that gene was not inherited by all of his descendants and that is a shame. But for those who did receive his propensity to help others, it is the greatest responsibility they have in their lives. This yearning - to give of one's self to others - can become a curse, especially when malevolent people are present. Spiteful people spread intolerance, jealousy and narrow mindedness and this evil grows and festers in the minds of those all around. My great-great-grandfather's dream sometime seems like an unreachable dream and many, including myself, have faltered before reaching that lofty goal. But it is not impossible and you, my dear, have inherited that task. For better or worse, my child, you have received the genes that create the undeniable predisposition of civic duty. It is in your soul and though you have not recognized it yet, like cream in raw milk, it will rise to the top of your life, soon."

Salley wanted to protest and tell her father he was wrong, but she knew it was useless to argue with him and besides, she wanted him to be happy with her. Sully wanted to take her mind off of James' absence and he knew his story of the Sullivan family history would do just that.

"Your youth and inexperience will not permit you to appreciate the words I speak today, but if you will hear them and store them away in your subconscious mind, they will ring true someday and give you solace. Come close to me and listen to my words, for I want you to hear everything I say and hold it in your heart and soul forever."

Smiling, Salley pulled her chair as close to her father as possible and leaned in so she could hear his every word. Sully asked her to hold his cup and straw to his lips so he could take a drink of water. Then, with a twinkle in his eye, he launched into the history of his family. At first, he told her about the people who occupied the land before the arrival of the first James Anthony Sullivan. He said, "It took me a half century of gleaning every scrap of information available to put together the history of my family. One of the largest contributions was quite a surprise and came from a historical preservation group in Augusta. An old trunk was found in a building about to be demolished so a new highway could be built. The workers who found the old trunk knew it was a treasure trove of history, but they did not know how important it would be to me. The trunk was given to the local historical society and they preserved its contents. Among the items in the trunk was the diary of a woman named Lucy O'Cain. She was a close friend of George Galphin and his name became the foundation for my genealogical journey to find all of our family. George was the first of our ancestors to arrive in the New World and his name had appeared often in my search for the Sullivan family's history.

"Through my network of history buff friends, I was told of the find of the diary and its tie to George Galphin. It soon became an invaluable resource and revealed much about the first James Anthony Sullivan to arrive in America. Lucy O'Cain was one of the first women to live in Augusta just after its inception. She told of her association with George Galphin in her journal, but described in greatest detail, her friendship with an Irish indentured servant girl named Rose. Apparently, she had come to the New World on the same ship as my great-great-grandfather and the two had fallen in love during the crossing. It is a sad love story and the most fascinating bit of history that I have ever read. Knowing it was written by someone who actually knew and loved one of my ancestors took my breath away. I will admit that I had to use my imagination at times to fit some of the puzzle pieces together, but my imagination was fueled by reams of documented history from hundreds of hours of research. As far as I'm concerned, my story is the true history of the Sullivan family. It is as close as humanly possible to the truth!"

If Salley had been thinking of other things as Sully started his story, she was now focused on every word he uttered.

**

"The new colony of South Carolina grew quickly along the Atlantic shore, especially around the port city of Charles

18

Town. As the population grew, a coastal culture was quickly adopted among the civilized people in that area of the New World. However, when some of the more daring and adventurous settlers began moving to the interior of the colony, a new culture arose among the backcountry populations. As civilization stretched its needy fingers into the backcountry of South Carolina, the need for an overland route to the largest sea port of Charles Town became a necessity. The Savannah River, which separated the colony of South Carolina from the colony of Georgia, connected the backcountry with Savannah, Georgia. Indian trade goods and people could easily be ferried down river, but there was no settlement or center of trade along the fall line of the Savannah River at that time. The bustling port city of Charles Town along the South Carolina coast, however, was connected to the backcountry by a narrow path that soon became a road known as the Charles Town Road. One of the byway's western trade centers was the township of New Windsor, between Town Creek and Horse Creek, just inside South Carolina along the fall line of the Savannah River. Deer skins harvested by the Native American tribes were in great demand in England and trading with the local tribes to obtain them became a thriving business. The deer skin trade promised to make those who worked in this dangerous business very rich men. The little village of New Windsor quickly grew into a bustling community and trade center in the backcountry. The Charles Town Road became a busy thoroughfare with foot traffic and long trains of pack mules and horses moving to and from the port city.

"General Oglethorpe, a member of the British Parliament, was able to make a treaty with the tribes of the Muskogee Creek Indians. He also created a settlement at the fall line of the Savannah River, just inside the colony of Georgia. Oglethorpe offered greater inducements for immigrants to settle in Augusta. With greater incentives, Oglethorpe's Georgia township grew exponentially, but New Windsor began to shrink. The once promising little village eventually disappeared from the map. Augusta soon became the major trading center in the backcountry and the western terminus of the Charles Town Road.

"George Galphin, an Irishman and renowned Indian

trader, obtained a large tract of land along the sparkling riverbank of the Savannah River. He became the largest landowner in the waning New Windsor township. He created a plantation and trading center only 8 miles below Augusta, on the South Carolina side of the river. River traffic increased daily along the Savannah and Galphin's trading center, named Silver Bluff, became a thriving community. He rapidly gained a wide-ranging influence. With a notorious sense for business and excellent interpersonal skills, Galphin's trading impact ranged far and wide into South Carolina, Georgia, Alabama and what is now the Pan Handle of Florida.

"Galphin was the owner of two huge plantations, Silver Bluff in South Carolina on the eastern bank of the Savannah and Galphinton on the south bank of the Ogeechee River in Georgia. Both were large and productive. By 1760, this semi-literate Irish immigrant was by far the richest and most influential man in the backcountry of South Carolina. At his pinnacle, Galphin was looked to as a leader of the region and his sway was felt at the highest levels of government in both South Carolina and Georgia. Many families today who inhabit the South Carolina side of the CSRA (Central Savannah River Area) have ties, in some way, to George Galphin.

"Success, as it always does, attracts many to its bright and shiny aura. In the winter, sometime during the late 1760s, George Galphin would have a visitor - a young Englishman. The newcomer was a businessman/adventurer who had just been granted control of a large section of the longleaf pine forest not too far from Galphin's bustling Silver Bluff Plantation. The young aristocrat had been trying to find out as much as possible about the highly lauded and successful Irishman and had traveled up the Savannah River to seek him out. He hoped to glean from Galphin the secrets of his abundant success in the colonies.

"Fresh off of the Savannah-Augusta Trail, he stepped out of his carriage at Silver Bluff and tossed a warm scarf around his neck as he drank in his surroundings. In the same venue as the fine homes and estates along the Thames River, east of London, this prosperous backcountry lord had a fine Federal style two story brick house. The brick outbuildings were a site to behold. As the Englishman gazed at the compound, he covetously concluded to himself, *If some Irish trash can do this well, I should easily have success beyond all measure.*

"Taming the cutting edge of the New World frontier took a special breed of individual, one who sought adventure and didn't mind risking his all from time to time to better his lot. George Galphin was just that kind of man and the young Englishman admired him and, as well, desired what he had amassed. He observed the Irishman's operations, including large open fields producing crops, herds of cattle scattered about the woodlands, along with a very busy sawmill and gristmill being operated by slave labor. The Englishman's spirits were bolstered by his visit to Silver Bluff and he felt his success in this New World was guaranteed.

"Well-heeled and well-connected, the recently arrived European opportunists fueled their egos with the thrill of entrepreneurial risk-taking in the colonies. This included the arrogant young Brit who appeared at Galphin's home asking questions. As an American Patriot, Galphin was not sure what to make of the stranger. With the hostilities in Boston now being called the Boston Massacre, all Englishmen were viewed with a suspect eye by the colonists in the South. Though Galphin did not think much of the Englishman who introduced himself as Alister Abrams Alwhite, III, he was polite and agreeable in answering the visitor's questions, giving as little information as necessary. King George III's Redcoat soldiers were now in Massachusetts and New York and most of the 'independent-minded' colonists in the South distrusted all things British. Business, however, was business and whenever an opportunity presented itself, George Galphin would be the first to take full advantage of it, even if he was dealing with the devil himself. George had not publicly renounced his loyalty to the King, but he hated anyone who wanted to stick a hand in his till, including King George, III. That said, if there was money to be made, George Galphin always had his hand in the pot, especially be it an English pot.

"After their original meeting, Alwhite bid Galphin adieu and climbed back into his carriage to travel the 8 miles further to Augusta. Taking a room at a travel house and establishing his base, he enjoyed the convenience of the pub next door and quickly threw back a few shots of whiskey as he settled in. He had been emboldened by his little detour to Galphin's place and was anxious to climb back into his carriage and began reconnoitering the area. Hoping to gain insight into just how others were harvesting the profitable pine trees from the indigenous forest, he felt he had much to learn. Careful and calculating, he was well aware of the troubles in New England and the ill feelings among the Southern Rebels, but he felt sure there were enough Loyalists and Tories in the area to keep things civil. As for doing business in the colonies, he felt sure the King would at some point squash the little rebellion and exert British dominance and control over the colonies once again. He assumed it would be just a matter of time before the colonists came to their senses and realized their foolish desire for independence would never come to fruition.

"Having spent most of his first year traveling from one logging operation to another in the backcountry, Alister Abrams Alwhite, III soon had a plan for harvesting the prized trees. Having visited a logging operation in the Barnwell district, he was on his way back to his base of operation in Augusta. The weather was freezing and it was drizzling rain as his carriage traversed the bumpy, rutted, unimproved road. Thinking of Galphin's fine home, he bumped the top of the coach with his cane and yelled for his driver to stop by Silver Bluff. He was hoping for a few shots of whiskey and a fireplace by which he could warm.

"The coachman reined the horses to a stop in front of the brick house and the Englishman stepped out of the carriage. As he approached the front entrance of the fine brick home, a young, well-dressed Black man opened the elaborately carved door and bowed. Alwhite entered the warm home and shed his cloak, handing it to the doorman. Turning back to enter the foyer, he immediately encountered an Indian man who looked to be between 25 and 30 years old. The Indian was loudly berating the house wenches in his native tongue and seemed at home in the huge house. He had the servants and slaves scurrying about with his orders. Upon noticing the Englishman, the Native American's first words were very abrupt, but spoken in perfect English.

"'Who are you and why are you in my father's house?'

"Politely, but sarcastically, the visitor said, 'I am Alister Abrams Alwhite, III from London, England and I was invited to visit by the owner of this house!' Then he curtly asked, 'And just whom might I be addressing?'

"In a very out-of-character move for a house wench, a light-skinned mulatto woman standing in the shadows scurried in from the periphery for an introduction. She looked at the floor as she offered introductions for the two men.

"'May I offer to you, Mr. Alwhite, George Galphin the Younger, Mr. George Galphin, Sr.'s son and namesake. He is from Coweta of the Lower Creek Nation.' Offering a little decorum to the situation, she hoped to make the encounter amicable as she continued to face the floor and avoid eye contact. With their questions somewhat answered, the two lowered their hackles, but each kept an eye on the other.

"Very matter-of-factly, the Creek man said, 'George Galphin is not here!' It was at this point that a beautiful and very precocious young girl came rushing into the parlor. She was not the least bit taken back by the presence of the Englishman, but seemed overjoyed to see the self-assured Indian and the timorous servant.

"The young girl was Salley Halona Galphin, George the Younger's daughter by Clarissa, the very house wench who had introduced the two men. Dressed in European clothes, Salley had earlier returned from Augusta where she attended school. The Englishman was immediately taken by her charm and appearance as she curtsied to him and spoke.

"'Hello, Mama. Hello, Father. Goboy brought me home from the academy in Augusta. I am so happy that you are here together.'

"George the Younger, however, did not enjoy the niceties of European conversation, nor did he like to see his daughter in the White man's clothes. Before his wife could introduce her, he quickly instructed his daughter to go upstairs and change her clothes. He also told her to stay there until he came up to get her.

"Without an argument, she said, 'Very well, Father, I will change and wait for you. I want you to tell me about your travels in The Nation.' With a flourish, she moved to her mother, hugged and kissed her and said, 'Oh, Mama, I have so much to tell you. You won't believe what I've heard from Boston.' Then she turned to the Englishman, made a little curtsy and dismissed herself to climb the stairs to her room.

"As she disappeared at the top of the ornate stairway, the visitor stood with his mouth agape. He could not believe she was the offspring of this Indian and house wench standing in front of him. The woman kept her eyes on the floor and was told gruffly by George the Younger to return to the kitchen and finish preparing the evening meal. As his daughter had done, he then disappeared up the stairs.

"As Clarissa made her way to a doorway in the back of the house, the Englishman bluntly ask her a question.

"'Is that girl really YOUR daughter and is that INDIAN really her father?'

"With a smile, but looking down and not making eye contact, Clarissa replied, 'Yes, she is my daughter. George the Younger is her father. He first came to Silver Bluff when we were young and we played together in the red brick stream. When he visits his father's house he often chooses to sleep with me.'

"Startled, the visitor continued his questioning. 'But she is as white as I am! How can that be?'

"Just before she disappeared through the rear door of the house, she looked down at the floor and quietly said, 'My mother was French Creole. She was the first house slave to work in George Galphin's home. I was born here at Silver Bluff. My father was Irish. He worked with George Galphin in The Nation. He was killed before I was born. My mother's master is Mr. George, as am I. I began working in this house as a little girl and George the Younger would come here with his father from his home at Coweta. We played together and when we got older, he took me to his bed. Now, we still sleep together, some. My daughter, Salley, was born here and George Galphin, Sr. is her master, too, but he dotes on her. George Galphin. Sr. has many children and grandchildren. Most have mixed blood, but he makes them all go to school. He is kind to all of us!'

"With that pronouncement, she withdrew from the house and the Englishman turned for the door that had been opened by the doorman. Shaking his head as the Black man helped him don his cloak, he headed back to his carriage and was thinking to himself, *That Irish trash has fathered more mongrels than a cur bitch!*

"In the early spring of 1770, after a period of reconnaissance, the young aspiring timber mogul traveled to Charles Town and hired an experienced logging crew. He also purchased a man slave and a woman slave to tend to his needs and cook for his men. Once back at the pine forest, he had the crew of loggers first build a small building with a bunkroom and kitchen. He then had them construct an abode for himself, after which he had them begin cutting the tall pine trees. His plan was to float the logs down the South Edisto River to the Big Edisto River and then on to Edisto Island, where a sawmill would mill them into the highly sought-after lumber. He was in a hurry to begin logging.

"Not fully understanding the problems he faced, a year later he realized he was losing far more logs than he was milling on the island. It was obvious that the locals along the river were profiting more from his trees than he. Facing such a loss in the shipment of his trees, he decided to mill the lumber at the source and haul it overland to Augusta. That, he figured, would be a much better alternative.

"He remembered that George Galphin owned a gristmill and sawmill at Silver Bluff and he also remembered that they were built by and were being profitably run by an old man who lived on his property. He was a free man of color and a talented millwright who had been a slave as a boy, but had been manumitted at the death of his elderly owner. Now, he saw to the operation and maintenance of millworks on Galphin's plantation.

"The Englishman believed he had found the answer to his conundrum and in the spring of 1772, he made his way again to the Irishman's fine home."

***

Salley was fascinated with Sully's story, but she knew

he needed to rest. When the nurses came in to check his urine bag and give his medications, she insisted he try to sleep for a little while. After promising him she would be sitting right beside him when he awoke, his eyes became droopy and finally closed. The nurse told her he would be sleeping for a few hours and she needed to get something to eat and try to rest some herself. She dashed down to the cafeteria and grabbed a sandwich, then hurried back to Sully's side. Sully was asleep when Dr. Baughman came into the room. He did not wake up, so the doctor talked to Salley and told her that her father was a strong-willed man. He said that most people in Sully's situation give up and begin to wither away. That was not happening with her father. His vital signs were good, his food intake was good and his determination was excellent. Salley was encouraged by that news and she also had a request for the old doctor friend of Sully's.

"Would you by any chance have a recording machine I could use until I can buy one for myself? Sully is telling me the history of our family and I want to make sure I don't forget any part of his story."

The gentleman in the white lab coat smiled and said, "I have exactly what you need in my office. It won't take me but a minute to walk back and grab it." With that statement, he dashed out of the room and was back in a flash with an old wheel to wheel tape recorder. He set it up on a rolling hospital tray table and pulled it up next to Salley. After plugging it in, he put on a new wheel of tape and showed her how to start the recording by pushing two buttons at once. Salley gave him a hug and he seemed as happy as if she had given him a million dollars. He was truly glad he could offer her his assistance.

Sully continued to sleep and soon, Salley joined him in a fitful sleep. Before she realized she was awake, she heard Sully's voice.

"You are truly the most beautiful thing in my life, sweetheart!" Wiping the drool from her mouth, she sat up and pushed the hair from her face, then smiled at her father.

"Oh, Daddy, you tell me that every time you wake me up. If you keep doing that, I'm going to start believing you!" Wiping his eyes and face with a damp cloth and brushing his unruly mop of hair, Salley kissed him on the forehead and began to tear up. Quickly, Sully tried to change her train of thought.

"Where had we gotten with the story of your ancestors?"

Thinking back, Salley easily remembered the old, white-haired free Black man named Clinalee.

"Oh, yes, that's exactly where we left off. Clinalee was the cantankerous old millwright who worked for George Galphin. He was an odd individual of few words and did not like being around White men, especially English White men."

Salley stopped him, saying, "Hold on just a minute. I borrowed something from your doctor and I want to make sure we use it every time you tell me part of this story. Placing the microphone near his head, she pushed the two buttons to start the recording, then settled in beside him and said, "OK, now we're ready."

Sully was so proud of her. He beamed as he began his story again.

***

"Other than the Irishman for whom he had worked for 30 years, Clinalee seldom acknowledged the presence of a white man, only offering 'yassir' and 'nawsir' when prompted. He had grown up in Savannah and learned the trade of millwright from his father while they were both slaves. At age 20, his master died and his master's wife, a Quaker, freed all of her husband's slaves. He and his father were very careful not to announce they were free men of color and continued working in their old shop. That shop was where they met George Galphin and upon his father's death, Clinalee made a beeline to Silver Bluff to work exclusively for the Irishman. That had been over 30 years ago and after showing George Galphin he could harness the power of the creek to run a mill, he had built a very profitable business for his boss man. Over the years, old age had crept up on the mechanically-minded old African and he had a talk with Mister George about getting him some help.

"The millwright did not associate with the slaves whom his boss man owned. He was a freedman and his attitude about slavery was very unusual. He did not want a slave as a helper.

Clinalee deplored slavery, but he worked daily with those enslaved, never acknowledging their plight. He always seemed gruff and irritable to the others who worked at Silver Bluff and most did not try to communicate with him. He was a boss man and was to be treated as such and he never let any of those who worked for him forget that fact.

"After a bout of back trouble had pretty much stopped his day-to-day toil in the mills, it became obvious he needed a helper and his need could no longer be deferred. Confiding in Mister George, he told him his days of working in the mill were over if he didn't get some help soon. No longer a spry young man, he explained that he needed a capable apprentice. He needed an able-bodied person who could work with numbers and also help complete the work his old body would no longer allow him to accomplish.

"After their talk, Mister George assured his old millwright he would find him some help. However, he didn't tell him he was sending notice to his family in Ireland of his need for a young millwright apprentice. Across the ocean, a divine intervention was materializing.

"James Anthony Sullivan, a young Irish lad, was just entering manhood. He was from a poor tenant family and his homeland did not offer him much of a future. Having faced starvation and plague, he had lost his entire family and now faced uncertainty. However, for reasons he had yet to understand, he was about to travel to the New World.

"He watched as his family had methodically succumbed to the plague and his last surviving brother, who had guarded and protected him, had now been taken by the scourge that swept the land. As a boy too young to understand, he watched as each member of his family slowly dissolved before his eyes. In the first 15 years of his life, hardship and grief hounded him daily, causing him to create a facade behind which he hid his emotions. He used hard work as an escape from the misery, but lately, the sweat and aching muscles could no longer mask his inner hurt.

"Now 17 years old and in the throes of despair as his struggles reached a low point, the younger sibling found himself digging his older brother's grave. Pounding the rocky soil with a borrowed pick and shovel, sweat mingled with his tears and stung his eyes. Stopping to wipe the flow of moisture from his face, he watched as the aged parish priest, a family friend, ambled toward the newly opened grave. Arriving without a word, the old priest sat on the pile of soil from the new grave and puffed on a short-stemmed pipe while he gazed onto the green glen that merged with the blue skies beyond the valley. Stopping to catch his breath and wipe his brow, the weary boy looked to the Father, exposing a long tired 'what do you want' grimace. Removing the stubby, knurled pipe from between his teeth, he turned his head and focused his full attention on the lad.

"With a deep Irish brogue, he said, 'I have been in this land of hurt and hunger for over 20 years and I have loved every member of your family that entire time. Not just because your mother, God rest her soul, did everything she could to keep me fed and not because your father, may he rest in peace, never forgot that I love a shot of whiskey now and again and not because you boys kept me and the church in firewood during the cold damp winters, but because every one of you truly cared for my well-being. I did nothing to gain your love, but each and every one of you sought my company only out of kindness. That is a rare thing to find. Yes, indeed, rare among the clans is a family that all love the Church, but yours certainly did. The English tried to kill and enslave us all, the famine threatened to starve us all to death and the plague finished us off. Now, it's only you left and I want to hold on to you like the last remnant of an old and tattered quilt that has given me comfort for so many years, but I am told to let you go. A new quilt of comfort must be started from the last vestige of the old - your family's goodness must survive. James Sullivan, you must be the beginning of a new and different blanket that will spread solace over a new group of family and friends.'

"The puzzled boy with a firm, chiseled body leaned on the shovel he was using and looked with earnest toward the old man of the cloth. 'What do you mean, Father?'

"Standing up on the pile of dirt, the preacher told him, 'Stop by my place at the back of the church after we say the rites and finish the funeral this afternoon.' With those puzzling words, he ambled toward the church where the boy's brother lay in repose in a coffin made from scraps of wood.

"After the graveside rites were spoken and the newly turned soil was covering the coffin, the lad shook hands with the few who had come to watch the burial of his brother. After one last glance at the mound of fresh soil, he turned away and walked alone to the back of the church and knocked on the Father's door. As James opened the door, the aged padre beckoned the boy into the dark room adorned with only a simple table, two chairs and a crucifix hanging on the wall. The oil lamp flickered on the table, illuminating a crude wooden bed with a trunk at its end. Motioning the puzzled boy to sit in one of the chairs, the old priest began speaking.

"'Your father was a man of odd ways in these green glens. Whiskey was never his problem, nor did he gamble or chase after skirts. On the outside, he was one of the jolliest of men I ever knew. In the confessional though, I could feel his hurt as he spoke of the guilt that cloaked his soul. Each time he asked for forgiveness, he was absolved of the things he felt were his misgivings, but in reality, they were just the burdens of a life over which he had no control. His cross to bear was his family, his church and his community and he felt he had let them all down. He struggled in so many ways to improve, but never felt satisfaction from his toil in life. As a self-imposed atonement, he started giving me a few coins and continued for the entire time I knew him. He told me to keep the funds in reserve in case there ever came a time when the church really, really needed to use it. Never thinking of his own hard times or his family, he gave me something every time he could. I kept it in reserve as he had requested and now I believe the church really, really needs to use the money.

"The boy spoke quickly, saying, 'Sure Father, if the church needs the money, I know my father would want you to use it.'

"Walking over to the boy, the aged priest put his hand on his shoulder as he sat in the simple chair. There was a moment of silence before the old man of the cloth spoke.

"'I know he would, my son - I know he would.'

"Placing the stole around his neck, he kissed the cross hanging around his neck, then pulled his chair close to the boy and asked him to confess his sins. After absolution, he crossed his chest and said a prayer. Standing up, the aged priest reached down slightly to grasp the boy's hand and pulled a small leather purse and an envelope from his frock. He placed the money pouch in the palm of the boy's hand and dropped the envelope into his lap. Pulling the boy's head against his body, the old man of God kissed him on top of his head and then placed his hand there as he spoke a prayer in Latin. After the prayer, he took the boy's hand and led him to the door. Giving the lad his blessing he said, 'A new world awaits you, my son. Do well as I know you will.' As the boy stepped over the threshold, the old man shut the door.

"He stood stunned at the back door of the old church for a few moments as he opened the envelope and found a note of passage aboard a ship bound for the New World and a contract for indentured servitude as an apprentice to a millwright in America. James had heard of George Galphin, the Irishman that had become rich in America. His success story had been repeated in most every pub in Northern Ireland. An offer from this legendary man took the young man by surprise and left him stunned with his mouth agape. Understanding a few of the words taught him by his mother and brother, he realized the unsigned document required a strong, sturdy young man of good moral character to agree to work for a period of seven years in the new colonies across the Atlantic. The ship was leaving the port of Belfast on the high tide that very evening."

***

Sully was forced to stop his story while the nurses tended to the equipment handling his bodily functions. While they were in the room, Salley made a beeline for the bathroom and as she was returning, she met Jon Chesterfield, Jr. standing at Sully's door. Again, he embraced her and she smiled for him. After all, he was taking care of Spot and that was a load off of her mind.

"Hello, Salley, you look beautiful this morning!" Salley was not impressed and knew he was lying because she hadn't washed her hair in three days and was wearing the same blue jeans from three days back. "I just wanted to let you know that Spot is doing well and starting to really enjoy his new home. His coat is shiny and he loves to run and kick his heels up in the Coastal Bermuda grass in his paddock. He hasn't warmed up to me yet, but I'm trying to win him over."

Salley nodded and said, "Yeah, he's kind of a one-person horse. There are not many people he likes or will allow to touch him." As she made the statement, she remembered James was one of the few people he tolerated and she knew it was because he knew James was kind. "Just keep him fed and groomed. I'll go by and show him some attention soon. We are trying to get someone to sit with Sully so I can run errands and things, but so far, we haven't found anyone that he likes. He and Spot are much alike."

"Well, set your mind at ease, I'll send some folks by who can help with that task and I know your father is bound to like one of them. Our house staff has many helpful people and all of them are very nice. You try each of them until you find the one that fits Sully's bill."

Salley was adamant. "Please don't do that, it's too much of an imposition for you and your family. We'll find someone real soon."

With his usual inability to take 'no' for an answer, he insisted and with a hug and a kiss, he was off to make arrangements for Sully's care giver. Salley just shook her head because she knew Sully would not have one of the Chesterfield staff helping him if he knew they were sent by him.

On his way out, Jon, Jr. ran into Salley's mother. She flashed a smile and Jon, Jr. asked how she was doing and if she liked Aiken. Polly told him she hadn't seen much of the town, but hoped to soon. She added, her son, Andy, who was parking the car, would soon be going out to try and find a place for them to stay in town. They didn't want to go out to Salleys Kitchen and stay in the Sullivan mansion because of the people there. Of course, young Chesterfield jumped on this opportunity to ensnare Salley's family in his web.

"Why I have the best possible place in Aiken for you to stay and it won't cost you a thing! I will have the staff open our guest house and put it in order. There are three bedrooms in the cottage with plenty of room to relax and I'll see that the refrigerator and pantry are stocked. Please let me help your family this little bit. It's no trouble and we'll be glad to have you use it."

Just as he finished, Salley's brother walked up and Jon Chesterfield insisted the two come with him to get settled in the cottage. Following young Chesterfield's little red sports car in his truck, Sully's son and his mother made their way to the palatial Chesterfield compound. They pulled into the parking area of the little bungalow just out away from the huge family house. It was nestled under the limbs of a group of huge oak trees. With their mouths agape, the two mountain people followed Jon, Jr. into the luxuriously furnished little house. Once again, they told him it was too much to ask of him and he flatly refused to take no for an answer. Hurrying back to the pickup truck, the rich kid, himself, grabbed the suitcases and hauled them into the bedrooms. He showed them around for a little bit and then he smiled and left them alone. They walked around stunned for quite a while, checking out everything in their new home away from home. In a few minutes, maids arrived to change the bed linens and a van arrived with all sorts of groceries. The man delivering the groceries seemed to know his way around and quickly put the provisions away. As he was leaving, he left a list of things available through his company and told them to call the number and tell the girl answering the phone what they needed and he would deliver it as quickly as possible. With a smile, he thanked them and left.

Two hours later, they arrived at the hospital and walked into Sully's room. They explained their lodging arrangements and both Sully and Salley were not happy. Their protests did little to dissuade the other two family members from taking full advantage of Salley's rich friend. After staying a couple of hours with Sully and Salley, the mother and her son left to return to their new accommodations. Father and daughter discussed what had happened and decided they would not make a big fuss about Jon, Jr.'s overwhelming hospitality, but Sully said, "Beware of Greek gifts. That house, my dear, is the epitome of a Trojan Horse and you are Helen!"

Unaware of the younger Chesterfield's other maneuverings, Salley returned to her chair beside Sully. She automatically started the recorder and Sully remembered exactly where he left off before the nurse and everything else had interrupted him. Returning in his mind to Ireland, he continued the story of James Anthony Sullivan, his great-great-grandfather, coming to the New World.

***

"Returning to his sod home, the Irish lad felt as if he was dreaming. After reading the few words he understood, he realized it was real. Still in a daze, he gathered his few belongings and left. Stopping once and turning to see his meager home one last time, he thought to himself, *I'm leaving alone with few belongings, but I will always hold close the love we shared and will cherish everything my family taught me about life.*

"After hurrying to Belfast, the lad was still in shock as he stood in line at the gangplank of the ship. He looked again to make sure the name of the ship was the same name on the paper. With his few worldly possessions wrapped in a blanket, he stepped forward when he became first in line. The grizzled seaman guarding the gangplank looked at the papers in the envelope and growled, 'Well, Poseidon himself may kiss my arse! Finally, the capt'ems por pilgrim has decided to show his face. Take yer gear and git aboard, my boy!' As he pointed, he said, 'Go to the wheel house where der Capt'ems making her ready. He's a'wait'n on you and chewing on our butts 'cause you ain't a'board.' With a shove, he pushed the boy onto the floating freighter, then yelled, 'NEXT!'

"Upon entering the wheelhouse, the boy stood and waited for the Captain to notice him. After what seem like an hour, the busy commander turned to notice him.

"'What is it boy?'

"To which the timid young man answered, 'The first mate sent me to you, sir.' Then in a softer voice he said, 'I'm James Sullivan, sir, your poor pilgrim.'

"The Captain spat, 'What the hell are you talking abo… ohhhh! Come here, boy, and bring me that envelope! Have you signed that contract I sent?' Reaching for the envelope, he snatched it from the boy's hand and unfolded the manuscript. Turning to the last page, he spread the document on top of a nearby counter and said, 'Make your mark here!' as he offered the lad a feather quill from the table that held his charts. Confidently taking the writing implement offered by the Captain, he signed his full name, James Anthony Sullivan, just as his mother had taught him over and over many years earlier. With pride and a smile, he handed the papers back to the uniformed man who said, 'Well done, lad, I believe you may be just what was ordered,' as he looked at the signature. The Captain was thinking to himself as he inspected the documents, *There's nothing worse than disappointing your friends or a priest, especially if the priest is your brother.* He folded the papers and put them back into the envelope. With a shout, he ordered, 'Take your things to the galley and see Adolpho. He will get you bedded. With that, the green young man from the Emerald Isles quickly became an indentured servant for seven years. As he left the wheelhouse, he heard the gruff old man say, 'Now, just one little jewel left and we'll be ready to make way.'

"Just as the new galley boy was about to step through the hatch into the darkness down in the bowels of the ship, he heard a commotion near the gangplank. In a fleeting glance, he saw the grizzled old sailor who had greeted him still guarding the gangplank. The old salt had taken off his hat and was bowing in an overly dramatic way as a young girl stepped on the boardwalk that was moving up and down with the sway of the ship. Attired in a long homespun dress with a tattered old shawl around her shoulders, she stood erect and held herself like a lady of gentry. Just seconds before James disappeared below deck, her face turned toward the open deck and their eyes met. With a flat little hat brimming with flowers and flowing black velvet hair forming a frame around her face, she flashed a daring smile at the lad.

"But just a quickly, she disappeared as he was snatched into the interior of the ship by a nasty man dressed in a dirty white apron. He wore a faded red rag tied around his head and sweat stains were covering the worn-out old clothing stretched over his dirty body. He seemed angry about something. Dragging the hapless boy behind him, they descended to a deck below water level. They entered a dimly lit galley full of boxes of every kind of dried food and just as many crates of vegetables and such. The grimy cook pulled a half-chewed cigar from his mouth and yelled, 'Get this stuff stowed away in that larder and make it quick! And don't forget to leave room for you to sleep 'cause that's where you'll be bunking - what little time you get to sleep.' With that introduction, he yelled again, 'Don't just stand there gaping at me! Get moving! Grab those crates and stack them in that room!' It soon became evident there would be no room for all of the crates and a place for him to sleep.

"As the huge ship rose on the tide, it began to creak and crack and move from side to side in a gentle rocking motion. At first, James paid no attention to the floating motion, but as the ropes pulled tight and the ship began to move back to the docks, he could feel his stomach starting to rumble. Continuing to sway slowly from side to side, the big ship did not offer a steady place to stand. Slowly, a queasy feeling enveloped the Irish lad, when suddenly the rumbling in the greenhorn's belly surged upward until there was no doubt the young boy was going to wretch. He reached the rail up on the open deck and he could no longer control the contents of his unsettled stomach. He puked everything he had into the litter-strewn harbor. Woozy and cross-eyed from seasickness, he wiped his retched tasting mouth on his shirt and moved away from the rail. The smelly cook was yelling at him from below. Slipping in some of his own vomit, he fell on the deck and skidded to the hatch leading down below. Sliding through the door as the ship rocked to the starboard side, his right hand grabbed the edge of the opening and he retched again onto the deck, wiping his mouth on his sleeve. He was sick as a dog and not even at sea and wondered in pain just how bad this journey was going to be. Flipping over on his back to gasp for air, he envisioned the earlier glimpse of a beautiful girl with a captivating smile. Suddenly, he realized his vision was in the flesh, the pretty young lass.

"James was only half of the special delivery. A lassie made up the second half of the special delivery.

***

Chapter 3

Salley stopped the tape recorder and told Sully it was time for him to eat and take his medicine. He seemed perturbed, but resigned to his fate. He said something that Salley could not hear, so she leaned close to his mouth and he said, "I sure would like one of those little Country Club Malt Liquors right now!"

Salley smiled and patted his head. With a devilish smile across her face she said, "All we have is apple juice now, but we'll see what we can work out later." Sully face was beaming!

After carefully feeding her father his lunch of soup and crackers, Salley asked him a few questions. "So, the lassie getting on the ship was my great-great-great-grandmother? They met on the ship coming to America? Who was she? Where was her home?"

Sully shook his head and said, "No, sweetheart, Rose was not your great-great-great-grandmother; you'll have to hear the whole story before you will understand. There are many twists and turns in our family history." With that pronouncement, Salley started the recorder and without missing a beat, Sully began the story again.

***

"Though it was one of many pubs in the Port of Belfast, the one-eyed proprietor had served his customers in such a way that the ole watering hole had earned an air of notoriety. But in the beginning, it had been a struggle to make a shilling with which to buy a loaf. The famine, and then the plague, made life hard. Now, with a shift to the troubles in the New World colonies, things were calming down a bit and the soldiers left in port brought good English money to the watering hole. Ever the businessman, the old barkeep was friendly to Irish and English, but heaped special attention on the Redcoat officers who frequented his pub. Soon after he hired the young, buxom barmaid with raven-like hair, he found the secret to his success. She was a descendent of some few surviving Spanish sailors who washed ashore from the Spanish Armada. With her dark complexion and olive skin, she was considered trash, even lower class than the Irish. Realizing her few options, it was easy for the old pub owner to make her service the English soldiers. By threatening to throw her out of his tavern, he made the full-bodied lass start pleasing the captains and colonels with more than drinks. He added a stairway to a snug he fashioned in the cellar of his pub. The punch house became very popular. There, the men in red could satisfy their urgings. Away in Belfast, the soldiers missed their ladies of privilege at home and they could not - or would not - go without satisfying their carnal lusts.

"Making money from the English officers that bought a sack, the old man always managed to procure a generous tip to keep things on the mum. His business was good and everyone was happy. The full-figured damsel was kept happy and healthy and regularly checked by the Medical Officer, while her pleasure chamber was adorned with every fancy whim that excited her and the high-ranking callers. Soon her techniques were widely lauded and friends of friends lined up to partake in the pleasures she offered.

"With a smile on his face and a jingle in his pocket, the pub owner felt all was going well, until one month the big boned woman had a scare. As the second month came and passed with no sign of her monthly period, she confessed to the old bartender she was with child. Quickly enough, he told her he would arrange to have her problem taken care of just as he had all of the other times. She cried for days, not wanting to lose this baby growing inside her and finally, in a last-ditch effort, she told the old man it was his child. Reminding him of the few times he had tried his own product, she added up the months to convince him of the facts. At first, he didn't care, but as she whimpered and cried, he realized that he, himself, had been brought into the world under similar circumstances. At his age, it may be his only chance to see his own flesh and blood continue. With the pangs of fatherhood uncharacteristically pulling at his heart, he relented, but made her continue to serve those of high rank that didn't mind the signs of motherhood or actually thought it added to the excitement of the act. He did make her find a replacement for the business during her impending absence and with a few letters to her sister, that problem was soon taken care of with a smile.

"At her home, the bartender's harlot gave birth to a beautiful little girl. She named her Aine Roisin Kelly. The first and middle names were Irish names meaning 'beautiful rose' and Kelly was the bartender's clan name, but the baby girl was known to everyone as Rose. Having the baby was the best thing that had happened in the barmaid's life. In the few years just after Rose was born, the little princess was the hit of the pub and she was carefully guarded behind the bar by her supposed father while the sisters, now a tandem, returned to business with a renewed vigor. It was an odd thing that many of mom's customers gave thought to possibly of being sire to the beautiful child. Of those who had partaken of the subterranean sensuality during the particular time in question, the mother secretly encouraged that idea, for many of them were men of money. Most of the time, a jilt's paternity claims were scoffed at by the army aristocrats, but for some bizarre reason, the officers took a common interest in the baby's welfare, often surreptitiously leaving a gold token of appreciation for the mother's services and little Rose's future.

"While Ireland tried to rebuild after the plague and famine, Rose grew to become a teenager with a huge sense of curiosity and an intoxicating smile. She became a regular feature in the business as she served drinks to all of her army 'uncles' and they protected her from those who might harm her. Insulted if she were treated wrongly, one man was killed in a dual when an 'uncle' demanded satisfaction after a drunken officer pulled her onto his lap and groped her repeatedly. She never complained and said he was only trying to tickle her. But after a round lead ball from a custom-made dueling pistol found its way through the accused man's heart, the young lady began to be viewed with a great deal more trepidation.

"It became obvious that Rose had to be sent away. That reality made the sisters grief stricken and they sulked about for days. The drinking establishment took on a somber atmosphere even though the budding young girl did everything to change the mood.

"From the saloon of army officers and seafaring captains, there went out a call for a good deed, an act of kindness that involved most every man that had hoisted a pint in the most favored watering hole in Belfast. The appeal was important to all that heard, for the wee young lass that everyone watched grow up was in a precarious situation and for the good of all involved, she needed to travel to a safer land far away. Very soon arrangements were made for a most suitable exit for the young lass. Rose was booked to travel on a ship to the colonies in America and the Captain, though he had never visited the basement boudoir, was an ale swilling patron. He was also brother to a Catholic priest who helped him complete the other half of his special request.

"Though sad to leave her mother and aunt, Rose was thrilled at the prospect of a new life in a new world and found the adventure most exhilarating. With a small purse full of English shillings collected by the 'uncles', she boarded the ship in donated clothes and put her brothel birth in the past.

"Knowing well the extenuating circumstances that surrounded the young girl, the ship's Captain decided she just might fulfill the second part of his colonial friend's request. George Galphin had asked for his assistance in securing a young woman and a young man for indentured service in America. While there were many in Northern Ireland that desperately sought such a contract, the old Irishman wanted a pair with unique skills.

"The lad he sought was to be an apprentice for the old millwright at his Silver Bluff plantation. Though a man of color, the millwright was a free man of color and therefore, it would take a certain type of person to fit this bill. Cantankerous and gruff, George Galphin thought a lot of the talented millwright and the pair had formed a close and unique relationship over the years. Galphin was a laissez-faire plantation owner and this gave Clinalee a free hand in the operation of both his boss's mills. The old Black man took pride in making his boss man lots of money. The apprentice he needed would have to be a special person who could see beyond the gruff exterior of Clinalee and have the aptitude to understand the workings of the complex machines he created.

"The lass who Galphin had requested was to work in a mercantile store for a lady in Augusta.

"From the moment Rose stepped onto the gangplank to board the huge clipper ship, she seemed very comfortable in her surroundings. She was not sick a day on the voyage and made her way around the ship like she owned it. Her 'uncle', the Captain, had warned the crew that Rose was his 'niece' and was to be treated like a lady or all hell would come to bear. Like she had done in her barroom home, she flitted around and made friends with the crew, even though the Captain forbade her to talk with them. This restriction of association only meant she would do all of the talking when the old man was around. The sailors were usually superstitious and perceived a woman on board as bad luck. Strangely, they thought of Rose as an angel who had been sent to cheer them up on the long, boring crossing. Though tradition labeled any on-board female among the crew to be a mallacht (Gallic word for curse), Rose quickly debunked that fallacy. She raided the kitchen and left hard biscuits and jerky near where the crew toiled to drop and draw the ship's massive sails. They would smile as they chewed the tough bread and salt pork while listening with a smile as Adolpho gave James a tongue lashing for stealing the food rations before they were served to the crew. The old cook also realized his galley boy became a bumbling clown when Rose was around. Maneuvering about the greasy kitchen floor was something that took experience and the lad was often caught, during an extended sway, without a firm grasp on anything but the air about him. This always resulted in his wiping up the galley floor as he sloshed from one side of the galley to the other on his sore butt. Always trying to impress the ever-present lass, James tried to showcase his strength by bringing too many crates from the larder at one time. He danced around the tiny kitchen, trying to keep them balanced in his arms as the ship rose and fell. When the trough of a particularly large wave made the ship dip severely forward, he was virtually thrown against the old cook. Then, as the ship was pulled up and over the next wave, he was thrown backwards. The crates he held were tossed into the air, scattering leafy greens across the galley. Most of the flying greens landed on or around the grubby cook's head and triggered one of his patented conniption fits. With the pair of teenagers in pain with laughter, he chased them out of his domain with a pot. When they thought he had cooled, down they came sulking back and found him busily cooking without the slightest hint that he had a collard leaf stuck in the back of his bandanna. Upon seeing him with the green feather-like adornment, the naughty girl smiled and said, 'My dear, what a lovely feather you have in your hat!' Poofing up her hair and turning with an air of exaggerated elegance, she added to the hilarity. James tried to maintain his stoic face, but finally cracked up laughing as Rose pointed to the head of the clueless cook. Ole Adolpho gritted his teeth and wanted to unleash his wrath on the lass, but knew he couldn't. Instead, he turned to James, who was struggling not to laugh, and screamed, 'Get out of here and don't you be coming back or I'll don me cie bais (Gallic word for sabre) and feed you to the fish!' Still laughing, the young couple vanished and steered clear of him for the rest of the day.

"With time away from the kitchen, James headed for his place of seclusion with the 'mistress of the ship' right on his heels. Always full of questions, she asked, 'Where are we going?' Not wanting the furious cook to know of his hide-away place, James put his finger to his lips for quiet and motioned her to follow him. In the bow of the huge vessel, where the anchor hung, there was a large compartment just under a hatch. The shank of the huge anchor lay in a groove just inside the hull of the ship. A chain attached to the gigantic hunk of iron was fed through a hole in the upper bow and coiled in a snake-like pile on the deck below. The crown and flukes of the mammoth ship's tackle were stowed on the outside of the ship and pulled tightly against its outside hull. The compartment that held the anchor shank was built wider than necessary, leaving a small alcove on each side of the huge iron rod. The space was just large enough for two small adults to recline side by side. As they lay on their stomachs with their heads sticking out of the ship, they peered over the top of the anchor stock and were mesmerized by the great keel of the vessel parting the water. The mammoth ship sliced neatly through the ocean waves, dividing the sea green liquid into a foaming white curl that grew as it moved away from the hull. Mesmerized by the whir of the wind and sound of the churning water, they lay in awe at such a sight. Safely hidden and hypnotized by the movement of the sea, the young couple lay motionless in the little niche, just inches apart. From their private perch at the very front of the ship, the view of the ship's cutting edge offered the duo a sense of the strength and agility of the craft as it elegantly moved through the water. Often the spray, caught by the wind, reached the alcove opening and splashed over them, making their bodies tingle. But most spectacular were the dolphins. Their sleek bodies glistened as they effortlessly kept pace with the ocean freighter and frolicked in the wake created by the keel. From their little hideaway, the teenagers were captivated by the aquatic visitors as they appeared and disappeared in the frothing water, smiling and squeaking 'hello'. Moving near the hull of the ship, the graceful sea mammals looked as if they were inviting the pair of humans to join them among the dancing waves. It seemed as if the couple could almost reach down into the water and touch them. It was a breathtaking site for the two juveniles away from home for the first time and it caused goosebumps to climb up their arms and tickle their ears. The excitement of the moment filled their heads and spun the two into a dreamlike moment in which only they existed in the world.

"While the pair lay wet and tingling from the mist and flurry, Rose was giddy with delight as she glanced over at her shipmate. Suddenly, she realized what James was sharing with her. He had invited her into his secret place - his place of happiness that he had not shared with anyone else. A strange emotion rushed over her body and as this warm sensation combined with the tingling mist, it sent shivers over her body. For some innermost reason, she leaned over to kiss the handsome young man on the cheek, but James, a little startled, turned to face her as she moved close to him and the kiss landed squarely on his lips. Both teens recoiled quickly and looked away, but after an awkward moment or two, she broke the tension and said, 'This is the most wonderful thing I have ever seen. No one has ever shared such a special thing with me.'

"Since James, the cook's boy, made the ship's princess happy, there would be none aboard the vessel to stand in their way. Therefore, the two young people were pretty much allowed free roam aboard the floating freighter for the rest of the voyage. Of course, 'Uncle' Captain made sure nothing was happening that shouldn't be happening and the young man knew there was a ship's crew who would turn him into cut bait if they even suspected their princess was harmed. The young man was too entranced to even think of doing anything that might injure her in any way.

"Both of the young adults aboard the ship had been robbed of much of their childhood by circumstances they could not control. Neither had ever had the companionship of someone their own age. But now, with an age appropriate friend, they became preteens again and soon succumbed to those childish urges they had missed. Running and playing anywhere they saw opportunity, their glee was exhilarating to everyone aboard. They played hide and seek and Rose screamed when she was found. On a rope swing, they swept out over the side of the ship, scaring the old Captain and the crew into nervous prostrations. Marching like soldiers, they sang to the top of their voices and banged out rhythms on every part of the ship, including Adolpho's pots and pans. They ate constantly and ran about the ship with food in their mouths and hands. They stayed up until the wee hours of the morning, watching the moon shine its silver streak across the water and talked of fairytales and wishes. Rose virtually took over the Captain's stateroom, so the old man started spending most of his time in the wheelhouse to avoid embarrassing his teenage 'niece'. Making it known that James was not allowed in the Captain's quarters, the protective old salt stayed alert as to where the couple might be and what they were doing at all times. It was an exhausting watch, to say the least, and he felt sure he would earn his price with this delivery.

"More like brother and sister for most of the voyage, the pair was saddened when all too soon they heard the Captain instructing the crew. He directed them to begin looking for the sight of land. The wonderful time of fun and frolic was hastily coming to a close and in a somber mood, they lay in silence side by side in their no-longer secret alcove. As they watched the huge red ball of the setting sun, they realized their fun-filled time was drawing to a close. Their time together was about to disappear like the setting sun, as it eased its way down until finally it vanished into the awaiting ocean. With sea spray misting the innocent couple, they lay together without speaking as the dolphins swam and played in the froth thrown up by the great vessel. The warm trade winds filled the ship's sails and made Rose's long, raven colored hair dance across her face. James moved to touch her as she stared out across the vast ocean and as his fingers softly reached the back of her hand, Rose turned to face him with tears in her eyes. Impulsively, she threw her arms around his neck and cried until her tears wet his shirt. He held her awkwardly with his arms around her shoulders, but not too tightly as to pull her close. This time, when she made her move to kiss him, she was not headed for his cheek. With a statue like stance, he allowed her to wetly kiss him on the lips, then buried her head between his neck and shoulder. Flushing red, James didn't know what to do. His heart was pounding. His lips were wet, but the inside of his mouth was dry as a desert and a million thoughts raced willy-nilly through his mind, like a leaf in the wind. Ever so slowly, he moved his hand to the middle of her back, but he did not move to rest of his body for fear he would send the wrong signal. With the innocence of first love enveloping them, the fledgling couple lay together - her arms around him with her lips on his neck and her beautiful hair blowing across his face in the sea breeze. As the moisture she left on his lips began to dry, he wanted to lick them, but didn't because he wanted her taste forever on his lips. Not capable of rational thought at the moment, he couldn't decide if he were going to die from the sheer pleasure she brought him with the kiss or if the Captain and crew would cut him to shreds when they found out what he had let her do. Either way, the kiss was the most monumental thing to have happened to the Irish lad thus far in his life and he wanted the feeling to last as long as possible.

"Such drastic changes in the young couple's lives had taken place so quickly. The problems that held them captive for so long were now on the other side of the ocean. The unlikely shipmates had become very close and Rose didn't feel like James was a brother anymore, nor did he think of her as a sister.

"The scout in the crow's nest was yelling 'Land Ho!' just as the sun was breaking the horizon over the stern of the ship. Everyone aboard knew this was to be a momentous day. With deft and skill from years of sailing, the old Captain yelled orders to the crew and long before the noonday hour, without so much as a moment of trouble, the huge ship was resting quietly beside a dock in the Savannah River. Quickly talking with his first mate, the old salt gave instructions as to what was to be unloaded first and without hesitation, the work began.

"On the long voyage over the pond, the Captain's concern had grown as he tried to think of a gentle way to separate the infatuated young couple. It was obvious, even to a blind man, the two had fallen in love and he knew their feelings would only muddy the waters of the business transaction that was required of him. He especially wanted to handle the lassie with care, so he planned to make sure she sat beside him as the threesome traveled north toward Augusta.

"Yelling toward the bow where the young couple stood, he told James to gather his belongings and make ready to leave the ship at once. After he disappeared below deck, the Captain called Rose to his side and told her they would be traveling by carriage to Augusta very soon. He wanted her to pack her things and be ready in a short while.

"Both knew this time was approaching fast, but its arrival seemed so sudden and without preparation. The Captain was first down the gangplank. Once on land, he quickly arranged for a carriage to be brought to the dock, then he went back aboard his ship. As soon as the four-seat carriage arrived, he gathered the couple and the three left the ship.

"As the Captain had planned, Rose sat in front, beside him. She fought to hold back her tears and keep her eyes forward. She resisted the urge to turn and look at James sitting in the back. Without a word being spoken, they traveled for hours, following the bank of the Savannah River as the sun passed noonday and dropped to its afternoon position. In what seemed to be the blink of an eye, the carriage pulled to a stop in the shade of a large live oak tree just off the bank of the river. Across the river, they could see a busy dock with people scurrying about, moving things here and there. Stepping down from the rig, the old Captain struggled to get his legs acquainted with terra firma again as he looked across the river. He pointed and said, 'This is Silver Bluff, James. This is where your new life in the New World will begin. I'll cross over the river with you and introduce you to your new charge, but you'll be on your own the rest of the way, son.'

"Turning to his other passenger, he left explicit instructions for her. 'I'll leave you with the carriage, Rose. My pistol will be on the seat beside you, cocked and ready. You are to fire it at anyone or anything that might bother you while I'm gone. You will be in my view the whole time and I will only be gone a few minutes. Then, you and I will travel on to Augusta.'

"The Captain left the couple alone to say goodbye and quickly walked down the bank to the dock. There, a ferryboat waited to take them across the river to Silver Bluff. Smiling, with tears forming in her eyes, Rose held James' hands as they promised to reunite in the New World. No matter how long it took, they vowed to be together again. With big tears running down her cheeks, she let go of his hands as he turned to leave. After two steps, he hesitated and turned just to see her once more. Suddenly, Rose threw her arms around him and kissed him passionately. Then, just as suddenly, James stepped away from her and headed for the makeshift steps leading down to the dock. As the ferryboat moved out into the current of the river, James strained to gain one last glimpse of her as he sat in the boat with all his worldly possessions in a bag on his back. Rose was nowhere to be seen. Sobbing, she was hidden by the large oak tree that she was kicking with her foot. She could not bear the sight of her friend, her companion, her shipmate, waving goodbye for the last time."

***

Salley held the cup and straw to her father's lips often as he dictated his story. He would suck water into his mouth repeatedly as he continued to tell his family history. Salley listened to every word Sully was uttering and she smiled when his story included the colloquial words and expressions of the people he described. It was obvious he had given much thought to his ancestors and what they might say in any given situation. As he described each character, it seemed as if he had been right there beside them in their daily lives. Salley wondered just how much research it had taken for her father to describe the Sullivans and the people in their lives so well. After a sip of water, he continued his saga.

***

"James stood beside Clinalee on the covered walkway as his new boss watched a barge in the distance headed down river. In a few minutes, George Galphin, himself, walked out of the back door of the house, followed by a pretty little Indian girl who looked to be 8 or 9 years old. James was struck by her attractive features and he wondered if she was Galphin's daughter or granddaughter. She was wearing a plain homespun dress with a beaded belt and deerskin moccasins. Her coal black hair was braided into two braids that hung down her back and they were tied off with brightly beaded bands at the bottom. She did not speak, but stood close to Galphin and stared at James.

"Offering his hand to the old Black man, the big man said, 'Well, hello, Clinalee, what do you think of the help I got for you? I'm told he's a strong and smart Irish lad who likes to work!'

"'Yassir - he seem ta beez ha goot boy, but wat's dem white foks gwine thank 'bout mes habin ha white boy workin fa me?'

"Galphin, a portly man, was wearing leather shoes with buckles and tall heels, white stocking to his knees and breeches. In addition, he was wearing a frock coat over a white shirt with a starched collar. Puffing a whale bone pipe with smoke about his head, he said very matter of factly, 'I don't give a damn what they think! Ain't neither one of you workin' for them. Tell 'em to see me if they have a problem. I'll straighten out that horse crap, quick!'

"Clinalee laughed and said, 'Yassir, I's bets yous will!'

"Pausing for a moment to puff his pipe, the backcountry lord continued addressing Clinalee. 'That Englishman has returned, the one who was here a while back, looking around and asking questions. He wants to pay me to make you build him a sawmill over next to Pine Log on the South Edisto River. I told him you were a freedman, but he still thinks you belong to me.'

"'Yassir, I dooz works forz yous, but hi haint yos'is slave. He's ain't da kind to udderstan, he hits me as a calf-killing dog. He lick yo hand in da daytime, den be in da pasture killin' calves hat night! He's hain't up to no good!'

"'I know, Clinalee, but I've dealt with many a scoundrel in my time. You just have to mind your purse and watch your back. I know you, Clinalee - you'll know what he's up to before he does and that's just what I want! I need eyes and ears everywhere these days. He knows well the people who want me dead. You know me, Clinalee, I keep those with my heart close enough to feel, but I keep those that want to put a lead ball in my heart close enough to see.'

"'Yassir! Wins he's wants to do da bild'n?'

"'He's a babe in the woods, Clinalee, and you're going to have to lead him around like a blind mule. The only two things that backstabber has are trees and money and I'm figuring he'll be losing both of them soon. We could use a mill over in that vicinity. There are some fine trees in that neck of the woods. Aye, my friend, the bad wind that blows may blow good our way - 'twill be handy when you're a mind to retire, my old friend. That is, if the British will leave us be, but I don't think they're a mind to do that. We're all King George's slaves at the moment!'

"Clinalee smiled and said, 'Yassir, I ain't node yous ta beez no man's slave! Hi fig'ur yous gwine stic yoz's nose hen ebbertang 'roun hea, buts I truss yous Misser George. If'n yous say bilt da man ha mill, I's dooz hit. Yooz wants James to stays heah or goes wid me?'

"'Clinalee, he's your charge and you will do with him as you please! I did not demand his presence. It was you, my man, who asked for help, so use him as you will!'

"After those words, the lord of the manor turned and said, 'Come with me, Salley, my girl. Let's go see what your mother has on the fire for us.'

"Walking back to the barn, Clinalee asked James if he understood everything the man said and James nodded his head 'yes'. Hearing Clinalee tell his boss that he stuck his nose in everything around, made James smile. They rode the wagon back to the mill and James left his belongings in the storeroom where he was to sleep. Afterwards, Clinalee took him to his house among the slave row. He had a fine house that put the slave shacks to shame and his wife, Mattie, welcomed James into their abode without a moment's hesitation. After eating catfish, collards and cornbread at their sturdy table, James and his mentor went back to check on the mills. Just before dark, a bell tolled that could be heard all over the plantation. Clinalee said loud enough for the mill workers to hear, 'Seben bells - quit'n time!' The dust covered slaves headed to their shacks on slave row. After James thanked Clinalee for his hospitality, the old man walked him back to the storeroom and deposited him for the night.

"As he laid on the meal bags in the storage room of the gristmill during the early evening, James kept thinking of all of the events of the day. Excitedly, he tried to remember every part of the mills and everything Clinalee told him. But that night, he dreamed of Rose; he could feel her kiss on his lips and see her looking at him with those unbelievable blue eyes. As he opened his eyes in the early morning light, he hoped they were lying together in the anchor alcove of the ship. But as reality dawned on him, he realized that it was just a bag of cornmeal - not the girl he loved."

***

Protesting, Sully paused his historical saga of the Sullivan family and Salley pulled a tray of food up next to his head. The doctor told her that if he did not eat, they would put in a feeding tube to give him nourishment. She did not want that to happen. Still, it was hard for him to swallow, because he was lying flat on his back. With each spoonful of soup, he smiled a silent thank you to his daughter. She treated him with the upmost care and concern at all times. Finally, Sully tried to tell her he had had enough, but she wanted him to take one more spoonful. He refused and reminded her that he did not need to be fattened up. Smiling, Salley gave up and put the spoon down and reached for a section of the New York Times newspaper. The only thing besides the story of his family that interested him was the crossword puzzle. She could never figure out the words, but Sully would always complete the puzzle. Finishing up the last of the puzzle, she put the paper on the portable table with the food tray and rolled it over next to the door so the nurses could get to it without any trouble. She heard the lightest of knocks at the door and Jon Chesterfield, Jr. stuck his head in and gave Salley a cheesy grin.

Under her breath Salley was saying, *Just damnit! He is the last person I wanted to see right now. He's like a spider hiding in a corner waiting to snare a fly in his web. Just damnit!* But instead of giving him the heave-ho, she painted on her Miss America smile and was cordial.

"Well hello, Jon. I don't know if we will ever be able to thank you enough for letting my mother and brother stay in your guest cottage. They are very comfortable and very appreciative. Have you been lavishing my Spot with that sort of care and concern? I really miss him! How's he doing in his new surroundings?"

Like a man receiving his pay check, he graciously accepted her kindness and thought of the other things he would do to make her like him. "I checked on him just before I came over here to the hospital and he was snorting and kicking up his heels in one of the paddocks behind the stables. He's not real fond of me, so I haven't tried to get too friendly with him."

"Yeah, he kind of has a dislike for anyone he doesn't know, especially if I'm not around. What can I say? He's a one-woman horse." Moving away from him, Salley made her way back to Sully's side and sat down. Jon followed her, holding his flat, preppy cap in his hand and stood just out of Sully's view. Acting as if he didn't know who was in the room, Sully spoke loudly to Salley.

"Is that James that's come to visit? I knew he would be back as soon as he could get here. How's he doing? Tell him to move over here so I can see him."

Sully could read Salley like a book and Salley could read him like a book.

"Sully! You know very well that's not James' voice; stop it, you're embarrassing me! I'm sorry, Jon, you know how frustrating parents can be at times. Come over and sit down and talk with us."

Just as the disingenuous young man pulled up a chair and sat down, Sully boomed out, "I am almost certain I smell my colostomy bag! It must be at its limit. Salley, my dear, please summon one of the medical staff to check it for me. I know your acquaintance detests that odoriferous aroma!"

Even more embarrassed, Salley blushed and pushed the button to call the nurse. While they waited, she maneuvered young Chesterfield out of the room.

Just to make sure the rich kid was on his way out, Sully spouted, "Salley, ask your friend if he would go out while they work on me and if you would, please stay here with me." She knew exactly what he was doing and with a smile, she escorted her unwanted caller to the door. As they stepped out, a nurse entered Sully's room. She apologized to Jon, Jr. for Sully's crudeness and told him she would see him soon. Crestfallen, he wanted to give her a hug, but she quickly took his hand and shook it, then went back in the room. Once inside, she let Sully have it.

"Alright, Sully, why are you trying to embarrass me? I wasn't going to let him stay long, but he is doing us some huge favors, so let's be nice."

Salley saw the embarrassment on the nurse's face, so she quickly told her that it was a false alarm and everything was fine. Avoiding eye contact, the nurse smiled and hurried out of the room.

Sully was quiet for a few moments while Salley stood by the door with her arms crossed across her chest, thinking. Her father did not like Jon Chesterfield, Jr. one iota! The truth was, she detested him, too, but he had made her family so comfortable while they were in Aiken and he was taking care of Spot and that had lifted such a burden from her shoulders. Salley knew there was more to his kindness than met the eye, but she was between a rock and a hard place. As she dropped her arms to her sides and walked over to sit next to Sully, she could tell by his expression, he was going to say his piece.

Sully started by asking his daughter a question. "My dear, do you love James?"

"Yes, Sully, you know I love him very much and he is the only man for me. I believe we are meant to be together and we will be soon."

"My dear, since the beginning of time, men have had to leave the women they love for various reasons. Historically, that separation from a loved one is a difficult period and it is helpful to have someone around to remind you for whom you wait and keep the wolves from the door. Like Penelope in The Odyssey, you are going to have many suitors and each will be vying to win your favor. But like Penelope's son, Telemachus, I will keep that unruly crowd of fortune seekers at bay until Odysseus, or in this case James, makes his return. In that I'm utterly incapacitated, I will employ any means necessary to keep you true to your soulmate. It may be unfathomable for you to believe, but I am as fond of James as you and I intend for him to be part of this family. There are damn few men that can tolerate the audacity that you and I bring to bear!"

Leaning over from her chair, Salley kissed her father on the cheek, then smiled and said, "You are very correct, it is hard to be away from James, but I have you, and together, we will make it. I have known your feelings about James for a long time. For a while, I thought you thought more of him than you think of me!"

Sully's laughter filled the room and spilled out into the hallway. One of the nurses stuck her head in the door and inquired, "Is everything OK?"

With a smile on her face, Salley shook her head and said, "I've never heard him laugh so much. I guess he's making up for lost time!"

Salley wiped Sully's face with a damp cloth and he seemed to enjoy the attention his daughter was showing him, but he was anxious to resume his story. He did not want to be delayed any longer. "Bring your recording machine back over here and let me tell you more about your great-great-great-grandfather. I don't want to stop until you have heard the complete story. This is your heritage!"

Pulling the recorder over close to his head, she placed the microphone beside him on the small platform on which his head rested.

***

"After his first night at Silver Bluff, James awoke and was excited to start the day. Fully awake, he remembered the friendship he created with Clinalee during the afternoon tour of the mills. Not once did either mention the other's color or status in the world. Somehow the mesmerizing whir of the two mills became music and the machines were performing a perfectly timed waltz in the most delightful ballroom with the most intriguing atmosphere. The odd pair couldn't have wanted more. As their number of days together grew, James and the old man had no problem figuring out what the other wanted. Clinalee seemed to know instinctively what the boy had on his mind and the boy intuitively knew what the old man was thinking without ever having to ask. In that first hour of their friendship, an amazing connection had been created between the old man and the lad. From that time forward, either would have done anything to aid the other.

"To most, it was an unusual bond, a white boy and an old Black man, acting as if they were father and son, more correctly like they were best friends. James honestly never gave a thought to Clinalee's color and the only reprimand the aged millwright gave the boy was, 'Nows we's needs ta git one thang scrait! Yous ain't ta bees acall'n me Mister! I's ain't a Mister, I's a man dat nose how'ta bilds hand make thangs, dat's hit, no Mister! You hair me?'

"James quickly answered, 'Yes, sir, what do I call you?'

"I'z thank yous done node my's name be Clinalee!'

"In a matter of days, the pair would begin a major construction project on a bank behind the dam of an enormous millpond. After furnishing power to the mill, the water then continued on its way to join the black water of the South Edisto River. The people from the community often stopped to see their progress and admire their handiwork. Clinalee enjoyed a well-earned reputation for building or fixing anything and James became known as his right arm."

***

After a few sips of water, Sully began telling Salley the story of the girl James could not forget. Rose's new life in the New World would begin, unbeknownst to James, just a few miles up the Savannah River. Sully was so proud to have had the opportunity to read Lucy O'Cain's long-lost diary, for it chronicled Rose's short life here in America. He so wanted to share it with his daughter.

***

"With her feelings pulling her in opposite directions, Rose was an emotional shipwreck. She could hardly wait for the Captain to return to the carriage and continue on their journey to Augusta. But she longed for James, for he had offered her such security and comfort. Their surreal journey across the sea seemed to be only the fuse of some great fireworks that had been lit when she stepped onto the Captain's ship. She felt the moment she stepped off the sea-going vessel, her life would burst into many wonderful, new escapades and she wished James could be part of all of it. Trying to control the emotions tearing at her heart as the Captain climbed back into the carriage, she fell over on the Captain's arm and buried her face in his coat, thinking of James. She knew he would never leave her thoughts and as her heart quivered with new emotions, she hated thinking she may never see him again. He had made her feel so good each time she saw him. After melding their lives on the ship, she knew they had become more than close friends during the long voyage.

"Though not dark, the sun had long since faded behind the western horizon as the Captain nudged her to look at the city of Augusta on the sandy plains near the river. To his

56

sorrow, she refused to take her face from his coat and he prodded her.

"'But what is wrong, my dear?' the tired, old seaman asked the girl. 'I thought you were excited about life in the New World.'

"With determination in her voice she said, 'Yes, Captain, I have had the most wonderful luck an Irish lass could have, but I'm scared. James was my anchor and now I have no one to hold me steady and keep me safe.'

"Having no ability whatsoever to tolerate anything that upset her, the Captain said, 'Here now, lass, I will have none of this! You're my spitfire lassie from the Emerald Isles and I would never allow anyone or anything to bring harm to you. Now dry your eyes, you're about to meet a lady who will walk beside you into a whole new life. It's with a smile you should start that journey!'

"With that, 'Uncle Captain' pulled her up straight on the carriage seat and handed her his handkerchief. Bolstered by his words, she hugged and kissed the old commander on his whiskers. Then they were off to find the settlement of Augusta before complete darkness fell across the western bank of the Savannah River.

"As the Captain's carriage finally pulled to a stop in front of a storefront in the bustling little river town, a matronly woman hurriedly put her writing down and made her way out of the double door entrance. Fashionably dressed, she stood erect on the stoop in front of the store. With a smile and a wave, she offered, 'Hello, Captain, I'm so glad you made it before dark. With all of the Loyalists and Tories traveling the roads these days, I certainly didn't want you to have trouble.' With that pronouncement, the stately woman smiled and stepped forward to greet her guests.

"'Aye, me lady, but I, too, am a subject of the King, only not as devoted as some would like.' Smiling, she offered her hand to the Captain and he bowed to kiss it.

"The busy little settlement had grown so fast, as of late, it seemed to constantly hum with commerce. But at this hour, the hustle and bustle of the little village had calmed down in the late afternoon sun. It was warm, but not hot, as the sun secluded itself behind the horizon on the frontier's edge. In the glow of the sun's final rays, an ethereal mistiness had engulfed the area around the store. Just as day was turning into night, the surreal atmosphere had Rose feeling as if she were walking on air. In the final throes of the dying light, Rose stepped out of the carriage in front of the commissary. Finally, at her journey's end, she was anxious to meet this woman, the one and only person chosen to help her start a new life."

***

It was well past midnight when there was a tap on the door of the hospital room. Jon Chesterfield, Jr. stuck his head in and announced that Salley's mother wanted her to come to the guest house and get some sleep. She had sent him to fetch her. Salley protested that someone had to stay with Sully and her suitor had a quick answer.

"This is Maude. She has worked with our family for decades and she has graciously agreed to sit with Mr. Sully until you return. She will take good care of your father and I know he will enjoy her company."

A nurse entered Sully's room and announced she was giving Salley's father something to make him rest. She was concerned he was trying to do too much for too long. With Sully being made to sleep, Salley finally agreed to go with Jon, Jr. to be with her mother and brother.

In a drowsy state, Sully watched Maude take Salley's seat. He was still conscious enough to warn Salley, "Remember, Odysseus WILL return!" Salley smiled and before she followed Jon, Jr. out of the room, she heard his new sitter offer her two cents.

Maude chimed in, "That's from the Odyssey. I read that as a little girl! That man was trying to get back to his wife and she had all of those men around her wanting to court her!"

Sully smiled and closed his eyes as the pill he had been given ushered him into the land of sleep.

That night at the guest house, Salley had the best sleep she had had in quite a while. She awoke refreshed and ate the breakfast of grapefruit and waffles that a Black woman in a white uniform had prepared. As Salley sat on the terrace in back of the little house, she could see the sun shining on a group of horses in the paddock just beyond the well-manicured yard. As she finished her grapefruit, Spot trotted up to say hello. She was overjoyed to know he was nearby and accessible whenever she could find time to ride. One of the staff came to the little patio area and told Salley he would take her to the hospital when she was ready. Salley was completely awed at the service her friend Jon, Jr. was lavishing on her and her family. It was nice for a change to know there were some people who liked her family and wanted to help them.

At the hospital, Sully was in a foul mood. He had found out about the guest house and everything else that morning from his wife. Unlike Sully, Polly saw nothing wrong with taking advantage of the Chesterfields' generosity. Sully explained, "I have done nothing to warrant such gratitude from that family. I am well acquainted with the Chesterfields and they offer nothing gratis, my good wife. There is always a quid pro quo. What, my dear, do you think they might hope to acquire?" As he was finishing his curt words with his wife, Salley entered the room and the ole cotton farmer's mood lightened considerably. "Hello, my beautiful daughter! How are you this fine day? Are you ready to hear more about your illustrious ancestors?"

Salley replied with a smile and a kiss to his forehead as she took her seat near his head. She gazed around at nothing and seemed lost in her thoughts as she placed the microphone beside him.

"As well I am, my good Sully. I am ready for you to pontificate on the illustrious Sullivans, the people from whom I am descended!"

With an exuberant smile, Sully offered, "Why, my dear, your vocabulary has improved greatly! People will soon know you are my daughter not only by the beautiful facial features we share, but also by the quality of your words, as well!" Salley hooted as she looked upon her father's grizzled beard protruding out from his prune-like face. She kissed him again, started the recorder and then prompted him to continue his family saga.

"Now tell me, Sully, who was this George Galphin guy who wanted the first James Anthony Sullivan to come to America and why did he want Rose to come, also?"

***

"George Galphin arrived in the New World in the late 1730s and took to his new vocation of Indian Trader like a man possessed. Leading a 20-mule train at times, he moved about the towns and villages of the Lower Creek Nation with a work ethic second to none. During this time, George met Enoch O'Cain and his wife, Lucy, fellow Scots-Irish by way of Charles Town. They made quick friends. Lucy made George come to their house for dinner, which was not something with which the Irishman was familiar. He did not know the proper protocol of a guest at a formal meal in a lady's home, but using his wit and charm, he evidently passed her muster. She insisted he return on a regular basis, for she thought he looked undernourished. Having already learned through the village grapevine of his multiple bed partners, she may have thought he was spreading himself a little too thin. In any event, George and Enoch were 'up and coming' men in the little settlement of Augusta. Both were movers and shakers in the lucrative Indian trade of the Central Savannah River Area. Their friendship was mutually advantageous.

"Lucy kept a diary and she religiously recorded the events of each day of her life. Writing each night before bed, she usually sat near a whale oil lamp with a feather quill in her hand and carefully described the happenings of her life, as well as her thoughts. Originally, she didn't have a formal diary, but after she married Enoch, that changed. Her husband had obtained a large package of parchment paper from a riverboat that had been poled upriver from Savannah. While the boat owner was away from the dock, the boat had sunk. When the owner returned to his boat, it was completely under water. He salvaged what he could and discarded the rest of his load. Wet and seemingly unusable, he tossed the large package of parchment paper on the river bank and left it. Enoch had found it and brought it to his warehouse. For his wife's birthday, he used a deerskin and some thin birch bark to fashion a blank book as a gift for her. Using pine pitch and thread, he attached a large amount of the now dry parchment paper on the spine of his homemade book. He knew the one-of-a-kind journal would become his wife's most prized possession. He was very correct! Gifts like her journal were the reason Lucy loved Enoch more than anything else in the world.

"During his early days in the New World, George was always eager to please and curry favor with the powerful chiefs of the Creek tribes. He catered to their wants and needs in a shrewd and cunning manner. Galphin quickly realized the importance of taking a Creek wife and in the first few years after becoming involved in the trade, he took an Indian wife. Nitechucky, a prominent tribal woman from a powerful tribe in The Nation, became his Creek wife. She became known as 'his woman' in 1741 and they had one child. He provided her with the things the other Creek women coveted and she became his bedmate when he traveled to her village.

"During this time, George was also able to take ownership of the rather large track of land along the Savannah River known as Silver Bluff. Through his contacts in Augusta and his Indian confidants, he obtained the property that had once been the site of a major Creek trading center. It had been all but abandoned, but its location along the route connecting the Lower Creek Nation to Charles Town made it an ideal home for Galphin.

"Always seizing the ready opportunity, Galphin established a trading center and warehouse on his newly acquired property, but his Creek wife continued to reside in her clan's village. Galphin's farm and trading center quickly grew to what most would call a thriving and self-sufficient plantation. In that he traveled extensively, the growth and success of his home base was due in large part to a unique method of operation. Galphin allowed many of his slaves to have near full autonomy on his plantation. They ran his farming operation and conducted his business while he traveled. Owner of many slaves, George was an unusual slave owner and had a unique view of slavery. Most plantation owners along the coast would have never allowed their slaves to have such freedom.

Galphin trusted his slaves and gave them ample incentives to handle his affairs and think for themselves. This unheard-of system was a great success and Silver Bluff became a premier business location. It made it possible for this Irish entrepreneurial genius to grow his trade among all inhabitants of the backcountry. His all-consuming commitment to be wealthy and powerful was paramount. Throughout the Upper and Lower Creek Nations, as well as part of the lower Cherokee Nation, he was a force with which to be reckoned.

"It was during this time that he met Bridget Shaw. She was a widow of high standing from Charles Town. Her father, William Shaw and her brother, Alexander, were wealthy participants in the lucrative Indian trade of the backcountry. They owned land along Shaw's Creek and operated a trading post near the settlement of New Windsor. In his travels to Charles Town, George Galphin was introduced to Bridget. Her husband had died from disease and after his death, she continued to live in Charles Town, for she enjoyed the bustling city life. George was never one to miss an opportunity to extend his commercial network. He considered marriage an excellent means of expansion. As a zealous young Indian trader, George had a promising future. William Shaw thought he would make his daughter a fine husband and provide for her a comfortable life. She reluctantly followed her family's advice and not that of her heart.

"After having taken Bridget Shaw as his latest wife, he began plans to build a new stately brick house where she could live a comfortable life. Her presence in his new home, however, never came to fruition.

"After meeting and marrying Galphin, she discovered her new husband's insatiable passion for women. She learned that he had produced children with a number of his slave women. Adamantly refusing to live at Silver Bluff among his concubines, she did not want to be constantly reminded of his infidelity. George made no pretense about his Creek wife and her importance to his success or the children he produced with his slave women. Bridget Shaw would not live at Silver Bluff and have George Galphin's multiple wives flaunted in her face on a daily basis. Therefore, George, the consummate peacemaker, quickly purchased her a nice home in Augusta.

"His marriage to Bridget, however, did secure a firm tie to a prominent family in the Indian trade of the backcountry. After moving his newest wife into her fine home in Augusta, he introduced her to Lucy O'Cain. They quickly made fast friends because both women had the city of Charles Town in their blood. It was impossible for the pair to avoid becoming inseparable friends and close confidants. They vented their frustrations and confessed their concerns to each other. Their friendship became a mutual means of support while their husbands were out doing whatever they did in the Indian trade.

"Bridget's home in Augusta was very nice and it was where she and her new best friend occupied themselves, while their husbands were in The Nations. Enoch O'Cain owned a store in the settlement and most of the prominent white men in the Augusta area traded with him. He also warehoused Indian trade goods for Brown, Rae and Company, the largest and most successful of the firms in the Indian trade. As a merchant and part-time trader, Enoch, too, was well on his way to becoming wealthy in the bustling little river settlement. Putting most of his earnings into building his business, he and Lucy lived frugally, but comfortably, in a flat above the store. Enoch, however, had promised his wife a fine home in the near future and she had written his promise in her diary.

"The relationship that Lucy and Bridget shared was much like that of twin sisters. They seemed to know what each other was thinking before the words were spoken. Their flash friendship was the sustenance for which each had longed during their time in the backcountry. The two former Charles Town women spent most every day together. Enoch, like George, was often away, leaving Lucy to run the store. Lucy's new friend now made that chore much more enjoyable. With a staff of newly arrived Irish immigrants and a couple of slaves to do the manual labor, Lucy did not do too much in a workday. Each afternoon, they took tea on Bridget's verandah that over looked the river and there they discussed every happening within the settlement, often at length.

"They also discussed their marriages. Bridget felt she had been pushed into marrying George Galphin and believed she had made a mistake. George was not the husband she had hoped he would be and she did not like living away from her beloved Charles Town. Bridget's catharsis occurred when she was told by one of Lucy's Irish workers that George Galphin was legally married to a woman back in Ireland. That knowledge became the straw that broke the camel's back. Bridget traveled to the village of New Windsor and cried as she told her father what she had found out. He told her she was lucky to have a man such as Galphin to support her lifestyle. Bridget's father said she shouldn't be worrying about another woman across the ocean.

"Frustrated with her father's answer, she immediately instructed her brother, Alexander, to begin the process of obtaining a house for her in Charles Town. She planned to return to the Holy City as soon as possible. Bridget longed to be back in the city that wrapped its blissful Low Country arms about her and made her feel at home. Lucy was trying to talk her into staying in Augusta, but Bridget was adamant about leaving as soon as the arrangements were complete. George seemed quite ambivalent about the entire affair. He said he wanted her to be happy and did not seem upset in any way.

"As the time for her to leave neared, Bridget increased her efforts to get Lucy to come with her, but Lucy would never think of leaving Enoch.

"Tragedy struck the O'Cain family just as Bridget was completing her plan to exit Augusta. On one of his trips to trade for deer hides in The Nations, Enoch was robbed and killed by either bandits or marauding Indians. No one knew the identity of his killer and all efforts to find out the identity of the perpetrator met dead ends. His body was found by some of George's traders and they brought his remains back to Augusta. Lucy was inconsolable and secluded herself in the living quarters above the store. Devastated, she could not understand - nor did she want to hear - Bridget's offer of condolences. George's soon-to-be-estranged wife tried to comfort her, but it was all in vain. In her sorrow, Lucy sobbed as she yelled at her friend.

"'I loved my husband with all of my heart and soul and wanted to be with him, yet he was taken from me. You detest your husband and can't stand to be with him and yet he is still alive. There is nothing fair or equitable about love and marriage. They too often become a cold and cruel tragedy!'"

***

Chapter 4

"Lucy's fair-weather friend left for Charles Town in just a few days. Lucy's grief was just too much for Bridget to accept and she wanted to be removed from her grieving and suffering acquaintance as quickly as possible. Boarding one of her husband's trade boats, Bridget floated to Savannah and was ferried to Charles Town in a sloop her brother had arranged for her.

"George Galphin came to offer his condolences to Lucy a few days after his wife left for Savannah. Stopping his carriage in front of the O'Cain store, he entered the commissary and found many items missing from the shelves and the cash drawer was bare. The employees had taken many things with no intention of paying for the items. George could see they were blatantly stealing from their former boss. Pulling his flintlock pistol from his frock, he made them all leave the store, after which he locked and bolted the doors. Making his way to the steps on the outside, he climbed up to the door of the comfortable apartment that Enoch had fashioned for his wife. When he knocked, Lucy came to the door looking very ghostly. She wore the same dress that George had seen her wearing at the funeral and did not appear to have done a thing since that mournful day. Entering the once happy abode, he wrapped his big arms around her and asked if she wanted to stay at Silver Bluff for a while. She shook her head 'no' and George stepped back out the door and told the boy driving his carriage to go back to Silver Bluff and fetch Clinalee's wife, Mattie. George stayed with Lucy until Mattie arrived, then he instructed the midwife to stay and help her. He told her to see that she bathed and put on clean clothes. He also instructed Mattie to make sure Lucy ate something so she could keep her strength up. He left for Silver Bluff and returned with his house wench, Hannah, the next morning. Hannah took over and allowed Mattie to return and resume her responsibilities as midwife at Silver Bluff. Every few days George would drop by and check to see if Lucy was progressing through her grieving process, often with Mattie by his side. As Lucy gained her strength and made her way through the tragedy of losing Enoch, George asked her about her husband's business. Quickly, she told him she intended to reopen the store and continue serving the people of the river town. Her friend George smiled and nodded his head in agreement, but he knew it was not something she could do alone. In his cordial, but always pragmatic, way he suggested she obtain an indentured servant with the wherewithal to help her in the store. He would not have anyone taking advantage of his friend's widow.

"Lucy had been a young Irish lass, too, when she came to the New World with her parents. Raised in Charles Town, she had met Enoch O'Cain on one of his many visits to the port city. He was a sturdy and strong man and Lucy was quickly smitten by his kind nature. They became husband and wife in 1740, just a few years after George Galphin had arrived in Charles Town. The couple settled in Augusta to be close to her husband's work and started a mercantile business. Lucy was a city girl, but quickly learned to help her husband and she had done her share of hard work to get the business started. As he began his trading in The Nations, Enoch refused to take an Indian wife. This made him an outsider. But he warehoused all of the Indian trade items for the traders that were offered to the tribes of the Creek Nations. This had permitted Lucy's husband's business to become profitable enough to hire a staff and purchase a slave or two. She had not worked as much since that time and was, instead, a respectable woman about town in the days just before her husband's death. She had only seen the inside of the store a few times in the last several months.

"Even though Lucy was best friends with George's estranged wife, George could not be so callous as to abandon Lucy as Bridget had done. He did not have it in him to be cruel to a woman. As he did for all widows, George Galphin felt he needed to watch after her and cater to her needs. After losing the love of her life, Lucy was going to need help if she were to survive and keep her husband's store producing a viable income. George knew Lucy well enough to know she would never marry just to obtain a helpmate. Through his connections, he thought he could arrange for just the right 'someone' to fill Lucy's needs. Agreeing with his suggestion, Lucy was elated when a few weeks later George told her of contracting with the

Captain to obtain a young Irish lass to help in the store. She had been walking on air since she found out about the impending arrival of the girl.

"Lucy was not one to do things in a half manner. This was true in most every aspect of her life. When she committed to something, she put her whole heart and self into the endeavor. This was especially true with the personal relationships she formed. As her friendship with Bridget had illustrated, all of her friends, once decided upon, were to receive her undying attention and loyalty. With Bridget's departure and her husband's death, Lucy felt as if a huge chasm had opened and she was falling further and further into her abyss of sorrow. Life on the frontier of the New World was a place where death occurred often. Diseases and common maladies took their toll on the weak and weary. The loss of a loved one often had to be suffered from within, for the hard work of sustaining a subsistence lifestyle did not allow for grieving. Lucy, however, could not adapt to living alone. She so longed for a friend with whom she could talk and share her weight of grief, someone on whom she could focus her attention. Close relationships sustained her and without them she was lost in a sea of despair. George was an old friend of her husband, but she knew very well she did not want to become entangled in his complex life. The moment George spoke of the Irish girl, Lucy was filled with hope and for some unknown reason, she felt as if she was about to enter a new and exciting stage of her life.

"Lucy's intuition was overwhelmingly correct. From the moment Rose first looked into her eyes, Lucy understood, without any doubt, that an unusual bond of extreme friendship and affection had been formed. To those around the two women, it was as if they were an older and younger version of the same person. The instant they met, both cried and threw their arms around each other's neck. In his best decorum, the old Captain had tried to introduce the two women, but quickly realized they were not listening to a word he said. In another realm completely, they held each other and snubbed for quite a while, then turned and walked up the steps to Lucy's apartment. The Captain, as if a delivery man, brought Rose's bags to the steps and then, with great labor, took them one by one up to the owner. Exhausted, he did not go back up the steps to say goodbye, rather he hurried to the local tavern and lifted a pint or two while having some food. He found a room above the tavern for the night.

"By morning's light, the Captain heard George Galphin's voice downstairs and when he appeared at the top of the steps, his old friend was smiling, as usual.

"'Come down here, ye old salt and let me gaze upon what treasure you have brought me from the grand and green isles. I know 'twill be wonderful, for you are incapable of anything less, my man!' Once down the stairs, the two old codgers hugged and slapped each other on the back. No one could deny they were old Irish friends.

"Together, they walked to the O'Cain store and climbed the steps to the apartment. There they found Rose and Lucy having morning tea and talking incessantly. They hardly noticed the knock at the door and only gave heed to the two gentlemen when they opened the door and said hello. Inviting the two men inside, they continued to ignore them and returned to their conversation. While Lucy and Rose sipped their tea and talked to each other, the men waited patiently until the conversation slowed just enough for them to get in a few words. Laughing and crying, the women admitted they had tuned out the world and apologized for their behavior. In a cordial manner, they thanked the two men responsible for their meeting and assured them that their friendship had been divinely inspired. It was obvious to both men that they were no longer needed. Chuckling, they walked together down the steps to the Captain's waiting carriage. After placing a small purse of gold coins in the Captain's hand, the two old gentlemen said their goodbyes and promised to arrange another reunion soon. The Captain left to return to his ship and George looked warily up the steps to the apartment above the store. Knowing it would be polite to go back up and bid adieu to the ladies, he thought better of climbing all of the stairs only to be ignored. He knew his work was done and he smiled with contentment as he headed to his carriage.

"With the excitement that a new adventure brings and ideas filling their brains to overflowing, Rose and Lucy dashed head long into remaking the O'Cain store. They hired workers to do the carpentry work and painting and kept them on task constantly. They had a plan to change the store and make it into something for which the little village longed. They could not wait to stock the new business and invite the people of Augusta into their establishment. They felt in their hearts that as soon as the new store was opened, the people would love their business. They marveled at the changes they made as Lucy grumbled at the amount of money she was spending. Even with the excessive spending, she could not have been happier with what was happening. Through the town gossip line, it was learned that there would be no loitering in the new O'Cain store. It was also found out that the men were to be moved outside to gather under the shed with the feed and tack. The rumor of frilly things and ladies' items being added to the store filled the conversations in homes around the river settlement. This caused excitement among the usually ignored fairer sex. With many walking by the store front and peering in the windows, anticipation was building and both Lucy and Rose were lost in the excitement. After working hard each day to complete the task at hand, both Rose and Lucy collapsed into bed at night, but invariably sprang to life with the morning's light. They just knew in their bones that their business would soon be booming and the pair was enjoying every minute of their anticipated success.

"As a month of days rolled off the calendar, the two female entrepreneurs felt as if they were about to explode when the day to reopen the store arrived. The relationship that had begun between the two women had grown into a working partnership. This well-oiled business alliance had taken place without either of the women realizing it had been formed. The storekeeper's widow was always concerned with the money and the young Irish lass was absorbed in offering the items that customers wanted. Together, the newly empowered team greeted their new customers with smiles permanently painted on their faces. Their new business approach was exactly what the bustling little river town wanted. As a new clientele entered the store, their customers were awed at what they saw and experienced. In the first few days after reopening, their business exploded and the earnings from the new patrons took their profits to a place beyond their dreams.

"Each had a natural place in the partnership and they worked together with perfection. Being the prettiest available female for miles, Rose was the object of many advances from the single males in the settlement. Lucy, however, was very protective of her appealing partner and deftly kept possible suitors at bay with her broom or the sea service pistol left her by her late husband. He had taught her to load and prime it and she had no problem using it if needed. After several men were thrown into the crude calaboose to sober up for a couple of days, it was quickly understood that unwanted advances toward the beautiful Irish lass would have dire consequences. Gradually, the male populace began to understand and tolerate the new female business approach and though not accepted by any means, they soon relented and at least tolerated the new rules of trade. Augusta's women and children had their first experience shopping in a store with their wishes in mind. Their money would be spent exclusively in the new O'Cain store and happily placed in the hands of Lucy and Rose.

"Rose soon became lost in the exuberance of her new life, helping the woman she felt was her soul sister. The locals called Lucy 'The Widow O'Cain' and Rose was called 'The Irish Beauty' and together they became an integral part of life in the small settlement. With new people always in the store, Rose was never one to meet a stranger. She greeted everyone with her wide smile and welcoming attitude. Together, the new store owners required each of the Irish women they hired to work in the store to wear a smile at all times and always dash to the customer's side to help. Their approach, they believed, would bring the women of Augusta into their store to shop and the men would follow.

"Most backcountry women did not venture far from their frontier homes without their husbands, especially with the talk of war looming. The Loyalist and Tory ears were always listening and could cause trouble for those with sympathies for the Patriot cause. The talk of war had all of the men up in arms and Lucy did not want that sort of talk in her place of business. She had been loyal to the King up to a point and George III had passed that point. As the New World colonies inched toward war, all inhabitants were being forced to make a fateful decision as to their allegiance. While Rose's leanings could not be measured, Lucy had not declared herself a Patriot, but she was clearly hoping for independence. With Rose's exuberant smile and Lucy's stability, the two women were constantly pressured to declare their fidelity to either the Patriots or the British. They had successfully postponed that declaration, but as the hostilities grew, they knew it was an inevitability they dreaded.

"As a new atmosphere swept over the once male oriented commissary, new items began to appear. Unabashedly, the female duo fell into their new business challenge like two beavers building a dam. Products were moved, inventory was changed and unseemly items were banished to the outside of the store. Without a thought of failure, they instituted their new and revolutionary business philosophy, then with a smile, offered it to the people of Augusta and the surrounding area. As with any revolution, however, there were those who didn't like the changes and most of those individuals were male.

"Many more items needed by the female population began showing up on the shelves. Bolts of printed cloth were stacked on shelves behind the counter along with a complete line of sewing products. Most of the same items offered before the renovations were still available, but they were now kept in an orderly fashion behind the long new counter that stretched nearly the width of the store. The large brick fireplace was now behind the counter.

"With business growing like never before, Lucy and Rose pushed to make everyone who walked into their store happy while shopping. The men who once used the store as a hangout and gossip center, now gathered outside. As the lady-folk bought things from the new O'Cain store, the men-folk never fully accepted the female twosome as their equals. Understanding the resistance of the men to trade with women in the store, George Galphin gave the Widow O'Cain a little male advice. She soon hired an old, white-haired man to handle the store's male clientele. He had worked for Enoch O'Cain and knew the business, but working for two women was something that took him awhile to fully accept. Soon, he was the liaison between the male customers and the female businesswomen. An uneasy truce was formed and the business continued to prosper.

"No longer was the store a gathering place where men talked, smoked and spit tobacco juice on the burning logs. A huge iron kettle now simmered over the coals, which made tea and coffee the beverages of choice. Liquor was still sold for medicinal reasons, but it was not consumed in the store and foul language was prohibited in the new female arena. Large items such as leather goods, tools and kitchen items were kept in the front corner, but many of the other large items were locked in the outside shed. Milled flour and corn meal from Silver Bluff were offered in large bags, but small quantities were kept behind the counter and scooped out of a barrel as the customer's needs dictated. Also behind the counter were household goods and soap, but guns, powder and ammunition were kept locked up in a rack a good distance behind the counter and only brought forward upon request. Horse and mule supplies along with animal feed and guano fertilizer were kept under the shed, as was anything with an odor unsuitable for the ladies.

"A rare new item, hard cakes of Baker's chocolate from Massachusetts, became a fancy new item in the store, as well as traditional molasses and sugar. These items were dispensed from barrels behind the long counter. Rose used the molasses to make a new treat that brought in a lot of new customers. After heating the sweet, brown semi-liquid in a pot over the fire, a little brown sugar from the barrel was stirred into the bubbling mixture. At just the right time, Rose would swing the crane holding the stewpot off the fire. Then with Lucy's help, ribbons of the amber liquid were ladled over a cool marble-top table. After the ribbons had cooled just enough to handle, she and Lucy would coat their hands in butter and pull the brown ribbons until they turned golden yellow. When the two women felt the sweet ribbons were just right, they braided three of the sweet blonde ropes together. After it cooled for a longer time, they chopped some into foot long ropes and still others into bite size pieces. Soon, children began to stare at the jars of sticky candy and begged for just a taste of the golden delight. Often, if a large order was made and paid for with gold, Rose would chop up a small piece of the candy and give it to the children. She quickly became a saint in their eyes.

"Men soon learned that sweet treats for a female friend went a long way in fostering a relationship that yielded what they sought. This new section of the long counter became the center of attention for a broad spectrum of patrons and many ogled the delectable delights. An often-heard phrase heard in the commissary became, 'Give me a sixpence of that yellow, Rose.' It was only natural that the candy became known as Yellow Rose.

"In the subsistence existence along the frontier, strength and force usually triumphed. The genteel milieu of ladies and gentlemen remained something for the metropolitan areas near the coast. On the edge of civilization, the fear of getting scalped in an Indian attack was a far greater worry than being snubbed for inappropriate behavior. In the backwoods, the safety and practicality of having a firearm in your hands at all times far outweighed the civility and decorum of walking the city streets with a cane. Wearing blood stained buckskin trousers seemed much more practical than sporting breeches with tall hose. Many of the tough frontiersmen wondered - sometimes out loud - if candies should be the items displayed on the long counter or should the more practical muskets, knives, shot and powder take a more prominent place. Under the lean-to shed where the men now gathered, it was often stated, 'Just let one of them females get grabbed up by a war party and see if they want us in the house with them, then!'

"This new style of business in the backcountry village seemed to spread many more smiles across the faces of those who inhabited the river port. Lucy and Rose's friendship grew even closer as the days turned into weeks and the weeks rolled into months. Together, the newly empowered women became a finely tuned machine in the hamlet's business center.

"With all of the talk of independence and the trouble in New England, the business people and civic leaders of the backcountry community were struggling to walk the knife's edge between loyalty to the King and loyalty to the Patriot cause. To slip either way could mean being ostracized and often physically attacked. Death also became an increasing possibility if the wrong people heard your opinion voiced. With the always present stress of Indian attacks in the backcountry, the advent of fighting between Loyalists and Patriots made the tension escalate beyond an acceptable level. Anxiety over the idea of allowing the fairer sex to trade in the community paled in comparison to the political issues of the day.

"While the women and children shopped exclusively in the new O'Cain store, George Galphin, the backwoods diplomat, spent time among the men who were gathered around the outside fireplace. Here, the Patriot men congregated with their guns and knives to discuss the King, the Loyalists and the Indians. Gravitating to the outside fireplace's warmth in the winter and the cool shade of the shed in the summer, the area beside the O'Cain store became a Patriot stronghold. Those loyal to the King knew of this Rebel hangout and watched it like a hawk. Lucy was uneasy with the talk that came from under the shed, but she did not know quite how to handle the situation. Her friend, George Galphin, was an outspoken Patriot leader and she did not want to alienate him or lose his friendship.

"In this rough and tumble area just to the side of the store, Rose had often noticed a certain woman moving in and out of the area in the shadows. She had long, raven colored hair like Rose and the same Irish manner. The mysterious woman never stayed long in the male area and the men seemed to treat her with distain. They often laughed and ridiculed her, but still she returned to the shed. Rose asked Lucy about the puzzling woman and she was told she was a prostitute. Her husband had been killed shortly after the couple had arrived in the New World and she had struggled to pay for a modest room and enough food to keep her alive. The destitute girl captured Rose's heart and she quickly befriended her. Ridicule was swiftly heaped upon the younger mercantile partner as the men sneered and made lude comments about Rose's relationship with the girl named Delilah. Their friendship led to many confrontations with the foul mouth men. Lucy always ended the clashes by brandishing her Sea Service pistol and threating to unload a lead ball. The men laughed at the women, but each of them knew Lucy was not bluffing. Rose was determined to help the down-and-out young girl and Lucy could not help but admire the goodness that poured from her business partner's heart. She remembered the situation that Rose had left behind in Ireland. Lucy did not chastise her for helping the girl, even though rumors flew through the small settlement. She knew the empathy Rose offered to the girl was a natural reaction. Lucy had grown to love her business partner's concern for others. She loved Rose as if she were her daughter.

"Rose's befriending Delilah was not a question of principles and it wasn't a problem for Lucy. The problems were created by the morally superior members of the community who pushed Lucy to the edge of her civility. Men and women began making snide remarks in front of the entrepreneurial pair as they tried to be business-like and pleasant. Both had decided to ignore the sanctimonious comments and act as if they didn't hear them, but this only infuriated those making the comments.

"Weeks after the two Irish women began their friendship, the pastor of the largest church in the village used his time in the pulpit that Sabbath to remind his flock of Jesus' reaction to the woman at the well. His simple, yet eloquent, description of the way Christ handled the situation gave many pause. While listening to the sermon, Rose and Lucy turned to face each other with tears trickling down their cheeks. With smiles on their faces and not a hint of self-righteousness, they joined the others as they left the church after the sermon. Most of the greatest offenders hung their heads. Both Lucy and Rose were amazed that the pastor's few well-placed words could create such a change in the attitude of so many among his flock. Gradually, the ill will passed away over the weeks following his sermon. Rose continued her friendship with Delilah, but it became strained when she told Rose she would not give up practicing the oldest profession in the world. Though never judging her, Rose tried to dissuade her, but she desperately needed the income and she simply refused to keep taking her friend's money. With strong misgivings, Rose watched her friend continue to sell her body to make a living.

"Strong and tough, Delilah maintained that the time she spent with men did not amount to anything more than money. She told Rose she was like a tavern owner, in that she offered men what they enjoyed as a way to make her living. Reluctantly, Rose said no more about her friend's profession, but she did notice Delilah no longer plied her trade in the shed. Moving to a higher class of customers, she now brought them into her home for service.

"Rose hoped Delilah would sooner or later find a good man who would take her away from the life she was forced to live. Rose also hoped to soon reunite with the man of her dreams, James Anthony Sullivan. Wherever he might be, she waited for him to return to her and she longed for his touch. At the most inopportune times, his image flooded her mind and she often shed tears in secret silence, hoping and wishing he would come for her soon."

***

As Salley listened to the story of Rose, her eyes teared up. She, too, knew the pain of missing a man named James, but in her case, it was five generations removed. She so wanted to feel her James' arms around her and smell his clean, Ivory soap fragrance. But she had not been back to Salleys Kitchen since the night Blackie was poisoned and James had had to put him down. She thought he would have called the hospital and asked about Sully. *What was wrong? Why had he abandoned her? Why had he not called her?* The story of Rose and the first James Anthony Sullivan had rekindled the pangs of love she had for James. His absence was becoming unbearable.

It was time for Sully's meds and bath. This was always a stressful time because the breathing machine had to be stopped in order for the nurses to bathe Sully. The orderlies then had to position Sully in a different iron lung so the other one could be cleaned. Stopping the iron lung meant Sully would struggle to breath. Each time this procedure took place, Salley had to sit and watch her father battle for air and turn blue. It sent Salley out of her mind, but she would not leave Sully. Even though the nurses worked as fast as they could and were as gentle as possible, it was still a very trying time for Salley and torture for Sully.

Each time the cleaning procedure concluded, Salley had to step out of the room and stand in the hallway to try and erase the image of Sully's face as he struggled for air. She knew Sully could not continue to endure the torture. Often, as she stood alone in the hallway of the hospital, the thought of James would flood her mind. Though she tried not to think of him, she couldn't help herself. *Where was he and what was he doing?*

What Salley didn't know was that Jon Chesterfield, Jr. had instructed the switchboard operator to deny all calls from James Williams to Sully's room. Along with the $50 bill he had given her, he told the operator James was not someone they wanted to talk with at present. The lady at the switchboard took the money and left a note for the other operators not to take calls from James Williams. Salley had no idea who or what was taking control of her life.

Back in the room, Sully looked as if he had been drained of all of his energy. He struggled to talk and could only offer a weak smile as he asked Salley for a drink of water. She held his water cup close to his lips and put the straw in his mouth so he could take a sip. With a sly smile, Salley asked him, "Is there anything you would like instead of water?"

Sully's eyes opened wide as she popped the top off of the Country Club Malt Liquor bottle with a church key and poured half of it in a cup. Putting a straw in the cup, she stuck it in his mouth. He sucked in a swallow of the golden ale and announced, "Ahhhhhhh, that's the taste I've been missing! Sweetheart, you are my savior! If I passed through the Pearly Gates tonight, it would be with beer on my breath and a smile on my face. You didn't, by any chance, bring some of that blackberry brandy, did you?"

With a smile, Salley told him she had not been back to Salleys Kitchen since the dreaded night. With his eyes, Sully let her know he understood. She let him drain the cup of beer and after a loud burp, he wanted to start the family history saga again.

Salley asked him, "Why is it so important that I hear this story? I'm not really getting into it right now. The story makes me miss James so much! Do we have to continue?"

Sully was adamant about his family history. "It may seem inconsequential and perhaps even trivial, at present, my dear - but its value will increase immeasurably as you mature, grow and evolve. I would not hesitate to say, you will return to this story many times in your life. The story of your heritage will help you understand not only who you are, but also what you are made of! Allow me this pleasure, sweetheart, and let the blood of our family flow until it courses within you."

Without further discussion, Salley placed the microphone in its usual place beside Sully's head and smiled to give him the go-ahead. He began right where he left off and Salley had to think of what he had already told her to keep it straight in her mind.

***

"With all of the help running around Silver Bluff that could have taken the wagonload of cornmeal over to Augusta, James could not understand why Clinalee had insisted he go alone. For weeks, they had been working together near the South Edisto River and they had nearly finished the little mill for the arrogant Englishman. The obnoxious Brit was constantly pushing them to complete the facility and they wanted to be shed of him. So, why in the world would Clinalee suddenly decide to take the day off and send him on a delivery run to Augusta?

"In a hurry to finish the delivery and get back to Silver Bluff, James had Galphin's old draft horse, Big Mac, backing the wagon up to the side door of the store near the shed. Just as the rear of the wagon was nearing the edge of the loading dock, Big Mac grunted and gave an extra hard push. The wagon hit the dock with a resounding BOOM! Cringing, he knew everything in the store rattled a little with that lick. He was not surprised to hear the genteel old widow woman yelling as she came around the corner. But as soon as she saw him and the wagon from Silver Bluff, she suddenly stopped her rant and began a civil conversation on the spot.

"Inside the store, Rose smiled and thought to herself, *It must be a handsome young man who she thinks would make a great husband for me.* She chuckled and kept her place, for she knew it would only be a minute before her widowed friend would rush in from outside, extolling the good looks of the man on the wagon. Sure enough, in less than a minute, the door of the store flew open and Lucy scurried in, bubbling over with glee.

"She blurted out, 'You need to come see this guy! I saw him with Clinalee the other day and he made my heart skip a beat! Come on! Come look at his muscles, they could hold you tight like a bear!'

"Rose knew it was useless to reject her invitation. No amount of refusal was going to stop her from having to go out to the loading dock and join Lucy as she eyed the young man.

"Determined to prove himself, James had dismissed almost everything from his life, but his apprenticeship. The mill he and Clinalee were building was foremost on his mind. With the British stirring up the Loyalists and Tories in the area, he and his partner were always watching their backs and saying very little. Working for Alwhite was not making the local Patriots happy, whatsoever. George Galphin, however, being profit-minded, had insisted that the local Rebels allow James and Clinalee to finish work on mill. He knew they could possibly overhear news of the movements and actions of the Loyalists. With their ears to the ground and their eyes wide open, they continued construction of the mill with a crew of slaves acquired by Alwhite.

"The night before, at Silver Bluff, as James lay on his cot in the storeroom among the bags of flour and corn meal, he tried to keep his focus on the inner workings of the complicated millworks. Invariably, his thoughts would drift back to the anchor alcove on the huge clipper ship and the taste of her kiss on his lips. No matter how hard he tried, he could not get her completely out of his mind. Rose was part of him, but he fought the urge to find her.

"Putting the last of the load of 100 lb. corn meal bags on a stack near the inside wall of the store shed, the sweaty mill apprentice was about to climb back onto the seat of the wagon and head back to Silver Bluff. Reaching to grab his shirt from the brake lever of the wagon, he had it nearly over his head when he saw the widow lady watching him from the front of the store. Having barely avoided being dressed down by the feisty woman for hitting the loading dock and shaking the store, he smiled, remembering he would probably be making deliveries to her store often. The smile on her face had a hint of curiosity and he wondered what was on her mind. As he wiggled the shirt over his head and down onto his shoulders, he noticed someone had joined her and the pair was staring at him. Suddenly, James recognized Rose's dazzling blue eyes framed by her shiny coal black hair. Both of the former shipmates stood frozen with their eyes on each other. Nothing was said until Lucy realized what was happening. She turned to her helper and said, 'I know you want to see him! Go!' Puzzled as to how Lucy knew of her feelings for James, she put that thought out of her mind and focused on the man she loved. Still frozen in place, lad and lassie stood without moving, searching each other's eyes.

"Lucy gave Rose a little push and said, 'Go! He's waiting and is just as nervous as you!'

"Rose was captivated and silent as she slowly started taking steps toward the boy she had dreamed of for months. Stepping down from the wagon, the Irish lad mirrored her motions and slowly took steps in her direction. The old woman stopped talking and put her hand to her mouth as if she was about to cry. She watched intently, as the couple slowly came together. Awed, she sensed this was a special happening and she wasn't about to interfere.

"Inches apart and silent, with emotions overflowing, their eyes were still locked. So close, but not touching, Rose was finally overcome and as she reached for his hand, she softly said, 'Oh, James, I have thought about you so much.' Without further thought, she embraced him and buried her face on his shoulder. Then, as she remembered the dictates of social decorum, she stepped back, still clasping his hand. Bubbling over with things she wanted to tell him, the words began to pour from her mouth. So much had happened since their parting hug and kiss on the river bank. She told him of meeting Lucy and how wonderfully accepting she had been to her in the first few weeks after she arrived. Rose could not believe she and James had been just a few miles apart. Telling him of her partnership and the transformation of the store, James could see the pride she felt about her accomplishments. He listened to her every word and drank in her emotions with the greatest interest. Never saying a word, he let her talk and eagerly tell him about her new and exciting life in the New World. When she finally stopped talking, she sighed with glee and impulsively threw her arms around his neck and pulled his head cheek to cheek against her head. Startled, but delighted, he stood like a statue. Unaccustomed to such public displays of affection, he certainly didn't want the widow woman to scold him about touching Rose. She pulled him by the arm to the steps leading up to the stoop on the front of the store.

"Realizing the love of his life was just some little ways up river from Silver Bluff, the lad was elated inside, but stoic outside. Love was a new emotion and he had never felt its pangs in his heart before - he was not sure how he should react.

"Lucy sensed a lull in the impassioned reunion and moved over to the steps where they sat and quietly said, 'From the looks of things, you two must know each other pretty well.' A smile beamed from both faces.

"Finally, looking at her former shipmate, the lass spoke, 'We were on the same ship during the crossing.'

"With a smirk on her face, Lucy said, 'It would seem you two became more than friends on that ship!'

"Remembering her earlier comment, Rose asked, 'How did you know I wanted to see him?'

"Pointedly avoiding Rose's question, Lucy walked up the steps and entered the store. Like she did onboard the ship, Rose stood up and grabbed James' hand, pulling him into the store behind her. Excitedly and almost shouting, the Irish lass said, 'Come see what we have done!' She explained how it was setup before and proudly pointed to every improvement they had made. Then, she grabbed her new best friend whom she had been ignoring. She pulled her close until she and Lucy were side by side.

"'And this is Lucy, the woman who has opened up this whole New World to me. She is my best friend! She lost her husband and I lost my home in Ireland, so we have started over together. We have done all this work to change the store from a backcountry commissary where men hung out to a store that has something for everyone. We fixed it up together and it was the hardest work I've have ever done! It's my greatest accomplishment in the New World and it was all because of Lucy!' The mercantile partners beamed with pride.

"As people started coming in the store, the young Irishman became very nervous and his senses were on high alert. He certainly did not want the widow woman to think bad of him, even if Rose did think she was the kindest woman she had ever met. Noticing he was ill at ease, Lucy smiled and put her arm around the young man as if he was her son. Her first words were motherly.

"'I'm glad to finally meet you, James. I thought Rose was going to pine away if you didn't show up soon.' There was an awkward pause in the conversation until Lucy continued, 'Well, I guess I will be the one to tell you both the truth. George Galphin and the Captain are old and trusted friends of mine and my late husband. The Captain told George of the friendship you two made aboard his ship during the crossing. He watched as you and Rose became friends and he revealed to George that he believed your relationship had a real chance to grow beyond friendship. The Captain also told George how sad you two were when you had to part.' With a sly smile on her face, she looked to Rose and said, 'I know James is trying to be manly and not show his emotions, but I promise you, my darling, he's just as happy inside as you are.' She looked at them as they both beamed from ear to ear. 'After George explained everything to me, we decided to give you both a chance to get your feet on the ground in your new home before the two of you were reunited. We didn't know if you might become homesick, my dear.' Looking softly at the Irish lass, she said, 'We wanted to make sure you wanted to stay here in the colonies before anything or anyone kept you from going home. Also, we thought it best to let James settle in at Silver Bluff and get started on his contract before he became distracted. If James had not worked out for Clinalee, his contract would have been sold to someone else. If that had happened, you two would have been torn apart again and that would have been cruel. We wanted to find the right time to bring the two of you together again.'

"James had dropped Rose's hand when the older lady began to tell them the true story, but the matronly woman smiled as she took their hands and put them back together. Finally, she said, 'Now that you are together again, you two can find out how you feel about each other.' She paused, then said, 'We only want the two of you to be happy and for that to happen, you two must decide if you want to be together permanently.' James' and Rose's faces blushed red as they looked at the floor and smiled.

"Overwhelmed, the inexperienced young Irishman didn't know what his next move should be. Gathering his nerve, he spoke for the first time, saying, 'Well, I need to get back to the mill, Clinalee might need me.' With that said, he moved toward the door, but his sweetheart did not let go of his hand. She followed him out the door, holding onto him tightly as Lucy watched. Rose was beaming that 'happy' smile again as the two walked back to the wagon.

"When Rose finally let go of his hand, James hurriedly climbed up on the wagon. Grabbing the reins, his attention was again diverted as he watched Rose's beautiful midnight hair dance in the breeze. Momentarily, he was taken back to the small anchor alcove and he recalled the sensation of her velvet-like hair softly cascading across his face. Like a magnet, his eyes were pulled to the two azure pools that were her eyes and his heart seemed to skip a beat.

"Longingly, Rose asked, 'When are you coming back? Please come back soon! I am so happy that you are here - I want to see you a lot more!'

"Whipping the reins across Big Mac's back, he said, 'OK.' Then he started the mammoth horse back toward Silver Bluff. On the way back, he said over and over in his mind, *I should have stayed! I should have stayed! I should have stayed!*

Earlier, before leaving the mill, Clinalee had helped him load the wagon and strangely told him to go into the store and get some soap before he came back. Puzzled, James told Clinalee he had a cake of soap and he didn't need any. Flustered, Clinalee said, 'Then go into the store and get ME some soap!' Now James understood the reason for the soap - but he forgot to get it.

"When James arrived back at the mill, the aged millwright was waiting for him at the entrance. 'How was your trip? Did you have any trouble? You sure got back quick!' Hopping off of the wagon, James started unhooking Big Mac so he could put him back in the stable. The curious old man followed him step for step. Finally, when they were back in the mill, Clinalee could not stop himself from bluntly asking, 'James! Did you go in the store? Did you see her?'

"James nodded in the affirmative, but said nothing and moved to the grinding area to start tying up some bags full of meal.

"'WELL?!' the frustrated millwright shouted. The tone of his voice made James stop and look his way. The old guy continued, 'DID YOU SEE HER?!' Again, James nodded in the affirmative and stood with a worried look on his face. Still perturbed, the fatherly man interjected, 'AND?!'

"James shrugged his shoulders and started tying up more bags. The old man huffed off. After just a bit, James heard Clinalee backing Big Mac into the traces of the wagon harness and then he took off in the direction of the big house. About an hour before dark, the white-haired, old man returned and entered the mill. Walking straight to where James was working, he got the boy's attention and gruffly said, 'Mista George say fo yoozta wash yos self extree goot han puts hon sum clothes wat ain't nasty afore yooz taks da wagon tooz Hagusta danight!' Then he turned and walked toward his home.

"Puzzled, James pondered, *Take the wagon to Augusta? Why would... Ohhhh!*

"When James pulled the wagon to a stop on the side of the store that evening, the widow woman yelled down from the top of the stairs, 'Come up here James, this is where we live.'

Once in the door, he quickly saw the reason for the extra cleanliness instructions from George Galphin. The raven-haired beauty was standing near the fireplace hearth where the older woman was taking food from a griddle above simmering fire coals. With a smile from ear to ear upon seeing James, the girl curtsied and said, 'Hello, James. Come over here.' Rose motioned for James to join her near the heat source at the end of the house. Once James came over to her, she leaned over and softly said to her nervous friend, 'Just watch what I do and do the same.' A little puzzled, he nodded affirmatively and displayed his usual statue-like stance that he automatically assumed when he was afraid.

"After putting the prepared food on the table and filling the cups with milk, the females stood near the table, with the elder saying, 'Well, I believe dinner is ready.' With that announcement, Rose asked James if he would pull Lucy's chair out for her and help her to be seated. Afterwards, he did the same for Rose, then he sat down and pulled up to the table. Waiting for her to move, James watched Rose intently. Once in the chairs, the widow reached to grab Rose's and James' hands. Quickly figuring out his next move, he took the beautiful girl's hand and listened as the woman prayed to God. This was not the way James was taught to pray. Making the sign of the cross over his heart was the only way he knew to pray. This would not be the only religious difference he would encounter while living in the mostly Protestant colonial world.

"The food was probably very tasty, but James chewed and swallowed without giving much thought to the flavor of the cuisine. He just wanted to get through the meal without making any mistakes that would embarrass him or the girl he loved. No matter how they tried, they could not get James to join in the polite dinner conversation. Using a quick 'yes' or 'no', he avoided lengthy answers and smiled a lot. Upon finishing the meal, the lady pushed her chair away from the table and stood. James sat stoically and wished he were back on the huge clipper ship with his friend. Having thought about her every day since they left the oceangoing vessel, he wanted to be with her. This situation was just not how he wanted to spend time with her and from the look on her face, he could tell she was very dismayed with the situation, too. Always the bold one, she finally looked at her host and said, 'Ma'am, would you mind terribly if I asked James to escort me on a walk to see the moonlight?' With a smile, the elderly woman looked at Rose and quickly said, 'I know James is a perfect gentleman and I'm sure he would be happy to walk with you to see the moonlight.'

"James quickly stood to take her hand and led her to the door. Once outside and down the steps, the couple walked slowly. In the cool evening air of late fall, they headed toward the river and watched as its current danced like silver in the moonlight. Pulling her shawl closer around her shoulders, the Irish lassie took James' hand and pulled him closer. Never looking in the direction of the river, they reached the point where they needed to turn around and head back. Standing under a large white oak tree that overlooked the river below, Rose reached up with both of her petite hands and pulled James' face to within millimeters of her face. Absorbing every feature, she closed her eyes and guided his lips the few millimeters to hers. The familiar feeling of 'weak knees' struck the lad as she put her arms around his neck and pulled him as close as she possibly could. Having longed for the taste of her lips and having dreamed every night of having her in his arms again, it was hard for him to think this time it was real. The moment was surreal and both felt as if they were floating above the ground.

"Watching from the window, the old woman swooned. 'They're in each other's arms, finally! I don't think I have ever seen a more tender moment in my life. I remember how wonderful it was to be young and in love for the first time.' Holding both hands to her mouth, tears began to trickle down her cheeks. Softly, she said, 'Oh, Enoch... I miss you so much.'

"Rose had experienced homesickness more than she wanted to admit and even though her home had been a bar and brothel, the beautiful girl often remembered how far away she was from her home on the Emerald Isles. The lonely feeling often invaded her heart when she was by herself. This melancholy feeling at times hijacked her mind, reminding her of her mother and Ireland thousands of miles across an ocean. With no shoulder to cry on and no one to hold her, she had longed for her mother's soothing voice telling her that things would be alright. It was an empty feeling that brought her to tears. She was never able to explain it to Lucy, who tried to comfort her. Knowing she had been offered a chance to go home, she had at one time contemplated sending a letter to ask her 'uncle', the Captain, to take her home.

"James, however, was the tonic that cured her homesickness. Listening to his Irish brogue gave her a feeling of home and while she was in his arms, she never felt that haunting, lonely feeling. The quiet, unassuming young man rescued her heart and gave her renewed strength. Just knowing he was close had returned her eagerness for the future. Again, she was the bright, beautiful lass that yearned to run with the wind. After their walk, James and Rose sat on Lucy's couch and listened as she told them of the small Irish village in which she was raised. Very few of her words fell on listening ears, instead, the couple held hands and looked deeply into each other's eyes. Finally, as James was leaving, they walked out onto the stoop at the top of the stairs and they kissed goodnight. Rose didn't care if it was proper or right - she could not wait to have his warm, strong arms holding her and his wonderful lips pressing against her lips. James did not remember much of the trip back to Silver Bluff - he was thinking of Rose.

"From the moment they had reunited, Rose was a new person. She sang and danced her way around the store and never lost the smile on her face. Bubbling over with eagerness, she greeted each customer at the door and did everything she could to meet their needs. Each time Lucy looked her way, she was in awe of Rose's effervescence. Never had she ever seen such a lovesick girl. Rose's mood was intoxicating and she made everyone smile. Visiting the old store seemed to put everyone in a happy mood and Rose was the initiator.

"With James living so close, Rose was determined to find a way to see him as often as possible. She began to talk with Lucy about getting a buggy or a carriage so she could make the less-than-an-hour trip to Silver Bluff whenever she could slip away. Lucy said it wasn't proper for a young lady to go flying off to see a man, especially in a buggy, alone! Pleading with her older partner to get her a rig, Rose knew

James would teach her how to drive a buggy. She did not want anyone driving her; she wanted to handle the reins herself and travel at a time she chose. Much to Lucy's chagrin, Rose quickly blew away all of her excuses. Reminding her partner of the dowry left for her by her 'uncle' Captain, the cost of the rig would not be a problem. She also pointed out that she was strong, determined and very capable of handling a buggy horse. Rose's final appeal was to George Galphin and it came wrapped in one of her patented hug-around-the-neck and peck-on-the-cheek tactics. She so wanted him to find her a horse and buggy. Two days later, about mid-morning, George pulled up in front of the store in a brand new, shiny black rig with a solid black, high-stepping filly in the harnesses. The filly's name was Sassafras and true to form, she was as frisky as the Irish lass who wanted to take her reins. Climbing in the sleek new buggy with the old man, Rose wanted the reins immediately, but the wise old codger would have none of that. He made her ride with him most of the morning, continuously giving lessons on what was permissible and what could never be done. Stopping for lunch at the store, Rose showed everyone her new rig and she could hardly sit down for lunch. After the filly had rested and Rose's food had digested, George took her out again. After Rose climbed into the buggy beside Mister George, he reminded her of everything he had told her before lunch. He told her she would have to go very slow at first until she got a feel for the reins. He gave her the reins and she whipped them on the back of the frisky filly and took off like a bat out of torment. Throwing the old man against the back of the soft, black leather seat, he grabbed his hat and the rail around the seat to keep from being thrown out on the ground. The men at the popular tavern two doors down got news of the fancy rig and came out to see it. As it flew by, they saw the horror painted on the old man's face and were very concerned. It was only after they heard her yell, 'HAROO!' that they bent over laughing and slapped each other on the back. One backcountry man standing outside the tavern with a pint in his hand made all of them laugh, when in his best Irish brogue, he said, 'Aye, matey! I pity the boy that tries to tame that filly!' He laughed and danced a little Irish jig as he made his way back into the tavern.

"With her new rig, Rose became a frequent visitor at Silver Bluff, most of the time with Lucy by her side. They even traveled a few times over to the South Edisto River area where James and Clinalee were in the final stages of completing the dual-purpose mill for the arrogant Englishman.

"Alwhite had become impatient with them and told them to forget the dual purposes and just get the sawmill running. With the local Patriot supporters trying to run him out of the country, he was now armed at all times and had several local Loyalists as bodyguards. As the project neared completion, the Englishman had become more and more distrustful of Clinalee and James. He knew both were supporters of the Patriot cause and he kept telling Clinalee that the British were going to free all of the slaves. Clinalee kept telling him he wasn't a slave, but a free man of color. Clinalee told the Brit, 'Yous is gwyne have a rite good chanc to leev dis hear area, but I's gots to stay hand lib wid deez heera folks.' James never spoke either way, just nodded when someone spoke to him.

"On a cold November day, the old millwright and his apprentice traveled along the recently cut Tory Road to their construction project. They knew this would be the last day to work on it and they were glad. All involved were happy it was completed, for no one like working for the Brit, especially George Galphin. The big man had invited Lucy, Rose and Mattie over to Silver Bluff that night to a small meal in the big house. It was his way of thanking Clinalee and James for their hard work in such a hostile environment. This gathering was a private affair and they did not want everyone to know of their get-together. The Brit was to make final payment to George this day and everyone was glad to end the association. James was looking forward to seeing Rose, but not at such a proper event. Clinalee, too, was uneasy eating at the table with the big boss. He told James, 'Sat'n hat da table wid ha white mans haint nuffin buts trouble! But he be mad hiffen hi don'ts. Seem lak no matta hows hards ha mans tries, yooz 'ust can't stays way from da devel!'

"All in their finest clothes, they sat around the large table in the dining room. Lucy sat between George Galphin and his most recent wife, Rachel Dupree. In their church clothes, Clinalee and Mattie sat on the opposite side of the table with Rose and James.

"The host was jovial and kept the conversation lively, except when he talked of the British and Patriots fighting in New England. In his conversation, he mentioned receiving a letter from Henry Laurens, one of South Carolina's representatives in the new Patriot government. Laurens had gotten wind of a rumor about the Redcoat Army coming to South Carolina. Though he didn't show much concern, everyone knew George Galphin had a price on his head. The British Indian Agent, John Stuart, wanted him dead and that knowledge, though never mentioned, made everyone very fearful. Galphin had spent much time with his Indian friends, the leading elders in the Muskogee Creek Nations, gathering assurances of their remaining neutral in the war with the British. The settlers of the backcountry trusted George Galphin and knew that he would do everything possible to keep the 5000 or more Creek warriors from joining with the British. If he failed, those living in the backcountry knew there would be a bloody massacre.

"As the meal was drawing to a close, a ruckus was heard in front of the house. Suddenly, the front door banged open and the Englishman from the mill barged into the parlor. Making his way into the dining room, it was easy to see he was drunk and furious. The mill James and Clinalee constructed had an 'overshot' wheel where water flowed over the top of the waterwheel. They had built a large trash rack across the flume, but someone had thrown huge blocks of wood down behind the giant water wheel and jammed it. The Englishman was fit to be tied and was aiming his fury at George Galphin.

"Indignant, George told the Englishman to get out of his house until he could keep a civil tongue in his mouth. With that, he showed the irate man to the door and slammed it behind him. 'And they call **us** backwoods people! Even I have better manners than to storm into someone's home while dinner is being served. That was no gentleman and I don't think we shall have any more to do with him. If he comes back, I'll make sure the boys know! They have been wanting to get a hold of him for a while now!' The boys he was referring to were the local Patriots who detested the arrogant Englishman. They would have been more than happy to handle him.

"With Loyalists and Tories trying to control the area, George Galphin had begun to store up arms and supplies that the local Patriot militias would need if the British decided to come south. For that reason, local Patriot men were on ready around the plantation and could come to Galphin's aid in short notice. Extra caution was taken when any stranger approached the plantation and Mister George had eyes and ears everywhere throughout the Indian Nations and the entire backcountry. His scouts and spies were always listening for any new information.

"Furious, the drunken Englishman grabbed the reins of his horse from the rough bunch of Loyalists accompanying him and struggled to climb into his saddle. Once he was mounted, the group departed in an all-out gallop, with their horses blowing vapor into the cold night air. They had decided to ride to Augusta and find a magistrate who was still loyal to the King. On arrival in the river settlement, however, Alwhite was told his problem was in South Carolina and he would have to seek legal recourse across the border on the other side of the river. Still fuming and starting to sober, the mob retreated to into the tavern a few doors down from Lucy and Rose's store and began to drink heavily. A couple of hours later, Alwhite was very drunk and he had infuriated most of the people in the tavern. The local Tories and Loyalists around him were the only things that had kept him from being beaten and tarred and feathered. Finally pushed out the door, one local Patriot yelled, 'Go back home and get on your knees for George III, that way you'll be at eye level when you wipe his nasty ass.'

"Grabbing a leather strap from one of the harnesses hanging nearby, the Brit yelled back at the loud mouth local, 'I'll show you whose ass I'll wipe - you worthless piece of scum!' He got about ten feet from the man when his hand came up from his side. He was holding a flintlock pistol and as he moved his coat to one side, another pistol was seen protruding from the waistband of his breeches.

"The outspoken Rebel offered the drunken Englishman an ominous reply. 'Let me tell you this, you English bastard, if you keep coming toward me, I'll turn you into a steer so fast, you'll be looking for some grass to graze before you hit the ground! Do you understand me?' The British timberman knew the Rebel meant just what he said and he stopped in his tracks. Throwing down the leather strap, Alwhite staggered into the darkness as he grumbled incoherently. The local Patriots were all laughing at him as he left.

"James had learned his way around the area and the surrounding communities. Soaking up the information like a sponge, he wanted to know everything about the people he served. After the meal, George Galphin told of his first coming to the New World and the trials and tribulations he had to face. When he finished and began working on his cigar, James, in return, told of his family and the tragedy that befell them. After hearing James' story, everyone acquired a new appreciation for the young man. His shyness was now understandable. Everyone at the table agreed that no one should have to go through anything like that. Then Rose told of her father and 'uncles' from the bar, but didn't elaborate and no one tried to pry information from her. Lucy told of her childhood, being raise in a comfortable family with loving parents. After her story, the old man perked up and said, 'Well, James, I believe you and I need to deliver these ladies home.' As the others gathered their belongings and visited a little more, James walked Rose out to her buggy and they kissed before the others came out of the house. He had been thinking about it all night and finally, as they stood between Sassafras' and Big Mac's stall, he blurted it out, 'Rose, I could drive you home and bring your buggy back to you in the morning. Sassafras can spend the night in the barn with Big Mac.'

"Big Mac was the solid black draft horse that pulled the wagon loads of flour and meal around the community and surrounding areas. He was bred to be a draft horse and had huge feet that clopped along the roads effortlessly, no matter the load or distance. The young couple had developed an attachment to the powerful, but gentle, animal, for he had ferried both around the community before Rose's buggy was obtained. He was their constant companion in the pre-buggy days. With an affinity for all animals, the lass was constantly cooing and softly talking to the huge beast of burden while she patted his wide nose. The affection she had for him was obviously reciprocated, for he always sounded off if she came near him without showing him some attention. She seemed to always have a piece of Yellow Rose from the store counter for him and he remembered her gifts. Watching her shower the old boy with affection gave James a warm feeling, for he knew it was a natural outpouring that she offered without expecting anything in return. It was her nature to show affection. She hung bird feeders around the old store building to make sure the little feather bundles had food. She always clandestinely stuffed her apron pockets with the biscuits left over after meals so Rummy, the old dog under the loading dock, could have a snack. Also, she secretly dipped milk from the milk bucket that the store help brought back from the cow shed behind the store. She left saucers full of the white liquid for the feral cats that had taken up residence under the lean-to shed.

"Pulling up her dress and running back to the house, Rose rushed in breathlessly and asked Lucy and George if James could drive her home. He would return the buggy in the morning. There was no one in the house that could say no to Rose. After receiving their okey-doke, she flew back out the door, happy as a lark. There, she found James waiting to help her get into the buggy. She blew by his outstretched hand and jumped into the fancy rig. Giggling, she grabbed James' arm and began pulling him into the buggy beside her.

"Big Mac whinnied from the barn as James grabbed the reins and stepped into the buggy with his love. He knew she wanted to drive the rig, but her breakneck attitude toward buggy driving was an experience he wanted to avoid. Turning to face her with a smile, James could see the pretend pout she was expressing. Leaning close to her face, he kissed her ever so lightly on her protruding lips. He always treated her with the utmost care and concern, for he worshipped the ground she walked on. That said, he was not about to have the bejesus scared out of him by letting her control the reins of that frisky filly. He knew well that the fast filly and Rose shared a 'devil-

94

may-care' attitude and both had a need for speed that scared almost everyone!

"It was a cool evening and the buggy blanket that Mattie had given Rose was appreciated by the couple. Leaving the compound with the big brick house in the background, James had to keep a tight rein on the speed-spoiled maiden pulling the buggy. In a high stepping gait, Sassafras was rearing to go, but James made her take it easy on the trip back to Augusta. Besides, he wanted the joy of sitting beside Rose in the cool night air to last as long as possible. Moving next to him, Rose snuggled as close as she could get and put her hands in his jacket pocket.

"A full moon illuminated the backcountry road and beamed sporadic light through the roadside trees. Sharing their warmth and feelings without speaking, the duo entered a realm of their relationship that had happened before. So often while together, the events, the atmosphere and their deep, abiding love blended to produce something not of this world. The two lovers, though they had never even considered intimacy, seemed to join their bodies and minds into one form as they hovered above earthly happenings. An 'out-of-this-world' ambiance had engulfed the couple on this moonlight night and neither wanted the amazing phenomenon to end. Alone together with the trials of life erased from memory, they floated in bliss.

"Crossing the river on the ferry, the nappy-headed boy was half asleep as he pulled them across the river. Telling the ferry boy he needn't get too comfortable, James explained that another carriage would be arriving soon. The sleepy boy pulling the rope didn't say a word, but his face expressed his distain. After Sassafras effortlessly climbed the sandy river bank leading to the little town, the couple turned left and headed down the street to the O'Cain store.

"Pulling up in front of the store, James sensed something was wrong as the filly skidded to the side of the road and nervously shook the bridle. Taking his arm from around the warm bundle beside him, he took the reins in both hands and spoke in a soothing tone to the wary animal. Scanning the scene for the source of trouble, he noticed two people standing in the street just beyond the O'Cain store. The pair was scuffling in front of the nearby tavern and James knew immediately this was the source of the horse's nervousness. Immediately upon spotting the ruckus, his heart jumped to his throat.

"From under the warm blanket, Rose followed James' eyes to the dangerous spot. With a full harvest moon shining brightly, she could see a man about twenty paces away as he stood with a pistol, waving it around. At the same time, the armed man was berating and cursing someone with the vilest language she had ever heard. Almost instantly, James realized the man was the Englishman who had stormed into George Galphin's home. It was the same man for whom Clinalee and James had built the mill. Now, he was staggering and trying to stand as he spewed his hatred on all those around him.

"Pulling the skittish horse to a stop, James handed the reins to Rose and stepped out of the buggy. Moving toward the scene, James could see there was a beaten woman at the Englishman's feet. Waving his pistol in the air, Alwhite spat out his words in a drunken drool, 'You sorry Irish filth, you're not fit to lick my boots!' The gun was being pointed in many directions, including at James, as the Brit stumbled and staggered.

"Stopping before he reached the intoxicated man, James could see the pistol had been cocked. In an effort to take the gun out of the equation, the mild-mannered boy said, 'How about putting that gun down, before you shoot someone!'

"The drunk quickly yelled, 'That's exactly what I intend to do - shoot this worthless piece of trash!' After spewing out those words, he grabbed the woman's hair and pulled her head back. Holding onto her long hair, he made her bloodied face appear. It was Rose's friend, Delilah! Alwhite staggered and stood with his knees buckling and feet spread apart. 'I'm going to put a lead ball through the head of this river whore!'

"Having trouble keeping Sassafras calm, Rose jumped from her buggy and began to console her horse. Pulling the bridle, she began leading her to the back of the store away from the commotion that was upsetting her horse.

"Full of rage and intoxicated to a point of danger, the Englishman saw Rose leading the horse away and began to protest loudly. Swinging the pistol in her direction, he shouted, 'Hey, you Irish bitch - where are you going? Stay where you are or you'll get it first!'

"Rose turned to look at the man yelling at her.

"That was the last thing the drunken Alwhite said before the pistol fired.

"James cringed and before the smoke could settle, he quickly walked over and took the pistol away from the drunk, shoving him to the ground. Never one for violence, the lad's Irish temper came rushing forward and he looked down at the soused man and said, 'Stay on the ground - if you don't want more trouble than you've already got!' The filly had bolted when the shot was fired and she was headed back toward the river. As James turned to Rose, he was struck with terror.

"Hearing her softly call his name, he saw her in a crumpled heap at the edge of the street. He ran to her and put his hand under her head to keep her beautiful hair out of the dirt. With horror, he noticed the small red spot on her bodice and realized the drunken fool had shot her. In shock with panic flooding over him, James began to tremble as he held Rose and repeated, 'It's going to be alright. It's going to be alright.' Rose's voice was barely discernable. He leaned close to her mouth trying to hear what she was saying. Finally, he understood - 'Kiss me, please, kiss me.' As he put his lips on hers, he could feel her life slipping away. Pulling his face back, he focused on her beautiful steel blue eyes, coldly staring at him. In disbelief, he screamed for her to wake up - but she was gone.

"As the men he had been taunting started coming out of the tavern, Delilah ran into the shadows. Alwhite realized he no longer had his pistol for protection, so he toned down his loud voice. Standing over the drunk, one of the men from the tavern saw James holding Rose's body and asked, 'Is she hurt bad?'

"Through tears and sobs he screamed, 'She's dead! He shot her!' Walking over to where James was holding Rose's lifeless body in his arms, the tavern patron bent down to feel her neck for a pulse. Without saying a word, the man from the pub walked back to the drunkard who was struggling to stand up.

"Standing over the murderer as he tried to stand, the angry man shoved Alwhite to the ground with his foot and shouted, 'You worthless piece of horse dung, you killed her!' Enraged, the local Patriot quickly stepped over to the porch of the tavern and with adrenaline pulsing in his veins, he ripped a picket from the porch rail. In the blink of an eye, the man returned to his intended target, who was now wobbling in the street. Cursing, he began to club the Englishman with the short picket. After inflicting much damage to the helpless sot, he broke his weapon. This made the bar patron even more infuriated and he began to kick and stomp the hapless drunk. Finally, he took his foot and rolled the beaten man over on his back and spit on him.

"Spitting blood and missing most of his teeth, the killer was beginning to sober. As his faculties began to return, Alwhite heard his attacker scream, 'You killed her, you fool! You killed Rose!'

"Suddenly, George Galphin's carriage came tearing down the sandy street with Sassafras and Rose's buggy in tow. Sliding to a stop in front of the store, George and Lucy had a look of horror on their faces. Leaping from the carriage, the gentle old man hurried to the boy holding the beautiful Irish lass's limp body in his arms. As tears streamed down his face, the Irish lad was rocking back and forth and talking out of his mind. With his head turned toward the night sky, his breath turned white as it billowed from his mouth. He screamed, 'I love you sweetheart, I love you! Please don't leave me!' Falling on his knees beside the boy, George Galphin realized the heartbreaking situation. Forcing the boy to let go of the beautiful girl's limp body, he immediately saw the small red spot on her white blouse. Putting his fingers to her neck, he searched for a pulse. After a few seconds, he hung his head and put his hand on his young friend's shoulder. Seeing the look on his boss man's face, the boy moaned sorrowfully and screamed, 'Why? Why? Why?' Standing, George walked back toward the carriage to stop Mrs. O'Cain from coming closer to the boy holding the girl's body. Offering her the truth, he stoically said, 'I know it's hard to believe my dear - she's gone.'

"In utter disbelief, Lucy cried out, 'No! No! It can't be! It's not true! She's my partner and my friend! She's the daughter that Enoch and I had always wanted! No, God, it can't be!' Completely distraught, Lucy fell into the arms of the backcountry gentleman as he helplessly tried to console her.

"Through the fog of a drunken stupor, the bleeding and beaten killer started to comprehend what he had done. As his faculties began to return, he realized his predicament and knew he needed to flee. With everyone in shock and looking away from him, he crawled, unseen, to the buggy tied behind George's carriage. Untying the reins, Alister Abrams Alwhite, III climbed in and whipped the filly, desperately trying to escape his deadly mistake."

***

Salley pushed the button to stop the recording machine and it made a loud click noise. Straining to see his daughter, Sully knew the story of Rose and the first James Anthony had caused her melancholy mood to reappear. Salley was crying and this frustrated Sully more than anything else. He knew why she was crying, and for whom she cried, but he was helpless to even console her.

Picking up the New York Times crossword puzzle, Salley tried to get her mind off of Sully's sad story. She began reading the clues to her father and he immediately began to give her the words to fill in the puzzle. Each time he gave her an answer, his eyes met hers and seemed to ask the question, *Sweetheart, what's wrong?*

Salley wondered if grief was consuming her, too. She had been forced away from the love of her life and no one or nothing could fill the void she felt in her heart. She was three months pregnant and Dr. Baughman was urging her to tell Sully about the expected child. She had part of James growing inside her and she did not want anything to jeopardize that precious gift from the man she loved.

Drying her tears and composing herself somewhat, she put her cheek next to Sully. He knew Salley needed to tell him something important. She had been focusing all of her time on him and he did not want her to be burdened with more sorrow. Salley had never kept anything from her father and he knew she needed to unburden herself.

Having finished the daily crossword puzzle with her father, Salley knew she had to tell Sully about the baby, but above all, she did not want to upset him. When he cried, his nose stopped up and just that little trauma was life-threating for him. She could not bear the sight of him struggling for air, but she could not wait any longer. Rubbing her hand across her father's unruly hair, she smiled and said, "Sully, this is the only thing I have ever kept from you and I can't hide it any longer. I'm expecting your grandchild." She was shocked when she leaned down to hear his words.

"I know my dear! I have known unofficially for quite some time and I am overjoyed that you and James are blessing me with a grandchild. It is marvelous news - I wish I had a cigar!" Salley smiled at him and kissed him on the forehead. She should have known she couldn't hide anything from that man!

With more reason than ever to record his family's history, Sully urged Salley to let him continue narrating his story. Depressing the two buttons that started the recorder, she knew, at least at that moment, Sully was happy.

**

"Word of Rose's death spread through the backcountry settlement like wild fire and the people of Horse Creek Valley and beyond grieved with George Galphin and Lucy O'Cain. Everyone wanted to avenge her death and a group of men quickly pursued the Englishman. He was caught three days later, hiding in the woods. Those who knew Lucy and George Galphin did not want to return the killer to Silver Bluff. They wanted to spare both Lucy and George the sorrow of having to see the man who had killed the girl they thought of as their own. The men hastily put a noose around his neck and hung him in the woods near where they caught him. Several of the men shot his lifeless body as he dangled from the tree limb, trying to achieve some form of satisfaction from such a despicable person. No one took his body down from the tree and it was left disrespectfully suspended from the rope. Days later, the Native Americans of the area happened upon the body and decided the area should be avoided. Any white man who was killed and was not buried, but left hanging from a tree, was bad medicine.

"Standing on the dock as the Captain's ship dropped the last of its sails and was guided skillfully alongside the dock, George Galphin met the Captain with news of the lass's death. In his sorrow, James had told George Galphin of the affection Rose had for the pod of dolphins that glided gracefully beside the ship on their crossing. Upon hearing those words, Galphin immediately had Clinalee begin the task of making a coffin for Rose's burial. After building a most handsome box of pine wood, the old millwright finished it with lacquer and adorned it with bright brass handles. On its top, he spent hours carving a magnificent rose and afterwards, at George Galphin's behest, he gilded the pedals with a thin layer of gold.

"Silently, they traveled down the Savannah River in one of Galphin's boats with the body of the Irish lass who had touched so many lives. As the Captain and crew began preparing for their voyage back to Belfast, the crew carefully took the coffin aboard and secured it on the bow near the anchor alcove. On their return passage, the crew waited until the dolphins were swimming alongside the ship and then reverently slid the exquisite box into the wake thrown up by the keel of the ship. As the Captain watched the beautiful box quickly drop below the surface, the usually stoic man wept. Many of the old sailors cried, but some held their sorry inside. The return crossing was a quiet, sorrowful voyage, during which the Captain spoke very few words. He spent a lot of hours in his cabin with a bottle of scotch whiskey, trying to figure out how he would tell her mother and the 'uncles' at the bar the devastating news."

Chapter 5

"The news of Rose's death spread an abiding sorrow across the backcountry and eventually down into the Low Country. The sad news crossed the Atlantic and brought sorrow to the green glens of the Emerald Isles. The young girl had touched the lives of so many people and each now felt as if something beautiful had been snatched from their lives.

"The initial tragedy that the first James Anthony Sullivan faced in the New World was enough to stop him in his tracks. In his young life, he had been consumed by so many heartbreaks, but this one seemed too much for him to handle. Rose was his reason for living, his hope for the future and nothing he could do from this point forward meant anything. Losing himself in the work at the mill, he was a shell of a person who had been rendered deaf and mute by his grief. The words that people spoke to him did not make sense and he did not respond.

"For months, James wore a shroud of grief after Rose's death. As if he was sleepwalking, his motions were automatic and he spoke very few words. He followed a daily routine of working in the mills from the moment he woke until exhaustion made him find his bed. After returning home from a delivery to Augusta, he told his mentor he could not go again for it tore his heart open each time he faced the people of the villages and saw the pity that poured from their faces. All of them knew of his tragedy and tried too hard, in their humble ways, to help him. The solitude of the mill became his refuge and the people of Silver Bluff allowed him the space to grieve alone. When there was no corn or grain to be milled, he worked on the elaborate mechanism or did maintenance in and around the mill house. He did not venture away from his safe harbor among the bags of grain and meal with the sound of the waterwheel. Clinalee's wife, Mattie, made sure he ate and that he kept himself clean as they grieved with him. They were never judgmental, nor did they try to hurry him through his healing process.

"In the months after Rose's death, James' grieving process came to an abrupt halt. His was not allowed to linger in his haven of solitude, for the British Army invaded the South and was bearing down on Silver Bluff. Each day brought more bad news as Charles Town and Savannah were captured by the King's troops. George Galphin finally had to move his family deep into the Creek Nation for their safety, but he returned to his plantation to face the inevitable onslaught. During this time, George Galphin dodged multiple assassination attempts because of a price placed on his head by the British Crown. As the Redcoats marched into the backcountry, they captured Silver Bluff and took George Galphin prisoner. He was held captive in his own house and told he would be sent to Savannah to be tried for treason and then hanged. Watching his plantation being pillaged and plundered was devastating, but when part of his family deserted him and sided with the British, Galphin was crushed.

"To reinforce their loyalty to George Galphin, their friend and advisor for decades, many of the Muskogee Creek chiefs from the Lower Nation demanded the British Army allow a meeting with their old enhesse (Creek for friend). Trying to maintain a friendship with the Native Americans, the Redcoat officer holding Galphin allowed the chiefs to visit with him. Using a little-known dialect of the Creek language, Galphin and his Creek friends discussed the fact that some of the other Creek leaders from the Upper Nation were offering to help the British. They told Galphin of their refusal to join the Upper Creek tribes in joining the British. Their refusal stemmed from their intense loyalty to George Galphin, who had asked them to remain neutral. Their loyalty to Galphin blocked the entire Creek Confederation of villages and tribes from wholesale joining with the British. George Galphin continued to implore them to remain neutral and not aid the British. They assured him their tribes and villages in the Lower Nation would not help the British. It George Galphin's greatest contributions in the fight for independence. Without his close friendships with the leaders of the Lower Creek nations, the Patriot cause in the backcountry would have likely faced a bloody defeat.

"After the meetings, Galphin was also able to get word out to the Continental leaders as to what he had discussed with the Creek leaders in his house. He passed word to the Patriot militias that James knew the locations of hundreds of stockpiles of arms he had securely hidden before his capture. The invading British Army thought Clinalee was a slave. They kept trying to offer him his freedom, but he acted like he was deaf and didn't understand. He continued to run the mill and did what the British told him to do. James, however, became part of the Patriot Militia and upon every opportunity, he clandestinely met with Clinalee. Delivering cornmeal, clothes and a major part of the arms hidden around Silver Bluff to the Patriots fighting in the backcountry, James Anthony Sullivan, the millwright apprentice, became an admired freedom fighter. With reckless abandon, he fought in every battle he could and most thought he had a death wish. He killed every British person with whom he was confronted. Several times, he defied death and plowed into the heat of a battle with nothing more than a bayonet and an empty rifle. In a year's time, James Sullivan was known as a ruthless soldier and had killed too many British, Tories and Loyalists to count. With nothing to lose, he was a killing machine and he lived in hiding among the Creek people, near Silver Bluff.

"Near middle of winter, word came from the big brick house that George Galphin had died and James felt as if the world was falling apart. Clinalee had been trying to stop the slaves from running off and joining the British, but his efforts had little effect on those who wanted their freedom. The slave congregation of Silver Bluff Baptist Church followed Preacher David George and fled south to Savannah as the tide of the war began to turn. After the fall of Charles Town and Savannah, most in the backcountry felt as if the War for Independence had been lost. It was told that 5000 Patriot soldiers were captured with the city's fall and most of the common people in South Carolina and Georgia were resigned to defeat.

"But the gods of war turned on the British and in the year after Galphin's death, the noose began to tighten around the necks of the British forces in the South. France and Spain had allied with the Patriot cause and James followed and fought with brave leaders like Francis Marion, Thomas Sumter and Andrew Pickens as they continued to use their guerilla tactics to weaken the spread-thin British Army. After the

Overmountain men defeated British Major Patrick Ferguson at Kings Mountain, the British Army seemed to lose their momentum. General George Washington sent Patriot General Nathaniel Green to lead the southern theatre of the war. When he arrived, he quickly sent General Daniel Morgan and his men to meet up with Andrew Pickens and his men. Together, they battled the British Army led by Lieutenant Colonel Tarleton at a place called Cowpens. The two Patriot armies thoroughly trounced the Redcoats and Loyalists and their victory swung the momentum of the war in favor of the upstart Americans. As the inevitable became clear, the local Tories and Loyalists who had supported the British had to make a grave decision - leave everything they had built and earned in the New World and flee with the Redcoat Army or be brutalized and probably killed by the victorious Americans.

"After George Galphin's death, James became even more involved in Patriot Cause and fought in every battle possible. During the British occupation of South Carolina, he took many chances and risked his life many times to smuggle arms and food to the Continental Army. He fought in quite a few skirmishes and also in the battle to retake Augusta. He was a dependable merchant of death when the British were involved and would fight whenever and wherever needed. His grief was replaced by rage and he fought unconditionally as a Patriot and American.

"Soon, the inevitability of fighting a guerilla war against a determined and entrenched group of rebels began to play out. Stretched too thin across the colonies, the main thrust of the King's Army worked its way into a trap. As news of the Patriot's victory over Cornwallis at Yorktown spread throughout the southern colonies, a huge transformation began to take place. The British Army began to retreat to Charles Town and when they finally sailed away in 1782, the remaining Loyalists and Tories who had supported them were at the mercy of the new Patriot government. Many were tarred and feathered, as Loyalist families were driven from their homes. Still others who had remained loyal to the King were killed on the spot. Their property was taken from their families and distributed among those who had fought in the Patriot Army. A surge of chaos seemed to consume the new nation as its leaders tried to figure a way to organize a new government.

"As the fighting stopped, James wearily began his return to Silver Bluff from the Low Country. In the late afternoon, just after he crossed the South Edisto River, he came upon the mill he and Clinalee had constructed for the Englishman who killed Rose. Enraged at the thought of the murderous Brit, the weary soldier was pulled to the sound of the water flowing through the millrace. The soothing sound of the water comforted him and as his anger dissipated, he decided to take a look at the mill, hoping it would offer him more comfort and a chance to reflect on everything that had happened as of late. Turning his horse onto the sandy lane that led to the mill, he heard nothing but the water falling from the from the millrace. Riding up in front of the building, he tiredly climbed off of his horse and headed into the millhouse. Once inside, the comforting sound of the water hypnotized him. Standing in the cobweb-filled building, he felt at home as he imagined how he could rebuild the mechanism and change it from a sawmill to a gristmill. In his mind, he could see a steady stream of corn dropping from a wooden hopper and disappearing between two huge turning millstones and emerging as corn meal from under the carved granite boulders. That site always offered him satisfaction. He realized he had within him the ability to build and manage just such a complicated mechanism. Such knowledge was a rare talent and he was filled with pride as he thought about the gift he had received from his mentor. As James stood staring at the idle mill in a trance-like state, he had an epiphany. *This is it! This is where I will cast my lot!* Looking around the rough walls of the building, he removed his hat and coat, smiled and hung them on a peg sticking out of one of the pine logs.

"The next day, James, with Clinalee by his side, traveled to Ninety Six, the district seat, and petitioned an official of the new government to allow James to take possession of the Englishman's land and mills. To his surprise, one of the men he had fought beside was now in charge of distributing land and property seized from the British. It was being given to soldiers who had fought in the War. When James inquired as to the ownership of the Englishman's land

and property, he was summarily asked if he would like to own it. With a quick 'yes', his fellow soldier completed legal papers and stamped them with official looking seals. He left the court house as a property owner and a happy man.

"Arriving back at the mill, he soon had it converted to a gristmill and with two millstones from a mill the British had burned, he soon had his mill rumbling again. At first, there was little to no corn or grain to be milled, but he continued to work on his millworks. Soon, traders and backwoods folk were dropping in to meet the Irish lad who had worked for George Galphin. The lad now owned the only business for miles around. James was excited and looked forward to returning to the life of a miller, but that idea was to be delayed. Selling merchandise and trading with locals was not what James considered his vocation, but it was forced upon him. Having seen Lucy and Rose doing business in their store, he threw himself wholeheartedly into that same task. Being the only supply station in the area, the little trading post prospered and grew into a regular stop on the soon-to-be thoroughfare between the backcountry and the newly named city of Charleston. In what seemed like the blink of an eye, farmers were stopping by to drop off corn and grain to be milled. He enthusiastically began milling again, but soon found the huge demand for alcohol to be much more profitable. Adding a new little tavern to the side of his mill, it became a popular spot along the well-traveled road. Clinalee came over often from Silver Bluff and taught James the process of making corn whiskey and home-brewed ale. With plenty of raw material from the mill tolls, the brewing business became a major part of James' overall income. Buying jugs and crocks from a potter near Edgefield, he peddled homebrew and corn whiskey by the glass or bottle. Catering to a wide range of clientele, he even sold whiskey to people as far away as Charleston. His tavern soon became a necessary stop for any person traveling in his neck of the woods.

"Once ingrained in the community, the business became a trading center with a stable income. A year passed and James could hardly believe he was doing so well. Continuing his hard work, yet another year passed and then, in the fall of his third year as a backcountry merchant, he was visited by a man he had seen only once at a distance. In his years at Silver Bluff, he had met and had a cordial association with Clarissa, an attractive Creole woman who worked in the main house and kitchen. Often, he had seen her daughter, Salley, with Mister George, whom she called 'Grandfather'. When not with her grandfather, he had often seen her playing with the other children about the main house. Even from a distance, it was clear she was friends with everyone at Silver Bluff. Clinalee told James that Salley was George Galphin's favorite among his progeny. She was regularly taken to Augusta to see her Aunt Judith and go to school. Whenever he had seen her around her grandfather or playing or traveling to school, she was dressed like a white person. But just as often, she could be seen dressed like an Indian with her hair braided and her beautiful blue eyes gleaming. Clinalee had pointed out her father, George the Younger, on one of his visits to the big house at Silver Bluff. He was an Indian from head to toe and not very cordial. Clinalee didn't give his opinion of George the Younger, but it was obvious he didn't cotton to him very much.

"George Galphin the Younger was the older Galphin's namesake. His mother was George, Sr.'s second Creek wife. She was named Metawney (Meh-taw-ney´) and was the woman with whose clan he was raised in the Lower Creek Nation near Coweta. With limited success, George the Younger had tried to continue his father's business after his death and was presently on his way to trade with the Beaver Creek Tribe between the branches of the North and South Edisto Rivers.

"The Beaver Creek Indians had befriended James when he first acquired the mill and for some reason, they had always brought their many deerskins to him for trade. George the Younger thought he should be the only person trading in deerskins in the area and was somewhat outdone with James moving in on his territory. He had stopped in to have a talk and hoped to stop James' incursion into what he thought of as his zone of business.

"Dressed in Indian regalia and wearing a feather hanging from his hair, he looked like a shrewd character and

James kept his eye on him while he was in the store. To his surprise, James recognized the very pretty girl who was accompanying him was the little girl who called George Galphin, Sr. her grandfather. He immediately remembered the first time they met on the whistler's walk behind the main brick house at Silver Bluff and recalled her name, Salley. She was, however, very different now and he was shocked to see how much she had grown. Dressed as an Indian, she was now a beautiful woman and she caught James staring at her on several occasions.

"George the Younger explained, in his gruff and unfriendly manner, they were just passing through the area and only stopped by the tavern to obtain the deerskins that belonged to him. James smiled, but never agreed to give him the deer pelts. As the day turned to evening, George the Younger continued to enjoy the home brewed ale, but was having no luck obtaining what he wanted. Pretty near drunk, he decided to stay the night and he asked about a room for his daughter. She was a dazzling woman with a dark complexion and looked to be 15 or 16 years old. James had no rooms to let, but he felt the young woman needed a proper place to spend the night. Cleaning a path onto his sleeping porch, he offered her use of his cot and tried to make her comfortable as best he could. After getting her settled, James was about to make his way to the mill with his pillow under his arm, when George the Younger announced he would stay in the tavern through the night. He said he had to protect his daughter, but James knew he just wanted to continue enjoying the rich barley beverage. James gave him a jug of the home brew, then locked and bolted the rest of the alcoholic drinks.

"The next morning, the Indian Trader was gone and he had left without paying his tab. Realizing he had abandoned his daughter, James was embarrassed for her, but she was not in the least. With her head held high, she matter-of-factly confessed that he had done this before and she was left to work off his tab. Though her father would not be returning for her any time soon, she never shed a tear and agreed to work as James' servant to pay off the amount owed.

"Besides being beautiful, strong and friendly, she was the most attractive and available woman for miles around. Showing a work ethic that impressed the rugged men and women in this backcountry region, she began cooking over the fire in the tavern. James quickly made arrangements with a traveling drummer to deliver a bevy of iron cookware on his next pass through the area. Salley began simmering wild game meat and catfish stews over the fire coals. In addition, she started baking hardy loaves of bread made from the mill's flour. She worked as hard as James and tried to please him in everything she did.

"Curious as to why he did not demand she sleep with him, she asked him one day while they were alone. 'Why do you not want me in your bed? I am here for you and will do everything to please you!' Embarrassed, James looked down as he told her he had never had sex with a woman. Shocked, she asked, 'Do you like boys?'

"Quickly, James spoke up and sternly said, 'Absolutely not! I like women just as well as the next man, but…' He stopped and looked at the floor again before continuing, 'I just never got around to doing that.'

"Salley Galphin could not believe what he was telling her. Walking away from him, she continued to think about what he had said. She knew about James and Rose and she had been told of the crushing grief that had crippled the Irish lad after her death. Standing silent for a moment, she stared at James. As he looked up to see her gazing at him, she suddenly stepped close to him and kissed him in a most passionate manner. Salley Galphin decided at that moment it was time to consummate their union and past time for James to lose his virginity.

"With her mind made up, she swiftly shooed the last two men swilling ale out of the tavern. Handing them a half-full jug of home brew, she hurried them out the door and locked it behind them. Taking James' hand, she led him to his bed that he had graciously given over to her when she first arrived. Very slowly, she began to undress the Irishman as he stood without protest. After pulling his over-the-calf moccasins off, she pulled his shirt over his head and wasted no time removing his breeches. Smiling at his arousal, she poured water from a pitcher into the bowl on the crude table. While bathing him, she was quiet and afterwards, she patted his body dry before she led him to the bed. Pushing him down on the corn shuck tick, she picked up his feet and laid him in the middle of the homemade mattress. Standing beside the bed, she stepped out of her moccasins and looked intently into James eyes. In a sultry, seductive manner, she slowly slid her hands down her doeskin dress. Grasping each side of the beaded material around the hem, she pulled it up and over her head.

"James' heart began to pound furiously as she pulled the beaded rawhide string holding her hair away from her face. Like raven-colored silk, it cascaded over her shoulders as she straddled James' body with her legs and leaned down to kiss him. The warmth of her breasts invaded his body as she probed his mouth her tongue. Every part of James' body was tingling as her ebony hair danced across his face. Slowly moving her breasts across his face, he took each into his mouth as she pulled his head close to her body. Feeling as if he were about to explode, the 35-year-old virgin was engulfed by the most warm and sensuous feeling he had ever experienced. Moving her body slowly up and down, she made his breathing labored and James felt a building crescendo like nothing he had ever experienced before. Suddenly, his eyes rolled back in his head as she slowed her up and down movements to extend his pleasure. The buildup and explosion eclipsed anything he had ever felt before. It was the greatest physical feeling James had ever been subjected to and he moaned with pleasure as she kissed his face and slowly ground her hips into his groin. Heaving for breath, James could feel her warmth as she lay beside him. As he caught his breath, she said, 'James Anthony Sullivan, I am YOUR woman now - and forever.' With a sensation that could not be explained, he leaned down to kiss her as she lay smiling next to him.

"With a sense of need, she pulled him on top of her and this time, with her guidance, he moved as her passion demanded. Staring down into her beautiful blue eyes, James felt he loved her with every being of his body. Urging him on, she arched her back and demanded he reach her deepest being and he obliged with wholehearted enthusiasm. As she closed her eyes and began to breathe heavily through her mouth, he did as she had and slowed his movements, making her pleasure last as long as possible. The sound of her rapid breathing and moans sent shock waves through James and once again, he exploded into a surreal world of pleasure and ecstasy.

"Completely spent, James lay beside her, breathing as if he had chased a runaway mule for a mile. With a huge smile on his face, he looked over at his partner - she was smiling, too!

"Regaining her composure, Salley was bubbling over with excitement as she totally engulfed the man who had brought her so much pleasure. Grasping her in a bear hug, James was over the moon at what she had introduced to him. He would look forward to being in bed with her each day for the rest of his life.

"Salley's father, George the Younger, stopped by to fetch his daughter several months later, assuming she had had time to work off his debt. She defiantly refused to rejoin his traveling group and told him she would be staying permanently with the Irishman. She then boldly unveiled a list of actions her father would be taking concerning her. First, he owed her money for his drinking debt that she had worked to clear. She told him he would be paying it before they spoke again. Second, she would soon be claiming the inheritance her grandfather had left her - 200 acres and 20 head of cattle - and he was to no longer consider them his property. Her grandfather, upon his death, had also given her freedom. In that she was no longer a slave, she could now, as a free person, own property. Her mother was not so lucky; she was given as inherited property to George the Younger.

"The sudden announcement of her independence did not go over well with her father. He felt everything she owned belonged to him. Standing her ground, she made her third declaration. In a clear, resolute voice, she announced he was to deliver to her, 20 head of cattle pulled from her grandfather's herd, to include 19 cows and one bull. And fourth and finally, she would be selling her 200 acres of property at Silver Bluff and if he wanted to buy it she would name a price for him, otherwise it would be sold to the highest bidder.

"Her father was incensed at her attitude and words. He had dominated her life since she was a little girl and now, not only had he lost her, he had lost her land and cattle. He was not about to let this happen, but he didn't know presently what he could do. He stormed off shouting Creek insults at her as she stood with a smile and watched him go.

"Her father's hiatus was not permanent, however, as he returned often to try and bilk her out of her inheritance. He tried on many occasions to deal with his daughter, but she refused all lower offers and demanded the cattle be brought to her or she would seek legal assistance. Each time he came to deal with her, James stayed out of the fray, but it was all he could do to keep from laughing out loud at times. She had her grandfather's business sense and was not going to allow her father to take advantage of her.

"While James Anthony and Salley Galphin knew they were man and wife, the others in the community began to wonder why they had not had a preacher to marry them. James Anthony knew of the community scuttlebutt and it began to bother him.

"For almost two years, they had worked together with smiles on their faces and did little things that grew their affection for one another. Having a chance to purchase a bathtub from a house owned by an Englishman in Augusta, James installed it near the fireplace in their sleeping room. He would heat her water and while she bathed, he would wash her long ebony hair and comb it dry. She could hardly keep her hands off of him and often in the middle of the day, she would appear naked in the mill and make passionate love to him in the storeroom. The frontier couple realized the immense joy they created in being together. As James Anthony and Salley welcomed the beginning of their second year together, James, with Salley's help, let Rose's memory slip into the further recesses of his thoughts. As the pangs of his first love waned, he realized his true feelings for Salley. Finally, after a winter together and a glorious spring of love blooming everywhere, James Anthony Sullivan, a former indentured servant from Ireland, took as his wife, Salley Halona Galphin, the daughter of a slave and a Creek Indian. They were married in early summer by a man who claimed to be a traveling preacher. While standing under a tall longleaf pine growing on an island in the middle of the creek feeding the millpond, they thanked the Creator for bringing them together. With each holding a dogwood blossom, they reached to the separate streams on each side of the tree and dropped the flowers into the flowing waters. Holding hands, they watched as the blooms danced on their way, swirling together in the main stream and rushing as one bouquet into the millpond. Salley would call him James Anthony and he liked that she did. His mother had called him by his first and middle names and it made him feel good. Happy with what had transpired, Salley became James Anthony's lifelong spouse, helpmate, partner and passionate lover while the backcountry population grew along with their business. Having the only food for sale for miles, her cooking soon became legendary along the backwoods trail and a stop at Salley's kitchen became a must if traveling overland from Charleston to the backcountry.

"Over the years, the area around the mill, inevitably, became known as Salleys Kitchen and a community was born. At one time, it was considered a village. The inhabitants of the sand hill community were a hodge-podge of people from different European countries, but the population was most heavily influenced by German, British and Scots-Irish immigrants. A variety of religions were represented, but most were Protestants. They all sought the freedom that was offered in the new nation. The hope offered by that freedom led them to uproot their lives and families to move thousands of miles to a New World across a vast ocean. Each person knew their decision to live in such a remote location near the wilderness carried great risk and all were aware of the hardships they would face. That is precisely why each understood the importance of having good neighbors. They learned quickly that helping a neighbor insured them of help in their time of need. By supporting each other, they were able to live together in harmony. The War for Independence was a world-changing event. In its aftermath, a sense of hope and optimism engulfed the homes and farms around Salleys Kitchen as it did all around the fledgling nation. As the new little nation struggled to get its footing on the world stage, its inhabitants were optimistic.

"As always happens after a revolution, there was a sense of bedlam in the air as those who had supported the enemy were purged from communities. Loyalists and Tories across the new country were forced from their homes as their property was confiscated by the new government. But after a time, the chaos began to wane as the new government created a constitution and laws were enforced. The country began to take the form of a civilized nation with rules and consequences. As it had since it was first explored, the backcountry around the Central Savannah River Area attracted quite a few timber and agricultural entrepreneurs. Some of the people coming into the backcountry were wealthy absentee owners who bought large tracts of land. For the most part, however, those who came seeking a new life were hard working people who enjoyed the liberty the new nation offered. The liberating promise of life, liberty and the pursuit of happiness allowed the locals, though diverse in many ways, to live together in the new melting pot society.

"As more people moved into the area, more parts of the old growth pine forest were cleared and the rich black soil in the low areas became productive farm land with the promise of a secure income and way of life.

"As an Irish indentured servant, James Anthony had miraculously escaped the starvation and plague in his home country and had been blessed with the opportunity to begin a new life in the New World. Rose's death and the War for Independence had changed all of his hopes and dreams. Now, as part of a new nation and a growing community, James Anthony Sullivan felt as if the sun was shining on him once again. With a thriving backcountry business, he was ready to continue his dream in the New World and take his place as a leader among the people of Salleys Kitchen. Vowing to follow in his father's footsteps, his vision was to bring together generous, hard-working people who wanted to grow and prosper together. He wanted to build a community in which everyone strived for things that benefited the entire community. The words of the new nation's constitution were ingrained in his heart: …that all men are created equal and endowed by their creator with certain inalienable rights, among them was life, liberty and the pursuit of happiness. With those immortal words as his mantra, James Anthony began his life's work as a community builder in the brand-new country, the United States of America."

***

When Sully reached this point in his family's history, Salley believed he would soon end his marathon recording sessions and relax for a while. He was, however, just getting started.

The story of Rose and James made Salley reflect on the loss she had endured. She, too, had lost the love of her life and was now pregnant, drifting alone in shark infested waters. She knew exactly what Jon Chesterfield, Jr. was about. Without asking, he had taken a lot of liberties and she was concerned about the boldness with which he was controlling her life. He had, however, made her life so much simpler and his latest gift was beyond anything she could imagine. With an unlimited pot of money, he had leased two iron lung machines and had them installed in the solarium attached to the guest house. In a complicated move, he had Sully transported in a portable machine to the guest house, so Salley could relax and be with her father. It was truly an unbelievable act and he had worked hard to accomplish it for her.

Jon, Jr. had new floor to ceiling windows installed in the sun room and they allowed Sully the opportunity to turn his head and see Salley riding Spot in the adjacent paddock. That, along with a copy of the New York Times being dropped on the front lawn every morning, was truly the best medicine available for a man who was completely paralyzed and unable to breathe on his own. How could she be mad at Jon, Jr.'s interference in her life after he had done so much for her and Sully? Salley now had only to come downstairs and get the newspaper to start the day with her father. There had never been a mention of money for any of the things he had done or the expenses incurred in keeping the Sullivan family happy. The Sullivan mansion, however, had all but been abandoned and Salley did not know when or how she would return to her home. Jon, Jr. had gone out and gathered all of Salley's clothes and belongings and brought them to his guest house. He was slowly gaining control of her entire life. She ran errands about town in Jon's little red convertible Mercedes sports car. He traded his old sports car for this new one because he wanted her to have an automatic transmission to drive. After driving up and down the dirt streets of Aiken, she had finally mastered driving and had gotten her driver's license. He never told Salley 'no' when she requested something. Sully had around-the-clock nurses and a doctor who visited him once a week to check on his wellbeing. He was cared for better than any hospital could have offered. Salley continued to stay by Sully's side as much as possible. She was rarely away for more than an hour or two and she was most often found in her comfortable chair beside Sully's head.

Though she did not have to worry about money whatsoever, she had paid a price for all of the amenities about her. Unexpectedly, Jon Chesterfield, Jr. had approached her in the massive brick barn and kissed her in a most passionate manner. It took Salley by surprise. She did not return the kiss, but it seemed to open the door to more of his advances. Late one night as she lay in bed, he tapped on her door and came in her room. Sitting on the bed beside her, he ran his hands over her legs and told her he was in love with her. Quickly, she told him she was carrying James' baby and she still loved him. Though she offered him an apology, he seemed undeterred as he kissed her again before leaving and this time he slipped his tongue into her mouth. Salley did not sleep a wink after he left, but lay in the dark rubbing her growing stomach as she stared out the window. The moon illuminated the horse paddocks and she wondered if the same moon was shining on James. She thought, *James, my dear James, where are you? Please come save me! I'm drifting in a sea of regret and can't do anything about it. I don't want to live without you! Please, James, please come save me!*

The next morning, Salley came downstairs very early and as the darkness began to turn to light, she sat beside her father and put her cheek beside his face. Since the moment she began to talk, she had a habit of telling Sully everything that happened to her. He knew well what she was going through, and what she was dealing with, but he was helplessly trapped in the damned hissing machine. His well-being depended on his daughter's actions with Jon Chesterfield, Jr. and he felt as if he was prostituting his own daughter. How much tragedy could he endure? He struggled to keep his sanity as he lay in the iron lung and focused on his one mission - he was ready to continue the epic story of his family.

As had been her practice, Salley was at Sully's beckoning call and upon his request, she was there to assist him. With a click, the recorder started and Sully continued to tell the story of his ancestors.

***

"Just after the War for Independence was won, the good citizens of the Holy City decided their city needed a new name. It was decided that they should change the name of their city from Charles Town to Charleston. As the unique and proud people of that thriving port city moved out of the 1700s and into the 1800s, many of its residents were well on their way to becoming wealthy. One of the nouveau riche families living in a stately house along fashionable King Street faced an embarrassing dilemma. One of their young house slaves had given birth to a beautiful baby girl with the softest alabaster skin imaginable. Though everyone about the house knew this child to be the result of repeated trysts between the master's youngest son and the coal black daughter of the cook, from all appearances, she was white. If she had displayed even the slightest bit of dark pigment in her lovely smooth skin, the problem would not have been such a burden. This child, however, was lily white, making the cook and the cook's daughter fearful of the severe repercussions that could occur from their raising and publicly proclaiming this white child as their own. The master and mistress of the house had quite the same misgivings and knew it to be impossible to keep this beautiful Caucasian-looking girl as a slave in their house.

"This dilemma, however, was not the first time such a faux pas had presented itself. The ruling White society of this up-and-coming seaport city had exacted complete and utter control over any slave they owned. Routinely using female slaves as sex toys was, though not discussed in mixed company, a common practice. Sexually gratifying oneself with a slave was thought of as nothing more than masturbation. While it might seem the adolescent slave girl may have too easily conceded herself to the master's son, to refuse him would have been an act of self-destruction. And while impregnating one's slave was commonplace, producing a child with such stunningly white skin was unusual. There was, however, in this genteel Christian society, a means of handling just such rare occurrences in a covert manner.

"With blunt orders from the mistress of the house, the child's mother and grandmother kept the baby away from any public eyes. She spent her first year in the back of the kitchen and slept with her mother in the coal storage area of the basement. Just before her second birthday, when the mistress thought it was appropriate to wean the child, arrangements were made and a man in a carriage came clopping down the narrow back alley behind the house. As the skittish young buggy horse was reined to a stop, the child's grandmother spotted the rig from the kitchen window. Hooking the horse to the fence post, the man of the cloth stepped through the back gate and walked up to the house. Dressed in all black with a white shirt and wide brimmed black parson's hat, he appeared to be a preacher from one of the many churches in the city. Expressionless, he knocked on the kitchen door. As it opened, a large Black woman in cooking attire appeared.

"Previous repercussions had taught her to wear the guise of a smile and smother the grief-stricken condition gripping her heart. Holding the innocent little ivory girl in her arms, the grandmother presented the child wearing a beautiful frilly yellow dress that the mistress had provided. The little girl seemed content sucking on her thumb. With little fanfare, the man reached to take the youngster into his arms. Quickly turning away, he began walking back to the buggy. As they walked, the toddler reached to touch his wide brim hat, but he pulled her hand down with a jerk.

"A couple of years later, just before the beautiful multicolored flowers exploded everywhere in the semitropical seaport, a young sea captain paced back and forth on the porch of his pastel beige mansion overlooking the Charleston Harbor. Captain Alfred Charles Rutledge was nervously puffing a cigar as he tried to calm his mind. Thinking back to the hardships of his youth, it was an unlikely journey that led him to this veranda amidst the quality people of this up and coming city.

"Never having such a home as a boy, the Captain remembered always being hungry as a child. Just before his 10th birthday, he was sold to sea by his father so bread could be bought for the rest of the family. While it should have been a tragic moment in his life, it instead became his greatest opportunity. Once shipboard, riding the rolling waves, he flourished and began to grow into a man. Learning the life of a seaman, he worked far beyond what was demanded of him and soon distinguished himself among his shipmates. Trying never to make an enemy, he had, at times, had to defend himself and he did so in a convincing fashion. Earning the respect of his shipmates, he caught the attention of the old Captain and he took the boy under his wing. The Captain of the boy's first ship taught him the importance of loyalty, hard work and remaining calm during adversity. His mates and the captain marveled at his 'take-charge' attitude and he soon earned his way to first mate, a position usually held by much older and seasoned sailors. Never hesitating, he was always ready to jump in and help and quickly became a steadying influence on the other members of the crew during times of emergency.

"On a voyage down the Atlantic coast, his captain took ill. By the time the multi-mast ship reached the bottom of the continent of South America and began its course around the Horn, the old commander collapsed and was forced to his cabin. With a look of confidence, the steadfast first mate took the helm and guided the ship through the most dangerous part of the passage, the Straits of Magellan. As his shipmates screamed for him to turn back, he fought to keep the ship on course as the torrential storm raged. Through the treacherous channel around the tip of South America, he barked orders and faced Poseidon's wrath without fear. His crew was in awe and blessed his name for snatching them from the grips of death. But his heroics could not stop the captain's demise and just a few days after passing around the Horn, he died of pneumonia. The crew agreed on the Captain's burial at sea.

"After the tumultuous mid-voyage events, the greenhorn captain completed the delivery of passengers and goods to the west coast of the New World. Sternly bargaining, he was able to garner a more than fair price for the freight on board. As the ship was unloaded, the rookie captain negotiated a return load for the vessel and made the trip home through the dangerous waters without incident. Sailing into Charleston Harbor, his crew cheered and fired cannons to celebrate their successful voyage. Offloading the freight and passengers, he walked into the offices of the ship owners and presented them with a handsome profit from the trip. They were surprised, elated and rich because of the exceptional young man's actions. Needless to say, they also celebrated, after which, the ship owners placed the conscientious young man in command of his first ship. With continued dependability through many voyages and some fortunate happenings, including his willingness to participate in the illegal slave trade, he purchased his own ship at a very young age. Wealth had found its way to the young commander, but true happiness was still an alluring mirage. With a new, fashionable young wife and palatial home in Charleston, he longed for the missing piece of the puzzle that would bring him happiness. The elegant mansion echoed with the emptiness of no children and after years of hoping, the wealthy and fashionable couple still had no offspring. Not one to be denied, especially with his lovely wife in tears, the impatient and demanding commodore forged ahead, arranging to adopt a child at his next arrival home.

"While pacing and puffing like a bull before a fight, his house servant came to the front porch and summoned him to the garden arbor in the rear. Throwing down his Cuban cigar, he dashed ahead of the servant through the ornately decorated house, crossed the rear veranda and scurried down the grand steps into the garden. Upon seeing his wife across the grassy yard holding a beautiful little girl on her lap, he slowed his hurried pace and drank in the sight of the stunning little creature wrapped in a bright floral dress. With his heart beating fast and adrenaline pulsing through his body, he dropped to one knee beside his wife and tried to absorb the precious little cherub with magnificent steel blue eyes. Gently touching her as if to ensure she wasn't a mirage, he fought to hold back tears.

"'And this gentleman is going to be your daddy,' the mother said, with tears already rolling down her cheeks. Continuing, she turned to face her husband, 'And sweetheart, we'll be your mommy and daddy from now to forever.' With the tender scene reaching emotional heights, the gentleman standing in the shadows, who looked like a parson, quietly backed away and returned to his buggy waiting in the alley. Clucking to the horse, he whipped the reins and the horse, buggy and man disappeared down the narrow back alley.

"Clara Ruth's childhood was one of opulence. Her father, being a highly successful ship's Captain, was away from home for extended periods of time and left his precious and only child in the loving care of her mother and the house slaves most of the time. His wife was a consummate socialite with strict adherence to the Charleston social seasons. When not entertaining, she was being entertained at the homes of the Low Country aristocracy. With frequent absences of both parents, a private tutor visited the gracious home three days a week to give Clara Ruth instruction and her music coach visited two days a week. During other periods of time, she was 'seen about' by an entourage of trustworthy house slaves who had nurtured her since her arrival. Once the help dressed her in the morning, she had breakfast with her mother, after which she began her daily educational obligations. While her lessons were being completed, her mother attended to the social requirements of a well-to-do woman in Charleston. During her mother's absence, the budding little debutante enjoyed total freedom in and around the beautiful home and gardens. Situated on the exclusive Charleston Battery overlooking the harbor, there was always activity on the streets in front and back of the house. Merchants daily hawked their goods and wares up and down the fashionable avenues, offering items from around the state and the bounty of the world that arrived in the harbor each day. Clara Ruth, privileged and precocious, took advantage of all the eclectic city had to offer. From an early age, she was immersed in the plethora of comforts and extravagances made available by her father's fortune. She wore clothes from Paris, enjoyed candies from Belgium and kept exotic birds and pets from Africa. In addition, she was offered books from around the world. Amazingly, the books were her favorite presents and she gobbled them up as soon as they were made available to her. She spent many lazy afternoons engaged in her favorite activities, swinging in the garden hammock, reading poetry or being transported to faraway lands in the stories from the library of books brought to her by her father.

"The Captain's daughter was the center of his universe and the thoughts of his precious Clara Ruth followed him from the moment he left Charleston Harbor until he returned to his home. On her 12th birthday, he sailed into the harbor at the helm of a brand-new clipper ship he had built to his specifications in the shipyards of Kennard & Williamson in Baltimore, Maryland. The ship was nearly 500 tons and one of the first 'Baltimore Clippers' to sail the seas. It had long, low, sleek lines and skimmed through the water with ease. She was built and finished without regard to cost. With a copper-sheathed bow, the decks gleamed with brass work and polished mahogany. She was a very handsome, yet fast, ship and the pride of her owner, who fittingly named her for the love of his life, *Clara Ruth*.

"Catching the eye of every maritime man in the harbor, she raised quite a stir as the crew dropped her sails and glided to a stop at the Captain's dock. The old salt walked down the gangplank as his excited daughter ran into his arms, squealing with delight. 'Oh, Papa! This is the best present you have ever brought home! I want to go aboard and see her!'

"He quickly said, 'No, sweetheart, shipboard is no place for a female - it's bad luck and I need none of that. You'll have to admire her from the dock. Come, let me show you her name!'

"Not understanding, but always wanting to please her father, she followed him around the dock as he proudly showed off both of his most prized possessions. This was the first time she had ever been to the dock to meet her father. It was only proper to keep her away from his ships, for they were slave ships. While clean and shiny above deck, they were filthy and foul-smelling dungeons below deck. Chains ran the length of the ship in the cargo area where his human payload was shackled to the floor. Covered in human waste and urine, it had to be thoroughly washed down each time his consignment of African captives was unloaded. On each trip, a portion of the enslaved prisoners died in the crossing and their bodies were tossed overboard before reaching the harbor. Seeing the light of the sun only once or twice during the 60 to 80 days of the crossing, the captives were chained below deck like animals. Once in port, the captured Africans were forced from the dark hole of the ship and offloaded at a prison-like holding facility. Only after the ship was thoroughly washed and cleaned was it docked at Captain Rutledge's dock and made ready to take on freight headed for Europe.

"All African men and women were brought to the shores of the United States as chattel slaves. Dazed and confused, they were dragged from the deplorable conditions on board the ships to a holding pen, where huge tanks of brackish water doused them numerous times. Warmed lard was poured over the subdued and starving foreigners huddled in groups. The liquid animal fat made them appear shiny for the auction that was held just days after they arrived. Rags were tossed into the holding pens so they could wipe off some of the filth that lingered on their bodies. They also used the rags to cover their private parts. Still wearing the shackles and chains from the ship, they were sold on an auction block to cotton, tobacco and rice planters from all over the South. After the auction, the Captain received his earnings from the slave sale and quickly reloaded his ship with the bags of rice, bales of cotton and hogsheads of tobacco the planters had hauled to Charleston. Once loaded, he would make the crossing to England with the valuable cargo and sell it to waiting merchants. After the first leg of the triangle trade, he quickly sailed south to the west African shore. Here, kidnapped natives were held in prisons along the African coast. Once the ships docked at the holding facilities, the slaves were shackled and loaded into the hold of the vessel. There, they were chained down for the duration of the return voyage to Charleston.

"As a seafaring businessman, the human cargo was the most lucrative freight of the Captain's Triangle Trade between the U.S., England and Africa. With profits in mind, the Captain oversaw his veteran and brutal crew as they methodically packed as many of the kidnapped humans as possible into the hold of his ship. He only hoped the death rate during the 6 to 8-week crossing would not eat into his profits. On New Year's Day, 1808, a law passed by the U.S. Congress went into effect. This law prohibited the importation of slaves from Africa. The Captain continued with the human trafficking by cunningly eluding the few British and American patrol ships that were making an attempt to prevent the illicit trade. With increasing pressure from Northern political entities, continuing his business in Charleston became difficult. Quickly adapting to the fluctuating world of commerce, he began offloading his now illegal cargo in Cuba. This enabled him to continue his lucrative enterprise with little interruption. The purchase of the speedy new ship had been a business necessity, as well as an occasion to display his success to the city of Charleston.

"As Clara Ruth neared adulthood, the old Captain explained his profession to his daughter and they discussed it often. She understood the commercial aspects of his trade and admired the old Captain, not only as her father, but also as an astute and reputable businessman. As a family, there were no ethical or social concerns about the slave trade. The dangerous voyages with seemingly endless days at sea yielded handsome profits, allowing the family to enjoy a life of luxury while amassing a very sizable fortune.

"Clara Ruth's childhood days were idyllic and though she had an often-absent mother and a faraway father, she was loved and nurtured by the Black women in her life. Discipline, however, was her mother's forte and she became the authoritarian figure in the girl's life. Never in her arms or lap, Clara Ruth's relationship with her mother was rather formal, regulated and not very nurturing. Her mother had the house slaves for bathing and feeding her child, in addition to comforting the little girl when she cried. She also encouraged the Black women to hold and cuddle the little girl and it was there Clara Ruth found the unconditional love she so coveted. Never wanting for possessions, she became a spoiled child surrounded by house slaves and she thought of them as her enablers.

"When the Master returned from his voyages, however, the household became a place of strict military-like rule. Spending months among seadogs of sordid backgrounds, the ship commander felt strong discipline was a necessity. Shipboard, he ruled with an iron fist and demanded complete adherence to his orders and procedures. Many of his crew had worked as privateers with other captains who frequently commandeered ships on the high seas and stole their goods. Piracy was a constant danger anytime a valuable cargo was aboard, therefore mutinous crew members were dealt with swiftly and without mercy. While underway, the Captain always kept a flintlock pistol near, if not on his person, and he did not hesitate to use it if warranted. Working with such an unscrupulous lot of men required a decisive and formidable rule, especially with a hangman's gallows possible if captured by the British or American patrol ships.

"Aboard the *Clara Ruth* the old Captain was king and his word was law among his deckhands. His authority and dominant manner continued at home, compelling the house servants and Clara Ruth's mother to longingly count the days until he returned to sea. But Clara Ruth could climb in his lap, pull his beard and melt the hard-hearted Captain by putting her head on his chest. Each night at home, the wide-eyed little girl begged him to tell her stories of his adventures on the sea. She, alone, loved the gruff old salty dog and treasured each moment he showered her with his attention. Marking off the days on the calendar during each voyage, she yearned for his return. As the anticipated days of his voyage would dwindle, she could often be seen on the widow's walk at the tip-top of the grand house, watching each ship enter the harbor through her telescope. The telescope had been a present brought home by the patriarch and she delighted in his generosity. A favorite keepsake, she used it often and he took immense pleasure in spotting her through his spyglass as she recognized his ship and excitedly waved her arms. She always yearned to see the colorful banners she had made for him whipping in the wind from the tallest mast of the *Clara Ruth* as she sailed into the harbor.

"During his long absences, though, she found refuge in her books. With directions from her private instructors, she and her father had put together an exceptional library. Imploring her father to bring her books as surprises, he bought cases with volume after volume of the finest manuscripts he could find. Though expensive, it thrilled him to make her smile and helped relieve the guilt of his being away. He lavished her with hundreds of leather-bound volumes. She was a voracious reader, but her father's reading skills were elemental at best. So, often she could be found perched in his lap with her latest book, reading as he marveled at her ability and she basked in his attention.

"Clara Ruth's mother loved her little girl, but enjoyed fashionable trappings much more than her daughter. While her mother strolled her down the sidewalk, little Clara Ruth was made to ride in a carriage with a moving horsey. She napped in a daybed with an elaborately embroidered mosquito net canopy and ornate sweetgrass baskets were filled with any and everything a little girl might need. Little Clara Ruth's bedroom was overflowing with frilly lace dresses and colorful outfits with matching bonnets. Motherhood was a fashion statement for Clara Ruth's mother and she surrounded herself, as well as her daughter, with the accoutrements befitting a member of Charleston's elite society. Presenting her beautiful little daughter in the latest fashions and showing her off at social events stood as the height of parenthood for the mistress of the house. She delighted in promenading about Charleston wearing the hard to obtain French gowns that were coveted by her elite clique. She always instructed her husband, the seafaring Captain, to bring her the latest Parisian creations. In addition, she spent her days searching the exclusive shops along King Street to acquire the latest fashions for mother and daughter.

"Clara Ruth, however, was never enthused by the elegant symbols of the privileged and shied away from the selected attention she received from her mother and her circle of friends. They constantly flattered her with remarks about her beauty and as she grew older, her splendor increased exponentially. The awkwardness of the teenage years bypassed the budding Charleston belle, as effortlessly she exuded loveliness. But the Captain's daughter preferred practical dresses with pockets for found treasures and wanted her hair to be braided by her house slave. On trips downtown or to the city market with her handmaidens, she wore large bonnets or sunhats that covered her face, allowing her a measure of anonymity. When allowed, she avoided attention and preferred the comfortable seclusion of the garden with her servants and books.

"In her middle teenage years, Clara Ruth's comfy and calm life was dealt a tragic blow as her mother was stricken with the fever that consumed Charleston during the summer months. When first afflicted, she became tired and felt nauseated, taking to her bed. As she suffered, she became delirious and finally, was stricken with 'black water' (dark urine). The first-generation African women in the house, born to field slaves, had often seen the fever strike and said it was a bad sign. After three days, she began to have convulsions and fell into a coma. The next day, she died of what is now known as malaria.

"It was a traumatic time in Clara Ruth's life and she was lost without her father. Her mother's socially elite circle of friends took over and her mother's pastor tried to offer condolences. But there had never been a loving relationship and the distraught girl was consumed with guilt. Falling into the arms of the Negro woman who raised her, she refused to greet anyone and withdrew to her room. While she secluded herself, her mother's circle of friends stepped in to handle the arrangements. Finally coming out of hiding, the 15-year-old girl watched as they buried her mother in the cemetery of St. Michael's Church. Social etiquette required the funeral of a well-bred woman to include an elaborate ceremony with a well-spoken eulogy. The mother's burial was presided over by a well-known clergyman and her interment occurred in a socially accepted graveyard. After ensuring all affairs were in order, her mother's refined friends mourned in their latest Paris attire, holding their composure throughout the entire ritual. It all seemed cold and formal to Clara Ruth and she only wanted it to be over. As she waited for her father, the house was adorned in the black of mourning. Clara Ruth often escaped the gloomy house by climbing to her retreat on the exposed widow's walk high atop the stately mansion. Knowing her father's voyage was nearing its end, she sat in a comfortable chair on the narrow walkway and read books above the canopy of stately oaks. Diligently, she searched for her father's ship and the colorful banners snapping in the wind at the mouth of the harbor. When at last she spied the three masts of the *Clara Ruth* and recognized her father's vibrant flags, she could not bring herself to joyously wave her arms, as was their ritual, for the joy in her life had vanished.

"Upon the Captain's entering the harbor, he cheerfully searched the skyline of the port city to locate his grand home. When the mansion finally came into focus, he could see his daughter watching him through her telescope. Waving his arm as he always did upon his return, there was no return wave. Instead, his cherished daughter stood stoically on the widow's walk, watching his ship enter its home port. Instinctively, he felt a forewarning of trouble riding the winds and blowing through the sails of the *Clara Ruth*. Unconsciously, his heart began to race and his stomach became queasy as the seasoned seaman sensed a whirlpool of upheaval waiting after he docked.

"Instituting his regular shipboard discipline among the servants of the house, the Captain hid his grief behind an impassive façade while handling the affairs of the dead. Made aware of the particulars surrounding his wife's death, he suddenly feared losing the one who meant the most in his life. On the recommendation of his physician, he insisted Clara Ruth leave the mosquito infested city during the fever season. He demanded she take up temporary residence, as did many of the Holy City's residents, in the upstate of South Carolina. Quickly, he arranged for Clara Ruth to move to the home of some dear friends in the town of Pendleton in the newly formed county of Anderson. Sending his daughter away from the only home she had ever known, just as she was becoming a woman, would be a tumultuous change. The physical move alone would be arduous and adding the task of obtaining both academic and music teachers would further complicate the change. The Captain stuck to his decision and arrangements began with earnest. Soon, a fine coach followed by a caravan of wagons with a saddle horse in tow left the Holy City and began its journey along the Charleston-Augusta Road. Stopping at roadside inns along the way, the grueling trip was finally concluded as the Captain and his daughter arrived in the small town at the foot of the Blue Ridge Mountains."

Chapter 6

"After greetings and introductions, the Captain and his daughter enjoyed their first 'upstate' meal, a hearty beef stew served with potatoes and garden vegetables. While the ladies talked and sipped tea in the parlor, the men sat on the porch smoking cigars while having a taste of some local corn whiskey. The visit was enjoyable and the Captain emphasized the importance of protecting his only daughter as he sat with his old friend. Clara Ruth was moved into her meager room and settled. Staying the night, the Captain dreaded leaving, so he said his goodbyes before Clara Ruth fell asleep and was off for Charleston, on horseback, before daylight.

"Offering a quiet, rural atmosphere, Pendleton did not have the hustle and bustle of the port city. The absence of noise was the most dramatic difference. With few businesses, the little hamlet offered adequate provisioning, but the overabundance of merchandise available in her home city was not present. The sound of the harbor with ships bells, gulls squawking and the street peddlers' cries were all missing. The smell of the marsh and sea was no longer in the air and the gentle coastal breeze did not blow. The talk of ships and fishing changed to mules, plows and farming. The changes were dramatic and Clara Ruth cried, longing for her home on the Battery and the sight of the *Clara Ruth* dropping her sails as she approached the docks on the rising tide. During Clara Ruth's stay in the home of the well-to-do lawyer, many Charleston friends, also avoiding the fever season, stopped by to visit. She was also introduced to a number of the socially elite locals and even had a chance to meet Vice President John C. Calhoun at a barbeque. Later, she visited his daughter at their home, Fort Hill, and had lunch. In their attempt to be gracious hosts, the prominent couple invited her on many outings and adventures about the village, but Clara Ruth continued to seclude herself in quiet places around the house and village, always with one of her beloved books.

"As always, Clara Ruth marked off each day of her father's voyage and as the Captain's expected return neared, the homesick teenager brought unease to the Pendleton home.

Seeking some way to calm the Captain's daughter, every avenue of entertainment was offered, until the desperate homeowners finally gave in and made arrangements for her to travel back to the coast. The hosting attorney gave orders to Clara Ruth's servants to make all ready for travel to Charleston. The arduous journey would again be attempted. As preparations were made, the hesitant host became worried about sending the carriage with one white face among an entourage of Black servants on the trek to the furthest corner of the state. Appreciating the bond between father and daughter and certainly not wanting to incur the ole seaman's wrath, the gentleman from Pendleton arranged for a trustworthy, experienced guide to escort the group to the coast.

"Having made the strenuous trip to Charleston on numerous occasions, the upstate aristocrat recalled his meeting an honorable young man with an impeccable reputation. His father owned a mill in the sand hills along the border of the Barnwell and Edgefield Districts. From a well-known family with a reputation for honesty and generosity, the young man was a skilled outdoorsman on good terms with the native Indians. His family would be a gracious host to the Captain's precious cargo for one of their three overnight stops. Sending word with a drummer headed to that area, he asked the trustworthy young man to come to Pendleton and escort a young lady to Charleston. He was sure this was the answer to his problem, but he had not a clue as to the far-reaching implications of his decision.

"Arriving on a fine paint horse and attired in buckskin breeches and shirt, the experienced guide with a dark complexion could not have been 20 years old. When introduced, Clara Ruth was quite taken with the handsome boy, but did not listen closely enough to recall his Christian name, James Anthony Sullivan, Jr. Hearing only the name by which he was called, Lil' Sully, she assumed his was one of the rough and daring backcountry ruffians who lived along the edge of the frontier. He was holding a musket in the bend of his arm, accompanied by a flint lock pistol in his belt and a powder horn with a shot pouch on a rawhide strap around his neck. As he tipped his well-worn tricorne hat and said, 'Ma'am', the pair's eyes lingered on each other.

"Clara Ruth curtsied somewhat and with a cutting smile said, 'Experience comes at a young age here in the backcountry, I assume?'

"Turning to mount his horse, he returned, 'Yes, ma'am, but we don't get called upon to protect a little girl on her way to the coast, too often.' He tipped his hat and she did not see him again until they reached the border of Abbeville and Edgefield Districts.

"The backcountry young man had made arrangements for the group to stay overnight near Hard Labor Creek at the home of some family friends. Here, the troupe would enjoy the safety and comfort of their plantation compound. With a constant fear of highway bandits, outlaws and renegade Indians, the protection of a of well-known and strong White person was tantamount to survival for the Black entourage. For slaves, the possibility of being stolen by white bounty hunters, separated from their families and sold before anyone knew what happened, was all too real. The slave servants were afraid to travel with just a young white girl to vouch for them. Without a strong master to dissuade marauders, they were sitting ducks. Clara Ruth, of course, would be an honored guest of the plantation owners and would sleep in the comfort of a huge feather bed. With the thought of him lingering on her mind at breakfast, she mentioned the buckskin boy to her gracious host. 'He is quite confident, but I guess that comes from his Indian heritage.' The host just smiled and said nothing.

"The second day's travel would take them across the Edgefield District to the border of the Orangeburg and Barnwell Districts and the site of their second overnight stay. The halfway point of the arduous journey from Pendleton to Charleston was a stop in the sand hills at a crossroad known as Salleys Kitchen. Stopping at Salleys Kitchen, the slaves sighed with relief, for here they reached the Charleston-Augusta Road, a well-traveled thoroughfare with much less chance of trouble.

"Arriving at the little junction of sandy trails, their young scout had arranged for the slaves to use the storage house of the mill as their accommodations. There, they could sleep on the bags of meal and flour. Of course, Clara Ruth would stay the night in Mrs. Salley Sullivan's home. Though not as grand as the home of the first night's stay, this home was warm and inviting and the homesick girl felt comforted as she dined with the older couple. Once the meal was over, the gentleman excused himself to fetch his son. As Clara Ruth retired from the dining area of the house, she watched as the lady of the house cleaned the table. Clara Ruth sat by the fire sipping tea. Once finished with her chore, the older lady joined her beside the fire. As both enjoyed the warm beverage, they began a comfortable conversation and Clara Ruth asked her host why she didn't have slaves to take care of her house work. Mrs. Sullivan smiled and very politely said, 'I was born a slave. My grandfather gave me my freedom upon his death, but my mother is still a slave owned by my father. James Anthony and I believe chattel slavery is an abomination and not only contrary to Christian beliefs, but completely contrary to the constitution of our new nation. It is rare that James Anthony allows slaves on his property, but he and the gentleman from Pendleton are close friends and he made an unusual exception for your servants. James Anthony fought in the War with your father's attorney friend and they are very close.' Apologizing profusely, Clara Ruth stood as if to go tell her slaves to vacate Mr. Sullivan's building, but Salley Sullivan sweetly told her not to worry. All had been worked out in advance and no feathers would be ruffled by their stay on the Sullivan property.

"Gently, but firmly, Salley explained their beliefs as if a fact of life a mother would tell her daughter. 'We are well aware of the attitude toward slavery in the Low Country and we vehemently disagree with our friends who condone chattel slavery. We in the backcountry, however, are the minority and must accept that fate, but it doesn't mean we condone it or want it to continue.'

"Clara Ruth accepted her host's explanation with a smile and spoke nor thought any more about the subject. She was anxious to broach another subject that had been following her since Pendleton. Infatuated with her unsophisticated guide, she mentioned his demeanor and rough attire as she smiled.

Having been disarmed by Salley Sullivan's obliging way, Clara Ruth was very comfortable talking with her. Pausing to take a sip of tea, she was on the verge of asking for details about the intelligent Indian boy, but her wise host seemed to know what was on her mind.

"Shocked and almost choking on her tea, Clara Ruth listened as Mrs. Sullivan disclosed she was the buckskinned boy's mother. Smiling at her guest's reaction as she revealed her progeny, it was evident the visiting girl was a little embarrassed for her uncouth reference to the young man's Indian heritage.

"Comfortable with her family and lifestyle, Mrs. Sullivan spoke freely of the backwoods life her son had chosen. 'I am the daughter of a Muskogee Creek warrior, and as I told you, my mother was a slave. She was owned by my grandfather, George Galphin, and he insisted I be raised as a white person and educated in a proper manner. George Galphin the Younger was my father; he was born and raised in the Creek Nations, so I guess you could say, I'm a Creek Indian, too. I have never tried to force my son to be either white or Indian, he has chosen the path that his soul told him to choose and as long as he is happy, I will be also.' She told of her son having eight years of formal education and many opportunities for employment in his daddy's businesses, but his love was the forest and she would never stand in the way of her son's happiness. 'He is a hunter, fisher, trapper and guide and is everyone's friend; a mother couldn't ask more of a son. I am so proud of him!'

"The homesick girl was stunned and embarrassed, but felt a kindred spirit with her new friend and was at ease in her home. Telling her host of the relationship she had with her late mother and her seafaring father, she said she dearly loved him, too, even his crusty ways. Describing her father, they laughed and agreed men were easy to love but hard to tame, sometimes. As their comfortable conversation continued, the door burst open and her backwoods scout appeared, holding out a dead bobcat by the back of its head.

"In a proud, loud voice meant to refute the inexperience accusation at their introduction, he yelled to his mom, 'No more missing chickens! I tied a hen down and let her squawk, knowing this rascal loved the taste of chicken. Sure 'nuff, he came sneaking up to the coop and BOOM! one shot through his ear.'

"Acknowledging his expertise and cunning skills, his mother admonished him for his rudeness in bringing the dead animal into her house and scaring their visitor. From behind the buckskinned boy, his father was smiling as he grabbed him around the neck and proudly decreed, 'There ain't no one better in the woods than you, Lil' Sully. Let's go skin 'em and tack his hide to the mill wall so everybody can see 'em.' Once the door was closed, the females laughed and rocked back and forth in front of the cozy fire. Clara Ruth wondered why she had such a weird and excited feeling come over her at the sight of the young outdoorsman, but figured it was the comfortable setting and anticipation of seeing her father. As he and his father stretched the pretty spotted hide on the wall beside the many antlers and trophies he had bagged, Lil' Sully felt the same type of feeling. Looking back at the house, he figured it was just the excitement of the kill.

"For two more days, Lil' Sully led the caravan out of the sand hills into the coastal plain, traveling out of the Barnwell District into the Colleton District. The group overnighted near Walterboro at a crossroad named Hickory Valley. The Walter brothers had established a retreat for those escaping the fever in Charleston and graciously hosted the old ship captain's daughter and her servants. They always enjoyed seeing their friend, Lil' Sully, from the sand land. In the plush surroundings of her room, Clara Ruth could hardly sleep and didn't know if it was the anticipation of seeing her father or her fascination with the young frontiersman who was leading their group. He seemed to always occupy a place in her mind.

"Finally reaching the sulfurous air of the coast, Clara Ruth saw her father's ship at its mooring and knew he would not be far away. She knew the old salt would be furious, but as usual, she sat in his lap and draped her long legs over his and the old salt melted like sugar in a hot skillet. With her head teetering above his, she leaned over and kissed his balding spot on top. The anger was gone and the old man was again filled with the feeling for which he had searched all over the world. Clara Ruth was his joy and his life and though the journey was dangerous, he could forgive her so quickly, for he worshiped the ground she walked upon. Her presence, especially in the eclectic city she called home, made all frustrations disappear. But he did think it very unusual for her to invite the backwoods guide to join them for dinner.

"The old Captain was at peace with his daughter and took every opportunity to flaunt her beauty around the bustling port city. They dined and hobnobbed with Charleston's finest and in deference to his wife's memory, the father's bravado and abrasive attitude were cordially overlooked by the city's elite. His acceptance was also due, in large part, to the accompaniment of his much sought-after and gorgeous daughter, who far outshined his rough edges. One thing, however, neither the old man nor the elite of the city could accept was the sight of the backwoods and buckskinned young man. He often kept the beautiful socialite's company on afternoon outings in and about the city. The father, however, after much cajoling, finally bowed to her pressure and offered limited approval for the crude young man to escort his daughter. This had only occurred after he learned of Lil' Sully's family connection to Salleys Kitchen. Seems the Captain sailed from England with two finely honed grinding stones, hand sculpted, to be used in creating the finest of flours. There had been quite a few ballast stones used in balancing the ship as it made the crossing with its unique cargo for a mill in the sand hills. Having met the Irish miller when he picked up the millstones from his ship, he respected him as a businessman and thought him to be honorable. Their views on chattel slavery, however, differed greatly and kept the two from calling each other 'friend'. Knowing the boy's mother was George Galphin's granddaughter, however, did lessen the impact of her primitive son keeping time with his daughter. The Galphin name was often mentioned among the political elites.

"During the hired scout's time in the sophisticated city, Clara Ruth, for some unknown reason, insisted he offer his arm to her when she was about town. The couple was often sighted strolling the streets of the Holy City. The snobbish elite referred to them as 'the maiden and the mule'.

"Gossip quickly traveled through the social grapevine, denigrating the heritage of the Salleys Kitchen miller's son. The highbrow aristocracy soon put an end to the quaint appearances of the boondocks boy at their very modern events. Clara Ruth was left to decide whether she wanted to be part of the social scene, which included being pursued by the most eligible bachelors in the city or sit home with father and Lil' Sully. She chose to flaunt her taboo beau in the faces of the prominent and powerful by dragging him to church, having him accompany her on trips to the elite stores on King Street and walking along the Battery on sunny Sunday afternoons. Ignoring the beautifully printed invitations requesting her presence at social gatherings, she told the house slaves, 'Just toss those old things in the trash.' The snub was passed from house slave to house slave, with word of her actions finally reaching the sender of the pretty invites. Her message was received loud and clear.

"Alas, Clara Ruth took the snub as it was intended - an insult to her, personally. As a result, Charleston's most eligible beaus lost access to the season's most stunning debutante. As a child of privilege, the Captain's daughter was not one to be told what to do. The forceful ways of her father had melded with the Charleston snobbery of her mother, producing in Clara Ruth not only an air of superiority, but also an attitude of disdain for being bossed around.

"In her childhood, Clara Ruth had been without order and correction during her father's absences and this privileged lifestyle caused her to feel unhappy. Struggling with her inner self, she sought things that she believed would bring her satisfaction, only to find her conquests unfulfilling. Without true boundaries in her life, she constantly moved from project to project, tossing aside the remnants as she lost interest. She left flower beds without bulbs, she threw her embroidery sampler to the side and she left the garden pavilion she had drawn up a half-finished skeleton among the shrubs behind the grand home. Her truest contentment came from her father and his demanding discipline. Noticing her slothful ways, he soon began demanding she work to complete the things she had begun and lavishly praised her afterward. Beaming with success, she stood beside her father with his arm around her shoulder after completing the patio gazebo. The house slaves were happy, too, for she had bossed them unrelentingly once her father demanded the structure be finished. The Captain completed her and she completed him, each offering the other unconditional love and happiness. But this happy time was always short lived and she begged her father to give up the sea and let her be the only love of his life.

"Once again, Clara Ruth's happy days with her father dwindled to a few and she became melancholy. Feeling equally unhappy about missing his daughter, the old Captain had been maneuvering out of her sight and was smiling as he took her hand and pulled her to the little garden house she created. Bringing her beside him, they sat close together on a marble top bench. In the splendor of the grounds that surrounded their home on the Charleston Battery, among the flowers and shrubs of their grand garden, he gave her the news she so longed to hear: this would be his last voyage. Having arranged with the merchants to find a young and responsible replacement to command his ship, he wanted to grow old making his beloved Clara Ruth happy. To seal his intentions, his ship, the *Clara Ruth,* had been sold to those businessmen and planters who depended on his services and the funds had been placed in the new Bank of Charleston until his return. Needless to say, Clara Ruth was elated as she hugged his grizzled neck and there appeared a never-seen-before expression of contentment on the old salt's face.

"On his last voyage, there was no dreading his departure, no guilt of leaving Clara Ruth and no fear of returning home to bad news. As he prepared his vessel to be under way, Clara Ruth watched from the docks with her unsuitable suitor by her side. The old man had warmed to her roughshod companion, for he knew well any person meaning harm to his daughter would quickly meet a musket ball, a long skinning knife or the hands of a potentially brutal beau. Clara Ruth, too, felt safe with Lil' Sully. Other than being the undefeated champion arm wrestler in the pub near the docks, she didn't know why he had hung around so long. At first, she was flattered, but after the high society snub, she wasn't about to let him leave. She had a point to make and he would be good companionship while her father was on his last voyage. After that, she would send him home to his beloved sand hills.

"Only allowed to watch from the dock, Clara Ruth knew well the Captain's silly, superstitious rule of never allowing a woman aboard ship and of his spreading that foolishness among his gullible crew. They believed adherence to the absurd decree had saved them from doom on many occasions. The Captain attributed his longevity to strict adherence to the no-female order. Clara Ruth was giddy with anticipation, for she had planned a series of affairs for The Season. A coveted invitation to one of her over-the-top parties would force all of the socially elite to come crawling back to her. This Season's social snub would be avenged and the upper crust of Charleston would know next time not to arrogantly exclude Clara Ruth Rutledge.

"Having her fuse lit by the snobbery of the Holy City's elite, the Captain's daughter wanted to ensure only she would have the finest dresses and gowns for her exclusive social Season events. She wanted the latest Paris fashions to wear and the lavish European clothing that was the rage of Charleston. As she moved about the city, she wanted the crème de la crème residing between the Ashley and the Cooper Rivers to envy her every move. To persuade her benefactor, the man who would buy her anything, to purchase the latest and greatest ball gowns and the ultimate trappings for her takeover of the port city's social scene, she listed her needs. But offering the list to the Commander was tacky and certainly not the manner that befitted a lady such as she. Remembering the joy they shared when he lavished her with gifts upon his return from sea as a little girl, she wanted these fancies from his last voyage to create the same elation. She so loved her father and knew he would delight in presenting her with the latest Parisian styles and the most astonishingly expensive jewelry he could procure for her on his last voyage. In an effort to put an end to the silly 'no women aboard his ship' superstition, she planned to sneak on board and put the spoiling list she created in the Captain's quarters for him to find. Sure of her plan, she had her backwoods guide escort her to the dock late on the night before the clipper was scheduled to leave on the rising tide. Slipping past the guard distracted by Lil' Sully, she followed the directions from her father's stories and wound her way straight to the shipmaster's cabin. Placing the note under his pillow, she blew a kiss to her absent father and tiptoed back to her waiting beau.

"After farewell hugs and lingering hands, the ship of many sails pushed away from the dock and dropped one main sail for the trip out of the harbor. Gradually adding sailcloth to the many sheets billowing in the wind, the *Clara Ruth* reached full sail at the edge of the horizon. While Lil' Sully stood by her side on the widow's walk high atop the house on the Battery, Clara Ruth peered through the telescope of her childhood. Watching the beautiful ship that bore her name as it clipped the waves near the horizon, she saw the crew set the last of her swelling sails. As the majestic ship reached peak sail and settled in on a tack against the wind, a sudden and monstrous explosion engulfed the magnificent vessel. Sending a column of bright orange flames high above the horizon, it littered the sky with millions of fragmented pieces. The once massive ship disintegrated and disappeared among the trade winds as Clara Ruth's breath left her body. Black smoke and charred pieces of wood were all that remained as the once splendid ship vanished into ocean and sky. The Captain's daughter could not believe her eyes. As her breathing momentarily ceased, she knocked over the telescope as she fainted and fell to the floor.

"Lil' Sully was as lost in Charleston as if he had been in a foreign land. Clara Ruth was delirious with grief, the house slaves were spooked and the Captain's business associates were calling on the house to pay their respects. While offering condolences, they were desperately seeking information as to how the old salt's affairs would be settled. To make matters worse, even though there was no body, three preachers had approached about the price of burial plots offered at their church. The brawny sand hill boy had not a clue of the social etiquettes of a funeral among Charleston's high society, but in a cruel quirk of fate, he was now in charge of the Captain's funeral.

"With no one to lead him through the Charleston decorum of death, he followed his father's advice and let his instincts take over. His first move was to have an elaborate pine coffin made by the finest cabinet artisans in the city. With his heart leading, he left the fine pine box at the harbormaster's office and had the old sailors who hung around the docks to carve scrimshaw on the sides with a large depiction of the *Clara Ruth* at full sail. The cabinet artisans put holes in the bottom under the silk lining and hand forged the wrought iron handles to adorn the sides. Ship cleats were fastened to the top of the box, making it identical to the signature rope box that rode the deck of the *Clara Ruth.*

"On the 2nd day after the explosion, an advertisement appeared in the *Charleston Courier* inviting anyone with ties to the late Captain Rutledge to call on his home beginning the next day at noon. Each mourner was instructed to bring a small ballast stone in remembrance of the Captain. On Saturday, the 3rd day after the ship's explosion, the gleaming pine coffin with nautical features abounding was placed under the portico in front of the Captain's house on the Battery. As the noonday sun beamed down on the harbor, a gentle trade wind blew through the ancient oak shading the covered area and cooled the guests offering their condolences. Lemonade and punch were served from two huge crystal bowls to those who gathered on the porch. A painting of the Captain standing in front of the *Clara Ruth* was placed on a pedestal behind the coffin that was engulfed with a plethora of multicolored flowers and greenery. As his close associates arrived, they were invited onto the shielded side porch to await a possible audience with the daughter. The other mourners passed the elegant pine box and deposited their small stones.

One hour before sunset, the last of the Captain's close associates walked to the coffin and placed their small stones in the burial box. Once everyone contributed their stone of mourning, the top of the coffin was closed and a group of the Captain's closest associates carefully placed it in a black hearse drawn by one black horse for the trip to the dock. There, the same group unloaded the box of rocks and placed it aboard a small sloop docked nearby. With a somber crew aboard, a black sail was raised and the little ship glided to the middle of the harbor on the dying evening breeze. Everyone who had gathered at the Captain's home walked from the covered portico to the Battery and lined the seawall. Clara Ruth was the last to arrive and took her place of honor among the crowd of mourners at the harbor's edge. As the fine pine box of rocks was positioned for burial in the harbor, three cannon blasts were heard, one at a time, from ships near the outer edge of the harbor. At the sound of the last cannon, a bell on the sloop pealed three times and the box of rocks was allowed to slide over the side of the black- sailed sloop and into the water at sunset. Standing on the Battery as the sun slowly slipped down behind her, Clara Ruth cried as Lil' Sully held her close and wondered to himself, *What has happened?*

"Monday's headline across the *Charleston Courier* read, 'Monumental Memorial for Monumental Man'. The backwoods boy from the sand hills had pulled off the most talked about social event of the season. The newspaper went on to say, 'The moving memorial brought tears to the eyes of all who knew the old Captain.'

"Clara Ruth was so proud of Lil' Sully. He had found a permanent place in her heart.

"The day after the funeral, Clara Ruth took her backcountry friend out to the garden gazebo she had designed and built. Sitting in silence most of the time, the Captain's daughter began to cry softly and Lil' Sully rushed to her side and asked her what was wrong. Looking straight into his eyes, she said, 'Lil' Sully, take me away from Charleston. Everything reminds me of my father and now he's gone. I don't want to be here anymore!' With those words, she burst into deep sobs and for the first time, Lil' Sully put his arm around her and told her he would take care of her.

"On Sunday morning while everyone was attending church, Lil' Sully loaded her things into a carriage and waited in front of the beautiful mansion for Clara Ruth to join him. Leaving the house staff in charge of what was now her home, she tied down the large hat she wore with a big bow under her chin. With Lil' Sully's help, she climbed in the carriage and settled in for a long, long ride. They slipped out of Charleston before the church services were over, bound for Salleys Kitchen. Traveling through the night, they reached Lil' Sully's home the next morning as the sun rose over the eastern horizon and shined its first few rays of light on the weary pair. Coming to a stop in front of Lil' Sully's home, Salley Sullivan hurried out to meet them. Quickly recognizing the grief on both of their faces, she lovingly scooped the distraught young lady into her arms and ushered her into her home. There, Clara Ruth was doted upon and petted for weeks while Lil' Sully moved about like a ship without a rudder. Remembering the many times her father had abandoned her in different parts of the wilderness, Salley knew the feeling of being all alone in the world; she comforted the grieving girl and helped her through the pain and loss."

* * *

After his marathon session describing Clara Ruth Rutledge, Sully was beginning to slur his words and Salley knew he had to stop and rest. He was so determined to finish the epic story until he was dismissing his own welfare and pushing himself much more than was healthy. Talking incessantly into the microphone, he seemed to be a man on a life or death mission and it was beginning to take its toll.

Jon Chesterfield, Jr. was continuing to stack the deck against James and Salley's reunion. Placing a $50 bill on the switchboard table, he convinced the telephone operator at the hospital to refer all calls for Salley Sullivan to the main house at the Chesterfield estate. He left instructions for no information to be released about James Anthony Sullivan, V. All phone calls were answered in the Chesterfield mansion before they were transferred to the guest house. He left explicit instructions with the house staff not to offer any information about Salley Sullivan staying in the guest house or her father. His orders to the entire house staff were emphatic and he alone was to handle all phone calls inquiring about his guests, especially from a person named James Williams. Filling out a change of address form, he had Salley sign it and told her he would have her mail forwarded from her Salleys Kitchen mailbox to the main mailbox at the estate. All of her mail came to the main Chesterfield home and Jon, Jr. scrutinized each piece before it was delivered to Salley. In effect, he was controlling all information that she received. With Sully needing almost all of her attention and the impending arrival of the baby, she did not realize what was happening and if she had figured it out, there was very little she could have done. She was completely ensnared in Jon Chesterfield, Jr.'s web of deceit and he was moving ever closer to obtaining what he wanted.

***

"With Clara Ruth Rutledge nearby, Lil' Sully was as lost as a duck in a desert. There was no fishing and hunting or nights in the swamps; he stayed near the house and did not seek the comfort of the woods or his Yuchi brothers of the forest. Each opportunity that his mother allowed, he timidly visited the distraught girl, kneeling in front of her to demonstrate his concern and intoxicate himself on her wine. She enjoyed his visits and coyly acknowledged his attention with a momentary smile that transformed the backwoods brawn into a man with a passion to please and a heart that seemed to be tamed. Asking Mrs. Sullivan to order a nice flannel shirt from one of the peddlers that called on the store, Clara Ruth gave it to Lil' Sully as a thank you for all he had done. The shirt immediately became a cherished item and was worn only when visiting her. She often complemented him for looking so handsome when wearing the flannel shirt and asked him to sit next to her so she could feel the material. Well noted by the Sullivan matriarch, she took the initiative and ordered her son a coat and pants when the peddler next called upon the store. Upon their arrival, the cunning females made sure Clara Ruth presented them to the bamboozled boy. As a reward for wearing the complete ensemble, she hugged his neck and purposely tried to kiss him on the cheek, but withdrew with dissatisfaction after his rough beard pricked her lips. That would not be a problem on the next visit, for Lil' Sully was a changed man. Now, the rough bearded, buckskinned backwoodsman was a clean shaven, well dressed and polite beau. His transformation happened so quickly, he was surprised one afternoon when he passed near the millpond and saw his reflection in the water. This, however, was not the most shocking development of the relationship. As he began to escort the fair young maiden to church, he befuddled the worshipers with his dress, his politeness and his citified air. Clara Ruth referred to him, when talking to his mother, as her diamond in the rough. It was soon obvious to everyone in the sand hill region, except Lil' Sully, that matrimony would soon be broached."

***

Salley's stomach was growing larger by the day and at the end of her seventh month she was so confused. She had tried many times to get in touch with James and each time she left a message with anyone who answered the hallway phone at his dorm. Every message was a plea for him to call her at the guest house. It was as if he had disappeared and as their child grew larger in her womb, she needed him more than ever. After she started showing, Salley did not venture out into public very much. There was not much reason for her to go out, for Jon, Jr. would bring her anything she wanted or he would have it delivered. Besides, she did not like having to explain who the father of her unborn baby was. All of Jon Jr.'s friends assumed it was his child and he did nothing to dissuade them. To make matters worse, he had started to kiss her in public and put his arm around her as if they were a couple. She was ashamed that she had not stopped him from doing things like that in the beginning. Now, if she acted perturbed at him putting his hands on her body, he would act hurt and do mean things. The scheming young Chesterfield would lock Spot's stable so no one could let him out to run, then he would stay gone all day. Upon his late return, he would tell Salley he was sorry, he just forgot. He would take the car keys with him and leave her stranded when she needed to run to the drugstore for Sully or lock the garage and stay gone in the car all day when she needed to go see her doctor for a baby checkup. His message was plain and Salley knew exactly what he was saying - either I'm your man or you'll lose everything I've done for you and your father will go back to the hospital ward. Alone for a few minutes, she thought, *My God, how could I have gotten so wound up in his web? Where is James and why is he not coming to help me?* She shuddered and was so afraid of having their baby, she just didn't know what to expect. Her mother had all but abandoned her and she felt so all alone. Sully was all she had and she could only talk to him.

Sitting with Sully and listening to his narrative had become Salley's escape. Over the months, his voice had become gravelly and she noticed he was laboring much more to get his words out. He was trying so hard to finish his story and Salley needed to hear him talk, not just for the family history he was offering, but to soothe her anxiety and give her a small window of peace. Most all around them soon learned that the time they spent recording was a precious thing that they alone shared and was not to be interrupted. Most adhered to that notion, but Jon Chesterfield, Jr. seemed to delight in interrupting them when he wanted Salley's attention.

As the Viet Nam War became the center of controversy across the nation, the Augusta Chronicle began listing the local young men being deployed to the southeast Asia theatre of war and placing a picture, if available, of each new soldier. Jon Jr.'s father spotted James' high school picture in the paper and recognized James from their meeting on the polo practice field. He immediately showed it to his son and as a grin spread across Jon, Jr.'s face, he folded the paper and headed for the guest house. It was now his practice to forego knocking and as he barged into the quiet of the house all he could hear was Sully's hoarse voice. With a smile on his face, he blasted into the sunroom and said, "Salley, honey, I have something you might want to see."

With a frown of aggravation painted across her face, Salley stopped the recording machine and looked toward the cause of the interruption. "Jon, we are recording in here and you knew that. What in the world do you want with me, now?"

With a spring in his step, he walked to the far side of the iron lung that held Sully and dropped the folded newspaper into her lap. He was still smiling like the Cheshire cat. Salley glanced down and straightaway recognized James' high school senior picture among a line of others. Silently she read, *Six Young Men from the CSRA Join the Ranks in Viet Nam.* Below the pictures and headlines, the story explained that those pictured had finished Basic Training at Fort Jackson and had received orders to join the tens of thousands already fighting in South Viet Nam. Below that article was listed, without pictures, those who had died in the fighting and had come home in flag-draped coffins.

Salley Sullivan was now 9 months + pregnant and due to give birth at any time. Shifting in the chair to sit up, she struggled to stand as Jon, Jr. offered her no assistance - just watched and smiled. Looking intently at the folded newspaper, she walked over to one of the floor-to-ceiling windows and continued to read. Suddenly, she dropped the newspaper, grabbed her lower stomach and said, "Oh, my God! My water just broke! Oh, Sully, your grandchild has finally decided she wants to see you!"

In a raspy voice, the grandfather-to-be joyously reported, "Hallelujah Jehovah! I had ample reason to believe my journey through the Pearly Gates would occur before my eyes were allowed to gaze upon my granddaughter! I have miraculously stayed conscious until the blessed event!"

Grabbing one of the many towels stacked near Sully's machine, Salley stuck it between her legs and even in that moment had words for her father. "How do you know it's a girl? It could be James Anthony Sullivan, VI!"

Sully laughed out loud and replied, "This child is indisputably female - of that I have no doubt. In veritable Sullivan style, that little cherub will make her fashionably-late appearance today!"

Salley hooted as she bent over her huge stomach. Sully's nurse, who had been silently sitting in the corner working a puzzle, dashed to Salley's side and ushered her to a chair. Jon, Jr. had planned every detail of the birthing process and he jumped into action. Picking up the phone, he ordered his father's limo to be pulled to the front of the guest house and he led Salley to the back seat. In what seemed like only seconds, she was helped out of the pretentious vehicle by Jon Chesterfield, Jr. and led through a seldom-used side entrance to

Aiken Memorial Hospital. Two nurses were waiting just inside the door and they escorted her into a private suite that had been prepared just for her. Moments later, Dr. Baughman came to her side and took her hand. "I will be here with you through the delivery and I will take great care of both you and your baby. I must say, though, I have never seen such enormous preparations made for one little baby, but we'll get you through this and have you back home in a day or two. How's Sully taking all of this?"

Salley was listening to the doctor as a contraction was waning. When she was finally able to catch her breath, she told the doctor, "He has decided that I am having a little girl, so please, if at all possible, make sure I have a girl baby!" The ole doc hooted and patted her hand before moving to the end of the bed to measure the dilation of Salley's cervix. After removing his rubber gloves, he gave his patient the ole hand pat again and said, "She might have waited a while to show, but she's in a hurry now!" Then he dashed out to scrub in.

Feeling the grip of another contraction, Salley prepared to weather it as she began to shed a few more tears. Through the pain she shouted, "Damn it, James, where are you! I need you so bad and I want you to see your daughter. Oh, James, I love you so much!" The nurses looked at each other and said nothing. They knew Jon Chesterfield, Jr. had arranged the private suite and he had led everyone to assume he was the father - now they knew he was lying.

It seemed to Salley that the contractions would never end, then in the moments just before the delivery, time sped up and everything flashed by so fast! She screamed in pain as the ole doc told her how well she was doing and suddenly he said, "OK, sweetheart, when the next contraction hits, we are going to push and push hard. We'll know very shortly if Sully was right!"

Suddenly, Salley felt as if the dam had burst and through all of the pain, she felt a great sense of relief and happiness. The doctor wasn't talking and the nurses were busy assisting him with the baby. And like a clarion call, the newborn cried out, announcing its arrival into the world.

The old country doctor seemed to take great pleasure in proclaiming, "Well, I'll be damned! Sully was right! My dear Salley, you have a beautiful baby girl!" Emotions flooded Sully's daughter as she sobbed with joy! Seconds later, she was holding her beautiful baby girl, who was crying at the top of her lungs and blinking her lovely blue eyes at her mother.

The ole doc inquired, "Have you decided what you will name her?"

With a quick reply, Salley told him, "Her name will be Lucinda Ruth Sullivan. We will call her Ruth. Lucinda was her great-great-grandmother's name and Ruth was her great-great-great-aunt's name.

Dr. Baughman had one last question, "So her last name will be Sullivan?"

Without hesitation, Salley Sullivan boldly said, "Yes! She will be a Sullivan through and through!"

After an easy delivery and quick recovery, Salley was picked up by the limousine once again and taken home to the Chesterfield mansion.

Holding little Ruth over Sully's face, Salley slowly lowered the baby's face to Sully's lips and he kissed her in such a loving way. It had become an every-morning routine when Salley came downstairs to be with her father. A bassinette had been placed next to Salley's chair and as she listened to Sully, she watched over her daughter. Often during his recording sessions, Salley would breast feed Ruth and the sight of the two people he loved most in the world often brought Sully to tears. Salley would lovingly wipe his tears as she held Ruth to her breast. Sully was beyond ecstatic to know her last name would be Sullivan. Ruth was very vocal and after she added her voice to Sully's recording on a couple of occasions, Sully and Salley had to postpone some of the recording sessions. Now, with Ruth sleeping peacefully beside the two of them, Salley knew they had a window of opportunity to record more of Sully's family history. Quietly, Sully began his story again.

***

"Now that his son was on the verge of taking a wife, James Anthony could look back over his life and think of the hard road he had traveled. He and Salley Galphin had worked hard for what they had and the most precious thing they had created was their son. In a quiet moment as James Anthony watched his boy trying so hard to please Clara Ruth, his mind drifted back to the day Salley came into his life. With maturity comes the ability to see clearly. Now, having that clear vision, he knew he had fallen in love with Salley the moment they met. The rituals of courtship had only delayed the inevitable and their years together had proved their love to be true. Often, though, he wondered what would have become of him if things had been different. *What would my life be like if I had remained in Ireland? What would my life be like if Rose had lived?*

Quickly dismissing the 'what-ifs' of his life, he was happy with the decisions he had made during his youth and he was glad Salley had come into his life. Thinking back to the good and bad times they faced as Salleys Kitchen grew into a community, he was filled with a sense of pride. Any man would have to be greatly pleased with the life they had carved from the sand hill wilderness. He was equally proud of his son, but concerned, for Lil' Sully's love of Clara Ruth had caused him to turn his back on the life he loved. Remembering the feeling that had captured his heart when Salley entered his life, he understood love's attraction, but hoped Lil' Sully would not surrender his core principles to the woman who now controlled him.

"Sitting on the porch late one evening with his son, James Anthony asked his son if he was ready for marriage. Lil' Sully was hesitant, for he had never given it much thought, but he answered, 'Yes.' Then he asked his father, 'Why?'

"Though his father's answer was crude, it spelled out the true tack of his son's future. 'Boy, you have been lassoed, hobbled and laid on the ground. All that's left is the gelding knife and you will soon be fat, contented and ready for a life of service.' He laughed out loud and slapped his bewildered son on the back. 'You might as well lay back and let it happen, for to put up a fight might bring harm to us all. Find a wee something special, boy, and give it to her. Then ask the lass to marry you and get the hell out of the way, for it'll all go quickly downhill from there!'

"Following his father's advice, Lil' Sully remembered the

small coin-shaped ballast stone he had picked up around the docks for Captain Rutledge's funeral. He had not put it in the pine box, but instead kept it in his buckskin pouch. It was smooth, flat and round from centuries of tumbling through a glacial stream in Ireland. It had then been used as ballast for a ship as it traveled to the new world. After the crossing, the stone was no longer needed and it was summarily dumped with thousands of others into the Charleston Harbor. With the turbulence from thousands of ships entering the harbor, it had washed ashore, only for Lil' Sully to pick it up as a memorial for the old clipper ship captain. He remembered showing Clara Ruth the stone that he had chosen to place in the coffin at her father's funeral. Now, he was glad he had kept it in his pocket, instead.

"After days of careful work using the centuries old skills taught him by the Native Americans of the sand hills, he lovingly tapped a hole in the top of the stone. He then etched a message on the smooth stone and poured a tiny bit of melted gold into the indented letters. A delicate gold chain was threaded through the tiny hole and the once ordinary little stone was now his priceless engagement gift to Clara Ruth.

"After church on Sunday, Lil' Sully asked Clara Ruth to take a walk with him. They walked arm and arm, Victorian style, as they had walked along the Charleston Battery as the high society scrutinized their every move. This walk was much more relaxed and as they approached his favorite spot near the millpond, he put his hands around her tiny waist and effortlessly swung her across a small stream. There, where the stream split and traveled around each side of a remarkable old pine, he held her delicate hand and placed the lovingly carved stone in her palm. Clara Ruth recognized the stone immediately and remembered the moment he picked it up along the harbor shore for his stone of remembrance at her father's memorial. She never knew he kept it and now, as she read the intricate letters he had carved, it became a precious gem of unmeasurable value. On the front was engraved one word, *Forever;* on the back, *Clara Ruth and Lil' Sully.* So hard and primitive, the stone embodied Lil' Sully. To Clara Ruth, the stone was part of her father's homeland and their home in Charleston and its unsophisticated simplicity represented Lil'

Sully in every way. The shiny gold letters now made it a unique and precious jewel. He could not have chosen anything that better embodied the makeup of their love. Once again, Lil' Sully's unpretentious and modest spirit had captured Clara Ruth's heart. The small, etched stone became a gem of immeasurable value. It would be, for now and forever, a keepsake she would wear around her neck throughout their married lives. She looked to his face as her eyes began to submerge in tears. Ever so tenderly, Lil' Sully put his hands on each side of her face and gently wiped her tears with his thumbs. Softly, he said, 'Clara Ruth, will you marry me - forever?'

"Following Lil' Sully's romantic afternoon proposal and Clara Ruth's resounding answer of 'Yes!', the love-struck couple made their way back to Salley and James Anthony to announce the great news. Of course, it had been arranged for months and prompts were given to Lil' Sully as necessary to keep the ball of matrimony rolling down that hill his father had mentioned.

"Excitement captured the community, for everyone knew this would be the wedding of the century for all of the inhabitants of the sandy crossroad. Anticipation zoomed to a new height as the preacher paraded the intended couple before the congregation, thanking them for bestowing upon him the honor of being first to formally announce their nuptials in June. With a prayer that would have brought joy to anyone's heart, he lavished them with praise and in general proclaimed them to be down-right fine examples for everyone else. After such a fine invocation, most of the congregation opened their eyes and hoped for a quick summation and equally short prayer of benediction. With the wedding season having just been officially opened, there was much to discuss, plans to be made and no time to waste listening to a sermon. The backcountry parson knew, as well, this was not the time for his best sermon. He knew most of the congregation was present only for a good look at the stunningly beautiful girl and the shockingly transformed Lil' Sully. With that in mind, he had the congregation to stand and he offered the benediction. Afterwards, the newly engaged couple stood with the preacher at the door and shook the hand of each member of the congregation as they exited. Most of the men wanted nothing more than to go home, eat and get comfortable, but they were left sitting in the buggies, wagons and buckboards while the women huddled for a long time in the churchyard, talking about the wedding. The frantic search for the things they needed to complete their attire for the wedding of the century was about to begin with great anticipation and fervor.

"With the wedding season having been officially opened, parties, fish fries and bar-b-ques had to be planned. Dress patterns were dug out from the bottoms of sewing baskets. Materials of every sort, along with thread of every color, were stockpiled in homes around the community. Anyone scheduled to take a trip to Charleston, Augusta or Savannah took orders and graciously brought back the fashion accoutrements the other ladies needed. Absolutely all stops were pulled out in the name of sophistication and style. The men of the community begrudgingly tolerated the bother and expense. Backcountry women were afforded few opportunities to dress up, fix up, accessorize and, if only for a short while, become fashionably adorned. The wise men who realized this did not stand in their wives' way, for they wanted to avoid sleeping in the barn, if at all possible.

"The men, however, talked of bar-b-ques and fish fries without a thought to planning or fashion. Their gatherings would take place later, as a man, on the spur of the moment would say, 'Let's do that fish fry Friday night, want to?' and that was it. A fish trap would be put in the millpond in the morning and baited with some rancid meat. That evening, it would be pulled out brimming with forearm-sized brown, slimy catfish. Most of the men would gather early and talk about their hunting exploits and their meager crops while they helped dress the catfish. The man considered to have the best fried cornbread recipe would mix his secret ingredients with cornmeal, eggs and chopped ramps in a crockery bowl and start dropping spoonful after spoonful of yellow batter into the boiling hog fat. Another member of the party would wash and quarter some freshly dug potatoes. The potatoes would be roasted and added to a seemingly unending table of hardy food.

Not long in planning, not long in preparing, but extra-long in what was considered good fellowship, the fish fry was sure to create a happy crowd. A few toasts to the bride and groom would be made as corn liquor was sipped out of the preacher's view. When most were beginning to get liquored up and the toasts became too raunchy, the preacher would gather everyone's attention and say grace, then give the Lord's blessing to the intended couple. Afterwards, he would graciously say, 'I think it's high time for me to go home.' With a basket piled high with fried catfish and all of the trimmings in hand, the preacher would receive a bevy of hardy handshakes and slaps on the back. His exit would allow the real celebration to begin.

"During festivities, many fruitless attempts were made to gather the crowd's attention, but too much liquor had been sipped, so a pistol was fired to quiet the rowdy partygoers. Afterwards, James Anthony Sullivan climbed up on a barrel head and began to speak in a strong Irish brogue, 'It takes a while for a man to find a good place to start a life in this world and then it takes a lifetime for that man to grow his family and make them a comfortable life in that place. When the day comes that he realizes his task has been completed, its then he looks back across the miles he has traveled and makes peace with what he has done. Knowing his time is drawing nigh, he can only hope his hard work has made the world a little better. Every man also wants to know his transgressions will be forgiven with peace and harmony to follow behind him. There is a longing in a man to leave what he has created with his blood and sweat in the hands of someone who will continue his work and make the place he leaves even better in the future. That is what I hope and pray for tonight as I pass my place to my boy, Lil' Sully.'

"A cheer roared from the boisterous crowd with whistling and applause. Raising his hand to quiet the crowd, James Anthony Sullivan calmed them down and continued to speak.

"'He is a fine man and a son who makes his father proud, but I will not let go of the reins just yet - not until I know his sweat will join mine in this good land. The road will be hard, but I will be there with him as he gradually takes the reins. He best not think he's taking over tonight!'

"Everyone laughed and he continued as the crowd quieted down again, 'I can't take all the credit, even though I was the one who whipped his butt enough for him to know right from wrong. You good men of Salleys Kitchen had a lot to do with him growing into an honest and fair man. You helped me keep him on the straight and narrow because he followed most of you down that right road. I want to thank all of you because every one of you had a part in his rais'n!'

"There was another roar from the rowdy crowd and James Anthony quieted them one last time. From his place above the crowd he said, 'Son, I expect you to do right and I know you will while I'm still about, but if you don't do right when I'm gone, I expect every one of the fellows here to let you know when you ain't right. I hope they won't hesitate to jerk a knot in your ass if you don't straighten up and fly right!'

"A huge roar bellowed from the crowd that made even the women folk in the house peek out the window to see what was going on. Lil' Sully laughed, too, as he hugged his father and was slapped on the back by a multitude of tipsy friends. All of the citizens of the sand hill crossroad knew for certain and were happy that the torch of leadership would soon be passed to James Anthony Sullivan, Jr. As the community of Salleys Kitchen continued to grow and prosper, it citizens would look to the next James Anthony Sullivan for guidance."

***

After Sully described how his great-grandfather had fallen in love with a rich girl from Charleston, Salley began to understand why the Sullivan mansion existed. She still wanted to hear the whole story. There seemed to be a fly in the ointment somewhere and she was sure he would describe it in his next recording session. Her comfortable armchair beside Sully had been replaced with an equally comfortable rocking chair and as she rocked Ruth and held her close to her heart, she sang her to sleep. The song that Ruth seemed to enjoy the most was 'Flying Purple People Eater' and Sully found that to be outstanding! Salley soon began to understand Ruth would follow no one, but carve her own path in the world. Salley's first child would not be a conventional little girl - Sully readily agreed and told Salley it was very apropos!

With little Ruth well-fed and asleep in her bassinet beside her grandfather, Salley started the tape recorder and nodded to Sully to begin. He was careful not to wake up the little one, for he knew that would end the recording session. She would certainly not lie still and listen to him!

***

"As the men of Salleys Kitchen sobered the next day and rubbed their aching heads, the women continued to frantically search for just the right dress pattern. They made many lists of needed items and practiced putting up their hair for the big day. All of the menfolk grumbled, for they knew they would be made to bathe and put on their new Sunday-go-to-meeting clothes that their wives had made or bought for the wedding. They tolerated the wishes of their womenfolk, for to cross them at this important time would surely set them to sleeping on the porch with the dog.

"The wedding was to take place in a fine new church. Though James Anthony was raised Catholic, Salley had been reared in the predominantly Protestant traditions and attended Silver Bluff Baptist Church as a little girl. In that there were no Catholic churches in the region, James Anthony had followed her to church, but had never converted. In the early days, they attended services in a hastily built little church. James Anthony realized his community needed a new church, for a community's church spoke volumes about the community itself. At his behest, a new worship building was built by the people of the community and with James Anthony Sullivan's influence, a fine church was constructed. The new church became a landmark that indicated to all that Salleys Kitchen was a Christian community. The inside, however, had yet to be completed. The push to put the finishing touches on the handsome building began with earnest, as the wedding was just around the corner.

"Ordering lavish accoutrements for the interior of the church, a community effort soon had the interior of the holy house matching the gorgeous outside of the Georgian style structure. With state of the art embellishments, the country church now rivaled churches in Charleston and was the pride of the community.

"All in all, by the time the big day arrived, just about everyone was either in a tizzy or madder than hell. Either way, there was a church full of tension as the organ, rented from Augusta just for the occasion, began to play the wedding march and the well-dressed ladies made their way down the aisle. With no father to give her away, Clara Ruth stood in the rear of the church, alone, wearing the stone she received for her engagement around her neck. Trying to meld her feelings for the two men she had loved in her young life, she gazed at the portrait of the old sea Captain displayed prominently on a table near the altar. His memory was permanently engrained in her heart - Lil' Sully was working hard to achieve that rank.

"Alone, Clara Ruth took the first step down the aisle and was determined not to cry, but tears of joy from the past and for the future streamed down her face. On her own in a quiet world with no sound but the beat of her heart, she looked to the picture of her father and made her way down the aisle. Wearing a fabulous Parisian gown with an 8-foot train, she took measured and deliberate steps, lingering for just a moment after each movement. The candlelight danced among the silk, satin and sequins on her gown - she was a mesmerizing vision. Two little girls dressed in white tended the bride's long train as it flowed behind while she slowly moved to the front of the grand country church. The tears sparkled on her face as she reached the man to whom she would join her life. Waiting patiently, as he had learned to do, he gazed through her veil into her eyes. Tenderly, he put his hands under her veil and cupped her lovely face, then once again, gently and lovingly swept away the tears with his thumbs. Taking her hand, they turned to face the stressed-out preacher, ready to repeat the vows they would keep for life.

"Filled to the brim, the stately church struggled to contain the overflowing crowd. The large and beautiful stained-glass windows had been opened inward and platforms were built outside each window for the overflow of people. Each window platform had a white awning overhead to shade those peering through the windows at the once-in-a-century occasion. From every opening and space, the people of Salleys Kitchen watched in awe as the monumental ceremony unfolded before their eyes. For decades to come, it would be the benchmark by which all weddings would be judged. No marriage ceremony would come close in comparison to the wedding of James Anthony Sullivan, Jr. and Clara Ruth Rutledge. Over the years, each time it was recalled, it grew larger and grander."

Chapter 7

"On the third day of the wedding celebration, the exhausted community sighed as they waved good-bye to the happy couple. Climbing into the handsome black carriage, the newlyweds seemed lost in love as they made their way to Charleston and the ship waiting to sail them to Paris.

"An enchanting carefree voyage gave the couple much time to consummate their vows. Their time on the ocean also did much to explain to Clara Ruth why her father had such a love of the sea. With chills running down her spine, she watched the dolphins play along the front keel of the ship and spotted the blow spouts of whales off in the distance. Thinking of her father, she beamed with joy. Lil' Sully wondered if the water on her face was the result of tears or the salty spray that she loved to feel. Those waves crashing over the front of the ship seemed to wash away her grief and bring renewed vigor to the woman who had so dramatically changed Lil' Sully's life. As he held her close on the deck of the clipper, she became his stability. He was consumed in her aura and eager to please her, for she was now his life. The crew of the ship and the others onboard shared in the glow of the newlyweds. The formal meals, attended by all of the first-class passengers, were delightful and happy with the lovebirds' presence. The Captain toasted their happiness and thanked them for making the voyage such a joyous event for all.

"For thirty days of blissful summer, the two young lovers enjoyed Paris and looked for adventure from the dress shops in the city to the vineyards in the countryside. Everything was fun no matter the setting, from snacking on cheese and bread with wine while huddled in a hayloft during a long summer shower, to exciting dinners in elegant restaurants with delectable cuisine. It was a time of no worries and no cares, just enjoyment, elation and ecstasy. The time passed too soon and the voyage home was at hand, along with the problem of finding a way for their many treasures to follow them home.

"At last, Charleston Harbor appeared over the horizon and the lovesick couple sailed into the home port of Clara Ruth's father. Entering the Holy City's harbor by ship allowed

Clara Ruth and Lil' Sully a view of her massive childhood home. It was a perspective she had never experienced. Seeing the widow's walk where she had paced so many times while waiting for her father to return made her smile. She realized she was finally adjusting to life without her beloved father.

"With the swagger her father once displayed, she stepped on land and immediately demanded to be taken to the office of her father's lawyer. She told Lil' Sully she wanted to discuss her inheritance and the ship captain's daughter took charge of the meeting the minute she walked into the counselor's office. She ordered the house to be sold in a way that would yield maximum profit and the house slaves were to be sold in the same manner, except for the two youngest girls. They would be coming with her. All monies were to be consolidated and easily accessible if she were to need cash in the near future. The old man of laws was puzzled and asked her to confirm that she wanted the men, women and children who had been keeping up the house - the families with whom she had grown up - to be split up and sold separately. Splitting the families would produce the most profit. Her reply was, 'Yes, I want top dollar! They are healthy and strong.' She thanked the attorney, then took Lil' Sully's arm and happily strolled to the carriage for the ride to her house.

"Once back at the mansion on The Battery, she ordered the slaves to pack up everything carefully, for some things would be taken to Salleys Kitchen while other items would be put into storage. She wanted nothing damaged or broken. She instructed them to pack up the things she was not taking with her and have them taken to her father's warehouse until she needed them. After giving the house slaves instructions, she arranged for a crew of men to build crates and pack the remaining items, for she wanted them safe while in storage.

"Satisfied with what she had done, she climbed into her waiting carriage and traveled to the offices of the most renowned architectural firm in the city. She had a long meeting with James Hoban, the architect who had designed the Charleston County Courthouse. The private meeting lasted over an hour as Lil' Sully sat in the foyer and waited for his wife. Exiting with a smile, she again took her waiting husband's arm and walked to the carriage. Stopping by the offices of her father's old business partners, she arranged for the storage of the items she was leaving behind and the old gentlemen were more than happy to accommodate her needs. Choosing a few household items and personal things to take with her to Salleys Kitchen, Clara Ruth was not the least bit intimidated by the many tasks she had to accomplish. Their new treasures from Paris and the rest of her belongings from her Charleston home would be carefully labeled, recorded and placed in storage. After a week of activity, final arrangements were completed and everything was in its proper and safe place.

"Lil' Sully watched the efficient and determined actions of his new bride and while he did not understand everything she was arranging, he knew in his heart she was a force with which to be reckoned. Finally, ready to leave the Holy City, Lil' Sully was more than anxious to get home after being away for more than a month.

"Still calling all of the shots, Clara Ruth ordered one of the slaves she had sold south to bring her carriage to the front of her home on the Battery. She told him to stop in front of the house, where a wagon and a group of men were waiting. The men were there to take possession of the slave families Clara Ruth had sold. She entered the house and hurried all of her former slaves out the front door. Once they were out, she looked around quickly, then exited the house with the two youngest female house slaves in tow. Clara Ruth instructed the young Black girls to get on the back of the carriage. Bewildered, they climbed up on the luggage area and grabbed the top rails. Looking at each other dumbstruck with fear, they held on for dear life, for there was no place to sit. The carriage suddenly jerked and started down the tree-lined street. Leaving the only home they had ever known, the two girls departed the city, looking back and wondering what was to happen next. Standing on the rear of the carriage like coachmen, they made the long, dusty journey across the Palmetto State.

"Arriving in Salleys Kitchen, the couple brought with them a new way of living. Wanting to emulate her life in Charleston as much as possible, Clara Ruth had brought two slave girls to a community that was adamantly against slavery.

This would not be received well by the community and her husband had traveled across the state with that dread gnawing at his gut. Lil' Sully had to face his father, the staunchest of the antislavery citizens. He was searching in his mind for a way past this dilemma. With seemingly no solution possible, he knew the time to pay the piper was at hand. If he was to keep his new wife, the love of his life, a solution had to be found – fast!"

***

Salley stopped the recorder when she noticed Sully's eyes closing as he nodded off to sleep. She knew it was time for him to rest. Giving her father a peck on his forehead, she said, "If you're still awake, watch for me out the window. I'm going riding for a while. Sully smiled and closed his eyes. Salley knew he would not be seeing her ride today.

With little Ruth now taking a bottle, Salley wanted to return to riding Spot and get away from the guest house for a while. The house staff loved having a baby around and they spoiled Ruth while Salley went horseback riding. The unpaved streets in Aiken reminded her of riding with James. Hitchcock Woods offered miles of trails to ride and explore, but they also made her yearn for James and Blackie.

Jon, Jr. was also glad to see Salley venturing away from the guest house, for he coveted her attention just about as much as Spot did. He wanted to ride with her, but with her Miss America smile, she asked him if he would mind letting her have that time alone. With a look of disappointment, he had nodded his head as if he understood, but he stomped away. Salley knew there would be repercussions from what she had just done, but she needed to be by herself for at least this little while. As it worked out, she did not get to ride alone.

On this Sunday morning, she walked into the mammoth brick barn and happened to notice the crew saddling a beautiful thoroughbred and making him ready for someone to ride. The grooms in the barn had tried saddling Spot a couple of times, but after a few hilarious attempts, Salley told them it might be less harmful to everyone if she saddled the frisky Appaloosa herself. This morning she wondered why they were saddling a horse. She immediately thought Jon, Jr. was again trying to hone in on her riding time. Walking to the end of the barn hallway where they were readying the beautiful chestnut gelding, she told them in no uncertain terms, "If you're saddling that horse for Jon, Jr. you can just unsaddle him, because he's not riding with me." Looking as if they had seen a ghost, the Hispanic grooms did not say a thing. A voice from the barn office boomed down the hallway.

"They are saddling Thunder for me!" A tall, older blonde woman wearing a riding outfit stepped into the hallway and began walking toward Salley. Turning quickly toward the voice, Salley saw the woman's face for the first time and immediately started to apologize. "There's no need for an apology! I wouldn't ride with my son, either! He's too much of an ass - like his father!"

Salley smiled and with a puzzled face said, "I don't believe we've met. My name is Salley Sullivan. I'm staying in the guest house for a while."

"Yes, I know who you are, but not because Jon, Jr. or his father told me about you. As usual, my attorney had a private investigator fill me in on their clandestine activities. I was surprised to learn that my son was offering to help someone in need. Like his father, that's just not in his nature."

Startled, Salley asked, "You had a private investigator to follow me and check into my background? Why?"

"My dear, let's go for a ride. I always feel better when I'm astride a horse and with what I have to tell you, we need all the help we can get." Leading their horses out of the barn, they mounted and trotted out of the yard, headed towards Hitchcock Woods. Salley was leery of Kellah Whitney Chesterfield at first, but after just a little while together, she became a breath of fresh air for Salley. Their serendipitous meeting in the palatial horse barn that morning, however, was not as coincidental as Salley thought.

Salley had never met Kellah Chesterfield, nor had she heard her name mentioned in any conversations with her son. Her surprise appearance intrigued Salley. The older woman seemed at home in the English saddle and as their horses neared the wooded trails, she slowed Thunder to a walk. Salley made Spot do the same.

Kellah Chesterfield began their conversation by saying, "Really, I should be the one apologizing to you for barging in on your morning ride. I very much understand the therapeutic qualities of riding alone in the woods. It's something I have done since I was a little girl. I'm guessing it's a favorite therapy of yours, too."

Feeling much less apprehensive, Salley began her long talk with Kellah Chesterfield. "Spot has helped me endure many trying times with rides like this. They have always helped me clear my mind and provide comfort when the crazy world sometimes overwhelms me. Why have I never met you?"

"I'm part of the Jon Chesterfield family in name only. I figured out their evil games years ago and managed to escape. I've never divorced Jon, Sr., partly because he doesn't want to give up half of his fortune and partly because I have carte blanche to do and have anything I want and have him pay for it. That, however, is going to end soon and I can't say I'm sorry."

Stopping along the sandy street momentarily for a truckload of hay to pass, the two women turned their horses onto a horse trail that led into Hitchcock Woods. Kellah continued her conversation with Salley. "My father was from New York and extremely wealthy. He was part of the elite group of New York sportsmen who loved to play polo and breed extraordinary horses. They thought of Aiken as a resort colony. He spent a lot of time here playing polo and partying with his gilded friends. My mother became his local mistress and I was the resulting love child. I never met my father; his lifestyle of drinking and partying led him to an early grave, but my mother made sure I had his name. After his death, his family gave my mother a large amount of hush money and a trust fund for me. I never wanted for anything as a child. I was allowed to play with the other boys and girls, but I never had a best friend - I was illegitimate. When I was a teenager, the boys all assumed I was a tramp. That's what their parents said about my mother. My life was a fight to prove I wasn't like my mother. My escape became horses. They have always been in my life and they have always been my surrogate friends. Then,

I met Jon Chesterfield, Sr. at a horseshow and he sucked me into his deceitful web. That's why I'm here - I'm afraid my son is doing the same thing to you and I wouldn't wish that on my worst enemy!"

Having heard her explanation, Salley instinctively knew she was telling the truth. Kellah Chesterfield's intuition and experience alerted her to the subtleties her son was using to control Salley and she wanted to know more.

Curious, Salley asked, "What makes you think they are deceiving me? They have helped me and my father beyond measure and made my life much less stressful, but I think your son is trying to push himself on me. I am in love with a boy from my home. His name is James Arthur Williams and he is the father of my daughter. We were forced apart and he is now fighting in the Viet Nam War. I love him very much and want only him. Your son doesn't seem to understand the love I have for James."

Kellah Chesterfield quickly replied, "Believe me, dear, it will only get worse. My son is trying to guilt you into getting in bed with him, and if you let that happen, he will continue to use and abuse you until he's tired of you. Then, he'll find someone new and throw you away like yesterday's garbage. You need to get away from both he and his father, now! The longer you wait, the harder it will be to fight your way out of their trap!"

During the rest of their ride, Salley told Kellah the story about James and how they met. She told her of James' friends of the field and his cruel father and of the men who tried to kill them. She told her how James saved her father's life and how he was driven away from his home by evil people. Over and over, Salley kept telling Kellah how much she loved James. But she also told her new friend that her father's welfare had to come first and that was why she continued to live in the Chesterfield's guest house. Her father was her world before James came along and he had to come first, even if it meant she and James might never be together again. Tears began to flow from her eyes and Kellah pulled Thunder next to Spot and put her arms around Salley. Kellah knew Salley's situation was one that no one should have to endure.

Arriving back at the barn and estate, Jon Chesterfield, Sr. was waiting in the hallway. He demanded to know why Kellah was riding his horse and why she was on his property without his permission. His estranged wife smiled as she handed the reins to one of the grooms. "Why, Jon, you seem more anxious than ever to give me half of everything you own. You seem to forget - I'm still your wife and I own half of everything you own. If you continue to be rude to me, I may demand your lawyer write my lawyer a very, very, large check."

The elder Chesterfield gave her a 'harrumph' and said, "Do what you will, you bitch, I don't care, but right now, get off my property!"

Kellah slowly sauntered out of the barn and climbed into a white Mercedes sports car, unfazed. She then sped away. Chesterfield, Sr. stormed back into the main house and slammed the door behind him. Salley unsaddled Spot and rubbed him down before she fed him, gave him an apple and put him in his stall. As she headed back in to see Sully, she went over what she had seen and heard in her time away from her father. She had a lot to tell him!

Once Salley was back in the guest house, she sat down beside Sully and began to tell him everything Kellah Chesterfield had related to her. Sully stopped her. He asked her to check and see if anyone was in the house with them. Sully's sense of hearing had sharpened considerably since he had been in the iron lung. When he was alone in the house, he keyed in on certain noises and had almost a sixth sense of when someone was near.

Walking into the kitchen, Salley found Jon, Jr. looking in the refrigerator as if he wanted something to drink. When she asked him what he was doing he said, "Nothing, just looking for something to drink." She reminded him that his favorite beverages were in the main house and there was nothing he liked in the guest house refrigerator.

Staring at her for a while, he smiled and said, "You're right. I guess I'll head back there and find me something." With that, he left the guest house and headed for the main house. Salley watched him until he entered the huge house, then she locked all of the slide bolt locks on the inside of the doors of the guest house and went back to Sully's side. His eyes were wide open as she told him who she had found in the kitchen. Salley spoke in a soft voice as she told her father of meeting Kellah Chesterfield and the warning she offered.

In a very concerned voice, Sully said, "My dear, we are in a very precarious position at present. I'm incapacitated and unable to extract us from the Chesterfield's labyrinth of control and you are the treasure they wish to steal. We must guard against letting these pirates get their hooks into us any further. Please, sweetheart, ask Doctor Baughman to have me placed back in the hospital and let's get out of this luxurious trap; there's nothing good that will come from our being here any longer." Salley promised she would talk to Sully's doctor friend and work something out. In the meantime, she thought it would be good for both of them to continue Sully's narrative.

Finding Jon, Jr. in the kitchen of the guest house was disturbing. It made Salley apprehensive and reminded her that she was in someone else's house and her conversations could be monitored at any time. The trap she had fallen into was more apparent now than ever before. Arranging the bedside table so it was near the iron lung, Salley placed the microphone near Sully's head. With the push of two buttons, she started the recorder. Sully immediately resumed his story of the Sullivan family.

***

"Lil' Sully knew it was coming, but didn't know what to do. In the back country, farmers did not own slaves. Most of the citizens of the small community were indentured servants, themselves, at one time and could not come to grips with the thought of a person owning another person. Aristocrats traveling through the area sometimes had personal slaves in tow, but it was not something accepted among the people of the community. There were many slaves in the Low Country, but the backcountry was a different world. Here, away from the coastal region, it was believed that sweat and hard work were the keys to success, not owning slaves.

"Lil' Sully believed the dilemma his wife had created to be a diplomatic challenge. He did not see, as his father did, the impending disaster the presence of the two slave girls would bring to the community. Dreading the thought of explaining his father's way of thinking to Clara Ruth, he knew it would not be pleasant.

"Lil' Sully's father had cornered him just outside his and his new bride's cabin immediately after their arrival back in Salleys Kitchen. In no uncertain terms, his father told him no form of slavery would be tolerated on his property or in the community, period. James Anthony Sullivan, a former indentured servant, told his son the girls would have to be manumitted or removed from the community.

"After his father's emphatic talk with him, the rumbling in Lil' Sully's stomach became much more intense. He remembered all too well that his new bride did not like to be told what to do. Watching her spread things around their new little cabin, he waited for just the right time to broach the subject of the slave girls. Clara Ruth knew the confrontation was coming and she had her strategy planned. When she sent the Black girls to find firewood for tomorrow, Lil' Sully summoned his courage and asked her to sit with him for a moment. Taking in a deep breath, he quickly said, 'We cannot own slaves and live in Salleys Kitchen; my father will not allow it.'

"Clara Ruth stared at her new husband for a while and then turned away. As she turned back to face him, she had crocodile tears running down her cheeks. She began to implement her plan to win this argument.

"'Then where shall we live?' she implored. With that quick and well-planned reply, she deflated her husband's assertiveness. Struck silent, Lil' Sully struggled to find just the right words for his rebuttal. He knew Salleys Kitchen would have to be their home, for he could never live anywhere else. Additionally, he knew for certain he could not live anywhere without her. Be that as it may, his father most definitely would not allow slaves on his property. He faced the first of many complex problems his new bride would create.

"Near panic, he tried to explain to his wife that his father had been an indentured servant and had come to this country as a boy and he just couldn't... Before he could finish his statement, a flash of inspiration made its way through the neurons of his brain. Stopping in midsentence to let his thoughts catch up with his brain, he saw a glimmer of salvation on the horizon. Knowing full well that the two dominant people creating the impasse would not compromise, he hoped his solution would suffice. As he teetered on the brink of disaster, he readied his solution. Gaining inspiration from, of all people - his father - he had a chance to avoid the current calamity, but he knew in his soul there would be many more clashes in the future.

"Painting on his best smile, he held her hand and looked to her with pleading eyes as he offered what he hoped to be an acceptable solution. 'Sweetheart, if you were to make the girls indentured servants and promise them freedom after an appropriate time, I think we could work this out. You will have to allow them some freedom around the farm, for no one will accept chattel slavery, especially my father. But for all of us to live together in harmony and keep peace, this is the best middle ground. Please, my love, understand it's our way of life and we want you to be part of our lives.'

"Without speaking, she walked across the cabin into the sleeping quarters and flopped on the bed. Quietly, he followed her over to the private room and asked her again if they could work it out.

"Looking at the back of her beautiful dress, he heard her sobbingly say, 'Yes, yes, whatever you want! I have no choice, for I have nowhere else to go. But this will be a problem, I know it will! They don't have a brain like you and I. Assuming they have the ability to think as you and I do, will lead to trouble! I know it will, I know it will!' He patted her back trying to console her, but she told him she wanted to be alone. He walked out of the cabin toward the millpond's edge and joined his father to take some abuse from the other side.

"James Anthony Sullivan, Sr. was adamant on the subject and once again reminded his son, 'Many have suffered and died for the cause of freedom and I'll not be the one to say their lives were given in vain! As for this house and this property, there will be no slavery and it will be that way as long as I am alive!' Honing his diplomatic skills on the fly, Lil' Sully told his father of their intentions to make the two slave girls indentured servants. He hoped this would appease each party. The elder Sullivan would prefer Clara Ruth grant the girls their freedom outright. He would, however, accept their becoming contract servants. James Anthony, Sr. was not satisfied with just talking about her intent to offer eventual freedom to the girls. He knew a verbal agree would not suffice and could be too easily forgotten. He had learned from Salley's dealings with her father that agreements had to be written down with witnesses observing. This would be the only way for the girls to stay, but James Anthony, Sr. was still not comfortable with the situation.

"Walking back to confer with his wife, Lil' Sully thought, *My God, will this be my life?* The answer to that question would obviously be 'YES', a thousand times over.

"Still in her room pouting, Clara Ruth refused to come out. After nights of bliss among sumptuous surroundings in Paris, Lil' Sully had finally made it home, only to find himself sleeping on the floor, alone. Knowing his wife would never allow the two servant girls to sleep in her house, Lil' Sully told them they could sleep on the porch.

"Leaving at daylight, Lil' Sully walked to the preacher's house as he rubbed the sleep from his eyes. He knew of no one better than Preacher Poole to formalize an agreement between his father and his wife.

"Upon their return, the preacher kept peace through all of the haggling and arguing. The terms were finally hashed out, but certainly not to everyone's approval. James Anthony, Sr. wanted the terms of servitude to be seven years, but Clara Ruth wanted it to be twenty years. Finally, with the terms settled, everyone gathered on the porch. Salley was the only person other than Clara Ruth who could write and she was, therefore, elected to draft the four primitive documents for all to sign. After 12 years of service to Clara Ruth, the ebony maids would be freed. Further, the documents stated that Clara Ruth had to feed, shelter and provide a doctor, if needed, for the two girls.

Additionally, it stated that if the girls were to marry and have children during their time of servitude to Clara Ruth, the children would be free and unattached to anyone. Clara Ruth insisted the documents have a clause stating the girls were never to leave the property without her permission. She also demanded Salley include a statement that required the girls to be obedient, well-mannered and presentable at all times while in service to the Mistress. One last note had to be penned on the four parchments before James Anthony, Sr. would sign. 'Slavery is not allowed on the Sullivan property and will never be allowed during the life of James Anthony Sullivan, Sr.' Adding to the tension, the elder Sullivan told his son that he would do well to remember his words and follow them!

"Lil' Sully finally began to breathe regularly again as the ink dried on the parchments. The girls made their X and Salley wrote LuDell by one and Naomi by the other. Clara Ruth insolently signed her name to the documents and the preacher looked them over and made them official by penning his name to each. What should have been a happy occasion was marred by resentment and tension from each side. Clara Ruth stood glaring out at the pond and refused the parson's hand. James Anthony, Sr. did shake the preacher's hand, but stood stoically with his arms folded across his chest as Lil' Sully and his mother tried to usher the two combatants to separate corners until the bell rang again.

"This incident drew the battle lines for James Anthony, Sr. and his daughter-in-law, Clara Ruth, for the rest of their time together. Lil' Sully and his mother, Salley, would spend much of their time and concern trying to avoid a conflict and listening to the spouses denigrate each other. Though they each tolerated the other's presence, the father-in-law and daughter-in-law never spoke to each other again. James Anthony, Sr. built a three-room cabin for the indentured girls and Clara Ruth fumed with anger as each peg was driven. She believed the barn was where the girls belonged. On Sundays, they sat on opposite sides of the church and never looked in the other's direction as the pastor's sermons regularly spoke of forgiveness and reconciliation. Gossip spread the news of the grudge by way of 'The Kitchen' grapevine and it was the hottest topic on the rumor mill. When Lil' Sully first brought Clara Ruth to the community, an aura of enchantment spread quickly among the backwoods people. With great anticipation, the people of the community took pleasure in watching their backcountry Prince court his chosen love. Thrilled with the state of affairs, they relished in happy anticipation of the mantle being passed from father to son and could see only peace and prosperity in their future. With delight, they had taken part in the wedding of the century and savored the prestige and notoriety it brought to the sandy crossroad. Having watched the fairytale couple leave on their honeymoon, they looked forward to their joyous return.

"With expectations so high, it was inconceivable that the celebrated couple could return with such tribulation in their wake. Everyone far and wide knew slavery was something that could never be brought to Salleys Kitchen. Everyone knew the founder of the community, James Anthony Sullivan, Sr. was adamantly opposed to even the discussion of the practice. Clara Ruth had to know she was committing a grievous mistake by bringing slaves to her new home. Though they never said it to his face, most of the men in the community felt Lil' Sully should have never allowed his wife to bring the slave girls to Salleys Kitchen.

"Unfazed by the conflict, Lil' Sully's new wife was not about to settle for being just a backwoods farmer's wife. She goaded her husband to clear the tall pines and dig up the stumps to make open fields. Always wanting to please her, Lil' Sully did as she wanted and soon had a sawmill up and running. Adding a pulley and a long belt to the waterwheel that turned the gristmill, the waterwheel now also turned a huge blade that screamed through the long pine logs cut from the forest. With Clara Ruth's urging, Lil' Sully made sawdust fly as lumber began to stack up. As fast as Lil' Sully's crew could cut the boards, they were purchased. Most of the time, it was hard to keep up with the demand. The tall pines fell as the crosscut saws inched their way through the virgin timber. Mules were purchased to pull logs from the woods and the little woman herself kept the men digging the stumps as large black dirt fields started to open up along the swamp. Thick smoke hung in the humid air while the heart pine stumps were piled up and burned to ash. It was an astonishing site for the locals to watch. For generations, they had enjoyed the seclusion and safety of the trees. Now, their world was changing and changing fast. Many of the locals sided with the elder Sullivan and were bothered with the openness creeping over the land. As the sawmill's loud up-and-down whine pierced the hot, heavy air, it alerted everyone that change was inching its way to them.

"Clara Ruth controlled the money and Lil' Sully provided the muscle and sweat. It was soon obvious that the newest member of the Sullivan family was determined to become wealthy and powerful. Though the couple was living a comfortable backcountry life, Clara Ruth wanted more. The former Charleston debutante was not happy with the status quo. She had plans greater than anyone dreamed.

"On a brisk fall morning, Clara Ruth's frantic voice rang out over the farm. She was hysterically begging for help and everyone dropped what they were doing and ran to her as the farm bell sounded the alarm. Running out on the porch, Salley heard her daughter-in-law scream over and over, 'It's James Anthony in the mill! He's not moving! It's James Anthony in the mill! He's not moving!' With her heart in her throat, Salley ran to the nearby mill and busted through the door to find her beloved James Anthony immobile on the floor. Distraught, she put his head in her lap and called his name, but he didn't move, not even to breathe. Others rushed to her side fearing the worst, but hoping he was alive. The crush of reality soon settled over those closest to him, as the knife of anguish pierced their hearts. All were stunned and shocked as Lil' Sully rushed through the door to hear his mother's words of woe, 'He's dead - he's dead! My love, my life - he's gone!' Lil' Sully flew to her side only to find his mother's hard words to be true. He cried out in pain as their friends tried to comfort and console them.

"After leaving mother and son alone for a time to say their final goodbyes, the men of the church finally pried Salley and Lil' Sully away from the body of the man they loved. Reverently, his body was taken to the parson's back porch. There, the body was cleaned and dressed in the clothes he wore to the wedding. His body was then carefully placed in a pine box that James Anthony Sullivan, Sr. had made for himself a long time back. His remains were placed in the family home and during that night of mourning it was told he had not a scratch on his body, not a sign of why he died. But everyone asked in a silent whisper, how was it Clara Ruth had found him dead, for they never spoke nor tolerated the other's company.

"The next day, the community leader's body was placed in the church for public viewing and the line wiggled out of the church and down the sandy lane to the main dirt road. But the question was still on everyone's mind: *How did it happen that Clara Ruth found James Anthony, Sr. dead?*

"Telling everyone who would listen exactly how it occurred, Clara Ruth told her story over and over trying to gain release for her imagined guilt. In the story she repeated, she had walked with Lil' Sully from their cabin to the front of the store and stood with him, holding his arm as he waited for the sawmill hands to arrive in the wagon. When the men arrived, she kissed her husband goodbye and started her walk back to the house. As she passed the mill, she heard something fall that didn't sound just right. Curious, she stepped over to the mill and peered through a crack in the door, only to see someone lying on the floor. Stepping in, she found the mill quiet and thought that was strange, in that the men had logs to cut and there was always corn to grind. There on the floor, she found James Anthony, Sr. grabbing his heart and begging for Salley.

"Clara Ruth asked the same question each time she told her version of what happened. 'Why did it have to be me? I'll never understand. Why did I have to find him dying?' Lil' Sully tried to console her, but grief was eating at his soul and her guilt was secondary to him. For a while, out of respect, the sand hill crossroad came to a halt and for some reason, the entire community of Salleys Kitchen failed to restart. The community remained motionless after the death of their leader, as an eerie pall engulfed the sand hill crossroad.

"It was Salley who made the mourning stop. She told the preacher she wanted to address the congregation after his sermon on Sunday. Standing before their friends and neighbors, she said their mourning and lack of work would have been the last thing James Anthony Sullivan, Sr. would have wanted to see happen. She continued by saying he loved the community and would never want his death to cause it to fall apart. 'All of you must get busy doing what you know to do. We will just have to work through our grief. Salleys Kitchen must continue and if my husband was your friend, you will get back to the business of our community. Each of you heard him on numerous occasions say he wanted the community he started to continue beyond his death and become a better place for our children. Tomorrow morning you must go back to work and do it to honor and remember my husband.' Taking Lil' Sully's arm, she left the church with the people following. On Monday morning after her words, the community once again hummed with activity and Salleys Kitchen roared back to life.

"In the early winter, as ice began to form around the edge of the millpond, 2 wagons pulled into the church yard. One wagon held a crew of 5 men and the other contained a huge marble monument that protruded out of the back of the wagon. After locating the grave of James Anthony Sullivan. Sr., the men quickly began preparing the sight and setting up the base upon which the huge obelisk would be placed. Using a 25-foot tripod with a block and tackle, the huge carved stone was permanently placed at the head of James Anthony Sullivan, Sr.'s grave. Fifteen feet tall with the family name on four sides, it was carved from one piece of stone. On the front facing the grave was engraved, Steadfast and Strong - He Helped All. When Lil' Sully asked who had ordered and paid for the huge tombstone, the workmen didn't know. The mystery buzzed through the crossroad, but most everyone assumed it was arranged by Clara Ruth. They wondered if it was a peace offering or a victory memorial.

"James Anthony Sullivan, Sr. would no longer lead the people of Salleys Kitchen and this caused many of the residents to question the future of their community. Could they continue to grow and prosper without their wise and pragmatic leader? While Lil' Sully was a good man, it was plain to all he was dominated by his wife. She was not concerned with the affairs of the little sand hill community. Clara Ruth Sullivan was building an empire and the other citizens of Salleys Kitchen only hoped their farm did not become part of her domain.

"In the months after the patriarch's death and well after the granite monument had been placed on his grave, the memory of James Anthony Sullivan, Sr. began to fade. The community continued to grow, prosper and change as the booming cotton economy in the Low Country caught the eye of Clara Ruth Sullivan. Many planters in the coastal region had become very wealthy growing cotton and this was not overlooked by the most ambitious woman in Salleys Kitchen. The void left after the death of the community's founding father was soon filled by a group of well-thought-of men. Lil' Sully took his place among this group. Though never a consensus leader like his father, he was an integral part of the leadership group. The men of this group, however, knew he took directions from his wife. Having watched her gobble up land - by hook or crook - in the community, they knew well behind her genteel façade was an ambitious and power- hungry manipulator. With this in mind, most of the citizens around the sand hill crossroad remained cautious when dealing with the Sullivan family.

"Most of the community remembered those years after Clara Ruth's arrival as a decade of change. James Anthony Sullivan, Sr. had been the most well-known and well-thought of man in the area. He had been a welcoming man and had never told the people of Salleys Kitchen what to do. However, the changes now taking place on the Sullivan property caused the others of the community great concern. Discussing it frequently, the citizens could not agree on the direction in which the community should grow. Their greatest distress came from watching Lil' Sully being manipulated by his new wife. She had brought two slave girls to the community and that had caused a slight fracture in the community's structure. The ambitious young woman was seen as a charlatan to some and was only concerned with wealth and power. Mistrust of the former Charlestonian spread through the community and made most of Salleys Kitchen's inhabitants view her with a wary eye.

"Clearing land and milling lumber required a labor force and the locals she employed were glad to have a steady income. But others detested the open fields that drove the wild game further into the forest. For those who had lived in the forest, it was as if they were now naked to the world. This forced most of those living in the area to choose sides and divided the harmonious community that had existed for decades around the tiny crossroad.

"Clara Ruth's drive to succeed far outdistanced her benevolence and she was constantly looking to expand her holdings. Often, she took advantage of a neighbor's bad luck to obtain their land and pad her acreage. Lil' Sully always followed in her wake, cleaning up the resentment and mending hard feelings. But her father-in-law had been the largest land holder in the sand hill region and instead of coveting his neighbors' property, he had helped his neighbors expand their property. Clara Ruth was just the opposite and took advantage of her neighbors' bad fortune to buy them out. Lil' Sully, though, had made it known that her land-grabbing purchases were not part of his family-held land.

"With the boundaries clearly drawn and the community divided on the issue of slavery, Salleys Kitchen entered its second decade of discord. Mr. and Mrs. James Anthony Sullivan, Jr. climbed the ladder of success two rungs at a time.

"At Clara Ruth's behest, Lil' Sully continued to cut the timber and clear the land she had obtained. Lil' Sully knew she had cotton on her mind as he opened up the new ground that was once a pine forest. When the South Carolina Railroad Company brought its new railroad through the sand hill region, the builders needed crossties for their track. The path of their railroad was just across the South Edisto River from the Sullivan farm. The new railroad would originate in Charleston, South Carolina and its western terminus would be Hamburg, South Carolina, just across the river from Augusta. This railroad project and the demand for crossties caused Lil' Sully to forgo milling corn and grain, as the mill was needed to produce lumber. The men of the community greatly benefited from working in the sawmill and pulling stumps from the newly cleared land. Though it was hard work, profits were climbing and Clara Ruth counted every penny. In the fall, after another exhausting year of cutting timber and clearing land, Lil' Sully decided that his wife's dream of growing cotton was just too labor intensive to be considered.

"Clara Ruth decided it was time to create a proper home on the Sullivan property. Pulling a dusty old leather tube from the hundreds of boxes of precious things she had stored, her endeavor began. Taking the cap off of the tube, she pulled a set of architectural drawings from the container and rolled them out on the kitchen table. Asking Lil' Sully to join her for a closer look, she gave him full access to the design. He gawked at the mansion illustrated on the parchment and marveled at the list of details designated for the magnificent home. Clara Ruth was talking in a manner that Lil' Sully knew well - the voice of a vixen who had her heart set on getting something done. With coyness in her voice, Clara Ruth began her pitch. 'Lil' Sully, let's build this house so we can be comfortable.'

"Lil' Sully smiled, knowing any protest would be in vain, but he knew in all actuality, the house in the drawings was not something they could afford.

"'Sweetheart, you know I would give you the moon if you asked, but this house would cost a rich man's fortune and, yes, we have some money, but as you well know, not near enough for this. We have several hundred acres of land that you insisted we purchase, but land will not buy material to build a house like the one in which you were raised.' Returning to the fire and his comfortable chair, he packed his pipe and pulled a flaming stick from the fire to light up the bowl.

"Undeterred, she turned to face him, but did not look him in the eye. 'If we had the money would you build this house for me?'

"Lil' Sully smiled while puffing his pipe, 'Yes, sweetheart, you know I would do anything for you.'

"She, too, smiled as she sat down on his lap. Pulling his head close to hers, she kissed him. The kiss left the taste of tobacco on her lips. 'Then I want you to start building as soon as possible.' she said confidently.

"He sarcastically replied, 'Of course, my dear, and where might I find a pot of gold?'

"Smiling even brighter, she returned, 'Why, in Charleston, my love, in the bank where my father's lawyer is holding it for me.' Lil' Sully felt a little nauseous as he gazed at her smiling face and saw the determination in her eyes.

"The next day was Sunday. After church and Sunday dinner, Clara Ruth took Lil' Sully on a walk to the highest spot on the land she had purchased. Excited, Clara Ruth kept urging her husband to hurry as they approached the place where she wanted her mansion built. Still feeling a little ill from the information his wife had dropped on him, Lil' Sully trudged along behind his wife. She had boxed him in and as usual, he was being cajoled and pushed into starting one of her patented monumental tasks. He knew she had some money in Charleston, but he did not know she had such a huge fortune waiting on her in a bank account. It was as if his wife had become filthy rich and extravagant overnight. Now, she would have the things she wanted that he could never offer her. There was nothing to do but share in her joy, for she had the best hand showing and had won the pot.

"But the thing Lil' Sully could not settle in his brain was why had she waited until now to become rich. Waking her up in the middle of the night, he asked her, 'Why didn't you tell me we were rich?'

"Irritated and sleepy, she put her head back on her pillow saying, '*We* aren't rich, *I* am! Besides, it wasn't our time - this was your father's realm. I did not marry him, so I didn't think it proper to invest in his farm. Now we will be living on our farm and we will make it a place people will look at in awe.'

"As she closed her eyes to rejoin her dreams, he had to ask one more thing. 'Did you have that monument put on my father's grave?'

"With a sleepy response, she said, 'Yes. Now leave me alone.'

"It was easy for him to love her with all his heart, but there would never be a prospect of him understanding her intrigue.

"At his wife's behest, Lil' Sully began scouring his wife's drawings as he tried to figure out where he would find all of the materials this mansion would require. For weeks, he worked on his list and tried to form a plan to begin construction. At his wit's end, he walked down to the place where he had asked Clara Ruth to marry him. As he sat chewing on a piece of straw, he began to contemplate just what had happened since that fateful day. His hopes and dreams were not meshing with his wife's plans.

"For ten years, Lil' Sully had yearned for him and Clara Ruth to have children. He hoped motherhood would occupy more of Clara Ruth's time, but even with his extra efforts, their hopes were an unfulfilled dream. His wife avoided the subject and passed it off with her favorite reply, 'It's just not our time yet.' So now, she was focused on building her mansion and the excitement was consuming her. She rigidly controlled every aspect of planning the construction and Lil' Sully was prepared for a long haul. Completely attentive to the task at hand, Clara Ruth exuded determination. Lil' Sully knew, without a doubt, his wife's mansion would be built on the very spot she chose and in the exact manner she demanded. They stepped off the area, outlined it with string and marked the trees that had to be removed. With an air of confidence he hadn't seen since he courted her in Charleston, she showed him the path for the tree-lined driveway she would create. It would connect her palace to the road and the world. The house site was a little distance off of the main road, but not so far as to make it hidden from public view. Once the unnecessary trees were felled, it would be easily seen by all who passed this way. As construction boss, the ship captain's daughter confidently led the way and felt her site to be the best location she could have chosen. She was ecstatic to be starting this part of her dream and Lil' Sully wanted her to be happy more than any other thing in the world.

"Six months into the project, it was well on its way. The extra trees were gone and the site had been graded by the new earthmoving equipment purchased just for the task. Mules were added and their barn overflowed with horsepower. The men working for her hooked the draft animals into teams. The muscular horses and mules strained as they pulled the heavy wheeled blades that cleared the building site. She took extra care in shaping and forming the long, sandy driveway leading to the main thoroughfare. Wagonloads of bricks were hauled from the railroad spur across the river. They had been shipped from Columbia, the new state capital. Clara Ruth hired skilled masons from Charleston and they laid the bricks to form mammoth footings in the deeply dug trenches around the building site. The bricks were also used to construct the basement that would be under the huge house. The plans indicated the need for an extra sturdy foundation to support the heavy load of the multistory mansion. With the huge first floor almost framed, Clara Ruth became the largest employer of craftsmen in the sand hills region. Lil' Sully was not as involved with the day-to-day construction of the palatial home; instead, he concentrated on the sawmill and clearing stumps from the large open areas left after the trees were cut. Clara Ruth had decided these areas would become cotton fields.

"The up and coming cotton planting couple made regular visits to Augusta, and only a little less often, they visited Charleston, to obtain special materials for the house. During their travels, Lil' Sully surveyed the huge fields of cotton for miles and miles along the way. Often stopping to talk with the planters who owned the sprawling plantations, Lil' Sully, at his wife's insistence, began learning how to grow cotton. Through that season, he watched the large cotton farms with particular care, while making notes of their growing process. Talking with the farm overseers, he soon became well versed in the equipment needed for the seasonal tasks. Realizing the labor involved, he knew slaves were used in their fields and was very troubled with the cost of labor he would have to pay. He would not be using slaves. Having seen and heard of the demand for the fluffy white fiber increasing every year, he knew the price of cotton was climbing astronomically. The sand hill sawmill owner soon decided there might be potential profit in planting a cotton crop, but the one point that made growing cotton improbable to him was the labor issue.

"Lil' Sully's focus was not on planting cotton, but his wife believed it to be the most profitable use of the eighty-acre plot of newly opened land. With determination, she set about making cotton their new venture. She continued to insist that cotton be planted in the new ground fields and urged Lil' Sully to step up the process of preparing the land. Buying the necessary plows and harrows, Clara Ruth had Lil' Sully divert many of his mules from pulling logs to prepare the land for the first planting of cotton.

"Finally, after investing in some very good seed, Clara Ruth had Lil' Sully to ready the new farm implements she had purchased for the farm. Her husband, however, every mindful of the labor issue, had found a new laborsaving device. He could not wait to try out the mule drawn cotton planter that he obtained from Maryland. A Black man named Henry Blair had patented the laborsaving device, but they were not readily available. Lil' Sully had his wife write a letter to the inventor and he agreed to sell them one of his used planters, but it was costly. They hoped it would be worth the money and trouble they had expended in getting it to the farm.

"The farm's best mule was hooked up to the unique little machine. As the strong draft animal began pulling the planter, it neatly opened a shallow v-shaped groove in the sandy soil. Evenly dropping the expensive ebony seed in the furrow, it lightly covered them with the rich new topsoil. It was such an efficient and easy task, that Lil' Sully worried for days if it had done the job for which it was designed. The large field looked as if it were biscuit dough that had been rolled out by a grooved rolling pin. It was a proud site for the new cotton planter and he hoped and dreamed it would be successful. It rained the next day as if Lil' Sully had planned it that way. Smiling, Lil' Sully called it the 'Luck of the Irish'.

"With relief and joy, the miller's son watched as his field of cotton sprang from the earth and grew toward the sun. The season was perfect and the virgin soil was full of nutrients from years of rotting and decaying wood. With no competition for food, the plants grew tall and soon were head high. The uniform rows of plants formed a dark green wave that rolled in the breeze across the field. First to appear among the waving plants were magnificent purple and white blooms that blanketed the field, attracting every honey bee for miles. Soon falling from the plants, the blooms were replaced by tiny green squares with feather like edges. A week later, round bulb-like bolls burst out of the small green packages and grew to the size of a first-year hen egg. The hardest part, Lil' Sully thought, would be waiting for the bolls to burst open. He couldn't wait for the soft downy ingredient to be forced from the bolls. His thinking was wrong, however, for that was the easy part, compared to the harvest of the fluffy white crop.

"The cotton appeared in surges that progressed from the bottom of the stalk to the top and was the most labor-intensive struggle in which Lil' Sully had ever been involved. He and his workers toiled for days picking the cotton and trying to keep up with the waves of white fiber that continued to appear for more than a month. Three crops were made in the maiden year: one on the bottom with full heavy bolls, then another higher up that wasn't quite the back-breaking work and finally, a top crop of light, airy plumps of pure white fluff. The top crop was easier to pull out of the sharp, pointed thorn-like bolls. His men were exhausted half way through the harvest, from dragging a heavy cotton sack up and down the rows of the eighty-acre field. Working their way across the entire field once was a tremendous task. All of Lil' Sully's men had sore necks and aching shoulders from the strap of a cotton sack being looped over their head. The bottom crop was the first to be gathered. It was the heaviest and hardest of the crops to be harvested because it had to be picked while crawling on your knees. For someone not accustomed to the extreme task, bending your back for such long periods of time could be crippling.

"Once through the bottom crop and sometime before the middle crop popped open, the bulk cotton was packed into bales. Clara Ruth did not want the workers to leave any of the fluff in the field, for in actuality, it was money left on the stalk. It was soon learned that any of the white fiber left in the field quickly darkened and became almost valueless, not worth the labor involved to go back and pick it. The top crop was by far the easiest, but on the third trek through the field, feet, knees, hips, backs and necks started to stiffen and seize with pain, resulting in sleep loss at night and fatigue during the day in the field. It took the utmost stamina to pick three crops and most of the hands who completed the task refused to ever try it again. Lil' Sully completed his harvest, but had worked ten good men too hard for too long and his prospects for next year did not look very good. He was exhausted and it took a month for everyone involved in picking the cotton to recover.

"As always, Clara Ruth kept the books and was jubilant after learning of Lil' Sully's success. After paying his help and giving them what she thought was too much of a bonus, their profits were surprising. The money made was tremendous, even with overpaying for labor. With the right type of management, Clara Ruth felt this could be a fabulous opportunity for increased wealth. Lil' Sully wasn't as thrilled with the prospects ahead, for he knew the problem of labor would not go away and his present help might leave if he put them through that again. His wife hugged his neck and told him not to worry, if he could make the crop, she would see that it was harvested. He heard her words and had an idea what she meant, but he didn't say anything, for her happiness was his life's work.

"The cotton was hauled to a cotton gin on the other side of the river at Windsor, where seeds were removed and the fluff was pressed into compacted bales. It was quickly purchased for more than expected and swiftly stacked on the railroad cars to be shipped to Augusta. During a leisurely fall trip to Charleston, the money was added to Clara Ruth's account in the Bank of South Carolina. With the satisfaction of depositing money in the bank, the couple enjoyed a taste of the city. Hobnobbing again with the Charleston elite who had once snubbed the couple, Clara Ruth felt somewhat vindicated, and therefore, victorious. Lil' Sully's first year cotton crop had been a success in many ways.

"Clara Ruth's house was nearing completion and with Lil' Sully's farming victory, she was giddy with excitement. She knew the mansion was an exorbitant expense, but with her husband having done well with the cotton, the future looked bright. Soon they would be living in the grandest house around. But Lil' Sully was not on top of the world, for he knew his wife was planning something he would have trouble accepting and that meant turmoil ahead. He could feel an ill wind blowing.

"Moving day was a monumental day in the community of Salleys Kitchen. Several events occurred that day that dynamically changed the community. The excited group of citizens who observed the happenings did not realize the significance or consequences of the events. The epic developments would bring peril to the people of the sand hill community. That early spring day would prove to be an infamous time for Salleys Kitchen, the Sullivan family and their legacy.

"All of the community, from poorest sharecropper to the best-heeled storekeeper, watched as wagons loaded with mounds of furniture covered with white canvas cloth arrived from the railroad station at Windsor. The arrival of wagons was not an unusual event, for much of the finishing materials for the manor had been shipped from destinations worldwide and arrived in the same way. Knowing it was Clara Ruth Sullivan's belongings from her East Bay Street mansion in Charleston added to the intrigue and caused the most interest. This would certainly be the grandest home in the tiny hamlet and imaginations were running wild with speculation on the opulence of the furnishings.

"The lavishness of the furniture, however, was not the thing that took everyone's breath away. As a solitary wagon snaked through the sand and into the community from the east, mouths dropped open. This wagon stole the limelight from the caravan of furniture wagons from the railroad. A single horse pulled the wagon as it slowly rolled onto the Sullivan property and stopped a ways from the side of the mansion. Paying no heed to the arrival of the single wagon, Clara Ruth was filled with glee and focused on the furniture from her childhood home. She had a place for everything and took pleasure in the supervision of unloading and arranging everything to her liking.

"Unnoticed by the joyous new homeowner, an unsavory character with a gun and whip rode his mule near the porch of the magnificent new home and asked for Mrs. Clara Ruth Sullivan. Attached to the wagon stopped in the side driveway, was a group of twelve black male slaves in chains. As the new furnishings were being moved into the house, the men carrying furniture stopped and stared in stunned disbelief at the chained Africans. The slaves' arms were manacled and chained. They were attached in pairs to a main chain attached to the back of the wagon. They moved with the wagon and shuffled along, dragging the chains attached to shackles around their ankles. After Clara Ruth spoke briefly with the seedy looking man, he returned to his wagon and told the driver to move ahead. Following the wagon, 12 African men hobbled to an area behind the huge new mule barn that had just been completed. The area behind the barn was a dumping area for the manure that had been removed from the old barn. It was kept here until it could be spread on the fields as a fertilizer. Here, out of sight, beside a smelly pile of rotting hay and animal feces, the first slaves ever to set foot on Sullivan property looked around at their new home.

"This night would be the first night for the couple to enjoy the spaciousness and luxury of their mansion. It should have been a joyous time of excitement and anticipation, but Lil' Sully could not come to grips with what was happening. The bound slaves were being managed by an overseer who quietly moved into the small cabin Lil' Sully and Clara Ruth had just vacated. The son of the founder of Salleys Kitchen could feel his father's rage as his words rang in his ears. *I will never consent to slavery no matter the circumstance! It's an abomination and a curse on our country! If we allow the scourge of chattel slavery, it will bring ruin to the nation so many fought and died to create! As long as I'm alive it will not be allowed on my property and I will fight every attempt to force it upon our community. If, when I'm dead and gone, you do not do the same, it will bring about your doom and disgrace to our name!*

"Like two peas in a wash pot, Lil' Sully and Clara Ruth hadn't had this much room since their marriage and it gave them a feeling of isolation. They were in a huge house and it would take some time for them to get use to the spaciousness, but the new living area was the least of the problems that night in the bedroom.

"After avoiding the question all day as the furniture arrived, Lil' Sully now had to ask Clara Ruth about the slaves. As she giddily came to the huge new bed, he ruined the mood by bluntly asking, 'Do you own those slaves?'

"With a look of righteous indignation on her face, she answered him. 'Yes, I do! A friend in Charleston purchased them, but they are my property and I intend to keep them. There will be more arriving before the harvest this fall and I hope you will use them instead of paying the other men. It is the most efficient method of working a large cotton plantation.'

"Lil' Sully knew it was a futile argument, but he had to make his thoughts known. 'We are not a large cotton plantation.'

"Clara Ruth replied, 'Not yet, but if you will use common sense and do what every successful cotton planter in the south is doing, we will be in three years. If you continue to clear land, we can grow each year. This will not only allow us to live like we want, but offer the same to those who come after us.' Lil' Sully looked at his wife, for he knew she still hoped, someday, for a child. He didn't speak, but flopped back on the huge feather bed and sank into the luxurious down mattress. It was a wonderful feeling and it made Clara Ruth so happy. She giggled as she slipped her feet over to touch him. That was the only hint needed and they made love in the mansion for the first time. Languishing in a lovers' embrace, sleep came quickly to Clara Ruth and floated her away with dreams of the future.

"Watching her sleep, Lil' Sully knew he was letting his father's legacy slip from his hands. Feeling the weight of everyone watching, he passed the night going in and out of sleep, waking only to have the burden of his conscience still crushing him with the load of decision. There was no question of right and wrong, for he had been taught from infancy the value of all human life. But the question of success or failure and many other things rode his back. The farm, his marriage, the community and his prestige, he felt, were all tenuously balanced on a knife's edge and his decisions meant success or failure in every situation. Putting it out of his mind, he hopelessly searched for sleep once again, only to have his torment return. Wincing from the words of his father, he was crippled and without any sense of moral strength. Deciding not to decide, he had decided.

"Lil' Sully never mentioned the slaves to Clara Ruth again, but he went to great lengths to make sure the people of Salleys Kitchen knew **he** did not own them. When people asked, as curious neighbors will, he always said, 'They belong to Clara Ruth, not me!' He felt by not claiming them as his property, he could somehow be released from the guilt of defying his father's wishes. Nevertheless, Lil' Sully had always been taught chattel slavery was wrong and the guilt continued to make a home in his gut. He comforted his conscious by saying it was a necessary evil if he was going to be a cotton planter and Clara Ruth's husband. But that did not keep his guilt from surfacing in his dreams, turning some of his nights in the fine feather bed into nightmares. Leaving his wife in blissful slumber, he spent hours of sleeplessness on the grand balcony overlooking the fields.

"Salley Sullivan was livid when she learned of her son allowing slaves on his property. She let Lil' Sully know of her disappointment in terms that were well understood. She told her son that he had let his wife take over his life and that she was sucking him into a dark whirlpool of doom. In exact and unmistakable words, she told her son that the land on which she lived still belonged to her and he would not bring slaves on her property. Showing her anger with her son, she told him she had not given her permission to allow anyone to live in the little house on her property. She promptly walked to her son's former home and told the occupant to get out. If he chose to stay, she would have him forcibly removed. He left with his belongings. Salley also forbade her son from bringing a slave to the mill. Trying to retain some relationship with his mother, he said he had no intention of letting slaves in his father's mill.

"Salley became acquainted with the slaves living behind the huge barn and made sure they were treated as humans. This bothered the overseer, for he did not want to dole out punishment in her presence, nor did he want any of the slaves talking while working. The slave master knew well the controversy he had injected into the community, for many of Lil' Sully's friends let him know of their disdain for his work. They repeated the words of the community's founder often, but the slave driver dismissed them and smiled each time Clara Ruth put the gold coins in his hand. Clara Ruth banned her mother-in-law from her fields, as Salley's relationship with her son continued to deteriorate. Frequently, the slaves sang as they labored and the sound of their voices made Lil' Sully cringe with pain each time he heard them.

"In another attempt to keep the slaves out of sight and out of mind, Lil' Sully had the slave quarters built behind the barn, just over one of the sand hills. This prevented them from being seen from the back of the mansion. Trying to avoid accountability, he had the cabins for the slaves built well and he gave them much food, which sparked another protest from the overseer. Lil' Sully told the veteran slave driver to do his job in the fields and he would handle the rest. Keeping the slaves barely clothed and sheltered, the slave master wanted the slaves to be fed only enough for energy to work. This was a method that had worked best for the cruel foreman in the past. After the slave boss spoke with Clara Ruth about his concerns, she had a talk with Lil' Sully and that conversation became 'the straw that broke the camel's back', of sorts. Lil' Sully, at his wit's end, furiously walked away from his wife's conversation. Storming out of the mansion, he was shouting, 'I've had enough! This is my farm and I will decide how people are treated on my own damn land!' In a fit of anger, he did not take the time to saddle his horse, rather he stomped across the fields, talking loudly to himself. With a scowl on his face, he stormed onto the porch of the house that had been built for the overseer. Pounding on the door, he demanded the employee listen, and listen well, to his instructions. Lil' Sully made it plain he would not tolerate any more abuse of his wife's slaves. Vehemently, he declared that any person working in his fields, whether slave or free, would be treated as a human and any punishments or physical harm doled out would be cleared through him. Further, he told the hired man that his authority would be restricted to only the cotton fields and the Sullivan family would decide all other matters concerning their property. In a parting ultimatum, he flatly told the overseer he could accept his terms or collect his wages and leave the premises, permanently. The wretched little man stayed on as field boss, but was often the source of controversy on the farm.

"The second year that cotton was planted in the sandy loam of the Sullivan farm, it was much less nerve-racking for Lil' Sully. But the overseer's attitude toward Clara Ruth's slaves was unchanged and this forced Lil' Sully to often ride through the fields to monitor his actions. From years of experience in Low Country cotton planting, the slave driver followed what he believed to be proven and proper methods of handling slaves in the fields. This included a mindset of subjecting the forced workers to his ill treatment like all other animals in his charge. Having successfully used this cruel method of oppression for years, he continued to pull every ounce of energy from the slaves with a whip and a gun. In his narrow-minded world, this abusive manner worked best and therefore, it was impossible for him to change.

"As the crop was harvested, it became abundantly clear how much easier and profitable slave labor made the cotton venture. At this point, *not* using slave labor was hard to even consider and with or without community acceptance, the immoral practice was being carved in stone. Small farmers, however, did not take up the practice, but continued using family, friends and occasional hired labor to eke out a living. Using a barter system and credit from the community store, the small family farms made much smaller profits and struggled to survive year to year. They knew Clara Ruth Sullivan was waiting, like a spider on a fly, for them to have a bad crop and have to sell their farm to her.

"The third year, Lil' Sully increased his acreage by double and had land being cleared for the same growth the following year. Year number three also brought double the number of slaves owned by the farm, with the addition of female slaves and the practice of encouraging family units in the slave row. Each Christmas, the female slaves were given a pig if they delivered a healthy baby during the year. The male slaves were given a ham when they jumped the broom and their wives showed signs of being in the family way. Everything was done to encourage procreation among the captured Africans living on the row. But there was one situation that would not be tolerated. There was never to be any white men enjoying the sexual services of the slave women on the row and any type of interracial sexual contact was strictly forbidden. Breaking that rule would result in banishment from the farm. The slave population was treated humanely and Salley made sure this behavior continued during her lifetime. Her relationship with her daughter-in-law was nonexistent and a continued source of pain for her son. He was again stuck between two opposing worlds and it was a source of misery for Lil' Sully. As the years flew by, Clara Ruth continued to hope they would be blessed with children."

Chapter 8

"In the winter of his 15th year of marriage, Lil' Sully visited his mother and found her sick. She had a persistent cough and sat by the fire, wrapped in a blanket as she sipped tea. She dismissed her son's concern and told him she had been much sicker on many other occasions. Assuring Lil' Sully that she would soon be well, her son kissed the top of her head and left her rocking by the fireplace. The next day when he checked on her, he found her much sicker and in the bed. Salley's cough was worse and she had a rattle deep in her chest. The family matriarch was ashen faced and weak. Lil' Sully immediately went for a doctor and upon his examination, the country medicine man announced Salley Sullivan had pneumonia. Lil' Sully stayed by her side for the next few days and watched her get weaker with each passing day. On the fourth day, the preacher came by to see her and she seemed to feel somewhat better. Encouraging her, he said a prayer and told her he would see her in church, soon. That Sunday, she sat by the fire with her tea and struggled to breathe her last breath. Salley persuaded Lil' Sully to attend church and on his return, he found her tea cup shattered on the floor. She was sitting in her rocker, wrapped in her favorite blanket, as if she had just gone to sleep. Lil' Sully soon realized his mother and the mother of the community was dead. It was a crushing blow for the up-and-coming planter. Both of his beloved parents had died without him by their side. He said the guilt of that filled his heart and was his punishment for not honoring his father and mother as the Bible taught.

"Salley Galphin Sullivan was buried beside her beloved husband in the church cemetery and as had happened for her husband, a tall granite monument arrived to be placed at the head of her final resting place. Lil' Sully would not let the men unload the expensive tombstone and made them take it away. He would not allow his wife, as she had done with his father, to pacify her guilt by buying a fine grave stone. Instead, Lil' Sully left her grave unmarked and the person for whom the community was named slowly faded from the memories of the people living in the area.

"Though the legend of how the community got its name was passed down through the generations, Salley Galphin Sullivan's final resting place would be a mystery to the generations in the future. Only one member of the Sullivan family would keep her memory alive and he would pass the location of her final resting place to only his daughter. Her grave has never been marked to this day.

"James Anthony Sullivan, Jr. grieved for the loss of his mother and moped about the farm for months. Gradually, he accepted the loss of his parents and dismissed the guilt of not following their wishes. He lived with his mistake and loved his wife until his dying day. Lil' Sully would never realize the repercussions of his grave mistake, but his decedents would rue his actions and feel the resulting pain for generations.

"Having never been introduced to books as a boy, Lil' Sully never saw a need for a library in the mansion, but Clara Ruth loved books. She had been surrounded by volumes in her Charleston home. She had been immersed in literature from the world over. She was dismayed at her oversight in planning her dream home, for a library was the only overlooked part of her building project. As her new home neared completion, she came up with a solution.

"Just off of the meeting room, there was an area planned as a sitting area and bedroom for her faithful handmaiden, LuDell. Now that she needed a place for her books, the bedroom and sitting area would be transformed into a small library. LuDell would just have to live in the basement. Clara Ruth knew Lil' Sully would not like the idea of LuDell being banished to the basement, but she decided her husband would just have to go along with the idea - because it was what she wanted.

"As the house neared completion, Clara Ruth had row upon row of bookshelves built in what was to have been LuDell's residence off the meeting room. As the changes began, Clara Ruth became aware of another omission she had allowed. She realized the need for an appropriate place to keep the records of her business transactions and maintain the general operations of her soon-to-be plantation. Changing the original plans, she added an office space by using a portion of the space that was to be the library. The rest of the area would serve as a site to display the huge collection of books that now resided in boxes brought with her things from Charleston. A neat little loggia above the office would serve as a quiet nook or secluded reading area and she loved that idea. Without discussing it with her husband, Clara Ruth made the changes and forged ahead. When the changes were completed, she excitedly pulled her husband into the house to see the additions. Lil' Sully stood in amazement of his wife's audacity and skill. She had added even more to the cost of her mansion and had done it without his even knowing. But as he knew well, to have protested would have been fruitless. The surprise changes made her happy, so, as he had become accustomed, he smiled and agreed with her actions.

"Before the couple had settled into their new mansion, Clara Ruth had been constantly on the go, deciding on things for her new home, keeping the workers on task and generally staying busy as a bee. After the mansion became their home and they grew accustomed to their large, comfortable surroundings, the lady of the house gave up her hectic day to day routine and began to enjoy the home she had dreamed of since she was a child. Though it was not in Charleston, it was on a large parcel of land that she felt was her realm. With the struggle behind her, she relaxed and became much more pleasant. Lil' Sully had taken notice of the transformation and enjoyed her company almost as much as he had on their honeymoon. In fact, he began to remember the girl who had stolen his heart and her sensuality during that infatuating time of love. Those memories manifested in the bedroom and changed the attitude of both husband and wife. The completion of the new house and being surrounded again with the things she loved sparked a renewed sense of passion in Clara Ruth. She began demanding her husband's attention to her needs morning, noon and night. Lil' Sully's life became centered on giving her complete satisfaction. Smiling most of the time, he began to spend much more time in the house with his wife. Lil' Sully's demeanor changed and he became much more agreeable, which even the neighbors recognized. At church, the couple sat together and acted as the community had expected them to act when they returned from their honeymoon over a decade and a half before. It seemed as if Lil' Sully and Clara Ruth had found love all over again. Soon, she began to give off a telltale glow. As LuDell finished helping her bathe and dress one morning, she looked at her mistress and blatantly said, 'Misriz Clara Ruth, yous gwine has a baby!' Clara Ruth laughed and told her handmaiden she was silly, for they had been trying for over 15 years and nothing had come to bear. The faithful black servant repeated, 'Whats ebber y'alls ha bens doing, yous gwine has a baby!' It wasn't long until all factors led the lady of the house to agree with her servant. Clara Ruth was pregnant.

"When she told Lil Sully, he was over the moon and to everyone with whom he came in contact, he proudly announced, 'I'm going to be a daddy!'"

***

Ruth was now 9 months old and already trying to walk. Salley was amazed at the determination her daughter exhibited. She could not balance herself, but she was untiring in her attempts to take her first steps without assistance. By ten months, she could walk from Salley's chair to the iron lung. Upon reaching the machine that consumed her grandfather, she would pound on it with her clenched fists. It was as if she knew it held a man who loved her beyond compare. She was pounding on the iron lung when she said her first word - "Out!" Soon, she was demanding, "Out, Papa!" and Salley almost cried when she realized what her daughter was saying. Sully smiled when she repeated her demand to his face, but inside he was in turmoil.

Almost at the point of giving up, Sully began to think it would be better if he died. He wanted to take the burden of caring for him out of Salley's life. She had been so faithful to him and the guilt he felt for causing her to miss out on her young life to care for him was pushing him in a bad direction. He had tried to talk to Salley about his feelings, but she told her father she needed him more than he needed her. She told him if he were to die, she felt she would fall into an abyss from which she would never return. She ended the conversation and said there would be no more talk about that subject.

Recording the history of his family was now paramount in Sully's life and he was unwavering in his attempt to complete the story. Ruth had added her voice to several of the recordings and now their sessions were limited to Ruth's nap time and at night when she was fast asleep.

Ruth often toddled about the sun room during the day. When Sully realized she was near, he began loudly pronouncing a particular group of words in an attempt to get his granddaughter to say them. He thought she was ignoring him, as Salley often did when she was a little girl. He soon found out she WAS listening to him.

Salley almost dropped the plate she was holding as she sat in front of her daughter's high chair one morning in the kitchen. She was feeding her and coaxing her to finish her food. "Now Ruthie, I know you don't like spinach, but I want you to finish this last mouthful and we'll go see Papa, OK?"

As clear as a bell little Ruth blurted out, "PREPOSTEROUS!"

Stunned at her pronouncement, Salley said, "What did you say?"

Again, her daughter replied, "PREPOSTEROUS!"

Quickly setting the plate aside, Salley wiped Ruth's mouth and pulled her out of the high chair. With haste, she took her daughter out to the solarium and held her over her grandfather's head and said, "Tell your grandfather what you said to me when I told you eat your spinach!"

Without missing a beat, the newest member of the Sullivan family exclaimed, "PREPOSTEROUS!"

Sully roared with laughter as tears filled his eyes. As Salley quickly grabbed a tissue to catch his tears, she announced, "We should have named her Little Sully! She's already trying to talk like you!" As Salley bent down to kiss her father, Ruth wiggled and stretched so she could do the same from Salley's arms.

Sully began to think he might like to postpone his death and teach his granddaughter a few more words.

Late that night, Jon, Jr. walked into the guest house without so much as knocking. He had removed all of the slide bolt locks on the inside of the doors. He told Salley it was in case there was an emergency and someone had to get into the house. Salley sat beside her father in her pajamas and robe and looked at Jon, Jr. with distain. Sully was asleep and Jon, Jr. motioned for Salley to come to him. Gathering her robe around her, she walked into the great room of the guest house and stood in front of him. Without mincing words, he bluntly said, "I think it is time. I want to sleep with you tonight."

Floored, Salley said, "What?"

Standing, without a smile on his face, he said, "I think it is time for us to sleep together. I've done everything I could possibly do for you and I want you to do this for me."

Stunned and speechless, Salley pulled her robe tighter around her body. Standing beside Jon, Jr. made her tremble with fear. If she was honest with herself, she knew this moment was coming, but she now had to face the music. Everything he had lavished upon her was for a reason - he wanted her! Standing silently facing her, Jon, Jr. reached down to grab Salley's wrist and began pulling her toward the stairs. She jerked her arm away from him and his attitude changed, as if she had flipped a switch. He locked onto her arm again and she could not get away from him this time. He began to drag her toward the stairs and she yelled at him, "Stop Jon! Stop! No, I can't, I can't do this!"

As Jon, Jr. continued to drag her toward the steps, Salley realized he was easily overpowering her. She quickly surmised her only hope was to talk her way out of his clutches. "Jon, you don't understand, I'm having my period! This is not the time - not now!"

Hearing those words, he stopped and let go of her arm. Having been stopped in his tracks, he stared at Salley and demanded, "When? When do I get it? I want it and I'm going to have it! When?"

Trying not to anger him, Salley softened her never-ever tone and reasoned with him. "Not now - you need to wait a while. I'm not ready yet. It will be soon, please be patient, it will be soon." She couldn't believe she was agreeing to have sex with that lech, but at the moment, it was the only way to stop him. Now, she realized she was so deep in his web she would never get out!

With his finger in her face, the younger Chesterfield said, "Well, it better be soon, because I'm not waiting much longer! I don't want to have to take it, but if you make me, I will! It better be soon, you understand, soon!" He stormed out the door and Salley stood in the great room with tears in her eyes.

After regaining her composure, Salley walked back into the sunroom and noticed Sully was crying. "What brought that on?" she asked.

He said nothing for a while, then, "If by a miracle I could have my body back for just 5 minutes, I'd kill that son of a bitch without a moment of hesitation!"

His words tore at Salley's heart, for she knew he had overheard Jon, Jr.'s demands. She began to cry, too, and through her tears she said, "Daddy, I'm a big girl and I have been through a lot as of late. I have grown and matured and if I have to do some things I don't like, I will do them for us. Please understand it's not much to ask of me to have you in my life and for you to have the best care possible. We'll still be together and nothing he does to me can ever stop me from loving you and James with all of my heart." She broke down and began to sob uncontrollably. Sully struggled to get his breath and tried to calm down. Once he was able to speak, he asked Salley to start the recorder.

* * *

"The minute she realized she was really pregnant, Clara Ruth began the process of getting her handmaiden, LuDell, to become pregnant, too. In the Low Country, it was a custom for a lady of means to have a wet nurse to relieve the pressure of keeping a feeding schedule after the child's birth. Naturally, Clara Ruth wanted her faithful and personal servant to handle these duties, so she blatantly told her formerly indentured servant to find a 'buck' and join her in pregnancy. Knowing

199

what Lil' Sully's reaction would be, she told LuDell not to tell him about her wishes.

"With a lifetime of serving Clara Ruth, LuDell would have walked into a fire for her mistress. She had traveled from Charleston to Salleys Kitchen as a 12-year-old girl with her cousin and best friend, Naomi. They were house servants for Clara Ruth. A few years back, Naomi's indentured contract had expired and as she had always planned, she left the farm with her papers in hand for Philadelphia, Pennsylvania. The preacher's wife had secretly played a prominent role in getting her to the Quaker community and she had recently married a freedman. LuDell missed her cousin, but was content to remain in Salleys Kitchen and continue to serve Mrs. Clara Ruth. She had become indoctrinated and felt her life was meant to be one of service to her mistress.

"Having been programmed to please her mistress, LuDell quickly approached a slave named Mary, who scrubbed the kitchen floor at times. Mary lived in one of the cabins on the row and had a man who had given her two children. With a pig as reward, Mary was five months pregnant again and as she worked in the fields, her stomach was beginning to protrude. Standing on the porch of her shanty late that evening, LuDell told Mary she needed her man, Lem, to get her pregnant. Asking her why, LuDell quickly said, 'Hain't naiern of yo bizness why! But I'z needs hit toos hap'n quick-like!' The woman of the field figured LuDell wanted a pig, too, so she smiled and took her friend's hand, leading her inside to her man. Lying with the other woman's man several times a week, LuDell was bred often. LuDell was known as a 'free house nigger' and she worked for Mrs. Clara Ruth. For that reason, neither Lem nor Mary mentioned the extra bedroom activity to anyone, nor did they offer a word of protest. They just did what they were told. Mary had a scowl on her face each time LuDell came to the cabin, but Lem smiled and enjoyed his task. He continued to smile for a few weeks, until it was believed LuDell was with child.

"The first Sullivan baby was a month late in his arrival and LuDell conveniently delivered just two weeks afterward, naming her child, Naomi, after her cousin. Naomi was not raised in the mansion, but lived with Mary after she was born. She would become part of the growing population of slave children destined for a lifetime of toil in the sand hill cotton fields. LuDell loved her daughter, but was told to keep her away from the big house. Mrs. Clara Ruth said another baby was not needed in the house and Mary could take care of two just as well as one. LuDell wasn't allowed much time to hold and love her daughter, for she was holding and nursing the newest member of the Sullivan family - Trip. Clara Ruth didn't like the nickname with which her beautiful baby boy had been tagged, but her husband was thrilled. He told everyone his son's name was Trip and it stuck. Mary nursed LuDell's daughter, Naomi, as well as her new daughter and raised them together in her cabin along with the rest of her children and she loved them all.

"Lil' Sully and Clara Ruth's first-born son was the love of both of their lives. James Anthony Sullivan, III, or Trip, as his father named him, had never been the kind of boy to run and romp through the fields and pine forests of the family's plantation. With beautiful olive skin, he looked as if he was a mulatto child, but no one ever dared to mention his complexion or question his pedigree. A mama's boy, Trip could always be found in his mother's lap and he was closer to her than anything in the world. Lil' Sully always assumed his son's 'problem' (as he saw it) was from her side of the family and decided his love for her trumped any of his son's strange habits. He never mentioned her doting on her first born. Clara Ruth soon realized her precious son had poor eyesight and made it her goal to erase the disability. The planter's son was fitted for glasses in Augusta and to his mother's pleasure, never allowed his astigmatism to be a hindrance. This, more than anything, changed his world and allowed him to open to full blossom.

"When Trip was a toddler, Clara Ruth began to get sick and started throwing up. She continued being sick for almost a month before LuDell once again proclaimed, "Misrez Clara Ruth, yooz gwine hava nudda baby!' This time Clara Ruth took heed of her servant's proclamation, because she continued her morning sickness for three months. LuDell waited on her hand and foot, staying beside her bed day and night. Lil' Sully was pushed to the couch in the office during the entire pregnancy. With her time being taken up with her mistress, LuDell was unable to join her in pregnancy and Clara Ruth was too sick to worry about her maid getting bred again. The house was in an uproar for the entire nine-month period. With everyone exhausted, the second olive-colored Sullivan baby was born early one Sunday morning, to everyone's relief. Ruth Rutledge Sullivan had been difficult in utero, but that was just a forewarning of her life to come. Trip's little sister would be his closest confidant and he would love her with all of his heart, but his parents would see her as their greatest nightmare.

"As a baby, Ruth roughly nursed at her mother's breast and Clara Ruth quickly stopped breastfeeding her daughter. A slave girl with plenty of milk was brought in as a wet nurse. Ruth was weaned as soon as possible. LuDell was the only one who could put a diaper on her and the only one who could make her keep it on. She was defiant from her first words and continued throughout her life to face the realities of the world without fear. She spoke out against wrong, then earnestly tried to make it right. She would be hated by most of the people in Salleys Kitchen her entire life.

"Pastor Poole and his wife lived in a cabin adjacent to the church. The preacher's wife was from a wealthy family who owned a rice plantation near Savannah. She was raised in comfort and educated beyond most women of her time. Having fallen in love with a poor preacher who had dedicated his life to God, she dedicated her life, as well, to God. She centered her life around helping her husband in his ministry. Her wealthy family promptly disowned her. Having cast her lot with the penniless preacher, she followed him and as the Bible taught, lodged wherever he lodged. The pastoral couple ended up in Salleys Kitchen and as her husband tended to his church members, she taught reading, writing and arithmetic to the white children of the area. Using the church as a school, she was not a paid employee however, she and the pastor did receive a regular love offering of food and supplies from the saved of his flock. He also worked in the mill and did odd jobs as needed on weekdays to keep the wolf from the door. With the preacher's wife, Mrs. Ann Poole, guiding him, Clara Ruth's boy was introduced to reading and learned to absolutely love the rows of books in his mother's library.

"The niche above the office became a favorite hideaway for Trip and he spent countless hours absorbed in the universe offered among the hundreds of leather bound volumes. Clara Ruth insisted Lil' Sully focus his attention on the pampered rows of cotton that were propelling them into the realm of wealthy cotton planters. As her husband farmed, Clara Ruth petted her son and tolerated her daughter. While protecting her son from anything that might do him harm, especially outside, she shooed her daughter out the door to play and learn from an outdoors perspective.

"As Clara Ruth's boy began to formulate a mind of his own, he was not at all comfortable with the slaves on his parents' farm. Trip detested the overseer from an early age and thought he was a dreadful man. When the slave master tried to assume control over the house servants, a small war ensued that almost cost the field manager his job.

"As fate would have it, Trip and Ruth became childhood friends with Naomi. But LuDell's girl was even more attached to Ruth. Forming a bond at an early age, Trip and Ruth guarded Naomi with the zeal of a parent. They had orchestrated her becoming a part-time house servant and waged war against anyone who tried to come between them. They played for hours in the sugar sand around the house and often fell asleep together in Ruth's room. Ruth pitch a fit if anyone tried to take Naomi away from her. Everyone soon learned that if controversy was to be avoided, Ruth and Naomi were better left to play as they pleased.

"As a teenager, Naomi was allowed to scrub the brick floor in the kitchen of Sullivan mansion and it was there she began her education and learned to read and write.

"Her greatest protector was Ruth. As a youngster banished to the outside of the mansion, Ruth saw the cruelty of slavery first hand and as a child, she railed against it in the boldest way. She brought holy hell on anyone who would abuse or treat her black friends cruelly. Her father watched her with a smile and never allowed Clara Ruth to chastise her. This became the object of many yelling, screaming, door slamming, not speaking for days, fights between mother and father. Watching the fields religiously for any sign of physical abuse, the preteen would run to her father, shouting to the top of her voice in protest. The overseer despised her for undermining his authority and dubbed her 'Run and Tell Ruth'. Having been caught more than once sharing her books and reading to the children of the slaves, her mother forbade her to visit the 'The Row' where the enslaved workers slept. Clara Ruth also instructed the overseer to have the children taken to the fields with their parents so they wouldn't be accessible to Ruth and her reading and writing lessons. Undeterred, she walked the long sandy rows of cotton with her black friends and taught them as Mrs. Poole had taught her. Labeling the end of each row with a number, she stood at the end of the rows and asked, 'Is that the third or fourth time you have emptied your cotton sack?' Labeling anything she could, she hung signs on the mules reading, 'This is a brown mule'. She hung a sign around her neck that read, 'My dress is blue'. The older she got, the more her older brother influenced her. Picking up his love of books, she read and became more determined to stop the abuse of the black people in the field. By her early teens she was an ardent abolitionist and had spoken out at church several times, to the embarrassment of her mother. Trip was very close to his younger sister, becoming her silent supporter. He protected her from the shadows so he would not draw too much attention to his true feelings and bring their mother's wrath upon him.

"Naomi, though, was Ruth's friend, confidant and special project. As a house slave, Naomi benefited the most from her friend's instruction. Hoping to appease her firebrand second child, Clara Ruth tried to look the other way in Naomi's case and Ruth took full advantage of the slight. Though strictly forbidden, as she had been since they were toddlers, Naomi spent nights in Ruth's room and wore her clothes. LuDell would have a conniption fit at the sight of Ruth and Naomi together, for she knew her Mistress would spread her meanness among everyone if she found out about the forbidden acts of kindness.

"As the girlfriends grew to be teenagers, a slip of the tongue by her father allowed Ruth to find out that LuDell had been an indentured servant. Ruth forced her father to dig up the old documents and upon reading them she realized Naomi was a free person. Clara Ruth was livid at her husband and even more so at her daughter. Ruth announced to the family that Naomi was as free as she was and demanded Naomi be accorded the privileges. She was the daughter of an indentured servant and was, therefore, not a slave. This brought a multitude of problems to the Sullivan mansion and threatened to split the family asunder. Ruth produced the parchments attesting to the agreement and pointed out the mention of any children of the indentured servants being free. Clara Ruth insisted Naomi's father was a slave and, therefore, she was a slave. Finally, in a fit of rage, Ruth moved out of the mansion and into the cabin her grandfather had built for LuDell and her cousin. She took Naomi with her.

"After much wrangling, Lil' Sully brought the two sides together and worked out a compromise. In his agreement, Naomi would remain in the cabin as a free black person; Ruth would return to the mansion and try to live peaceably with her mother. It was obvious to all, LuDell and Lil' Sully had been the ones to suffer the most during the strife. Both were sick to their stomachs for months during the battle of the strong-willed females.

"Two other young females in South Carolina were as adamantly opposed to slavery as Ruth. They also caused problems for their family, in that their father was a prominent judge in the Palmetto State. Learning of their efforts, Ruth quickly formed a bond with them, for she was cut of the same cloth as Sarah and Angelina Grimke. Joining their crusade for women's rights and the abolition of slavery, Ruth wanted to do more, but felt trapped in the sand hill community. After becoming friends with the Grimke sisters, Ruth joined their women's rights movement and echoed their belief in the abolition of slavery. Ruth felt a renewed sense of purpose and she hoped to join with Judge Grimke's daughters. The two sisters grew up in Charleston in the early 1800s. Two of fourteen children of a well-to-do family, Sarah and Angelina were part of the privileged aristocratic Southern culture. Judge Grimke, their father, was a prominent figure in South Carolina legal circles, as well as the owner of a large Southern plantation with many slaves. Much like Ruth, Sarah witnessed at an early age the horrors of slave punishment. Her protected best friend and personal slave had been beaten to death by a slave master. Never the same, Sarah lived her life fighting for equal rights for all people. The trauma of her friend's death followed Sarah through life and as she grew older she became more conscious of major differences in the rights of women. She began her battle for the equal rights of women as well as the abolishment of slavery. Bright and accomplished, Sarah was not allowed to further her studies in the field of law because she was a woman. Her crusade for equal rights led her to the Quakers of Philadelphia. As Godmother to her younger sister, Sarah's influence clearly impacted Angelina's belief in equal rights for all. Angelina Grimke was the first woman to speak to a legislative body in the United States. Active in human rights efforts for all people, the Grimke sisters were true South Carolina heroines, risking their lives for the rights of all people. The two sisters changed the course of history in both South Carolina and the United States of America. The Grimke sisters became Ruth's model and she corresponded often with them.

"As Trip neared manhood, he became well aware of Naomi's beauty and thought her freedom was wonderful. As their friendship blossomed, their association grew to more than friendship as he began spending a lot of time with the girl who did the laundry. Trip's father noticed the change and it worried him. His son's relationship with this free black girl could ruin his and the family's reputation. The people of Salleys Kitchen did not need to know this was happening.

"At age 17, a fateful decision was made by Trip's father. James Anthony Sullivan, III (Trip) was to start his formal education in Charleston at the South Carolina Military Academy. With no idea of how life changing the next three years would be, Trip left home with a kiss from his mama and a hug and handshake from his father. As Trip set out on the new adventure, his mind was occupied, in large part, by Naomi. Clara Ruth was not at all happy with Lil' Sully's insistence on him attending the military school and she cried for a day when he left. The father was hopeful that being away from home would transform the skinny kid with glasses into a man. Never mentioning the suspicions to his volatile wife, he took the abuse she heaped upon him for sending her 'golden boy' away. As he had done throughout his marriage, he kept his mouth shut and his head down as he moved forward.

"Trip's letters home to his parents told of the very rigorous routine the prestigious military school demanded. Telling them of the honor and pride he felt representing the sand hill region of the state at the esteemed school, his mother continued to cry. His daddy continued to hope for the return of a son of whom he could be proud. As Trip's now wealthy planter parents from the midlands visited him in the Holy City, they witnessed his gradual transformation and his father silently enjoyed a sweet vindication.

"After three years of absence, a strapping and erect young man rode back down the sandy lane to the Sullivan mansion. As Trip stepped off of his horse in his uniform, Clara Ruth cried for a different reason this time. Her handsome son kissed her on the cheek, but Clara Ruth threw her arms around her boy in prideful joy. She couldn't believe how big he had grown. He must have gained a hundred pounds of muscle and brawn and his mother had to stand on her tiptoes to put her arms around her son's neck. Lil' Sully was most pleased with his son's return from college. The bookworm mama's boy he had shipped off to school now returned as the son of whom any man would be proud. Lil' Sully wanted to scream to the top of his voice, *That's my son!* but he just smiled silently. Lil' Sully viewed his offspring in an entirely different light. He now felt that he had been successful in raising his son and his time on earth had been fruitful. The next generation of the Sullivan family looked to be in good hands.

"Trip's absence had only fanned the flames of passion between him and Naomi. He looked for opportunities to sneak away with her. He longed to hold her in his arms and feel her warmth. He and his sister, Ruth, were desperately wondering what would become of their love. With Clara Ruth leading the fray, the community had made it plain they considered Naomi a slave. She was threatened with being kidnapped and sold south and lived with that fear daily. Ruth kept most of the ill-talking riffraff at bay with her fiery rhetoric. She, however, had made her father teach her how to load and shoot his pistol. Lil' Sully didn't think it a good idea at first, but after a period of thought, relented and taught his daughter to shoot.

"Since Lil' Sully and his wife, Clara Ruth, had been living in the 'big' house, there had always been a low place in the front of their house where water ponded. The water that accumulated there after a large rain often flooded the end of the driveway and the main road. A lot of the horses and mules balked at the small rainy season pond and those who did ride through it, invariably slung mud and wet sand over the wagon, buggy or carriage occupants. It had become a ritual rainy-day mess. Fixing the problem had been avoided and postponed by others, but shortly after Trip's return from college, a deluge of rain brought the problem front and center. Surveying the huge puddle problem, Trip's father encouraged his son to find a solution to the problem. He explained to his son that it would be an excellent way of showcasing what he had learned in college. Eliminating the recurring problem of the seasonal swamp would benefit not only the farm but also help the community and secure goodwill among its leaders. Lil' Sully beamed with pride as he realized the three years of tuition he had paid for his son to attend the South Carolina Military Academy was money well spent. Trip was eager for an opportunity to display his economical and pragmatic approach to community affairs. The enthusiastic young man hoped to someday take his father's place as the unofficial mayor of Salleys Kitchen.

"With a drafting board set up among the young pecan trees, the college graduate set about his task with military-like precision. After weeks of taking measurements, grade levels and water flow tests, he presented his idea to his father while his mother and sister watched proudly from behind. The plans were to create a raised causeway from the higher grounds of the house area and connect it to the raised area of the main road. His design was essentially to build up the driveway so travel could proceed above the low basin that held water. The only problem the efficient and well-schooled young man found with the plan was the fact that the raised areas would create an even larger holding pond for rainwater. Without a way for the water to escape, it would stagnate and make the area unusable most of the year. The answer was to build a drainage system under the main road that would allow the water to escape. The water would then flow under the thoroughfare to the lower areas across the road to disperse. He proposed using ballast stone from Augusta to build an exit for the water.

"The ballast stones were brought over from Europe. They were used for balancing the loads of sailing vessels to allow for maximum efficiency (speed) on the voyage from England to America. These stones were discarded as cotton bales and hogsheads of tobacco filled the holes of the ships returning to Europe. The stones were starting to build up in the harbor and become a problem in the shipping lanes. Ship captains were no longer allowed to let their crews toss the unneeded rocks into the harbor. The stones now had to be removed from the vessels and hauled away from the city's dock area. Many were used to pave streets near the harbor but the practice was not continued in other parts of the city, as complaints of bone-jarring travel by carriage and wagon owners grew to a high level.

"With the new nation's free market economy, this burden soon became a business. The people of the coastal region and sand hill areas did not have access to stones or rocks for building foundations of lasting quality for their structures. For the price of labor to remove the unneeded stones from ships, an entrepreneur could offer a product for sale sought after by populations 50 to 150 miles inland. Recognizing the opportunity, enterprising businessmen in the port of Savannah began ferrying the stones on empty cotton barges returning to Augusta. They offered the stones for sale. Trip felt sure these stones were the best medium to use for the culvert. Bricks from Columbia were more expensive and more suitable for houses, walls or other aesthetic purposes. After all, once the culvert was covered over, durability was the only characteristic that mattered.

"With the formal approval of his father and the other leading men of the community, Trip's project began. Meeting with officials from the South Carolina Canal and Railroad

Company, Trip negotiated to have the stones hauled from Hamburg to Windsor and dumped from the railcars. It was a very pragmatic approach to obtaining the needed materials and was another tangible example of his abilities as an up-and-coming community leader. With little fanfare, the project began and the only college graduate from Salleys Kitchen began to showcase his abilities to the community.

"Rerouting traffic through the mansion's front yard, Trip began digging with a crew of six slaves. Three of the slaves were Clara Ruth Sullivan's property and the rest were from other planters in the region. With Trip as the overseer, they dug a wide ditch across the main road and began laying the floor of the culvert. But Trip, the engineer, had a large, room-size area dug adjacent to the culvert in the middle of the road. The puzzled onlookers asked, 'What's that for?'

Trip just smiled as the crew began constructing a 20-foot high crane with a counter weight that made it easy to swing flats of stones and place them exactly where they were needed along the ditch. 'Sure,' he admitted to his critics, 'the crane is not necessary with the slaves at hand, but it saves their energy for the field.' Everyone agreed that the young man was taking a sensible approach. This made some speak openly of electing the smart young man to represent them in Columbia.

"Invigorated, Trip's crews made runs to Windsor for stone, like worker bees bringing nectar to a hive. Stockpiling enough stones near the site of the dig, he brought more than enough to complete the drain. He also brought some loads to use in an area out back of the mansion where Clara Ruth was feverishly working her slaves. She was preparing a formal garden and planned a meandering cobblestone walkway through her perennial shrubs. She also wanted to build some for walls and borders for her other plantings. Overseeing her own project behind the mansion kept her away from Trip's cobblestone culvert.

"Trip had instigated the idea of the formal garden with the intent of pulling his mother away from the culvert project. He was hiding a secret part of his project. The dug-out area was needed for the crane, but its ultimate use would be as a hiding place for runaway slaves.

"The children of Clara Ruth and Lil' Sully were very close. This is why Trip's sister, Ruth, felt safe approaching him with her idea while he was designing the project. She had been inspired by her friends, the Grimke sisters, to become a conductor on the Underground Railroad. It was a network of safe houses for runaway slaves seeking freedom in the Northern states. Never surprised at Ruth's audacity, Trip had always tried to protect her. Though he would not have participated in the clandestine activity alone, he felt it his obligation to protect his younger sister. Knowing it futile to try and talk her out of the adventure, his participation, he thought, might keep her from harm. He did, however, think often of the consequences of his participation, but one person tipped the scale in favor of his participation.

"Once the floor of the culvert was covered with stones, the crane was erected in a carved-out area and used to swing a large box of stones wherever they were needed to build the side walls of the culvert. Upon finishing the walls, green, white oak boards were laid side by side to cover the top of the rock-lined ditch and again the crane was used to convey the stones that formed the top over the oak boards. When the masonry was finished, the only thing needed for completion was to remove the crane and cover over the water passage with hard packed soil. Without letting anyone know, Trip had the experienced slave men meet him after dark to quickly remove the crane and line the remaining dug out area with stone. They then placed boards over the top and covered them with stones. Lastly, the road was packed with the readily available sandy loam soil that had been dug from the culvert. The underground room was completed in one night and known only to Trip and a few trusted slaves, all of whom would have died before they told of its location. Most every citizen of Salleys Kitchen came by to admire the cobblestone culvert and extol the virtues of the stoutly-built, stone-lined ditch. They especially praised the up-and-coming designer and builder. With left over stone, Trip built two massive columns, one on each side of the driveway entrance. They had the blacksmith fashion two large coal oil lights to adorn them. Filling the reservoirs of the lanterns with coal oil and placing a wick in them, the lights were completed.

Once lit, the flames glowed brightly and became noteworthy beacons of the Sullivan mansion. Lil' Sully was very pleased, as was his proud wife.

"After two or three summertime rains proved the structure a most useful fixture, Trip crept silently one night to the culvert. He carefully pushed a narrow section of the top two rows of purposefully unmortared stones into the empty room. Passing a coal oil lantern through the opening, he then crawled over the remaining culvert wall and entered the hideaway. Lighting the lantern, he put the unmortared stones back in place. Completely hidden, he inspected the buried room and found it as solid as the rock from which it was built. After extinguishing the light, Trip crawled out of the hideaway, leaving the lantern behind. He later returned to leave a straw mattress, some clothes, shoes and food along with a file, hammer and chisel. Finally, he painted a primitive picture of a crescent moon with its tips pointing down over a fodder wagon and an arrow pointing to the North Star in the Big Dipper.

"With help from the Grimke sisters, word was passed of a new station along the Underground Railroad. It was near a sandy, tree-lined driveway in 'The Kitchen'. The two admired coal oil lanterns near the road burned brightly at night. They were a beacon to those who sought freedom in the North.

"One of the tasks required of the houseboy who kept the fires was to walk down the sandy lane each morning and extinguish the flames in the two lanterns. As he did this, he would also collect the eggs from the hen house on the way back. Returning with the eggs for LuDell, the boy would report the number of eggs he collected. The egg count was Ruth's way of teaching the boy to count, but it was also part of her undercover work as a stationmaster on the Underground Railroad. Having taught the slave boy the difference between odd and even numbers, the house servant was adept in using them. Each morning, Ruth checked the number of eggs the boy brought to the house and recorded it in her ledger. She said when egg production fell, she knew to allow some hens to set eggs and raise chicks for new egg producers. Actually, the number of eggs alerted Ruth as to whether there was a passenger in the station. If two lanterns were lit, it meant no passenger; if only one lantern was lit, it indicated a passenger was in the station. Each morning the boy let Ruth know how many lanterns were lit by the number of eggs. One lantern equaled an odd number of eggs; two lanterns equaled an even number of eggs. Often, to ensure passengers were present, food was placed on the floor of the culvert. If it disappeared, the confirmation was made. The boys who lit and tended the fires loved Ruth and would have died before they would have betrayed her. As their age required them to enter the fields and the overseer's reign, they too, often became passengers in the station. It was an intricate ruse that was only exposed in 1956 when the South Carolina Highway Department dug out the stone culvert to reroute the highway. Primitive messages of thanks were found scratched on the stone walls along with a file, pieces of chain and leg shackles. The message of the down-turned crescent moon and wagon remained on the wall. The local newspaper printed pictures of the message and a small article about its discovery.

"Seeing the signals drawn on the walls, it was hoped the runaway would know he or she should be ready to board when the crescent moon had both of it tips pointing down. When the moon was right, a wagon with a false bottom slowed as it passed the bushes hiding the cobblestone culvert. The petrified passengers crawled out of the culvert and into the narrow hiding space under the wagon. A string was pulled and a hidden trapdoor was closed, with the passenger not making a sound or movement. Traveling into the night with all of its tribulation and peril, each was well aware of the terror awaiting them if found. Following the North Star, hoping to make the next station, each sought the dream of freedom at the end of the arduous and secretive trail.

"In coordinating the stealthy movements in and out of the cobblestone station, Ruth was constantly sending letters to friends in both the North and South. Through coded messages in their friendly letters, each conductor synchronized the movements of their passengers heading north to one of the Free States or even Canada. Many of the Low Country planters, to their chagrin, had slaves willing to risk it all for freedom and board the covert train using the cobblestone station.

"Trip knew he was risking everything by participating in his sister's enterprise, but his secret love for Naomi was causing a great upheaval in his life. She had been living in his parents' old cabin since before he went to college. During his time away at school, he could not get her off of his mind. He tried to think of each stone he laid in the culvert as being a step closer to another person's freedom, but their liberty meant risking his sister's life and that bitter pill was hard to swallow. To compound the problem, the South, as a whole, was thirsting for war with the North. The curse of slavery threatened to divide the Union and the military-trained favorite son of the sand hills would be obligated to defend the beloved homeland of the South. He would be leading the soldiers of the South in an organized effort to kill the very men of the Union who were fighting to bring freedom and equality to Naomi and thousands like her. He felt as though fate had given him a 'hard row to hoe'. As his work on the culvert finished, the talk of war was increasing at a fevered pitch. Some of the war mongers and riffraff of the little community began to talk about 'putting that free nigger gal in her place!' A melancholy atmosphere surrounded the star-crossed lovers as they realized they would soon be separated again.

"Ruth continued as a conductor on the Underground Railroad using her proven method again and again. She was kept busy watching the lanterns, making contact with other conductors to move passengers along and restocking the cobblestone culvert. Her correspondence with others in the secretive network constantly put Ruth's life in peril, but helping those who risked it all for freedom kept her going. Now with Naomi's life being in danger, her massive network of friends began a plan to get her closest friend to freedom.

"Trip Sullivan, like millions of others, was forcibly prepped for the excruciating surgery of lancing the nation's boil of slavery. As the procedure began, he was quickly made aware of the torture he was to face.

"In the arrogant air of prewar rhetoric, most of the planter aristocracy urged their home states to secede from the Union. Southern regionalism reached a fevered pitch as reckless bluster and blind allegiance led many of the best men of the South into the ranks of a military poised for civil war. Honor and duty bound to the South, most enlisted with swelled chests, feeling invincible and expecting a quick victory with much bravado upon their return. Ultimately, nothing could have been further from reality. Realizing the impending doom, Trip Sullivan and other pragmatic thinkers could do little to slow the wave of disunion. As it swept through the South, it pulled all who called themselves southern gentlemen into the fervor of war and forced them to take up arms against the very nation that brought them prosperity. Those who realized the folly were helplessly swept into a tsunami of regional prejudice and could do little more than reel in the current.

"On April 11, 1861, Colonel James Chesnut, Jr., CSA, ordered the guns of Fort Johnson to open fire on the Union held Fort Sumter. The Charleston citizenry watched along the Battery and celebrated with mint juleps, toasting the beginning of the war. The news traveled quickly across the state of South Carolina and upon hearing of the momentous event, Trip Sullivan hung his head in sorrow. Having witnessed the hunger for war sweep over the Palmetto State, he knew it was inevitable and as well, knew what duty required of him. Traveling by train to Charleston, he joined his classmates as part of the South Carolina Military College Regiment. His hope was to become a military instructor and stay in Charleston for the duration of the war. The idea of staying in state was soon dashed, as his father used his influence to have his son transferred to Hampton's Legion, which was part of the 33rd Army of Virginia.

"James Anthony Sullivan, Jr. (Lil' Sully), at the age of 69, was in very good physical shape and looked much younger than his actual age. He had been one of the most outspoken advocates for war with the North. Urged along by his wife, the two were Salleys Kitchen's most ardent supporters of the Confederacy and regularly gave large sums of money to support the cause. Lil' Sully and his wife's reasons for supporting war were completely different. Lil' Sully believed the matter was centered around 'states rights'. He felt the Federal Government was dictating and controlling the South economically. His wife, Clara Ruth, made it plain that her reason for fighting was to keep her slaves. The couple was well known in South Carolina's Confederate hierarchy and their outspoken support, as well as their large monetary gifts, allowed them much clout in the political process of the Confederate States of America.

"Trip's father, (Lil' Sully) wanted to be part of the Confederate Army. He lobbied the hierarchy of the Rebel Army and insisted he had earned the honor of riding with Stuart's Cavalry. In an effort to appease the distinguished southern gentleman from the sand hills, he was awarded the rank of Honorary Colonel and became part of Hampton's Legion. With his honorary appointment, he quickly joined his son in Charleston, SC.

"As the first major battle of the war began to develop in Northern Virginia, Lieutenant James Anthony Sullivan, III (Trip), and his regiment boarded trains in Charleston to travel to Manassas Junction, Virginia.

"Hampton's Cavalry, in which Lil' Sully was an honorary Colonel, did not travel with the infantry regiments to Virginia, but Lil' Sully bullied his way onto the troop train with the infantry. Upon his arrival in Manassas Junction, Lil' Sully quickly began darting through the encampment like a bantam rooster, offering encouragement to 'the boys' and doing what he considered his duty - keeping morale high. Sitting astride a fine white horse, a long gold plume floated above his fine felt cavalry hat as he exuded confidence and predicted the boys of Dixie would rout the hapless Yankees.

"During that same night of July 20, 1861, Trip lay on his back in the grass near his camp and stared into the starry night. Thinking of Naomi and his home in the sand hills of South Carolina, fear hovered like a dark rain cloud in the back of his mind. Wanting to be a good soldier, he went over and over his battlefield duties in his mind, but his conscience would not give him ease. Consumed by a feeling of doom and foreboding, he doubted his ability to stand and fight. He felt unable to give his allegiance to the Southern cause because he knew it was wrong. Those feelings made the night before the battle a tortured hell of sleeplessness and self-doubt for the lieutenant.

"By morning, the honorary Colonel set astride his magnificent steed and epitomized the grandeur of a Confederate colonel. Not being attached to a unit, the greenness and disorder of the new Confederate Army was evident, in that Colonel Sullivan was allowed to ride at the head of a column of soldiers as they advanced to the prepared entrenchments.

"Skirmishes began almost immediately and gradually grew in intensity until they reached a crescendo of a Rebel Yell. With great fervor, the untested Confederate soldiers ran across the field to meet the enemy. During the early hours of the battle, the Confederate lines disintegrated with the onslaught of the Union troops. Foolishly parading back and forth in front of the troops and exhorting them forward, the Honorary Colonel Sullivan was blown from his mount as an artillery shell exploded near his horse. As he fell to the ground, his horse landed on top of him, breaking his ribs and in turn, puncturing his right lung. Conscious, but gasping for air, some of the men pulled him to the side of the battlefield and propped him against a tree. During the retreat, he was left unattended as the Union troops pushed the Rebels back to a place known as Henry Hill. As he lay mortally wounded and struggling to breathe, the battle waged and the Confederate Army retreated.

"When the retreating Rebel soldiers were gathered and organized, the left flank of the Confederate States Army was ordered to take the large guns being manned by the Union 111th New York Volunteers on a hill just above a small farm. There, in her house, lay Judith Carter Henry, an 85-year-old invalid widow, unable to leave her bedroom. Moving up the hill, Confederate troops began a barrage of small arms fire on the large Union guns. The Union Artillery Commander Griffin mistakenly concluded that the gunfire was coming from the Widow Henry's house and turned his artillery guns on the farm buildings. The old woman was unable to get out of bed as the shells hit her bedroom. The shots tore through the walls, taking off one of the widow's feet and leaving her with mortal injuries. She and the Honorary Colonel would succumb to death later that day.

"None of the troops, Union or Rebel, had ever been tested in battle. As other commanding officers were apprised of battlefield happenings, word worked its way to Trip of his father's injury. Begging his inexperienced commander, Trip was allowed to leave his reserve position to attend to his father. Foolishly racing through the battle lines with a rain of lead whizzing by his head, he searched the battlefield littered with bodies and covered with smoke. Finally spotting the elder Sullivan propped against a tree, he raced to his side. Placing his head near his heart to listen for a heartbeat, he was able to hear his last efforts to breathe and his barely discernable whisper, 'Clara Ruth'.

"Staring in disbelief at his father's face, Trip never heard nor realized the Confederate retreat as the Union charge overtook his position. Fortunately, the charging Yankee soldiers chose not to shoot him and instead, hit him in the back of his head with the stock of a rifle and knocked him unconscious. As the battle waged, Trip's hands were tied as he was thrown in a wagon with other captured Rebels and hurried behind the Union lines. As he was taken away, he looked back to see his father lying motionless under the lone tree, as if he were sleeping in the shade of the arbor behind the Sullivan mansion.

"The sight of his father lying dead revealed the magnitude of stupidity that had led so many good men to this point. Seeing the bodies lying on the battlefield and hearing the wounded crying for help above the gunfire validated Trip's premonitions. As if insane, the sand hill planter's son jerked his bound arms and helplessly thrashed about wildly, crying out in anger, cursing the war and swearing at the Confederate Army. He cursed the South for its insolent bravado and foolish arrogance. He cursed himself for not standing up for what he knew was right and denouncing slavery as an abomination. He cursed his mother for using slavery to become wealthy and rebuked his father for not honoring his grandfather's wishes to keep slavery out of his beloved community. He denounced all who supported slavery and proclaimed them to be neither Christian nor American, but greedy fools who were ruining the nation that had brought them a life of happiness. Though he knew society would have never allowed him to marry Naomi, this idiotic war was keeping him from being near her and protecting her from harm. He prayed God would pour out his vengeance upon anyone and everyone accepting the inhumanity of chattel slavery. The blatant greed and arrogance of the rich and powerful had knowingly pulled the peace-loving people of both North and South into the throngs of the warmongers. Helpless, Trip Sullivan cried out in vain as he viewed the horrid and revolting landscape of human carnage spreading for miles over the once green rolling Virginia hills.

"Crazed with hate, Trip was hauled into the festival-like atmosphere in the rear of the Union lines just as the tide turned against the Union forces. Several other captured Confederate officers were in the wagon with Trip. They were being taken to the Union command post in the rear of the battlefield, not too far south of Washington, DC. As the Confederate Army regrouped and formed a counterattack, the Union lines began to disintegrate. Panic soon ensued and the retreating Union soldiers began to run from the field. The Yankee soldier driving the wagon with the Rebel prisoners was swept up in the panic that raced through the once jovial crowd of onlookers picnicking on the hill above the battlefield. The Confederate Army regrouped and began ferociously driving the Union troops back toward the crowd observing from the hill. At the sight and sound of the Rebels charging the hill, the civilian audience panicked and began to flee in fear of losing their lives. The roads back to Washington soon became crowded and unpassable with people in a state of terror as artillery shells landed just behind them.

"Flailing the mules pulling the prisoner wagon, the blue-clad soldier began fleeing the attacking Rebel Army at break-neck speed. Coming upon a creek with only a single bridge across it, the driver realized it was hopelessly blocked by a wagon that had lost its back wheels. A terrorized crowd of people had backed up behind the wagon, making it impossible to cross. Joining the panic, the Union driver abandoned the wagon and fled on foot. With Confederate troops in sight, the other Rebel officers taken prisoner jumped from the wagon and ran to meet their comrades. Trip lay down in the wagon and cried, hoping to be quickly killed. As an artillery shell exploded near the mules, the terrified animals joined those fleeing the battlefield. Without a driver, the mules pulled the wagon to the rear and away from the noise of war.

"Exhausted, the Southern Forces did not pursue the Union Army in its panicked retreat. Trip was left in the wagon as Union soldiers hurried by on their way back to the Capital. Remaining in the wagon all night, he was found by Union soldiers the next morning as they attempted to retrieve the bodies of their comrades and salvage some of the abandoned equipment.

"Taken to the Old Capitol Prison, Trip could see the Capitol Building just across the muddy, nasty street from his cell. He was held there as talks of a prisoner swap ensued. Days marched by and weeks turned into months as the dejected soldier of the South was kept as a prisoner of war in a swamp filled with stagnant water known as the United States Capital. In ten months of imprisonment, Trip was housed at two different sites, the Old Capitol Building and the Carroll Building. In each prison, he met a varied group of prisoners from suspected spies to unscrupulous businessmen making illegal profits from the war effort. As the number of Rebel officers taken prisoner grew exponentially, talks of a prisoner swap wafted through the old brick buildings used as jails. Avoiding offers to become part of a POW exchange, Trip gave up a chance to return to the Confederate Army. He could not make himself fight for a cause in which he did not believe. Hoping to be offered a chance to take an oath of allegiance to the Union and be paroled, Trip's desire never materialized. In April of 1862, Lieutenant James Anthony Sullivan, III, was put on a railroad car and shipped to Johnson's Island, Sandusky Bay, near Lake Erie, Ohio.

***

Chapter 9

After the long session of recording, Sully fell asleep during Johnny Carson's monologue. Salley was about to go upstairs to bed when the front door opened. She knew when she saw it open it was Jon, Jr. It had been two weeks since he demanded she give him what he wanted and she knew it was time for him to collect. Without hesitation, she met him in the foyer and said, "I don't want to do this, but if you insist on pushing yourself on me, I will let you." His leering smile was answer enough for Salley and she told him, "Give me a minute and you may come upstairs to my room." She turned to walk up the stairs and he followed her. Again, she spoke to him, "I asked you to give me a minute. I need to go to the bathroom." He stopped in his tracks and let her climb the stairs alone. Salley went into the bathroom and washed her face with cold water and took a deep breath as her stomach twisted into a knot. Jon, Jr. was now waiting outside her bedroom with his ear against the door. The minute he heard her come out of the bathroom, he threw open her bedroom door. Salley was standing beside her bed wearing a robe and Jon, Jr. began taking off his clothes as he walked toward her. With his shirt off, he tried to kiss her as he took off his pants and she turned her face away from him. This made him angry and with his pants around his ankles, he grabbed her face with both hands and began to forcibly kiss her, putting his tongue as far in her mouth as possible. She squirmed away from his hold and held a condom in his face. "At least have the courtesy to use this, please!"

Taking the packaged latex from her, he threw it across the room and said, "I never wear a raincoat in the shower. You can save that for somebody else!" He then shoved her back onto the bed and ripped open her robe to find her naked. Staring at her body for a moment, he licked her nipples as she cringed and turned her head. Then, without any further hesitation, he entered her and began to hump at a fevered pace. In a matter of seconds, he was spent. As he backed away from her, he said, "Why, that was rather enjoyable! I'm going take great pleasure in getting some of that on a regular basis."

Pulling up his pants and snapping them, he reached for his shirt and said, "Too bad ole James won't be getting any more of that stuff. I heard today that he was killed in Viet Nam." With that statement, he stepped into his penny loafers and walked out of the room.

Salley lay on the bed and sobbed for hours. Afterwards, she took a shower and washed herself over and over before dressing and going downstairs to sit with her father. Sully was crying and she put her head next to his and they cried together.

Jon, Jr. returned to take advantage of Salley as often as he wanted for the next few months. Sully demanded they increase the frequency and length of his recording sessions and seemed to be racing to finish his family's history.

***

"As a Union prisoner of war camp for captured Confederate officers, Johnson's Island was one of the better holding facilities, though it remained a dreadful place. Not like the horrible situations he had heard about at Confederate POW prisons like Andersonville, Georgia, Trip found Johnson's Island bearable. As the number of prisoners increased, however, it soon evolved into outright neglect of human decency. Food and clothing became scarce as winter approached, forcing all of the prisoners to suffer from the cold and starvation. Soon, the struggle for food became a ruthless competition and staying alive turned into a horrendous labor. During the first summer, he thought of escape, but changed his mind as winter approached. Trip hoped against hope that he would be allowed to take the Oath and be paroled. During his second year, as the fortunes of war turned against the South, he realized there would be no parole offered. All hope of a negotiated peace was lost and conciliatory efforts were discontinued when the North announced it would trade black soldiers for white soldiers. He resigned himself to wait out the hostilities with the other officers of the gray army and take the Oath of Allegiance to the Union after the South surrendered. As a Son of the South, Trip found the freezing weather was nearly unbearable and that, combined with his constant hunger, forced him to recognize the opportunity of escape presented on Christmas Eve, 1862.

"Driving a team of mules that were pulling a wagon through the snow drifts along the causeway out to the compound, a man of Trip's stature and build rode through the wire gates of the island prison. He was bringing with him the last supplies and mail before Christmas. The southern sand hills boy could not get use to the cold and snow and he soon learned to hate it as much as the war. He and a fellow officer from Alabama had been assigned to push the snow from the rooftops of the hastily constructed buildings in order to prevent them from caving in.

"As the two pushed the foot or more of snow from the tops of the buildings, they were commandeered, being the closest prisoners, to unload the wagon that had just arrived. Ordered to carry the boxes of hardtack and buckets of lard from the incoming wagon, his eyes opened wide as he watched the driver guzzling whiskey with the guards in the back of the store house. It was obvious the civilian mule driver was about to become very inebriated, as he turned up the jug and swallowed long pulls of whiskey on more than half a dozen occasions. Once the wagon was empty and the two Confederate officers were leaving to resume their places on top of the building, they heard the whooping and hollering as the muleskinner took one last extra-long pull of the homemade liquor and staggered to the wagon. His drinking buddies, the guards, had to help him climb to the wagon seat. He grabbed the reins and flipped them on the mule's back, saying in a loud and slurred voice, 'Merry Christmas, you blue-bellied sons-of-bitches!' By the time the wagon left the store house, the driver was full-on drunk. Wobbling on the seat of the wagon, he teetered from side to side as he traveled out of the sight of the guards around the corner of the storage building. On top of the warehouse, the two Rebels watched as the soused wagon driver tumbled off the wagon seat and hit his head on the wheel. He fell into and was completely consumed by the white winter snow. Both of the men on the rooftop looked at the other as the moment of decision was presented. Trip quickly jumped off the rooftop into the snow on the ground and pulled the long great coat and cape from the driver, then grabbed his wide floppy-brim hat. Putting them on, he climbed on the wagon as the Alabamian pushed a load of snow from the rooftop onto the inebriated driver. All tracks around the area were covered by the rooftop snow. Afterwards, Trip's partner in the escape jumped from the roof into the bed of the wagon and crawled under the tarp. Trip swayed back and forth as if drunk while the mules slowly pulled the rig out of the front prison gate. Once out, he yelled back in a slobbering voice, 'Merry Christmas, you blue-bellied sons-of-bitches!' He waved his arm in the air and the soldiers in the compound laughed out loud as the wagon made its way across the causeway. Once on the mainland, Trip whipped the reins and stepped up the pace of the mules. The pair drove the wagon south, toward Kentucky.

"Traveling through that first night, both escapees thought it best to stay off of the roads during the daylight hours. They hid the wagon in the woods during the day. Trying to escape the snow and wind, they huddled under the wagon and propped evergreen branches against the side for a small measure of protection. The tarp was probably the only thing that kept them alive through that first miserable night. During the second night, they drove further south under a full moon that lighted the road. Not long after they started out, they encountered a black man walking down the road with his hat and coat pulled down against the wind and snow. Counter to the wishes of his Alabama partner, Trip stopped and asked the old man if he wanted a ride. Never saying a word, he nodded his head and they motioned him to climb in the back. After riding a few miles, the new passenger tapped Trip on the back and pointed to a shanty at the edge of a field, with smoke rising from the chimney. Driving the mules over to the old man's abode, he motioned for them to come in and they quickly agreed to come inside the warm house. His wife, son and little girl were huddled around the fire and turned suddenly to see the white men enter the house. As fear spread across their faces, the man pushed his family away from the fire and offered the men a warming spot near the hearth. Speaking to his wife, he told her to bring some cornbread to the men and they sat warming while eating and drinking buttermilk. Smiling at one another, they felt lucky for it was the first time in two days they had eaten and were warm.

"Huddling near the fire, they slept near the glowing coals under the fire logs. During the night, the old black man secretly sent his son on a mission. As the two Rebels awoke the next morning, Union soldiers had surrounded the house and were ordering them to come out with their hands in the air.

"Realizing the black man had turned them in, the Rebel from Alabama made a lunge for his host as he stood with his wife and children. Trip cut him off and told him to back off. Still infuriated, the Alabamian moved forward again and Trip hit him in the mouth, knocking him to the floor as blood started dripping from his lip. Holding his mouth, he cursed Trip and spat at him, then stood up and walked out of the shanty. Once his fellow escapee left the room, Trip looked at the man and offered his hand in gratitude. The black man shook his hand and Trip said, 'Thank you for feeding us and keeping us warm last night. You probably saved our lives.' After that, Trip nodded to the man's wife and patted his son on the head as he headed out the door with his hands in the air.

"The pair of escapees were treated rather roughly and taken forthwith to Rock Island, a government-owned island in the Mississippi River between Davenport, Iowa, Rock Island and Moline, Illinois. Immediately upon arriving, Trip was added to the thousands of other Johnny Rebs unfortunate enough to be captured. This prison offered much worse conditions and Trip quickly presumed he had made a very bad decision in trying to escape the Johnson's Island Confederate Officer's Prison.

"After just a few days at Rock Island, Trip was handed a flyer. The handout was an offer for Confederate Prisoners of War to join the Union Army and be assigned to a U.S. Army Fort in the Dakota Territory. Those Confederates who did switch sides would be assigned to protect the wagon trains that were passing through that far-flung land. Indians were regularly attacking those people migrating to Oregon Territory. The reluctant Rebel jumped at the chance to avoid prison life and escape the possibility of being returned to the Confederate Army to fight again. He gladly became a Galvanize Yankee.

Those 'swallowing the dog' (accepting the offer), were quickly moved to a different area of the prison with better food. As the days progressed summer arrived with Trip and the others who joined the Union Army becoming outcasts from both groups of soldiers. Giving up their loyalty to the Confederate Cause, they took an oath of allegiance to the United States and enlisted for Federal service with neither the Rebs nor Yanks trusting them. Their actions and whereabouts became meticulously scrutinized by each group and they found themselves constantly looking over their shoulders for the knife that might stab them in the back.

"There were varied reasons for switching to the Union side and becoming a Galvanize Yankee, among them, war weariness, letters from home with bad news, a realization that the South would ultimately lose the war and most of all, guilt from the inability to protect and provide for their families. Often, multiple factors caused them to make the about face. These same motivations resulted in many deserting the regular ranks of the Confederate Army.

"Drilling in a separate part of the prison dubbed 'The Calf Pen', the new recruits were the subject of jeers and slurs and often human feces being thrown over the high fence that separated the two groups. The sergeants drilling them just laughed at the attacks and kept them marching. In an effort to appease their former comrades, the turncoats often threw hunks of meat or a loaves bread over the fence to those being offered much less food.

"For most of 1863, the new recruits were still poorly clothed, but adequately fed. As the summer ended, news of the siege of Atlanta spread among the turned soldiers. That news gave the men a sense that the war would be ending soon. Thoughts of the one-year commitment they would soon make to the Union Army lingered in their minds as they began to wonder if they had made a mistake. With winter approaching, there was no indication that warm clothing would be issued by the end of the year. During January and most of February, food was plentiful, but the cold winter weather made times very hard for the 'turned' boys from the South.

"Finally, in late February of 1864, Trip, along his fellow recruits, were issued new Union uniforms and completely outfitted just before they loaded aboard trains for a trip to St. Louis, Missouri. Arriving at the Mississippi river-port, they boarded the steamboat Effie Deans and headed for Fort Leavenworth, Kansas on the Missouri River. Their destination and new home would be the remote outpost of Fort Rice, deep in the Dakota Indian Territory.

"Once on board the steamer, the turncoat soldiers were greeted with bloodcurdling news. The men aboard had heard reports from the previous summer of Indian raids leaving the plains littered with wagon train supplies and dead bodies of Indians, whites and livestock. Horror stories from individuals who had traveled through the areas and horrific newspaper articles spread through the ranks of the soldiers while they slowly made their way north up the winding Missouri River.

"Arriving at Fort Leavenworth in late March, the Galvanize Yankees signed their enlistment papers committing them, surprisingly, to two years of service in the Union Army of the West. Continuing up the Missouri River toward their new post, the newly assigned soldiers were puzzled when the steamer moved near the west bank of the river and the prow was lowered. Shocked and dismayed, they were forced to march off the riverboat, two hundred and seventy miles short of their destination. The water level of the river had become too low for the paddle wheeler to continue.

"Wearing their new blue uniforms and bathed in fear, the anxious new recruits formed a column with full packs on their backs. Most of the green soldiers gripped the army issued carbines tightly in their sweaty hands and faced the wide-open prairie with trepidation. The prairie wind, as well as the stories the men had heard about the wide-open expanse, chilled them to the bone. Each believed they would find the bloated and rotting bodies of whites and Indians lying among burned out wagon trains across the prairie. Though not as bad as they imagined, the dire situation had begun to settle somewhat. Lingering in the minds, however, was the report of many white people being killed in a bloodbath a year earlier. Every white person in the area now feared any Indian they saw and were looking for an opportunity for revenge. The Galvanize Yankees marched and camped on the prairie as they made their way to Fort Rice.

"Always seeking information, Trip learned that Colonel J.M. Chivington had led his Colorado Cavalry out to teach the heathen Indians a lesson. Attacking the Cheyenne, Comanche and Kiowa in November, he had foolishly massacred innocent women, children and old men and greatly inflamed the explosive situation. After Chivington's folly, stage coach drivers and train guards were once again returning from the plains, telling of horrific Indian attacks and brutal tortures. The firsthand accounts told of many whites being forced to suffer long, slow agonizing deaths at the hands of the war parties roaming the frontier of the American west. It soon became abundantly clear why the Galvanize Yankees had been chosen for duty on the distant prairie. Trip was terrified as each new story was spilled upon the new recruits. With uneasiness, his unit continued to march across the foreboding plains and prepared for the duty ahead, but many whispered of plans to desert.

"While James Anthony Sullivan, III was preparing to face the marauding and deadly Indian attacks on the Dakota plains, a much different foe was approaching his home in Salleys Kitchen. The news of Atlanta's fall and General Sherman's move eastward brought fear to Trip's heart.

**

With a lingering guilt and a hollow heart, Salley gradually accepted Jon, Jr.'s sexual advances. It was never a pleasant event, but like changing little Ruth's stinky diapers, it was a necessary evil with which she had to deal. Sully and Ruth were the most important things in her life and she would have done anything to protect them and make their lives comfortable. Ruth was growing up fast and now had a half-dozen of Sully's words that she repeated often. Sully beamed with pride each time she belted out one of his chosen words. Her favorite place to play was right under Sully's head and as she grew taller, she began to reach up and tousle his hair. Once,

Salley came back from the rear of the house to find Ruth had pulled one of her little chairs up to the iron lung and had her chin resting on the platform that held Sully's head. As Salley approached the couple, she saw Ruth rubbing Sully's unruly hair and saying, "Papa, Papa." Salley almost cried at the sight of the two together as Sully tried to get her to say 'magnificent'.

"Salley's tears were also an admission of something else bad happening in her life over which she had no control. Sully's health was declining and though she dismissed it as good days and bad days, he had gone downhill over the past few months. Dr. Baughman had a doctor from Augusta to join him in treating Sully and he had become increasingly concerned about his blood pressure. The new doctor had a group of orderlies to put the iron lung on a huge hospital table that could lower and raise Sully's head. He was trying to get Sully's blood flow to increase. The new doctor also wanted the iron lung to be opened and Sully's limbs moved as much as possible. This was extremely traumatic for Sully and Salley. Both wondered if it did more harm than good.

"The appearance of the therapy nurses was always a harrowing time. Dr. Baughman had explained in a gut-wrenching talk with Salley that, at best, they were prolonging Sully's life for a few years. Sully knew this, too, and that was the horrible fact that haunted him and those who loved the ole cotton farmer. Despite, or maybe because of, his situation he was driven to complete the mission of recording his family history. His monumental efforts, however, were taking a toll on him.

When Ruth fell asleep under Sully's head, Salley picked her up and put her in the day bed just away from the iron lung. With the little one sound asleep, Salley started the recorder.

***

"Many of the inhabitants of Georgia and South Carolina during the Civil War considered General William Tecumseh Sherman to be the Anti-Christ. Ordering the western wing of his army to leave the port city of Savannah, he instructed them to move up the Savannah River to Sisters Ferry. They were to enter South Carolina on February 1, 1864. With his top commanders well aware of his plans, he sent the eastern wing of his army by ship to Beaufort, where they would enter South Carolina. He hoped his perceived move toward Charleston would cause the Confederate troops in that port city to hold there in case they had to defend the city. Using the same move with his western wing, he hoped to freeze the Confederate troops in Augusta, Georgia for defense of that city. With both Confederate troop concentrations effectively frozen in place, he hoped to move more or less unopposed through the middle of the state to its capital, Columbia.

"Having his western army advancing up the western side of the South Carolina toward the Confederate gun powder factory just across the border in Augusta, he had the Confederate Army wondering which city was next to be burned and destroyed. Lacking the troops, supplies and ammunition to mount a complete defense of both Charleston and Augusta, Confederate war strategists continued to believe Sherman would choose to destroy at least one of the cities, if not both. Instead, the Yankee General had set his sights on the birthplace of secession and home of the loudest and most arrogant voices seeking to dissolve the Union. Sherman intended to leave the haughty loudmouths of the Palmetto populace with a fate so terrible they would beg to rejoin the Union and rue the day they chose to be the first state to secede.

"After the fall of Atlanta, many refugees fled to the city of Augusta along the fall line of the Savannah River. As the most southern of its railroad towns still operating in Confederate territory, Augusta was known to be storing bales of cotton and other supplies for the cotton mills in Graniteville, South Carolina. Certainly, it being the leading manufacturer of gunpowder for the Confederate Army, most Rebels felt that alone made the river city the most likely target for Sherman.

"Fort Sumter, in Charleston, had been the site of the first Confederate acts of war against Union troops. Besieged and blockaded during the entire war, it had been reduced to a mere symbol of the once proud South. Still, it was believed by many Rebels that Sherman wanted the Holy City, the birthplace of the war, to be part of his 'scorched earth' path through South Carolina.

As his advance troops or 'Bummers' as the locals refer to them, pillaged and pilfered their way up the western side of the state, they indiscriminately looted and burned many of the plantations and communities of the Low Country. Making their way up the eastern bank of the Savannah River, they destroyed everything substantial in their path. Towns like Gillisonville, Allendale, and Barnwell were burned to the ground. Railroads were torn up and the steel rails were heated and twisted around trees. The twisted metal was left as their calling cards known as 'Sherman neckties'. News spread quickly up to the Central Savannah River Area where the inhabitants were mostly women and children who could not - or would not - flee. The remaining Confederate Army regulars, left to protect the homeland, were small in number and their ranks consisted of mostly old men, adolescent boys and sick or wounded soldiers. As they braced and fortified for the impending onslaught, silver, gold, jewelry, family heirlooms and anything of value which had not already been donated to The Confederate Cause were hidden deep in the swamps. Other valuables were thrown down the well so the damn Yankees could not steal them. Food stores were hidden and livestock was driven into the forest, as resolute and brave mothers gathered their children around them and read from the Bible.

"A young neighbor boy of the Sullivan plantation was nearing his fifteenth birthday. As he frantically scurried from neighbor to neighbor, he borrowed any type of firearm he could cajole. At the end of his search, he possessed three old flintlock squirrel rifles who no one would take with them as they marched off to war, two fancy dueling pistols from a velvet lined wooden box and a Colt Navy revolver his older brother brought home on leave before he was killed at Chickamauga. Filling a leather bag with powder cans and shot, he had gathered all of the remaining firearms he could find. Grabbing the lone lame mule left in the Sullivan's eighty stable barn, he dragged a wagon missing both back wheels down the road just in sight of the intersection of the plantation's sandy driveway and the main road. Unhitching the mule, he left the wagon blocking the main road, then whipping the mule with the reins he hurried back to a rail fence that separated the mansion from the main road. He was about 50 yards away from the old wagon in front of the house. Using the trace chains hooked onto the harness, he pulled the rail fence apart. Then he made the balking old field animal drag the parts to each side of the main road between the wagon and the culvert.

"Going back to the barn, the boy pushed all of the old and rotting hay out of the loft onto a sled. Savagely beating the crippled mule, he made the decrepit old animal pull the hay to the road. Using the rails, he built up long thin piles of hay on each side of the road and continued his abuse of the mule, making it haul any and every object in sight to each side of the road. As he scattered the debris, he noticed a cloud of dust stirred by a rider hurriedly coming his way over the horizon. Hiding in the culvert, he made sure every weapon was loaded and ready. Jamming the six shot Colt into his belt, he grabbed one of the rifles and prepared to do battle. Concealing himself behind the hay shock and junk he had placed along the side of the road, he crept closer to the wagon blocking the thoroughfare. Appearing over the horizon, the rider was galloping fast and jumped the wagon, landing just out in front of the young fighter. The man on the horse was a Rebel scout riding to give a report of the advancing Union horde. Recognizing the comrade in arms, the greenhorn let out a Rebel yell, causing the rider to jerk back on the reins and simultaneously point a pistol at the boy's face.

"'I 'bout killed you kid! Get on that old piece of a mule over there and get out of here! Dem Yankees is right on my tail! I been a dodging they minié balls since I got on this hoss to run! Dey can't be more than two or three minutes ahind me!' With that, he spurred the lathered horse and continued his fast retreat. Looking back down the road, the lad heard horses and spotted the dust cloud just over the sand hill. Narrowing the distance by the second, the blue legion of death and destruction approached.

"As he crouched behind the hay sled turned on its side, he spotted the first of three blue clad soldiers cautiously approaching the wagon in the middle of the road. With rifles drawn and the barrels pointing to the sky, the butt ends of their rifles rested on their thighs as their index fingers nervously danced on the trigger. Scanning the area for any movement, they were on high alert. As the first one reached the wagon just 15 yards away from the boy, the Union rider laughed out loud and turned to the soldiers behind him, 'Dem rebels was arunning so fast they done run the wheels plumb off dis here old wagon!' As he turned back to look at the wagon, a bullet from the boy next door's Navy Colt entered the Yankee's ear and exploded the far side of his head. Just as quick, the boy fired at the second soldier. He lost his hat as his head snapped forward, reacting to a hot lead ball hitting his chest. The shots made the third horse panic and try to run. With his horse spooked, the sergeant from Ohio tried to rein in his steed. Both rider and horse pirouetted in the roadway and stopped, facing away from the boy. The boy fired his third shot and hit the remaining soldier in the back. The stricken man looked down just as the boy's bullet came tearing through the front of his uniform, along with part of his heart.

"Quickly squatting behind the debris, the young assassin scrambled on his hand and knees as fast as he could to the culvert. Grabbing one of the dueling pistols and one of the old muskets, he then crawled under the road to the far side. The rest of the Union advance party quickly dismounted and dove for cover in the ditch. From their protected place, they slowly raised their heads and peered to the side of the road where the shots originated.

"As the smoke and dust started to settle, the sneaky sniper was ready on the opposite side of the road. He peeked through the bushes, like he did when playing hide-and-seek with his sister. As the dark blue coats crept ever closer, they moved into the youthful assassin's comfortable shooting range. Each Union soldier scanned the area for gunmen on the opposite road bank as they crouched with their backs to the boy. Without a sound being made, the old musket was eased between the branches of the bush and the bead was lined up carefully on the buttocks of the closest pair of cobalt pants. As the boy squeezed the trigger, the hammer of the musket snapped and after a millisecond delay, the black powder packed into the barrel exploded. A lead ball screamed from the old musket on a higher trajectory than the boy had aimed. The lead projectile reached its intended target, shattering the man's cocci, splintering the base of his spine and eviscerating the clueless northerner. Before the cloud of battle cleared, the dueling pistol was pulled from the boy's waist band and aimed at a black strap across the chest of another blue target. Again, the shot was high, but it hit the Union soldier's Adam's apple, carving a path through his carotid artery and exiting out the back of his neck.

"The zinging sound of a minié ball sizzled by the boy's ear and the 14-year-old ducked for cover. He pulled the Colt and drew down on the man who fired the shot at him and hit him squarely in the stomach. Again, as fast as he could move on hands and knees, he fled for the culvert and crossed under the road. As he reached the roadside closest to the house, he grabbed the other old worn out rattling musket and the last dueling pistol. The straw from the hayloft provided cover, but not protection, and the boy next door was careful not to make the hay pile move in any way. Peering over the pile, the closest of the blue boys was yelling back to his Lieutenant on their progress, or lack thereof. The boy next door heard him yell, 'Dey's three or four of 'em on both sides of da road. We oughta have 'em rooted out in a minute or two.' As he turned to advance to the opposite roadside, a lead ball from the rickety old musket put a silver dollar size hole in his Union issued cap and plowed a tunnel through the cerebral cortex of his brain. Quickly pulling the trusty gentleman's pistol from his waistband, the want-to-be Rebel aimed again and pulled the trigger. The dueling pistol gave a smoky report and a boy in a Union soldier's uniform spun to face his killer just before he fell on his face.

"After the last shot, the zeal of the advanced group of Union soldiers began to falter. Their veteran leader, sensing the momentum shifting against them, tried to rally his squad. He shouted, 'There they are, boys!' as he pointed to the end of the culvert and lurched forward. 'Let's get 'em!' With that, they all rushed with bayonets fixed to the area of the last gunshot.

The boy next door was now a hunted killer. He scrambled back into the culvert and crawled under the road as fast as he could.

"Looking behind him, he saw the first sprinkle of sand falling near the opening and a black boot step onto the rock culvert floor. Aiming the Navy Colt, he fired his last shot at the leather bag that held the cans of black powder he had left in the gully. The blast from the gun shot reverberated in the elaborate stone waterway and momentarily deafened the kid. His last shot, as were all of his others, was true and on its mark. The powder cans exploded in the faces of the soldiers entering the culvert and sent a cloud of black smoke three or four feet up in the air. Tin shrapnel from the cans and loose shot were forced up from the Irish ballast stone floor, killing the closest charging soldier instantly and mutilated the legs of three others standing near the culvert entrance. One soldier, bending down to look into the storm drain, had a hole punctured through his cheek and his partner was blinded by the blast. The remaining soldiers beat a hasty retreat screaming, 'Dey's got a cannon! Run boys!'

"The soldiers who had been peppered by the blast retreated to the rear. The commanding officer in charge of the men had been waiting there for the men to clear the road and when they returned unsuccessful, he was furious. The Lieutenant angrily berated his men for failing to make the roadway passable for the advancing column following closely behind them. As his horse danced and spun about nervously, the impatient officer decided to take matters into his own hands.

"Riding his horse to the wagon blocking the road, he cautiously looked around at the carnage. It was as quiet as a Presbyterian Church service, so he dismounted and tethered the horse to one of the wagon's two wheels. He drew his service revolver and stepped closer to the smoking culvert. Jumping down into the crater made by the blast, he put his hand on top of the masonry drain and with a stick, slowly stuck his hat in the opening. Nothing happened, so he squatted down and cautiously peered into the dark channel. The light from the other end of the culvert illuminated the boy next door as he pointcd the empty Colt pistol at the Yankee officer. In self-preservation, the officer fired his revolver three times in rapid succession and stepped back away from the culvert. Smoke was coming from the barrel of his pistol as he waited for return fire. Instead, he heard the eerie cries of the boy next door as he writhed in pain.

"Two of the three shots hit the rock walls of the waterway. But as the youth turned away from the officer shooting at him, the third shot struck him in the right side of his back. Puncturing a kidney and deflating his lung, the minié ball cut a wide swath through the boy's liver and tore opened his stomach before making an exit near his navel. The boy next door screamed from the incomprehensible pain and his body shook with convulsions. Blood and bile pumped from the 14-year-old's body. As the boy's child-like screams reached crescendo, the rest of the officer's men joined him above the culvert on the roadway. The frustrated young officer barked out orders, 'Get that damn junk out of the road and make ready to move forward, NOW!'

"One of his men asked, 'Did you get 'em all, sir?'

"Curtly the Lieutenant replied, 'You bunch of damn fools, it was just one kid!'

"The gut-wrenching screams continued as the men cleared the roadway. Watching from his horse as the roadway was cleared, the Lieutenant caught a glimpse of a lone horseman approaching. As the single rider came into view, the rattled young officer recognized him as a major who was an attaché of General W.T. Sherman. Riding up on a big bay gelding, he asked,

"'What the hell happened here?'

"The under officer saluted and spoke, 'A Rebel boy, sir, but we got him. The road is clear.' The major stroked his whiskers and looked around at the nine bodies lying on the road bank and six wounded being attended by the medical officer. He looked back at his underling and asked,

"'Did just one boy do all of this?'

"With a quick report, the sick-feeling officer replied, 'Yes, sir.'

"Hoping the next question would not be asked, the Lieutenant cringed as the Major spoke again.

'"Where is this exceptional warrior boy? I want to see him.'

The Lieutenant did not want to see the face of the boy he had shot. Clenching his teeth, the under officer ordered two soldiers into the culvert to remove the boy. Each soldier pulled a leg as they dragged the boy next door from the dark cavern and dropped him on the road bank with the other bodies.

'"Hellfire and damnation, he's still alive! If we had men who fought like that boy, the war would already be over!' Shaking his head in disgust, the Major spurred his horse and rode up the tree lined driveway toward the mansion. The Yankee soldiers who were clearing the road regrouped and pressed forward toward the next bivouac, Johnson's Crossroad. (present day Montmorenci) The boy next door was left lying on the road bank, writhing in pain. He cried out for his mother.

"As he trotted his horse toward the Sullivan mansion, the Major tried to shake the image of the blood and guts falling from the kid's gaping side. Having been with 'The Red Head' since Vicksburg, he had seen a lot of carnage and never liked having the butchery of battle forced in his face. This day, though, he needed to focus his thoughts on his assignment. Returning his attention to the task at hand, he looked down the sandy tree-lined lane to see his soldiers standing guard at the entrance to the mansion. He had given orders for them to set up camp in the yard between the barn and the residence. Knowing his men, he figured they wanted to be near any livestock or chickens on which they could get their hands.

"Fires were smoldering and the chow detail was busy as sentries had been posted around the house. On a regular day, the Major would have watched as the Bummers freely pillaged and plunder ed the house and property, then burned it as they left. But his orders were different today. They read 'Arrange suitable quarters for meeting of advanced attachment of Red Senior Command.' The word 'red' was a code word for the commanding general himself. General William Tecumseh Sherman was riding out in front of his troops to manage the direction of his armies. In a feigned move toward Augusta, he sent a Calvary unit in the direction of the town of Aiken, just a little ways from Augusta. It was a ruse and now he wanted his armies to turn abruptly and start marching north toward Columbia, post haste.

"The capital city would be the centerpiece of his path of destruction through the Palmetto State. The capitulation of the 'epicenter of secession' would, he thought, crush the morale of the Southern populace and bring a much swifter end to the hostilities. In his plan to bring about a Confederate surrender, he needed to illustrate to those who wished to splinter the Union the devastating and horrific reality of war. He wanted to leave the people in his wake demoralized as they faced the consequences of their treasonous actions. Sherman predicted his 'scorched earth war plan' would be remembered in Georgia and South Carolina for centuries. He was, therefore, deliberate about his troop movements.

"The meeting that the Major was arranging was to be held at the tiny crossroad of Salleys Kitchen. It was a war conference to ensure all of Sherman's generals stayed on the course he had ordered.

"General Kilpatrick, who was leading the advanced Calvary unit, had a habit of wandering off and getting into trouble. He had, too often, caused unseemly news reports to appear in the Northern press. Having been victimized by the press himself, Sherman usually gave no credence to the occasional report of malfeasance among his generals. General Kilpatrick, however, his pint-sized cavalry leader, had to be reined tightly in order for his skills to be used effectively. Northern and Southern newspapers had printed accounts of Kilpatrick's reckless disregard for the lives of his men and the innocent civilians in his path. The little General's most blatant disregard for his men was the well published account known as the Dahlgren Affair. During this ill-conceived raid on the capital of the Confederacy, 324 of his own cavalrymen were killed or wounded and 1,000 or more among his ranks were taken prisoner. Immediately after the Dahlgren Debacle, while the remaining members of his cavalry were recuperating in Alexandria, Virginia, there arose another scandal among the men in his charge. The undisciplined conduct that Kilpatrick allowed among his officers was brought front and center once again.

"The city was garrisoned with Black troops and one of Kilpatrick's cavalrymen was stopped by a Negro soldier who informed him that only persons on active duty were allowed to ride horses through the streets. The white cavalryman found it insulting for a Black man to order him from the street and promptly struck him down with his sword. This disobedient and fiendish behavior was a direct reflection of the red whiskered reprobate's attitude that had spread among the men who served under him. After all of his antics were made public, he was considered a rogue among officers and generals in the eastern theatre of the war. Kilpatrick was soon banished to the western theatre of the war. Like most of the Union's misfit officers, he was promptly dumped into General W.T. Sherman's eclectic assortment of military leaders with questionable baggage.

"Called a 'flamboyant fool' by one newspaper, Kilpatrick too often put the soldiers under his command in avoidable jeopardy. He displayed a flagrant lack of concern for the lives of any human around him and he was very unpopular with most of the troops. Believing strongly in Sherman's, 'trail of destruction' war stratagem, the diminutive Kilpatrick immensely enjoyed the burning and looting of Southern property. General Sherman called him 'a damn fool' but he was just what Sherman wanted for this march.

"Entering South Carolina, it was said Kilpatrick spent an exorbitant amount of money on matches and issued a large ration to every soldier under his command. With a reputation for involvement with multiple prostitutes, his licentious tendencies nearly cost him his life on several occasions. The description offered by his officers and often repeated by his fellow Generals was that of a 'frothy braggart without brains'. His troops had narrowly avoided disaster the day previous during a skirmish in Aiken. Confederate troops led by Major General Joseph Wheeler set a trap and tolled the aggressive little General into a 'V' shaped ambush. The ensnarement nearly proved fatal for the cavalry leader and forced him to beat a hasty retreat, during which he lost his hat. Kilpatrick served under General Henry Warner Slocum, the Commanding General of the Army of Tennessee and he, too, knew to keep a tight rein on the rogue cavalry leader.

"The Commanding General of the entire western army, General William Tecumseh Sherman, had ordered the meeting to ensure the feisty and foolish cavalry leader followed his plan. He did not want the damn fool to get entangled in a skirmish from which he would have to be saved. Augusta, Georgia was just across the Savannah River from Aiken, well within Kilpatrick's sights and the commanding Generals feared Kilpatrick would try to attack the well defended munitions factory there. Kilpatrick's cavalry unit did not have the troop strength to wage a successful battle on such a large enemy concentration. Most of the other commanders feared having to pull troops away from the main force to rescue the little General from another one of his follies. The commanding Generals agreed the possibility of such brash actions were highly probable, given Kilpatrick's history. They did not want to jeopardize the maneuvers of the other armies already in progress.

"The meeting had been arranged to ensure General Sherman's orders were followed and his plans were executed. The Major chose the Sullivan mansion for convening the war council, hoping it would be a comfortable meeting place for such a significant encounter.

"Reaching the house, he stopped his horse at the front cobblestone walkway and tied it to the fancy hitching post. Met by a Lieutenant who snapped to attention and saluted, he banally replied, 'At ease son, have you been in the house?'

"'Yes, sir. We conducted the walk-through and visual search, following your orders not to disturb anything unless necessary, sir.'

"'Good. Is there anything I should know?'

"'Sir, the lady of the house is very formal and feisty. She has a daughter and a maid with her, sir.'

"'Thank you, son. I'll try to be careful. You may be dismissed.'

"Before he walked up the steps onto the painted porch, he knocked his boots against the post and cleaned them on the boot blade. Talking to himself as he climbed up to the doorway of the house, he mumbled, 'Women are women wherever you go.' Brushing his dusty uniform coat and pants, he slapped the knocker two or three times, with no results. Then, again, he slapped the door knocker, this time a little harder, and listened for movement in the house. He tried to turn the knob but found it locked, so his third knock was with his knuckles on the beautiful door. Displaying a carved sunrise (or sunset as the case may be) across the entire top, the engraved scene produced an impressive entrance. This time he yelled, 'Please open this pretty door so I won't have to kick it open!' After no answer again, he took his boot and kicked the door until it flew open.

"Pulling his service revolver from its holster, he entered the foyer and looked around. On his right was an ornately decorated meeting room with long purple drapes, a fireplace and two long sideboards. Turning to his left, he saw the three women together at the far end of a long dining table. Behind them was another fireplace above which hung a portrait of an older gentleman.

"As he put away his pistol and entered the grand dining room, he abruptly halted upon hearing the maid unleash a bevy of insults aimed at him. 'Yous Yankee scum, dat's what yous is, jus Yankee scum. Ain't got no mo sin' dan to kick de doe op'um. Can't yous tell yous haint wanted heah? Likes a animul wid no raisin. If'n you can't dos no bet'er en dat, yous jus need to git on out froms heah!'

"The Major put his hand to his hat and ducked his head a little, 'Ma'am.'

"The house maid began unleashing another barrage when the lady of the house spoke and put her hand on the house slave's arm. 'Now LuDell, not all men have been raised appropriately and they lack the chivalry and graciousness of Southern gentleman. Northern men are ignorant of proper civility and they do not know to extend the social graces of a gentleman when in the presence of ladies to which they have never been formally introduced. We cannot expect these barbaric people to offer the courtesy that is normal from Southern officers and gentlemen.'

"Unperturbed, the Major offered, 'Afternoon, ma'am, Major George Ward Nichols, United States Army. I'm here to commandeer your house for use by the Union Army. I don't suppose you're a Union Sympathizer?'

"'Sir! You disrespect me with those vulgar words and I consider the question an insult hurled upon me and my house. I am a Confederate down to my bones and though not serving in the army, I am a warrior for of the Confederate States of America. You play the fool if you think my civility is offered as assistance to you. Given the chance, I would put a bullet through your Yankee heart without a moment's hesitation and send your soul to hell for eternal damnation!'

"Again, without acknowledgement of the threat, the Major bade, "Yes, ma'am - if I could just look through your house, I'll try not to mess up or break anything.'

"The dominant matriarch spoke to her servant, 'LuDell, if you would show the ill-mannered officer around, we'll retire upstairs.'

"The Major broke in, 'Oh no, ma'am. You have way too much civility to be allowed free roam upstairs.' As he backed into the foyer, he called out through the open door, 'Sergeant! Place an armed guard with these women with orders to shoot to kill if they try anything.' With that the Major moved from the foyer to the meeting room.

"In the meeting room, he slid all of the furnishings against the walls and pulled the dark drapes over the two front windows. He rolled up the rug and placed it on the furniture out of the way of dirty boots. The shiny heart pine floor was reflecting the afternoon sun through the window as he remembered the sideboards and why they caught his eye. Pulling them away from the wall, he pushed them back to back in the middle of the room and gouged a groove across the stunning floor in doing so. He thought to himself, *So much for not messing anything up.* Thinking he'd better check for himself, he opened the doors of the two elbow high cabinets. There waiting in several crystal decanters beside cut crystal highball glasses, was a mix of dark, aged brandies. He smiled and thought, *I might get a promotion for this setup.*

"Clara Ruth Sullivan sat at the far end of the dining room on a floral fainting couch near one of the floor to ceiling windows across the front of the house. Her daughter, Ruth, stood looking out the window. A soft southern breeze made the long sheer curtains dance as it blew through the open window.

The early spring breeze also brought the agonizing cries from the boy next door to the ears of Ruth Sullivan. Tormented with pain, the neighbor boy lay writhing in the ditch at the end of the long, sandy driveway. At first, his cry was for water, then as dusk neared, he cried out for his mother and told her he was hurting real bad. LuDell walked up and down in front of the window and fumed. All the while, she was asking the Lord God Almighty to rain down his wrath on the blue-bellied animals all about the farm. They were stealing, pillaging and wantonly taking whatever they desired. Hollering for help, the boy next door's agonizing cries were clear as a bell. The women would sob and hold a lace handkerchief to their faces each time his screams reached the mansion. They prayed aloud, 'God of love, God of mercy, bring comfort to the boy next door and take him quickly to Your side.' But to no avail, the boy's piercing yells continued into the late afternoon.

"As the last of the setting sun could be seen over the horizon, a lone horseman made his way down the main road from the west.

"Through the dusk light, the first obvious feature of the man on horseback was the huge, gold plume dancing above a new, black felt cavalry hat, tilted at a rakish angle. The sentries knew this could only be the bantam-sized peacock, General Judson Kilpatrick, or as many of his soldiers referred to him - General Kill Cavalry.

"Reaching the stately tree covered lane, the flamboyant General heard the boy next door cry out, 'Mama it hurts so bad! Mama!' He glanced in the direction of the sound, but never broke the stride of his high stepping horse as he hurried up the sandy lane. Upon reaching the residence, he ignored the soldiers waiting to take his horse. Dramatically, he stepped down from the frisky steed and promptly dropped the reins. Before the spirited horse could be gathered, it bolted and ran into the pecan orchard. Kilpatrick ignored the incident and obliviously climbed the steps to the porch. Just inside the open door, the waiting Major took the General's hat and gloves and motioned him into the room with the brandies. Never one to drink alcohol, Kilpatrick poured a cup of the coffee the Major had ordered prepared and sipped it slowly.

"From the east, came a party of three riders. They approached the sandy lane at a gallop with the last of the sun's rays in their eyes. Behind the lead group followed three other horsemen who lacked ornate gold trim on their blue uniforms. The lower rank of those following was obvious, as they lacked the gilded trim of high rank. When in view of the posted guards, the lead group was recognized as Major General Henry W. Slocum, Commander of the Army of Tennessee and two generals under his command, Major General Jefferson Columbus Davis, Commander of 14th Corps and General Alpheus Starkey Williams, Commander of the 20th Army Corps. They slowed their mounts to a walk and prepared to turn into the sandy driveway.

"In the lead, General Slocum was first to hear the youth's cries for help and he pulled his horse to an abrupt halt. From the height of his horse he could plainly see the figure of a disemboweled kid lying prostrate in the ditch. It was evident he was in great pain for he had wallowed frantically and tumbled off the bank into the gully. Reining his horse in beside the commanding general, General Davis asked his aide to check and see what was wrong with the boy in the ditch. As the aide rolled him over, it was quickly apparent his wounds were extensive. The aide moved the boy's torn and bloody shirt from his wound. Wincing in dismay, he saw much of the boy's side was missing. Shaking his head negatively at the group of Generals and officers, he tacitly relayed the fact that the boy was nearing death and could not be helped. General Slocum said, 'If not for fear of The Almighty, we should put him out of his misery.' The aide climbed back on his horse and the group proceeded to the now amber lighted house.

"The Generals gave their horses over to the soldiers waiting, pulled off their gloves and hats and climbed the steps to the entrance of the house. Promptly they heard the loud, obnoxious voice of the dramatic little General Kilpatrick, welcoming them as if to his own home. All six of the recent arrivals entered the ornate meeting room from the foyer and helped themselves to the fine brandy.

"The matriarch of the home continued to project her regal air as she perched on the edge of the couch and watched the familiar road leading up to their home. Ruth, usually outspoken and forceful, was uncharacteristically quiet and distant. Just as the light was disappearing, she watched as three soldiers galloped in from the east with rifles at the ready. They deployed on each side of the well-used lane and across the main road near the rock culvert where the boy next door lay. The mortally wounded kid was delirious with fever and thought the sentry was his brother. 'Aaron, are you home? I did what you asked and stayed with Mama. Aaron! Aaron!' The mounted military man heard the boy's cry, but stared straight forward and sat on his horse at attention. The newly arrived sentry had the butt of his rifle on his leg and the barrel pointed to the sky. His index finger nervously tapped the trigger guard.

"The next traveler was alone and, likewise, came from the east. Puffing on a cigar, the latest to arrive cantered into view soon after the three sentries had arrived. He appeared disheveled and untidy. His hair was covered with a hat pulled down tight, but red strands of hair stuck out all around his head. The sleeves of his uniform coat seemed a bit too long and his shirt appeared to be buttoned up wrong. The occasional glow of the cigar bounced up and down with the gait of the steed he rode as the 'Big Guy' himself turned into the entrance way. Just as he passed the intersection, he heard the screams of a child in agony and he pulled his horse to a stop. Turning and looking in the direction of the sound, he yelled to the further soldier, asking, 'What was that?'

"The statue-like guard replied, 'Sir, it's a Rebel. It's a kid who's all shot up, sir.' The commanding General sat puffing his cigar as he looked at the boy next door. After a few seconds, he clucked to his horse and continued on to the meeting.

"Bringing his horse to a stop, the red-headed General patted him on the shoulder as he stepped off and handed the reins to the men waiting. Moving at a hurried pace, he climbed the steps. The door was standing open pending his arrival and the other Generals and aides were standing at attention, saluting the last and highest ranking General to enter the house. Giving his gloves and hat to the Major, he said, 'Who the hell is the kid at the end of the lane?'

"As the Major was about to relay the full story to his superior officer, the lady of the house interrupted. She had observed his arrival and knew exactly who had entered her house. Having moved from her place on the small fainting couch, she now stood in the archway between the mammoth dining room and the foyer. Standing composed and erect, she projected her voice across the foyer of her house toward the two Union officers and undauntedly addressed the highest-ranking Union officer in the Southern Theatre. 'Sir, I do not grovel nor ask anything for myself from such an abominable foe, but I implore you to have the human decency and intestinal fortitude to either put the boy out of his misery or fetch him to us so we may comfort him is his last hours.'

"The Major, with a perturbed look on his face, turned to the General and finally answered his question, 'Sir, he is the kid who killed ten of the advanced Ohio squad, put shrapnel in about 6 others and blinded the Master Chief. He held up the movement for more than an hour, by himself.'

"'My God! How old is he?'

"'I don't know, sir, but he is certainly young to have done that much damage.'

"The leading lady interjected again, 'He is 14 years old, and God rest his soul, will never see his 15th year.'

"The unkempt General looked to the distraught woman and asked, 'Is he your kin?'

"The staunch woman answered, 'He is not, but a boy next door, a brave and honorable soldier for his cause.'

"The General turned to the Major and asked, 'Have you had the women under guard all afternoon?'

"The major answered, 'Yes, sir.'

"Puffing on his cigar, Sherman appeared aggravated and barked out his orders. 'Send some men to get the boy! Bring him here so they can tend to him and for God's sake, let the women be excused!' With that, he tossed the smoking stump of his cigar out the open door and stomped into the meeting room.

"The Major ordered two men to retrieve the agonizing and delirious adolescent with a wheeled litter. Blood stained with much battle experience, the litter was pulled by two men of the same Ohio regiment on which the boy had rained terror. Griping and grumbling on the way to the fancy stone culvert, the soldiers pulling the litter wondered aloud, 'Why would 'The Red' want to help that lunatic Rebel filth? Our buddies are having shrapnel painfully picked from their faces and other areas of their bodies at this very moment! Why should that vermin who tried to kill them not suffer the cruelest of deaths?'

"At the main road they roughly swung the boy's limp body onto the cart and bounced him back to the fine country home. One soldier grabbed his legs and the other grabbed his arms. They roughly carried the boy up the steps into the house.

"LuDell had removed the empty candle holders and doilies from the massive dining table, leaving only the tablecloth and an oil-less hurricane lamp. The only light being emitted was from a small piece of a candle jammed where a wick once burned.

"As the boy next door was brought in, his body began to shake with convulsions and he was mumbling out of his mind. Swinging him on to the table, the Union boys took no pains and the lady of the house rushed to the injured boy's side. Using her dress to hold his entrails from falling further out of his body, Clara Ruth Sullivan's face was distraught.

"Ruth, the firebrand abolitionist daughter, was obviously experiencing a soul-changing upheaval in her innermost self. The cries of the boy next door echoed in her head as life slowly drained from his shattered body. She became repulsed at the sight of the blood and gore and started to cry and gag as she ran to the other side of the large room. From a drawer in one of the built in china cabinets, LuDell grabbed more pieces of candles and lowered the beautiful crystal chandelier. She filled the sparkling holders with short remnants of candles and lit them from the burning piece of candle in her hand. She then raised the crystal chandelier above the injured boy and the room became filled with refracted light.

"Replacing the one candle in the lamp, she scuttled out of the dining room and hurried by the Major who was standing in the foyer. She burst into the meeting room where several of the men were holding cut crystal highball glasses with brandy. Grabbing one of the brandy decanters, she started back to the dining room as she berated the generals over her shoulder, 'If air one dem good glasses hits broke, yous all gwine ansir toda big man hisself!' As she scurried out of the room, the Major came to the door and apologized to the Generals for the disturbance.

"The Generals smiled and brushed it off, but General Williams cautioned, 'Well gentlemen, I guess we'd better drink carefully'. They all roared with laughter.

"The boy next door looked very small as he lay on the large table. Covered in his own blood and dirt from the ditch, the boy begged for water. Clara Ruth Sullivan held a china cup of water to his mouth. The boy tried to gulp the water, but most did not make it down his throat. She handed the cup to LuDell and turned to a different cabinet drawer, grabbing a handful of folded linen napkins. As Clara Ruth turned back to the table, her handmaid saw the expensive cloths in her hand and instinctively said, 'Ma'am, yos good naptins?'

"The tears showed under the lady's eyes as she turned to the Negro help and scolded, 'My God, LuDell, he's dying, can't you see?' Sobbing softly for a few seconds, the mistress of the house regained her composure and said, 'LuDell, help me roll him over a bit so we can put this cloth under his side.' With the linen napkins under him, Clara Ruth liberally doused one of the napkins with brandy from the decanter. Carefully, she began cleaning his wounds as LuDell wiped his face with a cool wet cloth.

"As he lay on the fancy dining table, the boy next door passed from consciousness to delirium, speaking of things that flew through his mind. The blanket over his feet reminded him of his mother tucking him in each night as a boy and kissing him. Recalling his recent years, he remembered telling his mother he didn't need her to tuck him in anymore. In her loving way, she came to his room each night, anyway, and kissed him.

"She always told him, 'Something wonderful will happen in the morning.'

"Each night he would reply, 'I know, I'll see you cooking my breakfast.' He would always smile and blow her a kiss.

"The water they poured in the dying boy's mouth choked him and made him think of learning to swim in the millpond. His brothers had thrown him from the raceway. They laughed and told everyone he drank half the pond before he figured out how to swim. He smiled and called his brother's name - 'Aaron, Aaron.'

"After some time, the boy who so wanted to fight in the war realized he was watching the happenings in the room from above his body. The many glass prisms from the chandelier reflected a colorful and infinite array of light around the top of the room. As his spirit floated among the beautiful colors, the multicolored rays were passing through his image.

"Ruth was crying and cowering alone. He recognized her from their earlier encounter and went to her side. Wanting to comfort her, he said, 'Please don't cry. I'm okay and I'll come over and rake up the magnolia leaves for your mom real soon.' She didn't seem to hear or notice him, but she dried her eyes and smiled as she remembered climbing the tree just after the boy next door had raked all the leaves up. Mischievously, she shook more leaves onto the clean grass he had just raked. The neighbor boy didn't get mad at her, but smiled and raked the new leaves she had added. Afterwards, her mother sent her out with a Confederate dollar and she offered it to him before he left. Accepting the money, he started to walk away and for some reason, she hit him in the stomach and ran to the porch. Once on the porch, she turned and smiled and he smiled, too, gasping for air.

Chapter 10

"As the injured boy struggled to breathe air into his lungs, he saw Ruth Sullivan's face and the memory of her hitting him in the stomach flashed through his brain. But this time, the pain he felt was unbearable and he cried out for his brother again, but knew he wasn't there. Aaron was killed at Chickamauga, near Chattanooga, and he remembered his mother sliding her finger down the alphabetical Death List posted on the store wall. When she saw Aaron's name, she fell to the floor and he knew then, he would never be allowed to go and fight, like his three older brothers. He begged, but his mother told him no, three sons and a husband were already too much to give to the useless war that had nothing to do with her family or their way of life. His family had never had the money to own slaves and of that his father oft said, 'Why do I need slaves? I have three boys!' It never seemed funny to him and now they were all dead, so others could get rich with their slaves. But it was the Southern way of life that was in peril and that nationalistic fervor swept over the land and demanded his loyalty.

"Floating just above his body, the boy next door could see the Generals in the huge meeting room across the way and their faces were now the faces of the men he killed near the main road. Their screams echoed in his mind; their blood ran down his face. Their eyes stared at him with wide surprise after he shot them and they continued to stare at him as they fell to the ground, dead. Looking down, he saw the hole in his side, but when he moved his hand to touch it, there was no feeling. Looking back at the Generals, their faces became the faces of his brothers and he cried, 'I'm sorry! I didn't know! I'm sorry! I didn't know!'

"As the mantle clock ticked past three AM, the boy's spirit found complete release. His soul was no longer part of his bloody, mangled body. Hovering above the room, the boy next door understood he had shed his earthly body, never to need it again. The excruciating pain he had experienced was no longer a memory and Mrs. Clara Ruth's anguish puzzled him as he viewed the setting from his new prospective.

"Clara Ruth Sullivan recognized the last bodily reflex -

the grip of death. It signaled the boy next door's spirit was leaving his body. She pried his hand open to free hers. Away from his grip, but not from his presence, she pulled a white tablecloth from a nearby cabinet and placed it over his body. The boy next door's ingrained hatred, his sorrow and his grief, instilled by the realities of war, were now passed away. No longer did he despise the Northern troops, no longer did he detest the Yankee politicians who ruined his way of life and no longer did he feel contempt for the people who killed his brothers. In spirit, all his human frailties ceased to exist, but he remained in the room, unable to rise above or fall below.

"Resolute, Clara Ruth left the body of the boy next door and moved to Ruth who seemed so overwhelmed by the horrible scene that had unfolded before her young eyes. Clara Ruth's mothering instincts filled the divide that had long kept the pair apart. She moved to her only daughter and she tried to offer her comfort. But Ruth was no longer shedding any tears and the anguish she had experienced was no more. Ruth was smiling as she took her mother's hand. A divine awareness had engulfed her and she felt the voice of God speak to her. In an effervescent glow of blessedness, she softly spoke to her mother. 'Don't worry, Mother, we'll be okay. We'll never be the same again and that is God's choice. We should be strong and take comfort in the fact that God ordained this war, for he seeks change in His people. We must recognize His will and seek to follow the path He would have us travel. He requires us to repent of our sins and follow a new path that offers equality to all human beings. It was He who made all human beings in His image and we must be thankful for His grace. He gave us a choice and allowed us freedom. Though we chose the wrong path of war, He now wants us to come home to Him. His infinite love offers us an opportunity for redemption and forgiveness. He is showing us His way and once again offers us freedom through love and equally, as is His wish for all of his people.'

"Ruth had been rehabilitated and renewed as she felt the spirit of the boy next door pass from life to death. She felt God allowed her to experience his release from pain, his escape from suffering and the elimination of all of his human weakness that only God can grant. Ruth had experienced the presence of God and the experience left her with an urgent sense of purpose.

"Ruth, however, did not know of the brutal and inhuman fight she would face in the future. Naïvely, she looked forward to providing righteousness and equality for all people. While her intentions and heart were pure, she was ignorant of the horrendous fight she faced in her struggle to help the newly freed Negro. She had no inkling a century of heartache and misery would pass before black people would begin to experience equality in the American melting pot. Ruth was also unaware, that as a woman, she would have to fight for decades for full rights as a United States citizen. She had no suspicion that after her long struggle, she would have only one opportunity in her life to exercise her constitutional right to vote. Unknowing, she could not have comprehended the extent of hatred and bigotry she and her descendants would face. She could never have fathomed the horrors the fight would heap upon the Sullivan family and the Black people of the South for nearly a century. For if she had known of the utter vileness and atrocities the future offered, she would have prayed as Jesus had, for God to let this cup pass. But thankfully, her God did not allow her to see or understand the path ahead and she marched forward into battle, redeemed and filled with God's strength in her soul.

"In stark contrast, her mother bristled and gritted her teeth as she offered a small sample of the wickedness the future offered, 'With every drop of blood in my body, I hate the very air those Northern heathens breathe. They are butchers, murderers and Satan's henchmen and if I could, I would burn my beautiful home to ashes if it would send them back to Hell's Gates. Those Yankees and the black animals who caused this abomination to be heaped upon us should suffer horror upon horror until their kind is wiped from the face of the earth!'

"The daughter spoke as the spirit of the boy next door moved away from her. 'Mother, we will make it through this, I know we will and Trip will come home, I know he will and we'll forget all of this happened and live on this farm in peace with God.' The older adolescent was bolstered by her newfound spiritual vigor and she prophesied a new way of life with a comforting and optimistic strength.

"Still infuriated, Clara Ruth spat out her words as if they burned her tongue. 'This tyranny has been heaped upon us by the Northern hordes of infidels. You must see this and never forget it!' A chilling force passed through Clara Ruth's body as anger and hatred took command of her being. It filled her with a dark wrath that controlled her every thought and action.

"But Ruth was filled with confidence and courage as she experienced the warmth of righteousness from a Holy Spirit that enveloped her soul. She felt renewed and bolstered for the first time in quite a while. As Ruth reached for her mother's hand, sparks zapped her and she recoiled in shock.

"'Mother, God demands we have forgiveness in our hearts and offer peace to all.'

Clara Ruth filled the room with righteous indignation. "There will be no peace until the atrocities forced upon the South are vindicated and the Northern evil is driven from our land. I swear upon my soul, I will die trying to make that happen, so help me God!' Clara Ruth Sullivan did not understand that it was not God controlling her at present.

"The spirit of the boy next door became part of the room. His soul was trapped between Ruth's goodness urging his spirit to rise and seek peace and the wickedness that possessed Clara Ruth's heart and forced her down to a dark, evil hell. The epic struggle that began that night in the dining room of the Sullivan mansion has remained though the centuries. The essence of the boy next door would remain among the dancing lights of the crystal chandelier, seldom seen, but often felt, as the generations passed. As he wanders, even now, in the ornate dining room, he searches for a clear pathway to his judgment, whether that be in heaven or hell.

"Going forward, some few people visiting the dining room of the Sullivan mansion would tell of experiencing a wave of hot and cold air passing over their bodies. Sully told a story of his grandmother Lou cleaning and polishing the elaborate candelabra and filling it with new candles during the time she and her husband, Trip, lived in the mansion. Lowering the large mass of candles, Trip and Lou lit every wick, then they pulled the antique light up above the massive dining table. As they stood admiring the multitude of dancing flames, a boy's face, that seemed to be laughing and crying, appeared in the smoke rising from the candles. Trip asked Lou if she saw anything on the ceiling. She wouldn't say anything, just nodded her head, yes. Later, Lou asked Trip if the face he saw was laughing or crying.

"Trip said, 'I didn't tell you I saw a face.'

"So, she asked, 'Then what did you see?'

"He answered, 'A boy's face, laughing and crying.' They decided not to tell anyone of their experience and keep their encounter with the boy next door a secret. My Grandpa Trip took it to his grave, but a few weeks before my Grandma Lou died, she recounted the incident to me. Telling me of other encounters with the spirit in the mansion, she could not explain them and her stories have vexed me until this very day. She asked me not to repeat what she had told me while she was alive, because everyone would think she was a crazy old woman.

"Early in the morning hours, as the boy next door lingered between heaven and earth, the doors of the meeting room opened and the red-headed leader of the Generals entered the foyer. The Major jumped to his feet and saluted him. Grabbing the General's hat and gloves, he offered them to General Sherman as he was preparing to exit. Looking into the dimly lit dining room, the commanding General was taken by the sight of the white tablecloth over the body of the gallant youth. Slowly, he walked toward the corpse, leaving the Major behind and entering the presence of the dead, alone. With reverence, he placed his hand on the now rigid remains and stared straight ahead, looking into the darkness of the window. His face portrayed the story of a seemingly unending scene of battlefields with thousands of young men wounded and dying, crying out for help. As his thoughts returned to the boy who would enter his tortured dreams on this night, he reached into the pocket of his blue Union uniform and pulled out one of the stars missing from his shoulders. Carefully, he pinned it to the tablecloth on top of the boy's chest. Turning to no one, but as if leaving, he said, 'May God grant peace to a great warrior who distinguished himself with honor, giving the ultimate sacrifice for the cause in which he believed.'

"As he reached to the Major for his hat and gloves, he heard the woman of the house yell as she stood like a statue beside the deceased. 'Don't you dare disgrace the body of this Confederate Soldier, a true hero of the South, with that filthy piece of Union trash!' She yanked the star from the tablecloth and flung it with great vigor. It hit the shiny pine floor and skidded across the room, disappearing somewhere in the shadows. General Sherman put on his hat and gloves, tipped his hat and left the foyer for his waiting horse. As Clara Ruth Sullivan stood crying with rage, her daughter embraced her. Ruth was determined to follow her heart and do what was right.

"The other Generals exited the mansion soon after their leader. Slowly, the sound of their horses galloping away faded to silence. By noon, the soldiers around the house had packed up and marched down the sandy lane, leaving their wreckage and refuse scattered about the grounds of the mansion.

"The magnificent house would stand unharmed while many of the remaining houses in Salleys Kitchen were plundered and burned. To those in 'The Kitchen', the Sullivan mansion became an undeniable reminder of the peace and prosperity that was arrogantly tossed away at the behest of those with wealth and power. Most people of Salleys Kitchen had watched as their houses were plundered and burned. They lost everything and were left destitute. To the homeless and starving people of the community, the sight of the mansion, standing unharmed, was infuriating. The very people who whipped everyone into a frenzy for war had escaped the atrocities and they continued to occupy their fine home. In a disfigured landscape of burned homes and desolate fields, the mansion stood like a beacon, permanently reminding the community of everything they had lost.

"In later years, as the South faced the perils of Reconstruction, an unspoken question would be asked repeatedly: *Why had that mansion been spared, while so many other homes were ransacked and burned?* Resentment would grow through the years as the house was scorned and tales of Union sympathy were heaped upon the backs of the Sullivan family. Gossip would be disseminated throughout the community, accusing the Sullivan family of aiding and abetting the Yankees. There were even whispers of an orgy involving Union Generals and this, too, brought more ridicule to those living in the Sullivan mansion. Disparaged and ostracized, the family would continue to live in the great white house while others struggled to survive."

***

Salley did not need Dr. Baughman to tell her the results of the test. She had known for a couple of months that she was pregnant and had tried to put off thinking about it for as long as possible. That was no longer an option and after her visit with the doctor, she would now have to face the horrible music. Deciding she would not bring another child into the world without a father in its life, she faced the reality of having to marry Jon Chesterfield, Jr. She had been unable to find out if Jon had been lying to her when he told her James had been killed. Each time she asked him about what he had told her, he always just smiled and walked away. Certainly, this was not the way she had envisioned her marriage.

In Salley's mind, she had already brought one illegitimate child into the world and she was not about to do that to this precious child. Many tears had been shed while a man she didn't love used her for sex and now he had inflicted the ultimate disgrace upon her. As she drove his little red sports car back to the guest house after her doctor's appointment, she wondered how she could have gone from the bliss of loving James Williams to the horror of having to marry Jon Chesterfield, Jr. and have his baby. With the wind blowing through her hair, she recalled something James had told her. It was something that Wes had told James about bad things happening to good people. Wes told James, 'Life hain't by no waz fair - yooz ust hadda makes hov hit whats yooz can!' Salley's life was in tatters, but she was determined to make something good come of her tragedy. She decided at that moment to make the best of what she was offered.

As she turned into the driveway of the Chesterfield estate, her mind was not occupied with driving. James had often reminded her she was not the best driver to come from Salleys Kitchen. Thinking of other things, she plowed the shiny little German car into the huge brick column from which the large black gates swung. The new-fangled seatbelt she had put on kept her from any injury. Relieved she had not hurt herself or the baby, she put the car in reverse and backed up before getting out to see the damage she had caused. A smashed head light and some bumper damage didn't seem that bad, so she got back in to continue to the guest house. As she sat in the plush little car, she lingered at the crash site for a bit. Thinking for a minute, she clicked the seat belt back on and for reasons known only to her, she pulled the car into drive and floored the accelerator. For a second time, she plowed into the brick column and laughed out loud. With a smile on her face and steam spewing from the front of the car, she backed up, turned the car around and positioned the car so the rear was facing the banged-up brick column. Again, flooring the accelerator, she rammed the rear of the little car into the brick gate post and when she pulled away, she decided that for good measure, she would do it again. The final accidental collision made the column of bricks tilt to a 45° angle and Salley drove the sputtering, knocking and rubbing Mercedes to the guest house where it gave up its last gasp as she stopped just in front. Without a care, she walked inside and gave Ruth a big hug. She felt better than she had in long while.

***

"While the residents of Salleys Kitchen were dealing with the aftermath of General William T. Sherman's march through South Carolina, one of its most prominent citizens was dealing with a different life-threatening situation.

"Trip Sullivan was part of the six companies of soldiers in General Alfred H. Sully's First Northwestern Expedition of 1864. They were to be the Volunteer Infantry who marched into Fort Rice and replaced the Wisconsin infantry who had begun building the garrison. Arriving as fall began, they had orders to complete the fort and organize its defense. The Union Volunteers began their assignment looking over their shoulders. Winter was approaching and they were deep in Indian Territory.

"The temperature was soon well below freezing and the weather was bearing down on the mostly Southern regiment as they struggled to complete the structures and keep an eye out for marauding Indians. As the Dakota winter opened full bore, the soldiers had to suspend work on the garrison because temperatures often hovered around -20° to -30°. This also limited guard duty to 15 minutes per soldier. Most of the recruits had their faces and feet to freeze solid and some died in their sleep of hypothermia. Long before spring arrived, most of the garrison was malnourished and suffering from scurvy and other diseases caused by a lack of essential vitamins. The colonel provided vegetables for the men, but they were frozen and often not eaten.

"As a boy among the books in his mother's library, Trip had read of men aboard ships agonizing with scurvy resulting from a lack of vitamins and minerals in their diet. He ate the frozen vegetables as often as they were offered and was determined to survive, but sadly, he realized many of the soldiers would not make it through the winter. During his year and ten months at Fort Rice, Trip saw eighty-one men die. But as severe as the conditions were, the cold was not the big killer. Of his fellow soldiers, 37 died from scurvy; 24 succumbed to chronic diarrhea, 3 died from typhoid fever, while other diseases caused 10 more to give up the ghost. Surprisingly, only 7 members of his regiment were killed in combat with the local Indians.

"After the first brutal winter of '64/'65, spring's arrival brought with it a renewed effort to complete the fort. Repeated attacks, however, by the deadly Indian war parties plagued the Galvanize Yankees. The warring Indians often simultaneously swooped down on the post livestock while also attacking the loggers working in the woods. Coordinating their attacks, the Indians would suddenly begin firing on the sentries posted around the hoof stock and at the same time, they would attack the wood cutting details working out away from the fort.

"In April, news of Lee's surrender reached the fort and most of the Southerners who turned to the Union side were truly despondent. Not only had they lost face by changing allegiance, they were now stuck in the middle of nowhere, being attacked by savage Indians who wanted to torture them to death. Many thought of desertion and some disappeared in the night, never to be heard from again.

"By May, the garrison's soldiers had fought off a dozen or more attacks and were always at the ready for an assault. Once, while on a logging detail, a group of warriors rushed through the woods with tomahawks and lances as Trip and his fellow Southerners chopped firewood. With his gun in the wagon, Trip could only hide behind a tree as a young warrior galloped toward him, swinging his war axe. Trip dodged the deadly strike and in a flash reflex, grabbed the wrist of his attacker and pulled him from his horse. Both combatants were surprised at what had happened and Trip ended up standing over the young Indian warrior. There was a moment of indecision for both, as the two regained their senses. Evidently, the Indian war party thought the young brave, covered in war paint, was about to die, for they gathered his horse and uncharacteristically stopped at the edge of the wooded area to watch and attest to their downed comrade's honorable death. As Trip and the Indian brave stared at each other, Trip reached down and offered his hand to the young fighter. Frozen for an instant, the Indian relented and took Trip's hand. Still trying to best his foe, the young warrior suddenly tried to yank the soldier to the ground. Aware he might try to take him down, the strong and muscled army recruit held him at bay and smiled as he reached his feet. Looking momentarily at Trip's face, he turned and quickly began running toward the war party. As he reached nearly 20 paces away, Trip yelled loudly and forced the fleeing Indian to momentarily stop and glance over his shoulder. To his surprise, the soldier tossed the war axe back to its owner. Stunned again, the Indian brave quickly stooped to grasp it and for a split second considered attacking the soldier again. Instead, he continued to his awaiting party and jumped on his horse. With a final glance toward Trip, he galloped away, yelling and screaming his war call.

"In the summer of '65, an attempt to negotiate peace with the warring tribes was ordered by commanding General Sully. Some of the army representatives began meeting with their Indian counterparts in the Lakotas and the Upper Yanktonai tribes. A chief named Two Bears seemed to be the only leader wise enough to recognize the futility of a continuing war. The chief was a short, stocky leader with piercing eyes. Very influential and very brave, he sought a peaceful relationship with the strange, white aliens who were invading his homeland.

"During peace pow-wows at the fort, Two Bears was flanked by his two sons as he moved about. Trip had seen the Chief and his sons several times at the fort and shockingly recognized one of his sons as the warrior who attacked him in the woods. The Indian Chief and his sons made Trip think of his father's futile attempts to prove his honor in the war. With the wise chief's influence, the offer of peace interested most of the leaders of plains tribes. Cautiously, all of the tribes began gathering near the vicinity of the fort and preparing to stay for a while. As the women of the tribes set up their camps near the army garrison, the tribal leaders talked among themselves and prepared for the peace pow-wow.

"General Sully was the commanding general of the District of Iowa and as his detail approached the compound to attend the peace conference, a cannon was fired. This was the traditional salute offered at the Mountain Man Rendezvous where the Indian traders of the Rocky Mountain region gathered for an annual multiday drunken retreat. After the huge gun was fired, every Indian camped near the fort fled in panic. There was little trust of white men among the tribes and the sought-after peace treaty was greatly delayed.

"In the fall of '65, the soldiers prepared for another brutal winter, realizing they would again be facing temperatures often well below zero. When the year of 1866 arrived, the Galvanize Yankees were hanging on, trying to make it to spring. Many of the soldiers from the South were near the point of giving up. As March approached, the turned soldiers were bolstered, for they knew the end of their original two-year enlistment period was approaching. A brutal blow was delivered when the commanding officer announced that all original enlistment agreements would be extended indefinitely. A somber mood engulfed the garrison. For the next ten months, through the summer and into fall, most of the duped soldiers performed their duties as whispers of desertion continued and a few more recruits disappeared. As November approached, the unbelievable news of an end to the extended enlistment period was announced. The homesick Southerners were elated and made plans to leave as soon as possible.

"To muster out of the Union Army, Trip had to travel back to Fort Leavenworth, Kansas, before he could begin his journey home. Experience had taught him he should definitely make the trip before the brutal winter weather prevented his travel. He planned to buy passage on a paddlewheel steamer for the trip down the Missouri River, but he had great reservations after hearing and reading about the riverboat steamer *Sultana* explosion. Earlier in the year, the tragedy had killed nearly 2,000 Union POWs heading home, north from New Orleans. Many rumors blamed saboteurs, while others pointed to the overloaded steamer's fractured boiler. No matter, with winter bearing down on the territory, Trip decided the overland trek would take too long and his need to see the sand hills of South Carolina was immense. He felt the use of his limited funds was warranted and he began to make arrangements while his time in a Union uniform was quickly coming to an end.

"Two days before his enlistment time ended, he received his final duty assignment. He was ordered to help guard the last wagon train leaving for Fort Benton in Montana territory before the hard winter gripped the countryside. With a bad luck draw, Trip was given an old army mule to ride and he felt sure the old mule was 'knocking on death's door'. He only hoped the animal would pass to its glory after his return to Fort Rice. As he and the other soldiers bundled up and escorted the line of wagons, they kept a sharp eye out for attackers. Only two miles from Fort Rice, a dreaded site appeared on the horizon - a war party of Indians. The wagon train pilgrims began to panic and Trip had the other soldiers circle the wagons and organize the men in case of attack.

"After getting the wagons in order and making the frightened travelers take cover behind them, Trip, in a very un-military move, rode out to meet the war party. The sand hill planter's son had orders to protect the wagon train and he felt the best way to keep them from harm was to avoid a confrontation if at all possible. Nearly 200 yards from the caravan, Trip stopped his old mule and shivered as he sat in the old army saddle. He didn't bother to pull his carbine from the leather scabbard.

"Seeing him alone, the attackers began their war cries and galloped toward him like a swarm of hornets. Trip gambled that their thunderous display was only an effort to intimidate him. Holding his ground, Trip stayed in the saddle and sat perfectly still, showing no fear outwardly. His heart, however, was pounding out of his chest as the deadly group rode within 20 yards of him and abruptly stopped. With a cloud of dust engulfing everyone, there was a tense moment as the combatants all waited for the dust to clear.

"Trip was trembling, but he didn't know if it was from fear or the cold prairie wind blowing in his face. As the dust was cleared by the whipping wind, the war party appeared clearly in front of the terrified soldier. Covered in war paint, each had a rifle and a tomahawk at their disposal. Every member of the warring band sat on a beautiful spotted horse that had also been painted with war paint. The head of the war party had half of his face painted black with red spots dotting the other side of his face. With a feather dangling from the rear of his long hair, he stared intently at Trip as the sand hill boy continued to shiver.

"The leader of the warriors dismounted and walked over to Trip as he sat his mule. Walking 360° around the decrepit animal, he rubbed his hand across its skin and bones. Turning to his fellow warriors, he said something in his native tongue that made his fellow fighters laugh.

"As Trip remained in the saddle, he looked down at the Indian covered in paint and was shocked to recognize the young warrior. He was Two Bears' son, whom Trip had pulled from his horse in the woods near the fort. Oddly enough, the Indian offered his hand to the soldier. Trip quickly dismounted and smiled while he was gripping the stone-faced warrior's arm.

"Trip's grin quickly disappeared when his adversary suddenly moved toward his mule and unhooked the saddle cinch. The painted warrior pulled the saddle off and removed the bridle from the decrepit old animal's head and then placed the tack on the ground at Trip's feet. Just as quickly, he pulled his carbine from his back and shot the mule between the eyes. It crumpled into a pile of bones and hide in the prairie sand. Then, swinging the rifle over his shoulder, he walked over to the horse he had been riding and led it to Trip. Standing expressionless and mute for a brief moment, the Indian handed Trip the braided reins. Pulling his blanket from the horse, the warrior tossed it over his shoulder and walked back to the group of mounted Indians. In one swift movement, he leaped onto a horse behind another member of the war party. Trip briefly made eye contact with his wordless adversary just before the group galloped off. They vanished - just as they had appeared - in a cloud of dust. The perplexed soldier stood holding the reins of a beautiful Appaloosa stallion, a Yanktonai war pony.

"With the shock of new ownership suddenly thrust upon horse and rider, it took a few minutes for the pair to become acquainted. It was soon apparent that both members of this new team viewed their partnership with a different perspective. Control seemed to be the conflicting issue and it was obvious each would have to compromise for the new relationship to work. Two Bears, as Trip called his new mount, was not going to have a metal bit put in his mouth, but he did - finally - concede to having a saddle strapped to his back. After several 'how-do-you-do' encounters, the stallion sported a knot on his head and Trip had some of the skin scraped off his left arm. As neither wanted to incur further bodily harm, an understanding was reached and horse and rider slowly rode back toward the wagon train.

"Trip's new mount had bright red and black war beads noticeably braided in his mane. With war paint among the spots on the war horse's hindquarters, it was obvious to those who understood the ways of the prairie, the Yanktonai stallion had strong medicine. These symbols would offer Trip a measure of protection, for they signaled the rider was protected by a powerful shaman. Others on the prairie who might want to do the soldier harm would not want to deal with the strong spirits that had been ceremonially given to the horse.

"Nearing the circled wagon train, Trip saw the fearful travelers slowly emerging from the protection of the wagons. They looked at the soldier as if he were a ghost. In a hurry to complete his last assignment, the Son of the South yelled, 'Wagons Hooooo!' The lucky pilgrims obliged him and began regrouping to continue on their journey along the treacherous Oregon Trail.

"Those familiar with Chief Two Bears and the prized war horses of his tribe realized the blue soldier had great medicine. Trip completed his last assignment on the Great Plains and rode back into the garrison on the Appaloosa stallion, to the stares of every soldier in the fort. They knew he was riding an Indian war horse and soon the story of how he acquired such a fine mount infiltrated the entire garrison. This resulted in Trip's being ordered to the Colonel's headquarters. Explaining the events to his commanding officer, Trip was told he was a fool, but since he was mustering out, he would be allowed to keep the horse. Only saluting and saying, 'Yes, sir.' Trip walked away thinking, *It would have been a hell of a fight if he had said I couldn't keep Two Bears!*

"Trip had packed his belongings two days earlier in anticipation of leaving Fort Rice and the Union Army. Having heard the long, low blast of a steam whistle, the homesick Southerner quickly grabbed his pack and led Two Bears to the landing area along the river. The pair now stood watching with great interest as the paddlewheel steamer *Benton II* was guided to the river bank at the closest location to Fort Rice. All riverboats on the Missouri were built for shallow water and had a ramp across their bow that could be dropped to provide easy access to the vessel. As Trip led Two Bears toward the noisy, hissing vessel on a cold day in late November of 1865, his horse was very nervous and vapor shot like smoke from his nostrils.

"Approaching the riverboat, the former war pony was very nervous and skittish. At one point the stallion panicked and almost dragged his new owner into the river.

"After Trip made several attempts to load him, an old deckhand walked over and tied a flour sack around the horse's eyes and walked him to a pen where the horses were held during the voyage down river. Turning to Trip in a subdued manner, he spoke to him as if he knew he was a Galvanize Yankee saying, 'I'z wish dey had cobered my eyes so's I ain't had'a seen som er da thangs I'z is seen.' Smiling, Trip asked him how long he had been working the river and he said, 'I'z ain't neber not been on dey riber. I'z born on dey riber and I'z guess I'z die on dey riber.' Walking away, Trip heard the white-haired man say, 'I'z put yoz saddle in de tac room. Don'ts yous be worri'n none - I'z take good care of yoz's spotted hoss, sir.'

"Turning around and walking back to him, Trip pulled a gold coin from his uniform pocket and placed it in the old black man's callused hand. Trip smiled and inquired, 'You wouldn't know where a fellow could get some second-hand clothes to wear, would you?'

"For the first time, a smile came to the aged man's face. 'I'z sho do Mister! Wez run'd aground up riber two shree days hago and de Cap and sum udder men went up dey riber in the yawl to chek fo too shallow. Lack fools, dey pulled up to dey sho and fo deys no's hit, dem injuns fell on um and two dem fellers got arrows shot deep in dey backs wid anudder git'n cached by dem hedens. Cap and dem udder two ust dids make hit back to dey boat wid dem air-rows fly'n. Dat man what got cauched, he ain't gwin bees back and I'z got his clothes, but deys way-yonder toos fancee fer mees to beez ha wear'n and way yonder too's big, too. Dey prob'ly bout fit youz.' The boat hand led Trip down to the bottom deck of the paddle wheeler, to a little dark cubby and pulled a small satchel from under his cot. Handing it to Trip, he said, 'I knows youz ha want'n toos bees ha git'n dat blue off'un has quick-lak has youz can.'

"Trip offered him another smile and said, 'You got that right!'

"His new friend laughed and slapped his thigh. 'I'z nos youz fom dey South timez youz spoke. Youz ain't needn' toha beez ha wearn' dat blue down dare!' Quickly peeling off the Union blue, Trip pulled the clothes from the valise and found they were a perfect fit. In the travel case was a nice white linen shirt with a pair of gray plaid trousers that seemed brand new. Folded in the bottom were two pairs of white cotton drawers, two pairs of socks, two undershirts and a pair of braces, along with a gentleman's sack coat.

"As Trip put on part of his new wardrobe, the old deck hand remarked, 'Sirz - youz looks laks de gentleman youz is!' Grabbing his uniform, he stuffed it in his saddle bags and left with the case. Wearing an ear to ear grin, Trip placed another gold coin in his new friend's hand. Both had the biggest smiles they could manage as they climbed to the main deck. Looking every bit of a gentleman, Trip checked on Two Bears, then strode around the deck in his new outfit. It was the first time in four years he had worn civilian clothes and he felt liberated. Checking with the porter, he found the cabin he was sharing with three other soldiers and stored the valise under his bunk. Each of them had to pay $25 in Union greenbacks for passage on the riverboat to St. Louis. The first stop for them was Fort Leavenworth, to muster out. After that official and final duty, Trip would be homeward bound.

"At the Quartermaster's office, in typical army fashion, the men leaving the Union ranks stood in line to get their official release. Each was told he could keep his uniform and service revolver, but Trip offered his uniform to the Sergeant at the counter. He was quickly told to get that filthy thing off the counter, at which he tossed it into a growing pile of blue uniforms near the back door. Signing the necessary papers and getting his official discharge documents, he tucked the revolver in his waist band and quickly headed back to the boat to continue his journey. His bunkmates were three other Galvanize Yankees, but they were not going back home. They had heard too many stories of the destruction and devastation that blanketed the South. In addition, they had turned their backs on the Confederacy and had served in the Union Army. Not only did that make it impractical to return to Dixie, but also, dangerous. The gold mines of the west coast had been a hot topic in the barracks and the lure of gold was calling them west to find their fortunes.

"Back on the boat, they headed down river and Trip had plenty of time to contemplate his return to the sand hills. He had not corresponded with his family since leaving the POW camp at Fort Johnson. Knowing he had joined the Union Army would devastate his mother and cause major problems for him among the people of Salleys Kitchen. Not knowing how to explain the $200 he was bringing home, he decided his war history should remain undisclosed and careful discretion given to any use of the Union greenbacks. Moving his hand to feel the Navy Colt under his new coat, he intended to keep as much of the money as possible for the farm and his family at home.

"From all of the information he had gathered, the outer edge of Sherman's path of destruction had swept by Salleys Kitchen and he hoped against hope that his home and family farm had not been reduced to ashes. He trembled as he thought of his sister and mother facing the Union Bummers. He hoped against hope they were all still alive and able to hold out until he could get home. In St. Louis, he would have to pay again for traveling down the Mississippi to Memphis. Once in that Tennessee riverport, he and Two Bears would be on their own, traveling through Tennessee, Alabama and Georgia. How he longed for the feel of the sand under his feet and the smell of the longleaf pines. In her letters to him at Johnson Island, Ruth led him to believe Naomi had to leave Salleys Kitchen. Hoping she was safe, he shuttered thinking of the horrors she must have had to endure. As much as he wanted to be with her, he knew, in the back of his mind, that dream may have been lost.

"Trying to build a sense of hope to sustain him, Trip brought each of his father's cotton fields to mind and imagined plowing, planting and harvesting the cotton that his family would now depend upon to survive. But the memories left him with a heartbreaking realization of how much had been lost and the needless death and destruction of the last four years. The reality of his father's death and the disintegration of their way of life made him sick to his stomach. But he was just one person - the thoughts of so many young men lying dead on battlefields or returning home with mutilated bodies sent tremors through him. Lying in his bunk aboard the riverboat, he remembered the lead-up to the war and how reckless and out of control the fervor had become. The respectable people of Salleys Kitchen had shouted him down for offering caution as they blindly raced to start the war. A population of intelligent, Christian people had allowed themselves to be swept up in a fanatical movement and drunk on the wine of the rich powerbrokers, they blindly marched to their slaughter. With arrogance and pride, they created a hell on earth and now they sat dumbstruck among the ashes of the flames they had created.

"All civil wars begin with contempt and frustration that boils and bubbles like a cauldron of scalding, hot tar. Super-heated by a fire of discontent, the situation will burn out of control until the pot tips over and spills out death and destruction on those who stoke the fire, as well as those who innocently stand too close. Arrogantly dismissing those who spoke of caution, the South built an inferno under the boiling pot of tar. When it predictably tipped it over, it spilled its contents of death and destruction over all the southland. How could this have happened? Trip lay on his bunk trying to erase his memories of the unbelievable, self- inflicted suffering that had swept across the land.

"Arriving in St. Louis mid-morning, the three Galvanize Yankees happily shook hands and went their separate ways. Trip left Two Bears on the *Benton II* with the old river hand and quickly found a steamboat headed for Memphis. After booking passage on the first southbound riverboat, he returned to the original boat to gather his horse and belongings. Helping Trip secure his possessions, the old black man looked awkward, for he was wearing the nicest looking Stetson hat Trip had seen in a while. The old boat hand was grinning like a mule eating briers as he walked on the opposite side of Two Bears while Trip led him down the bow and off the boat. Once off the boat, Trip turned to take his new friend's rough, cracked hand and said, 'Thank you, sir!' Staring into the homesick Southerner's eyes, the old black man reached up and took his fine felt hat off and handed it to Trip. 'Dis hera forz yooz. Hit ain't sumpin' I'z can wares. But I'z tank hit purfit forz yooz!

"Putting the hat on his head, Trip was not a bit surprised that it fit perfectly. While both men smiled from ear to ear, they hardily shook hands and grabbed each other's shoulder. Then the old river hand changed his facial expression to serious and looked straight into Trip's eyes. Wearing his new hat, Trip listened as the old Black gentleman offered him some parting words of encouragement.

"Hits goot dat youz gwine home to Dixie. Mos dem boys wid youz haint gotz dey gutz to stands up for da right. I'z nos youz'll do 'ust dat. Duh South gwine need a heap of good mans like youz if'n dey gwine crawl outta da hole dey dun dug for demselves. Youz ha goodt man and youz'll do wats rat. I'z hopes sum uh dem udder Rebels wills follows youz lead. Gawd bless youz and gibs youz ha safe wayz home.' Turning loose of Trip's hand, the old river hand stood and watched as his friend and horse made their way to the local livery.

"Two Bears had not been on dry land for 5 days and Trip felt he needed to get his legs under him again. After feeding and brushing him, he climbed on Two Bears and rode him south along the Big Muddy on a path along the high bank overlooking the river. The hustle and bustle of St. Louis was not a place the horse or rider wanted to linger. Though cold, the two continued to follow the path along the levee for a mile or so out of town. Looking to his left on the Kentucky side of the river, Trip spotted a farmhouse with a handsome barn across a field from the dike. Wanting to save his money for home, he thought it might be worthwhile to ride over and inquire if he and his horse could spend the night in the well-kept barn. As they neared the house, a boy, who looked to be no more than 7 years old, ran out to meet them and began asking a variety of questions.

"Trip was glad to see the boy, for he had not been around children for quite a while. He smiled and patiently answered the boy's questions. The inquisitive little boy asked why the horse had spots all over his hindquarters and Trip told him he was an Indian warhorse, but that seemed a little too far-fetched for the boy. He continued his questions about the horse, but Trip changed the subject and asked the talkative little guy if there might be room in the barn for him and Two Bears to spend the night. Upon hearing Trip's request, the excited little fella turned and raced back to the farm house, yelling for his mother. Sounding as if he were in need of help, the mother appeared at the door as he caught his breath and asked if the man and horse could spend the night in the barn.

"By now, Trip and Two Bears were only 25 yards from the front door of the house. The woman of the house could see Trip was dressed as a gentleman, but she gave the stranger the once over. She was pleasantly surprised to find he didn't look like the riverboat gamblers often thrown overboard when caught cheating. Trip took off his new Stetson hat and bowed at the waist. With a smile he introduced himself - then humbly inquired about staying in the barn overnight. 'Good afternoon, ma'am. My name is James Anthony Sullivan, III, but most folks call me Trip. I saw your barn from the dike and wanted to inquire about my horse and me staying there for the night. I just got out of the army and I'm heading home to South Carolina'.

"Quickly, the lady of the house, who looked not to have passed the age of 30, said, 'You're a long way from home, Mister, besides, you'd freeze to death in that barn! It's still winter, here - this is not the time to be spending a night out in the weather. Put your horse in the stall beside the cow and come into the house.'

"The barn seemed too well kept for the woman not to have a man around. Trip unsaddled Two Bears and put some hay in the rack for him. Grabbing the valise with the new clothes, he walked back toward the house. Curious as to what he would find in the attractive woman's home, he hoped it would not be a large, jealous husband.

"As he tried to clean the Mississippi mud from his boots before entering the house, the back door was thrown open and the little boy appeared again. Grabbing Trip's hand, he began pulling him into his mother's warm kitchen. The woman admonished her son, telling him to leave the gentleman alone and quit pulling his arm. She was cooking on a stove and the entire house was filled with the aroma of bread baking. Before she turned back to the stove, the cautious visitor noticed the shape of a pistol in her apron pocket. Wanting to set the woman at ease, Trip quickly doffed his hat and asked her if there was a safe place for him to store his handgun while he was in her house. He added, 'My mother taught me that it was disrespectful to bring a firearm into someone's home without permission.'

"She replied, 'You had good raising - your mama taught you well!'

"Trip responded, 'In some ways she did, but not in all things.'

"Looking back at him, she wondered, *What type of man remembers what his mother taught him, only to say she didn't always teach him the right things?* Pointing to the pie safe near the kitchen door, she watched as Trip unbuckled the army belt and untied the leather cord just above his knee. Once the gun was off of his body, the ex-Union soldier wrapped the belt around the holster and put it on top of the cupboard. Putting his hat on top of the gun belt, both were well out of the boy's reach. Looking at her son, she warned, 'Randy, if you go near that man's gun, I'll stripe your behind with a green willow. Do you hear me?'

"The boy quickly replied, 'Okay, Mama.'

"Offered a seat at her kitchen table, Trip was glad to be out of the cold, however, he was still cautious, as he remembered the woman of the house was still armed. He pulled up a chair and sat silently until the woman spoke to him.

"The conversation began as the woman continued to cook. 'We get a lot of river trash washing over the bank here and you don't seem to be that type. Who are you and what brings you to our door?'

"Trip smiled and began, 'I just mustered out of the Union Army and I'm just passing through the area. The boat to Memphis doesn't leave the dock until mid-morning tomorrow and I don't cotton to spending the night in that city. Your barn appealed to me because it suits my present economic situation.'

"Trip's Southern drawl did not fit with a Union soldier and it stirred the woman's interest as she quickly asked, 'Where did you say your home is? You don't sound like you're from the North.'

"Realizing his answers were not fitting his profile, Trip knew his best bet was the truth. "'I'm from South Carolina, ma'am, a little place called Salleys Kitchen.'

"She looked at him with a very stern face and asked another question, 'How's a Southerner like you end up in the Union Army?'

"Having already decided to speak the truth, Trip said, 'I'm a Galvanize Yankee, ma'am. I was an officer in the Confederate Army and fought at First Bull Run, but I was captured by the Union forces. I ended up in the Rock Island POW camp. When offered a chance to get out of the squalor and starvation of the prison camp, I volunteered to join the Union Army and was sent to fight Indians on the Dakota Plains.'

"The boy jumped in, 'Is that where you got your warhorse?' Trip nodded yes and smiled at the curious little lad.

"The woman was not bashful and quickly responded, 'I've heard about you fellows, but you're the first one I've met in person. Do you tell everyone about switching sides?' "Responding honestly, the visitor said, 'No, ma'am, just the people I figure I can trust.' This time, she smiled and said no more.

"The boy wanted to know more about Two Bears. 'Did you kill an Indian to get your horse?'

"Again, Trip offered the truth, even if it sounded far-fetched. 'No, I got him by **not** killing an Indian.'

"'Huh?' spouted the boy, obviously confused.

"Trip told the true story of how he and Two Bears became partners, as the boy listened in awe. After he finished the story, the boy's mother made her engrossed son go wash up for supper.

"After he was gone, the mother asked, 'Is that really how you got that horse?'

"Trip looked straight into her eyes and said, 'I haven't told you a lie since I met you and I don't aim to before I leave.'

"She smiled and said, 'You're quite an unusual man.'

"Trip replied, 'No, just a regular man trying to survive. I was forced into a situation I tried desperately to avoid.'

"Looking at the stranger in her house, the woman said, 'My husband died of Typhoid during the second year of the war. He was a good man and didn't want to fight because he had very close friends on both sides. After putting it off for a year, he told me he was joining the Union Army. When I asked him why, he said it was because they were fighting for what was right. He never fought in a battle, but they said I would get his pension. I haven't seen any of it, yet. My husband's daddy comes by to help me with the farm, but he's too old to do much. I do what I can and pray the Good Lord will watch over us, because I don't know what the future holds for me and my son.'

"Trip again answered her honestly, 'I understand. There's no way of knowing what I will find at home, because I haven't heard from my family since I left the POW camp. I just hope they are still alive when I get there.'

"As they talked more, Trip found the woman to be very practical in her words and actions. He found her company to be very enjoyable. She equally enjoyed the Southern gentleman's company and found him to be very level headed and sincere. Without the slightest hesitation, the nice-looking woman set a plate for her visitor and invited him to break bread with her and her boy. Trip Sullivan did not hesitate in accepting her invitation, either. He hoped his good fortune was a sign that his luck had changed.

"During the meal, Trip told her of his home in South Carolina and about Sherman's army having marched through the area. Telling her of his family, he mentioned his mother and sister. Having heard nothing of a wife and children, the woman's blunt curiosity was evident as she asked, 'Did you leave a wife and children when the war started?'

"For a moment, there was an awkward silence. Immediately, the woman's face blushed red and she began to apologize for asking such a question. Trip quickly eased her embarrassment by saying, 'There is no reason to apologize for that question. I would be just as curious as to your marital situation had you not shared it with me early on. I did leave someone who I loved, but my situation never allowed me to make her my wife and I don't think she will be there when I get home. The war was a cruel executioner of many loving relationships.' As he spoke, he soon realized how much he missed giving and receiving love.

"As they talked by the warm cook stove and enjoyed coffee, her curious son soon fell asleep across his mother's lap. Instinctively, Trip scooped him up in his arms and followed the mother to the boy's little bed. As she turned it down, Trip laid him carefully among the cozy covers and she tucked him in, giving him a goodnight kiss.

"Heading back to the kitchen, the woman stopped in front of Trip in the hallway and turned to face him. Hesitating for a minute, she then looked into her visitor's eyes just before she blurted out her words.

"'Mr. Sullivan, would you favor me by sharing my bed tonight?' Stunned, the bachelor didn't know what to say and his hesitation brought another response from the woman. 'I don't want you to think me a loose woman, for I loved my husband more than anything in the world, but...' She paused and looked at the floorboards. 'I miss him so much and long for his touch, but I know that will never happen again. You seem like a kind and gentle man and I am so lonely in this house. I know I'm a plain woman and I will understand if you say no.'

"Trip quickly looked her in the eye and said, 'Ma'am, you are most definitely not a plain woman, but I haven't been with a woman in four years. I don't know...'

"She took his hand, squeezed it and smiled. Then she walked alone into her bedroom. After a quick trip to the outhouse and another cup of coffee, Trip pulled a pair of the new under garments from the valise and joined her in the warm bed.

"He arose while she slept and at daybreak was riding Two Bears back to the docks in St. Louis. With a smile on his face, man and horse soon made their way aboard the side-wheel steamer named *The City of Cairo*. Leading his horse to the holding pen on board, he secured Two Bears for the river passage to Memphis. Lingering near the rail on the top deck as the paddle wheeler moved away from the dock, Trip was lost in his thoughts.

"Entering the current of the river as it left St. Louis, the riverboat hugged the Kentucky side of the river for a little ways. As Trip looked up, he saw Randy standing on the high bank of the river, waving. The steam whistle on top of the pilot house let out a long low wail and prevented both the boy and his new-found friend from yelling goodbye. Trip waved his new Stetson at the boy and wondered if he should have lingered or even stayed, for he had no idea what he might find at home. As the little boy disappeared out of sight, the pleasant aroma of the woman's scent drifted up from Trip's new undershirt.

"After the long, winding and seemingly unending voyage down the Missouri River from Fort Rice to St. Louis, the trip St. Louis from Memphis seemed over in the blink of an eye. Maneuvering the side-wheel paddler through the muddy water, the veteran captain eased her to the Tennessee side of the river.

"The city was abuzz with former slaves now moving about and trying out their newfound freedom. The recently created Freedmen's Bureau offices were the busiest places in Memphis and were overflowing with former slaves anxious to experience their new liberty. The traditional power that had been enjoyed by the controlling white men of Tennessee no longer held status quo. The loss of their domination was building to an inevitable conflict as both sides jockeyed for control of the local government. Disputes between the white men and the Blacks had vigilante groups up in arms. The most powerful of these groups was the Ku Klux Klan and they set ready to rain terror on the former slaves who sought equality and those who offered them assistance.

"Landing after dark, the riverboat passengers unloaded among the tall bamboo poles stuck in the sand, holding coal oil torches. Ready to make a quick exit from the trouble-filled city, Trip and Two Bears cautiously and carefully made their way through the busy streets and onto a well-traveled road heading east. Trip gripped his pistol, ready for any problem that might arise as they nervously made their way into the dark countryside with a full moon lighting their way.

"As midnight came and went, Trip looked for a place to stop and safely catch a few hours of sleep before proceeding south across the Volunteer State and into Alabama. He slept holding his Colt pistol across his chest covered by his hat. Leaning against a tree, he slept in his bed roll as Two Bears stood with closed eyes under a sycamore tree on the Huntsville Road.

"At daybreak, Trip ate a cold breakfast of the last few pieces of Union hard tack that he had brought from Fort Rice. Breakfast for the stallion was some grass munched near the edge of the road. Daylight also gave the traveling pair a view of the fallow farmland left untended for the years of the war. It was obvious the fields had once been productive, but the war and fighting had put an end to any crop being raised on the land.

"As they made their way along, Trip noticed a sign lying in the ditch of the road that read, The Pillars, John Bills and Ezekial McNeal, Proprietors. It was obvious that it had been run over by many wagons and stomped by countless horses.

"Through the day the pair traveled southeast without stopping and crossed the state line, leaving Tennessee and entering Alabama. Following the Huntsville Road, scenes of destruction were seldom out of view. It was hard for Trip not to believe there may be ashes and ruins where the Sullivan mansion once stood. As he and Two Bears passed the burned-out shells of many fine homes, he was once again reminded of the colossal and immoral mistake made by the people of the South.

***

When Jon Chesterfield, Jr. saw his little red sports car crumpled, crashed and still smoldering in front of the guest house, he burst through the door and demanded to know what had happened. With a dismissing attitude, Salley said, "Oh, I had a little bump up as I turned into the driveway this morning. I'm sorry I made such a boo-boo on your car."

With his hand on his head, he asked, "A little boo-boo?! My car is totaled! How in the hell did you manage to bash in the front and the rear during the same accident? Were you drinking?"

Salley gave him a fake laugh and flashed her Miss America smile as she told him, "I guess I need to be more careful when I'm driving."

Turning to leave, he spat, "You're crazy! Stay out of my car from now on!"

Salley followed him outside and shut the door. "As much as I hate to say this, we need to talk about getting married – I'm pregnant!"

Chesterfield stopped in his tracks and turned to face her. "You're what?"

Salley unequivocally repeated her pronouncement, "I'm pregnant. What did you think would happen if you kept rutting on me and refused to use a condom? Has your father never told you about the birds and the bees? Now you have gotten us both in a fine mess!"

The rich guy standing in front of his destroyed sports car yelled, "I'm not in a mess. I'll make arrangements with a clinic in Augusta and you can just have an abortion."

With the face of a school teacher who had just caught a student cheating on a test, Salley replied, "You can forget that right now! I will never consent to having that procedure! You need to find a preacher or Justice of the Peace and get him to come here and marry us. I am not going to a church or anywhere else with you to get married. It's bad enough I have to marry you - I certainly won't do it in front of a preacher! Thursday afternoon will be fine, at 3 o'clock. I've cried enough tears over you; now it's time for you to ante up and get in the game!" As she turned to go back in the house she sent a parting shot, "Oh, and since I won't be having anyone from my family attending except Sully, you may invite your father. There will be no other guests!" With that she went inside and slammed the door!

Sully had figured out a while back Jon Chesterfield, Jr. had gotten his daughter pregnant and he agreed that Salley should marry him. For the moment though, he wanted to return to recording his story. His family saga had become his escape and with Salley by his side, it had become his way of coping with all of the bad things in his life. With the fine blackberry brandy in the basement of the Sullivan mansion no longer available to him, his story had become his crutch. Salley had also become absorbed in the recording sessions. She looked forward to sitting beside her father and letting the world 'go to hell' as they recorded his story. Once again, she put the microphone next to his unruly hair and pushed the buttons to start the recorder.

***

"Riding through the afternoon, the weary man from South Carolina and his spotted horse reached the foothills of northern Alabama. The road they traveled followed the banks of the Tennessee River and led to the top of a small mountain. The view was of udder devastation and stretched out on a vast scale as the burned rubble of the city of Decatur came into view. Every building had been reduced to ashes, save for a bank and three houses. Throughout the ruins, tall chimneys and iconic antebellum columns stood like tombstones. The smoldering debris was all that remained of a once vibrant town. The inhabitants could be seen searching through the rubble for anything with which to rebuild. The scene of such unwarranted waste was not a welcoming sight to Trip. In disgust, he and Two Bears followed the mountain road out of town.

Chapter 11

"Just outside of town, the smell of rotting fruit filled the air. Following his nose, Trip reined Two Bears off the road and onto a barely discernible, overgrown trail. Dodging low limbs and briers hanging over the narrow passageway, the pair ended up at a long-neglected apple orchard. The ground was littered with rotting apples and it was obvious the local wildlife had been feeding on the fallen fruit. Scavenging the area, Trip found several apples that were borderline edible. Cutting the spoil from the fruit, the hungry traveler devoured his find. Continuing to search the orchard, Trip found quite a few apples and he shared his bounty with Two Bears. Filling his shirt with half rotted apples, Trip tied the bundle over his saddle and then led his horse back to the main road. Though famished, he tried to limit the number of apples he ate. It would be far from pleasant to have a case of the back-door-trots while traveling through Alabama.

"Riding well into the evening, fatigue finally made the pair stop and rest. Searching in the dark, Trip luckily found a water source in a secluded neck of woods where the pair could sleep. The last night in Alabama would pass with Trip sleeping in a freezing drizzle. As had become his routine, he slept with his loaded pistol on his chest under his bedroll and his hat not quite covering his eyes. It was a miserable night and the morning light was a welcome sight. Washing his face in the freezing water from the spring, Trip remembered they were just outside of the mountain community of Collinsville. The area was nestled on the edge of the mountains and the entire region was covered with hoarfrost. Though brutally cold, it was a beautiful sight in the morning sun. But the South Carolina sand hills were calling and Trip needed to warm his body, so they did not linger in the pleasant little hamlet.

"Crossing the Alabama/Georgia state line, Trip entered the red clay hills of Georgia. This was an alien landscape for a sand hill resident. A cold December rain had turned the ruddy soil into a sticky red mass. The mud clumped together and stuck to Two Bears' hooves, causing him to become quite aggravated. He snorted and whinnied each time the red tar-like substance accumulated to the point of being twice as large as his hooves. Stopping often to remove the sticky red clay, Trip and Two Bears' progress toward Atlanta became long and drawn out.

"About midday, Trip noticed an overgrown farmstead just off the main thoroughfare. Riding over to the abandoned house, he climbed off of Two Bears and began to look around for anything useful. Out of the corner of his eye, he saw a guano sack just under the edge of the dilapidated house. Walking over to the old fertilizer bag, he pulled it from under the house and quickly realized there was something inside. Feeling around in the sack, he retrieved a half-dozen sweet potatoes that were still edible. Adding them to his apples, he kept one out for himself and Two Bears. Rubbing most of the dirt from the tuber, he broke it and gave half to his horse. Starving, he quickly began munching on the other half of the dirty root. As he chewed the raw potato, he continued searching for any food items that might have been left behind by the people who abandoned the house. Finding nothing else, he climbed back on Two Bears and made his way back to the main road.

"Trip and the stallion spent the night just a few miles from the Georgia/Alabama state line. They ate sweet potatoes and apples while sitting on a wooden bridge over a creek that crossed the road. With thoughts of home still invading his dreams, Trip slept under the bridge with Two Bears standing close by. At the first sign of light, they continued their journey, following a long and winding road that led into Atlanta.

"Approaching the Georgia capital from the west, Trip did not notice the telltale signs of the war. He wondered if the reports of Atlanta being burned to the ground by Sherman's army were true, but as the pair got closer to the city, the reports were confirmed. The devastated city, however, was abuzz with the business of reconstruction and it seemed as if an army of ants were rebuilding a destroyed anthill. In every pile of rubble, men were working judiciously to clean and salvage materials to rebuild. The city was teeming with activity as businessmen, both white and Black, frantically sought to be the first to offer their wares to the rebuilding metropolis.

"Stopping by a house whose owners had transformed its porch into a store, Trip bought a bag of hard tack biscuits for the unheard-of price of 5 cents. He grumbled as he took out one piece of the rock-hard bread, then put the rest with the other food items he had gleaned along the way. Climbing back on his horse, he gnawed on a piece of hard tack as he continued on his way through the city of rubble.

"Trip's time in Atlanta was short, for the noise and bustle of the city unnerved Two Bears and he danced and snorted his disdain at being forced through the clamor and clatter. Struggling to keep his steed under control, Trip marveled at the resolve and tenacity of the people of Atlanta. Climbing out of the ruins of the civil war, the city's residents were ignoring the Union soldiers who occupied their city. They were defiantly displaying their unyielding spirit to rebuild their city with renewed optimism. Trip hoped the people of Salleys Kitchen were working with the same zeal.

"With the sand hills dominating his thoughts, Trip and Two Bears did not linger long in the Georgia city and they were soon following a well-traveled road towards home.

"Once outside of Atlanta, Trip came upon the rolling fields of a large farm about the size and scale of the Sullivan farm. Like an island oasis in a large sea of open cotton fields, a lovely white Federal style home came into view. Showing stately alabaster columns, the comfortable-looking home was nestled among a cluster of tall pines and cedar trees. Obviously, this was not a huge operation, rather, a medium size family farm built with cotton money and hard work. The home, while stately and well adorned, was modest compared to the usual size home of a large plantation. Trip had seen much larger mansions in the Low Country of South Carolina. This home, however, was inviting and seemed to welcome Trip and Two Bears to stop and visit.

"The freedmen now working on the farm were pleasant and though the travelers were interrupting their work, their attitude was cordial and hospitable. When Trip reined Two Bears to a stop in front of the main house, a tall plain woman stepped into the doorway. A young girl was hiding behind her dress and peeking out to see the travelers. The woman offered a big 'hello' and the pair came out to greet the visitors. In a cordial manner, Trip held his hat in his hand and introduced himself. Explaining his journey home, he spoke of Salleys Kitchen and his family across the Savannah River in the Edgefield District of South Carolina. Mrs. Dolly Burge and her daughter, Sadai, welcomed him to the Burge farm and extended an invitation to stop and have some water. Within a day's ride of home, Trip knew he and his horse needed to rest before the pair made the final push to his sand hills home. Walking Two Bears to their watering trough, Trip let him quench his thirst while he washed his face in the cool water.

"Sadai, like the little boy in Kentucky, watched the pair intently and was enamored with the spotted horse. She asked Trip if he had painted the spots on Two Bears' hindquarters. With a smile, the weary sojourner picked her up and let her touch the roan spots scattered across the horse's white coat. She giggled as she told her mother, 'He's as spotted as a fawn, Mother, but he's so much bigger.' She asked the man holding her, 'Did his mommy and daddy have spots, too?' Trip told the fascinated little girl of the stallion's Indian pedigree and her eyes widened as she patted the horse with much greater zeal. Stepping in to free the beleaguered visitor, Mrs. Burge took her daughter's hand and made a veiled attempt to escort her back to the house.

"The lady of the house, however, stopped short of entering her home and turned to speak to Trip again. As if she was giving vent to her thoughts, she offered, 'It's good to see a man with civility and courtesy again. This war has changed people into savages and I'm glad it's over. It's time to put this awful mess behind us and start treating each other with respect, again. I have been a widow for seven years and faced many trials during that time, but I could never have believed the thievery and outright robbery perpetrated by Sherman's Bummers. Without a doubt, it was the worst horror I have ever had to face. They took everything we had and only left the house un-torched because one of the officers knew my brother in Chicago. I thank the Lord for His mercy in keeping us alive through that horrendous ordeal, but I will never show an inkling of gratitude to those thieves for not burning my home.'

Trip offered his empathies for her loss and did not voice his opinion of the Union soldiers who treated her so shoddily. She noticed his neutral tact and asked, 'Where did you serve during the war?'

"As had been his policy to anyone who asked, he offered her his war story in a 'condensed form'. 'I was a First Lieutenant in Hampton's Legion in the Army of the Confederacy at First Manassas and was captured by the Union Army. I ended up out west and was just released a few weeks ago. Since then, I have been making my way home to Salleys Kitchen, South Carolina.'

"Silent for a moment, his host said nothing of his military service. Her silence made it obvious she was trying to figure out the complete story behind this well-dressed gentleman on such a fine horse.

"After a moment, she said, 'Well, most folks would take you for a carpetbagger, but your voice would have them believe you're a scalawag. I don't see either handle fitting you, so I'll take you at your word. Thank you for showing me there are a few good Christian men left after they have fought in this war.'

"Trip smiled and ensured her he was neither a Northern money grubber nor a Southern swindler. He added, 'I can understand how my appearance might offer that impression and I think it only prudent that you question any man coming to your door.'

"His gracious manner had obviously disarmed the plain-spoken woman, for she called to the black woman cooking in the kitchen. 'Hassie, bring some of those corncakes and pork skins for this gentleman. He looks like he could use something in his belly.' After a few moments, Hassie came out of the house holding a flour sack with the contents the woman requested. She offered it to the lady of the house, but Mrs. Burge said, 'It's not for me - it's for the gentleman here. Give it to him.' As he took the food bag, Trip could not imagine his mother offering any stranger a bag of food. He knew this lady was a Christian woman.

"Thanking her for being kind and gracious to a wayfaring stranger, he excused himself, put his hat back on his head and climbed back on Two Bears. His homesickness for the sand hills urged him on. He and Two Bears camped for the night a ways west of Augusta, Georgia. The biting cold had subsided, somewhat, as Mother Nature gave the pair a brief reprieve. After Two Bears gulped down a few apples and a sweet potato, Trip laid waste to the corn cakes and pork skins. That night, Trip fell asleep and dreamed he was sleeping in his bed at the Sullivan mansion. Near morning, as his slumber was ending, he dreamed of LuDell's hoecakes and molasses.

"As the morning sun brought him fully awake, Trip could sense someone was watching him. Sleeping as he usually did, with his Colt pistol in his hand, he carefully cocked it under his blanket. Opening one eye slightly, he saw two men on horseback staring down at him. Neither of the two said a word, but the expression on their faces told Trip they were not there to welcome him to the community. As one of the two horsemen move closer, Trip flipped the blanket back to reveal the loaded and cocked pistol. Both men froze in place for a moment, then turned and galloped away. Relieved, Trip could think of nothing but getting home. Tossing an apple on the ground, he repeatedly looked over his shoulder as he saddled Two Bears. He barely gave the horse time to gulp down the fruity nugget and grab a few mouthfuls of grass along the roadside before he climbed on his back. The pair headed east, in a hurry, with Trip frequently looking back and on alert for any situation where he could be bushwhacked.

"Just after midday, the horse and rider boarded a ferry to cross the Savannah River. Reaching the far bank of the river, the weary rider was elated to, once again, be in the Palmetto State. The sand hills were a welcome sight and caused urgency in the returning soldier as he hurried along his way. With familiarity silently screaming at him, the exhausted traveler drank in the well-known sand hills scenes. With adrenaline coursing through his blood vessels, he breathed in the late winter air. Vapor, like smoke, poured from the nostrils of both man and horse as they moved onward. With only necessary stops to regain his breath, dependable Two Bears galloped across the ancient dunes as his new master urged him toward his final destination - Salleys Kitchen.

***

On July 21, 1972, Salley stood in the sun room with Sully and the iron lung to her left. Jon, Jr. stood to her right, beside his father. Both Chesterfields wore dark suits with ties and boutonnieres. Both of the suited men had frowns on their faces. The corsage that Jon, Jr. brought for new wife had been promptly tossed in the trash by Salley. She stood beside them wearing blue jeans with holes in them, a sweatshirt with Foxcroft written across the front and old tennis shoes. Salley told the Notary Public there would be no vows or rings exchanged. She told him she wanted as few words as possible spoken and the marriage completed as quickly as possible.

The gentleman stood in front of the couple and hurriedly read from his little booklet, "Do you, Salley Sullivan, take Jon Chesterfield, Jr. as your husband and do you, Jon Chesterfield, Jr., take Salley Sullivan as your wife?" They both answered yes. "Is there anyone here who can give just cause for this couple not to be married? Without so much as a pause, he announced, "Then by the power given me by the State of South Carolina, I pronounce you man and wife." The Notary turned quickly to the new bride and Salley handed him a check. She nodded her approval and then began to usher everyone out of the house.

"Following her new husband and father-in-law outside, Salley announced, "I'll be moving into the main house in a few weeks. We'll need the group of medical folks who moved Sully the last time to move him to the big solarium on the east side of the house. Ruth and I will be moving into the 3-bedroom suite just down the hall. I'll want to redecorate some and setup one of the bedrooms for Ruth and one as a nursery. If you would arrange for the workmen to come get me, I will explain exactly what I want." With that announcement, she turned and walked back into the guest house. Closing the door behind her, she fell back against it and smiled, *You are a fool, Jon Chesterfield, Jr. No one ever taught you to be careful what you wish for - because sometimes what you get ain't what you expected!*

Still wearing a smile, Salley sat down beside her father and moved the rolling table that held the tape recorder next to

285

Sully. Seeing her smile, Sully inquired, "I am somewhat reluctant to ask, my dear, but is the Cheshire Cat smile you're displaying the smile of a new bride or the smile of that mean little devil you were at Foxcroft?" Salley never lost the grin on her face as she pushed the buttons to start the recorder.

***

"Lathered and foaming, Two Bears sensed the urgency of the man on his back. The powerful horse continued to pound the road at his new master's insistence. Unaware of the cold temperature and his horse's struggle to maintain his pace, Trip's mind had already reached the tree-lined lane leading to the Sullivan mansion. He hoped beyond hope for his home to still be standing.

"Arriving just at last light, his fears were heightened as he hurried across the section of road that followed the top of the millpond dam. Suddenly, he had to rein Two Bears to a stop, as both breathed hard in the cold evening air. Facing a cavernous break in the dam, Trip recognized the thoroughfare was now impassable. Looking across the breach, he saw the charred remains of the mill beyond the gaping fracture in the dam. The millpond no longer existed and thousands of yards of soil had been part of the dam had washed into the South Edisto River. Facing, for the first time, the destruction around his home, Trip realized the people of the community had been left with no means of producing corn meal or flour. Those products had been the staples of the community.

"Backtracking from the ripped-open dike, he found a dried and cracked layer of mud across the area where the millpond had been. Following the wagon ruts, he crossed the unfamiliar landscape of the pond with fear and trepidation, wondering if his mother's mansion had met the same fate. Struggling to recognize landmarks among the now alien area, he finally reached the cobblestone columns on each side of the sandy lane. There was just enough daylight to see the outline of the mansion and the anxious man was elated to see if his boyhood home was still standing.

"To Trip, the sight of the house was an answer to his prayers. In the dusk of evening, it was still there, with dim lights glowing in the windows. Urging Two Bears toward the mansion, his heart was pounding. He slowed his mount to a walk. No longer the pleasant shady lane he once knew, it was now the heartbreaking scene of stumps and discarded limbs. The huge majestic oaks that had once stood, stretching their long limbs over the driveway, were no more. Every tree had been chopped down by the Yankee soldiers to fuel their fires and cook the meat and poultry stolen from the plantation. Dismounting in front of the mansion, Trip tied Two Bears' reins to the familiar hitching post. The mansion looked untouched, as far as he could see. Climbing the steps to the closed front door, he noticed the splintered facing where the door had recently been kicked in. Cautiously, he yelled out, 'Helloooo! Anybody home?'

"Listening for an answer, he heard the all-too-familiar sound of a gun being cocked. The voice of his mother then called out, 'Who are you and what do you want - as if I didn't know?'

"Trip shouted back, 'It's Trip, Mother, at least what's left of him.' A crack opened in the curtain covering the sidelight of the door. The next sounds he heard were his mother's sobs and the thud of the gun falling onto the floor. With a sudden movement, the front door was thrown wide open and he was immediately engulfed by his mother's arms. The haggard woman gripped her son in a speechless clinch while beaming a seldom seen smile. In a flash, Ruth and LuDell became part of the group sobbing and clutching Trip. It was as if he was their savior. At long last, the four family members had been reunited.

"It was a completely euphoric moment, for they had prayed and hoped for this moment over the five long years of Trip's absence. All had shed innumerable tears, faced uncountable nights without sleep and endured days of inconsolable grief. The death of James Anthony Sullivan, Jr., early in the war had taken away the family's core. But now, their world of trouble and woe seemed to be lifted from their shoulders. No matter what had happened in the past or what might happen in the future, at this moment, they were together again and there was hope once again in their lives.

"But for Ruth, it was a bittersweet reunion, for she knew she had to tell her brother Naomi was in Pennsylvania and married. Trip would never see her again. Recognizing the bad news in his sister's eyes, he knew it would be revealed later when his mother wasn't around. Staring at his sister, he was shocked at her appearance, for she was not the little sister he kissed goodbye from his saddle as he left for the war. She was now a full-fledged woman, beautiful like her mother, but with a much more subdued nature than he remembered before the war. He could only wonder what tragic events may have changed her life.

"LuDell was never one to cry, but she bawled like a baby at the sight of Trip. She said no one would ever tell her God didn't answer prayers, for she had prayed for five solid years for this very moment, and the Good Lord had answered her humble prayer. Raising her arms, she held her palms upward toward heaven and shouted, 'Hallelujah! Hallelujah! Hallelujah!'

"As darkness completely engulfed the devastated areas surrounding the mansion, the family laughed a lot, but cried much more and at times silently held each other as they recalled the separate hells through which they had lived. With tears in his eyes, Trip related the circumstances of Lil' Sully's death, telling his mother of his father's last heartbreaking words – *Clara Ruth*. It was the name of the woman he loved. He recalled the precious few minutes he held his dying father in his arms, just before he was knocked unconscious and captured by Union soldiers. Trip told his family, 'I would do it all again for the privilege of holding my father in my arms as he drew his last breath.' Trip also told them of his imprisonment and the awful conditions of the prison camp. Relating his arduous journey home, he said nothing of being a Galvanize Yankee. Knowing her brother, Ruth knew there was a lot he had not told them and she shed a tear, thinking of the horrors the full story might include. Long into the night, until the early hours of the morning, they talked and often just hugged each other in silence as the reunion became real to each of them.

"As the first few rays of the sun were peeking over the eastern horizon, Trip used the last of his energy to walk Two Bears to the huge mule barn. Once the hub of horsepower for the farm, all of the barn's elaborate stables now stood empty. Finding a straw brush among the manure, Trip brushed his steed and put him in one of the 80 empty stables. There was no feed for a hungry horse that night.

"The next morning, LuDell made hoecakes with honey from her hoarded supplies and poured coffee from grounds that had been used a dozen or more times. It was a wonderful breakfast enjoyed by everyone. Afterward, Trip stood in his father's favorite spot - on the balcony overlooking the farm - and grimaced as he viewed the devastation that covered the landscape. There were no animals in sight and no activity of any kind on the farm. The doors of all the buildings stood open and the contents that remained after the pillaging were scattered about. The arbor vines were ripped to shreds as the trellis was torn apart and used as firewood. The huge umbrella elm, however, continued to stand majestically by the well. The barn was still intact and seemed to have come through the war unscathed.

"As his mother joined him on the balcony, she began telling her son of the night General Sherman visited the Sullivan mansion. Clara Ruth cursed and spat to clear her mouth of the General's name. Her son had never seen such vileness come from his mother. With a demonic scowl on her face, she said, 'The death blow those Northern hordes tried to inflict upon us was unsuccessful and though it brought us to our knees, The South, with the help of the Almighty, will rise and be vindicated once again. We will send those Yankee bastards back to the devil's lair from which they came. We will stand and fight again and when we do, God will rain down hellfire and brimstone on those who did this to us. This atrocity upon His people will not go unpunished!'

"Looking out over the scorched earth, Trip replied, 'I think we have seen enough of hellfire and brimstone for a lifetime, mine at least.' As his mother sulked away, he noticed she had become an old woman, hunched over and bracing against the walls as she walked. Having filled her heart with loathing, this once proud woman was consumed by hatred and resentment. Her life was now ruled by a lust for revenge. The war had wreaked havoc on Clara Ruth Sullivan and inflamed her whole being.

"Ruth now joined her brother on the grand balcony as their mother retreated back inside the mansion. The siblings were now finally alone. Ruth began the conversation by telling her brother of having to kill the cruel overseer they had hated as children. 'After Lincoln's Emancipation Proclamation in January of 1863, the slave master tried to keep 'our mother's' slaves from leaving the farm. There were several clashes between him and the freedmen and I finally intervened. I told him to leave the property or I would have him arrested for trespassing. Furious, he cursed and promised revenge, so I asked each of the freedmen to help me watch for anything he may try to do. In only a few hours, he returned drunk and kicked in Naomi's door. The others alerted me and I ran to the cabin to find him on top of Naomi. He had ripped her clothes from her body and was attempting to rape her. I screamed for him to get away from Naomi, but he stood and kicked her in the head. Knowing I would probably have to shoot him, I cocked the pistol and told him to leave. Like a fool, he reached to his pocket and pulled out a knife. As he moved toward me, I warned him to stop, but he laughed and said he was going to give me the same thing he was about to give Naomi.

"Ruth stopped for a moment and composed herself before saying, 'I aimed at his head and pulled the trigger. The shot hit him directly between the eyes.'

"Trip held his sister in his arms as she cried and wished he could have been there to take care of that filthy piece of trash himself.

"After a moment, Ruth told Trip the home guard was summoned and after a bit of grumbling, the members of the community decided Ruth had killed the man in self-defense. After our mother heard he had threatened to rape me, she refused to allow his burial in the church graveyard. His body was taken to the paupers' cemetery in Aiken for burial.

"Continuing the account, Ruth said it was apparent Naomi's life was in danger. 'A few days after the attack, I heard rumblings of the Home Guard wanting to arrest Naomi. Quickly, I arranged for her to leave Salleys Kitchen'.

"Ruth told Trip that Ann Poole, the preacher's wife, had been one of the conductors along with her on the Underground Railroad. She and Ruth had worked together for years, helping runaway slaves, including Naomi, escape to the North. Even though she was a legally free black woman, she was ushered to safety by conductors on the Underground Railroad. Delivered to a Quaker community in Pennsylvania, Ruth said she received a letter from Naomi telling of her meeting a new man. He was a former slave who had escaped a wealthy family in Charleston. He was a trained silversmith and together, they traveled to Boston. He was working there and had become a respected member of the community of freedmen in Massachusetts. Naomi married him during the months just after the surrender and had delivered a healthy baby girl. Wiping her eyes, she spoke tenderly, 'I'm so sorry, Trip, but the war changed everything and we… she didn't know whether you were alive or dead. I urged her to follow her heart and I'm sure that's exactly what she did. I'm so sorry.'

"Trip hugged his sister and said, 'This war has broken many hearts. The loss of our love seems small in comparison to the thousands of husbands taken away from their wives by that senseless war. I'm happy for her and I wish her a long and happy marriage. She certainly deserves that opportunity. Our being together was just not in the realm of possibility, but I did love her with all my heart.'

"Trip remained on the balcony after his sister returned to the inside of the mansion. As he looked out over the barren land, his thoughts, for some reason, returned to Randy, the little boy standing on the river bank just south of St. Louis. Trip wondered how he and his mother were getting along and how it would have been if he had decided to stay with them."

***

As Sully told of his grandfather's lost loves, Salley's eyes began to fill with tears. She now knew she was not the only Sullivan to be ripped away from the person she loved. She felt sorry for her great-grandfather, Trip, and wondered if his heart had ached as much as hers. Trip Sullivan's story made James reappear in Salley's mind and she hoped against hope he was still alive. She had not heard a word about him and was starting to believe her husband's story was true.

Since they had moved into the main house, the staff now waited on Salley, Sully and Ruth around the clock. The nurses still came for Sully's therapy and both Dr. Baughman and his colleague from Augusta came every Wednesday to check on their patient. Salley had overheard them talking as they left the house one afternoon about how remarkable it was for Sully to have survived for this amount of time. The doctor from Augusta did not think Salley could hear him when he said, "I have worked with quadriplegic patients for all of my years in practice and I have never seen someone with a spinal cord injury that high on the spine live longer than a few months. It's remarkable he has survived this long. He must have quite a reason to live."

Sully's doctor replied, "His beautiful daughter is one of the reasons he is still living. She is his inspiration - but that damn story he's recording is his other reason. He is determined to finish the story of his family for posterity. I have known him since I came to this area to practice almost 3 decades ago and I've never known him to say more than a handful of words. Now he talks into that microphone for hours - go figure!"

It was now very obvious Salley was pregnant and though her husband came by to be serviced once in a while, he was not a regular presence in the house, nor was his father. As Salley's stomach grew larger, Jon, Jr. was seen less in the house. Now that her stomach was really extended, he seldom came by and seemed not to want to touch Salley. That left Salley, Ruth and Sully to use the house and its surroundings as they pleased.

During the remodeling that Salley orchestrated, she had demanded a TV be mounted in the ceiling, so Sully could watch it comfortably. The workmen had never heard of putting a television in such a place and scoffed about rich people spending their money foolishly. Sully also had another cutting-edge device. The doctor from Augusta brought over an electronic straw Sully could bite on to summon help if he needed it. It gave Salley more comfort than her father, for she always feared he would choke when she was not near him.

Ruth loved the horse barn and spent hours playing among the fine polo ponies and recruiting the stable hands to help her build forts in the hayloft. Each time Ruth persuaded her mother to follow her to the hayloft, Salley would tell her daughter, "Your father and I had a hay fort in his hayloft."

As the Christmas season arrived, Salley had a field day with the Sears and Roebuck and Montgomery Ward mail order catalogs. She was much too big to go shopping and in lieu of trudging through stores for hours, she spent her holidays filling out mail order forms from the back of the catalogs. When the mailman brought the mail one December day, he told Salley that a special truck would arrive that afternoon to deliver all of the items she had ordered. She thought it was decadent to have spent so much money, but what the hey, it was Jon, Jr.'s money and she had sure earned her part of it!

On Christmas day when Ruth got to open her presents, she enjoyed the boxes more than their contents. She was thrilled to put the cardboard boxes together as her 'hay fort'. Sully loved to hear her squeal and say the latest word he had taught her - 'tremendous'!

The holidays did not stop Sully's drive to finish recording his family's history. As the New Year approached, he became weak and could not record for more than an hour before becoming exhausted. Salley knew the inevitable was approaching, but she put it out of her mind.

In January, Salley returned to Aiken Memorial Hospital and the private maternity room where Ruth had been born. Little Jon Wesley Chesterfield arrived without the presence of his father and Salley was thankful for her husband's neglect. Throughout her pregnancy, Salley had wondered if she could love a child who had been forced upon her by someone she loathed. But when Little Wesley Chesterfield began to nurse at her breast, all doubts were erased from her mind. She knew she would love him as much as life itself. Salley arrived home after a quick and easy delivery. She walked into the sunroom and held Little Wesley over Sully's head. Sully cried at seeing his grandson for the first time. Though he was not named James Anthony Sullivan, VI, Sully was overwhelmed with pride that Salley had chosen Wesley as his name.

In the days that followed, Sully would record his family history while Salley nursed Little Wesley. Ruth, as always, played in her 'hayfort' of cardboard boxes under Papa's iron lung and regularly shouted the words her grandfather had taught her in the background – preposterous, tremendous, gargantuan, magnificent, astronomical and her favorite, inconceivable.' Both Salley and her father thought it very 'apropos' for Wesley's cries and Ruth's shouting to be part of the story Sully was telling. They recorded Sully's family story as often as he had the energy.

**

"Trip's return from the war brought with it many challenges for the entire Sullivan family. Ruth could sense a melancholy mood spreading over her brother. She knew the loss of Naomi had torn his heart asunder and he blamed it on a war that never should have happened. She vowed to bring happiness back to her brother's life, for he was a good and decent man who deserved a wife to complete him. Though he never revealed the whole story of being a POW, Ruth felt she shouldn't force him to relive the horrors he had witnessed. She hoped he would open up later, given time.

"Two Bears was the most intriguing element of Trip's unfinished story and that was the only part of his war experience Ruth insisted he explain. But her insistence was to no avail. He only told her Two Bears was a gift from an Indian friend and the two had formed a close partnership on the long ride home.

"Neither Ruth, nor any other curious inquirers, were ever successful in getting Trip to reveal his complete war story. The events remained shrouded in mystery for 80 years, until I sifted through thousands of Civil War Regiment Rosters and tens of thousands of Confederate papers. Having searched every South Carolina Confederate record for years, I was in my college library when one of my history professors happened to ask if I had ever thought about looking in the Union Regiment Rosters. Within a few weeks, I had found my grandfather's Union Army service records. Reading and researching the regiments of Galvanize Yankees, I finally solved the mystery of my grandfather's complete Civil War service. I traveled all the way to North Dakota to search the records of Fort Rice and it was there, I found the story of Corporal James Anthony Sullivan and his Appaloosa stallion. One of the army clerks had written up the incident and placed it in the official records. I was awestruck by the difficulties my grandfather endured as he attempted to stay alive on the wild prairies of the Dakota Territory.

"In that my grandfather never wanted the world to know of his time as a Union soldier, I have never revealed this information to anyone. You, my dear daughter, are the first to know of his being a Union soldier. There is a bevy of information about my grandfather's regiment at Fort Rice buried under the mound of papers on my desk. You will also find among that hoard of papers, the complete story of the gold star that stabbed my precious little girl's toe.

"In the days after his return to Salleys Kitchen, my grandfather rode Two Bears through the community of his boyhood. He was wearing the gentleman's clothes from the valise and the Stetson hat he had been given by the old river hand. As he slowly rode the familiar roads, he sadly surveyed a decimated and appalling landscape. The haggard inhabitants stared with vicious eyes and screamed at him in silent resentment. Attempts to talk to former friends were rebuffed with muteness as he followed the path of destruction through the community and slowly entered the sandy lane leading to the once grand church. The house of worship had been left standing, but the welcoming setting once offered by the many majestic oaks that cloaked the building was no longer. Limbs that extended like arms to shade, cool and protect the building were now gone, replaced by a naked and inhospitable landscape of stumps and charcoal discard. Sherman's Bummers had camped in the church yard and cut the trees to fuel their campfires, leaving their charred remains and trash scattered around the religious epicenter of the crossroad. The large gathering porch on the front of the church, once shielded by the trees, was now open and unprotected. The wide masonry steps were cracked and had large pieces missing. In the lead up to the war, the porch had been the stage of heated discussions and a place where secession was arrogantly demanded. On this day, Pastor Poole sat on the bottom step in a dazed silence, staring out at the scores of new graves dominating the cemetery adjoining the church yard. After his long hiatus, Trip longed to be among the familiar people of his boyhood and was anxious to renew the friendships that the war had forced him to abandon. Without being offered so much as a formal hello from anyone in the community, Trip now sought an explanation for his rude reception. Riding to the front of the church, he stepped off Two Bears and walked over to the subdued pastor. Speaking without a greeting or salutation, he demanded an explanation from the country preacher as to why he was being shunned. 'What's causing these people to turn their backs on me? I'm being treated as if I had killed their brother.'

"Looking up at the man standing beside his horse, the preacher straightforwardly explained, 'In their eyes, you did kill their brother. These people are filled with grief and despair. They have lost everything defending your way of life. You know these people; they worked with their families and by the sweat of their brow, grew cotton. They never even considered owning a slave. Now, their world has been torn apart because they chose to defend your mother's right to own slaves. Your family, to this community, represents the rich, slave owning planters. They watched as the General who ordered the destruction of their homes was allowed to be a guest in your fine home. His troops stood guard in your yard as he visited your mansion. While that visit was taking place, almost every other house was being looted and burned, yet your mansion was left virtually unharmed. As a mob of ruthless robbers laughed and ran off with everything they owned, many of your mother's slaves ran after those thieves, singing hallelujah for their Union saviors. Those once weak and powerless slaves are now free and openly mock the white people who owned and ruled them for decades. For the white citizens of Salleys Kitchen, their civilized and ordered life has been turned upside down and their once bountiful world is gone. They have been left destitute.

"Your sister Ruth has offered help to every freedman in our community and hasn't once offered to help the white people she grew up among. Now, she is pouring salt in their wounds by supporting every Negro seeking political office and they fear being stripped of the last remnants of dignity to which they desperately cling. With all of that happening around them, you return from the war, riding a fine horse, wearing a fine suit of clothes and Stetson hat, without a scratch. If their family members were lucky enough to survive the fighting, they walked, limped and dragged home wearing rags. Many came home in boxes and are lying in those new graves out there. Everything about your family reminds them of what they've lost defending your mother's right to own slaves. They have been robbed, pillaged and left without a means to feed their families and the provisional government who now rules their lives has embarked on a vendetta to take their land for the taxes they owe. You represent everything they now despise and they curse the sight of you.'

"Trip stood in silence as the churchman fed him reality. The first James Anthony Sullivan lying in the church's cemetery came to the New World as an indentured servant and hated the very idea of chattel slavery. He never allowed anyone in the community to even consider owning slaves. But now, just one generation removed, his son married a woman who not only accepted the immoral practice, but also exploited it to become wealthy. Most of the older men in this community knew Trip's grandfather or were told by their fathers of his prophesy of slavery bringing ruination to the community.'

"This was a hard reality for the grandson of the community's founder to accept. He wallowed in the guilt of its truth. The former warrior sat down beside the plain-spoken pastor and dropped his head into his hands. He could now plainly see the greedy grab for wealth his family had perpetrated was the reason for the resentment and shunning of his family. His father and mother were truly responsible for the situation and that realization was humbling. As the principle heir to the Sullivan family, Trip stood in a lonely place.

"With a broken heart, Trip realized the monumental struggle he faced, but he refused to allow self-pity to take control of his thinking. In his blood, passed to him by his grandfather, he had received a sense of community responsibility. He quickly recognized it was up to him to rebuild, strengthen and bring about the resurrection of his community and its people. As did his grandparents, he felt a sense of devotion to the people of Salleys Kitchen.

"Trip's character would allow him to take only one path, that being a lifelong attempt to right the wrong. With a tough road in front of him, he knew the first step would be restoring the community pride that the people of Salleys Kitchen had experienced before the war and to rejuvenate the attitude of working together for the good of all. But amid the ruins of the community, hatred and resentment filled the hearts and minds of the people and a return to the amicable times enjoyed before the war seemed to be a faraway dream. The prospects of facing the cruel and unforgiving world created in large part by his mother made him shutter. He realized only divine intervention could get him through the troubles he faced on the horizon.

"The pastor and the former soldier sat like two family members who had witnessed a tragedy. They had tried to separate a fight between brothers, only to witness one killing the other. Helpless to change the tragic events of the past, the two open-hearted men now felt saddled with the responsibility of bringing the family - their community - back together. Knowing full well they faced a seemingly impossible road ahead, the two men hugged as they sat on the church steps and vowed to each other and their maker, to work for reconciliation and rebirth among the people of Salleys Kitchen. Though jealousy and hatred would permeate every aspect of their daily lives, the pair would never relent in their struggle to help their community recover.

***

The birth of Jon Wesley Chesterfield did not instill within his father a sense of parental duty. After his marriage to

Salley, Jon Chesterfield, Jr. was given most of the day to day responsibility of his father's business fortune. This was an unsuccessful attempt by Jon Chesterfield, Sr. to avoid losing half of his holdings to his now ex-wife, Kellah Chesterfield. In a shady business move, he had transferred ownership of all of his holdings to his son through dozens of shell corporations. Though his efforts were to keep his former wife from obtaining any great amount of his money, his attempts failed. Kellah Chesterfield now owned half of the fortune he had amassed. Jon, Sr. was now an old man who had been bested - something that had never happened to him in his life. He had retreated to his New York estate and was now focused on his precious horses. Jon Chesterfield, Jr. was now charged with rebuilding the family fortune.

"The cut, gut and make profits tactics of his father's former business days were now taken up by Jon, Jr. The son emulated his father's unethical and ruthless business practices and seemed to take to the shady task like a duck to water. After taking the reins of the multimillion dollar cooperation, Jon, Jr. morphed into a money-making machine. He became even more cold-hearted and ruthless than his predecessor. While on his way up in the financial world, he amassed millions of dollars while shafting millions of hard working people. Jon Chesterfield, Jr. went well beyond rebuilding the family fortune. He became a billionaire and was known as a tenacious bulldog. The younger Chesterfield, much like his father, was an unscrupulous character who didn't mind stabbing a friend in the back if it meant he could own his company. In business circles, the Chesterfields were to be avoided if possible and if they did sink their teeth into your business, it was bad news.

"Fresh from a hostile corporate takeover in which he made millions, Jon, Jr. decided it was time he met his young son in Aiken, South Carolina. Landing his private jet at the Aiken airport, he then flew to his family estate by private helicopter and landed on the polo practice field across the street. Salley Sullivan Chesterfield knew the minute she first heard the whir of the rotors that it had to be Jon, Jr. arriving, but she was not impressed, whatsoever. She and Sully continued their recording session as if the arrival of her priggish husband was not occurring. She did not go out to meet him, but Ruth stood wide-eyed at the window as the loud aircraft settled onto the green field. Like his daughter, Sully ignored the arrival of his arrogant son-in-law and continued to chronicle his family history.

***

"From the beginning, Trip and the preacher's efforts to organize and conserve what little food remained in the community were rebuffed. Most of the broken citizens of Salleys Kitchen felt the situation demanded an attitude of *every man for himself and to hell with anyone one else.* Having been severely burned by joining the lost cause of the Confederacy, the community was in no mood to become part of a cooperative effort to help others, especially if it was led by the rich planter family whom they blamed for their current predicament. Ignoring the naysayers, the two good men worked to pulled together the meager remains of food they could and set about serving one meal every day to which all were invited to partake. None of the other, so-called community leaders, joined Trip and Reverend Poole to break bread and pray together. Worse, they ridiculed the idea of forming a community cooperative and threatened those who spoke of linking with Trip and the pastor in the joint effort. The community steadfastly refused to come together, so the preacher and the planter shouldered most of the hard work of rebuilding, themselves. Time and time again the citizens turned their backs on Trip and the pastor. Even as it became evident they were not gaining any support, the two continued to offer help and show kindness.

"One person who felt the full weight of the selfishness that had consumed the people of Salleys Kitchen was Lucinda Mae Plunkett. She, along with her brother and sisters, came to Salleys Kitchen to live with their grandmother after their father was killed at Gettysburg. In the two years since her father's death, Lucinda had been robbed of her childhood and forced to become an adult. The war had taken away the love and nurture traditionally offered by caring parents and forced the

300

responsibilities of being the family provider upon her all too soon. Her mother died right after the birth of her last child. Soon after her mother's passing, the death machine of war swallowed her father on that infamous Pennsylvania battlefield, Gettysburg. With no one knowing for sure what happened, Lucinda, at ten years of age, was saddled with the responsibility of taking care of an infant, a younger brother and a baby sister.

"While waiting for her father to return from the war, the orphaned little family simply could not survive at home alone. Walking together from the middle of the Orangeburg District, Lucinda carried her infant sister and urged her other siblings along as they traveled to their grandmother's home in Salleys Kitchen. The grandfather had died of typhoid just after the war began and her grandmother was living alone, but soon after the children arrived, she was stricken with tuberculosis. The grandmother became bedridden and Lucinda gained another responsibility. Each time the church doors were opened, the troop of children would attend. They never missed a service, for they depended on the goodness of others to survive. Lucinda was not afraid of work and never hesitated to do odd jobs when asked. She would broom a yard, do washing, work in a garden, help kill a hog or sit with children while parents worked in the fields and never ask for pay. She took only what was given to her, whether it be a few coins or food or old clothes. She always shared with her family. The community understood her position and tried to give her things to do, but Reconstruction took a terrible toll on every member of the community. As a whole, the people of Salleys Kitchen were reduced to living a subsistence life. Each family member constantly worried about his or her next meal. Often, parents were left with the inhuman choice of deciding which of their children would be fed. Usually, the older children who could work and produce were fed first and the least and most vulnerable were left without nourishment. It was a cruel and horrific time for every living thing left in General Sherman's path of destruction.

"Destitute, the ill-fated family was dealt a final blow when they were evicted from their house and they watched as it was auctioned off with the land for the price of back taxes. The

Christian folks of Salleys Kitchen had seen this brutal fate fall upon many of their neighbors and they watched without feeling as the auctioneer banged his hammer and sealed the little family's horrible fate. Ultimately, the sick grandma was taken to 'the poor house', which most considered a fate worse than death. The four children became homeless after being turned out of their house by the new owner so he might rent it to a sharecropping family. The people of Salleys Kitchen were helpless to intervene in any way. With barely enough food to feed their own starving children, four more would have turned a difficulty into a disaster. They looked the other way and did not want to know what happened to the evicted family, for atrocities and inhumanity were ever-present and might descend on their own family at any moment.

"Lucinda, acting as head of the family, appeared at the back door of the Sullivan mansion one morning just as the sun came up and asked to borrow a shovel. The house servant, LuDell, told her where to find it and lectured her on bringing it back. Later that afternoon, Trip was riding by the church and saw her digging in the cemetery. Curious, he rode over and got off of his horse to inquire what she was doing. Standing knee deep in a sandy hole, it was obvious she had been digging a grave for hours. As he walked up to her, he noticed the oldest boy lying motionless in the shade of some nearby trees. A little girl was fanning him with a pine bough to keep flies from his face while a baby lay swaddled and asleep next to the body. Trip stood shocked with his mouth agape as Lucinda did all the talking. 'Hello, sir. My brother died last night and I'm trying to give him a decent buryin'. He always liked this part of the graveyard. It's where we played Tag and Red Rover after church. The grass is worn out, but that don't matter to me and I'm sure he don't care. You don't know of anyone that was planning to bury here, do you? I want to make sure I don't get where anybody else might have their buryin' place already marked out. That's why we're over here next to the woods. It don't cost nothing to bury a person in the church cemetery, does it? My brother was hungry last night and I didn't have nothing to give him so he ate some kind of mushrooms. I've heard people call that kind of mushroom 'snake bread'.

Anyway, after dark, he started saying his stomach was hurtin' and 'bout two or three hours before light, he hollered out and gave up the ghost. I've been trying to find a blood-beat, but ain't yet and besides, he's stiff now, so I thought I might better get to burying him 'afore he starts to stink. I shoulda knowed better than to pick this here spot. There's a heap of roots over here next to the woods."

"When she stopped talking, Trip walked over to the boy's body and was horror struck to see the infant lying beside the corpse. The baby was wrapped in a nasty blanket, lying on the ground.

"Trip quickly stepped back to the girl standing in the grave and asked her to give him the shovel. He told her to see to the baby and her little sister. He then went to fetch the pastor from his house behind the church. Returning with the preacher, his wife and two other men, they were all horror struck. The parson's wife brought a bed sheet to cover the lad's body and sobbed as she covered him. 'We ought to be ashamed,' she said, 'to have starved this little boy to death.' Of course, the men that finished digging the grave said they didn't have enough to share. They insisted it was the Yankees, scalawags and carpetbaggers whom should be blamed, for they left the countryside in ruin and the people to starve.

"'No!' the preacher exhorted. 'This boy did not have to die! Someone, somewhere, could have shared something with this child. We have all sinned in God's eyes. **Inasmuch as ye have done it unto one of the least of these my brethren, ye have done it unto me.**"[The Holy Bible, Matthew 25.23] Silence and tears overtook the small group as the youngster's body was wrapped in the sheet and reverently placed into the fresh grave. Lucinda, like an adult, said a few nice things about her brother. The preacher, however, consumed with guilt, begged for God's forgiveness for himself and all of the community, saying, 'I am ashamed and my soul cries out in guilt, for I have allowed this tragedy to happen. The weakest of God's creatures, this little boy, was part of my flock and I didn't do what my soul and my Savior would have had me to do. May God forgive me and the others who caused this precious child to die so young.'

"Mrs. Poole took the youngest girl home with her and Trip took Lucinda and the baby home with him to the Sullivan mansion. His sister, Ruth, lovingly bathed the baby and swaddled it in clean linen. LuDell scrubbed Lucinda from head to toe and sat her at the huge stone table in the kitchen with a bowl of grits. Lucinda was 15 years younger than Ruth, but she dug out dresses she had kept from her younger days and shared them with the little urchin. The once dirty little ragamuffin was soon dressed in some hand-me-downs and was over the moon to be wearing a new frock. With both of the orphans fed, the baby soon fell sound asleep in a bassinet that had been hastily pulled from the basement. It was understandable why Lucinda sat grinning from ear to ear, but it puzzled some of the other folks as to why Ruth was just as giddy.

"As Trip walked down the formal stairs that evening and into the dining room for the evening meal, he felt good about bringing the homeless children into their home. It was, however, under Clara Ruth's staunch protest. 'You don't know what you're bringing into my house. They could have lice or bedbugs or something. I hope you didn't bathe them in our tub. My saints alive, where is your head, I declare, not a thought to others in this house!' she said, scolding LuDell as she held her lace hankie to her nose.

"LuDell acted as if she, too, was put out by the two new guests in the house, in a vain attempt to appease the lady she served. In actuality, though, she enjoyed the addition and reveled in the thought of having to change baby diapers in the Sullivan mansion again.

"LuDell was a peach of a lady and both Trip and Ruth loved her with all of her rough and uncouth ways. She loved them, too, and thought of both of them as her own children. She was one of the first African slaves brought to live on the farm and at the insistence of the Sullivan patriarch, had subsequently been made an indentured servant for 15 years. That period had long since passed, but LuDell stayed even after her freedom was officially granted. In her dialect she pragmatically said, "Wheres I gwine go? Naomi is don gwine north - I hain't got no body. Y'alls his mys family. I'z stay 'til y'alls trow mees hout!" And she did stay until she died. A very wise old

304

woman, she often said, 'A baby diap'r his ha telln' thang - hit tells youz wen dey sick, wen dey well and wen dey needs som'tang! Alls youz has to do is ust' lookz.' She took the care and wellbeing of all babies in the Sullivan house as her responsibility and she bore it with a smile - but not so the lady of the house could see.

"There seemed to be a little happiness returning to the Sullivan mansion. Though Clara Ruth moped around complaining all the time, no one paid her much mind. The other folks in the house seemed to enjoy their time together and soon formed a cohesive family unit who supported each other, gladly giving assistance without regard to the bloodlines in the hybrid family.

"Over the next few years, Ruth and Lucinda formed a sister-like relationship and moved about the house giggling and laughing as the younger was introduced to a new world without starvation and pressure. Coming in from the fields in which he now worked side by side with his hired help, Trip always found his clothes cleaned and pressed and his room in perfect order. His supper was always waiting for him, warm, on the huge stone table in the kitchen. His guilt made him remark once, 'It's almost like having a genie. I just wish and there it is!' He just smiled and enjoyed the service until one day he caught his clandestine personal servant in his bedroom. Coming home early and unannounced one day, he quickly opened the door to his room and found Lucinda standing on the threshold staring at him. Now a budding young woman, she looked nothing like the little pauper Trip had found digging her brother's grave. Nutritious food, decent clothes and freedom from the stress of taking care of her family had given the young girl the opportunity to blossom into a beautiful woman. The years had turned the caterpillar into a beautiful 16-year-old butterfly named Lucinda Mae Plunkett and Trip had noticed the metamorphosis.

"After cleaning his room and arranging his things just as he liked them, she had opened the door to come face to face with the man of her dreams. She had the biggest crush on Trip Sullivan. Stepping back to let her exit the room, Trip said, 'What were you doing in my room?' "She smiled and said, 'I was putting clean sheets on and straightening your bed. I can draw you a bath and fetch some hot water if you need it.'

"Trip smiled and answered, 'You don't have to do all of this for me. You don't owe me anything.'

"Coyly, she answered back, 'I know that, but I want to do it.'

"Puzzled, Trip questioned her. 'Why?'

"Walking away, she said over her shoulder, 'Because I want to be your wife one day.' Trip stood frozen, stunned by such an audacious answer to his question. Laughing to himself, he thought, *Why, I'm old enough to be her father.*"

***

Little Ruth continued to stare out the window as the helicopter's rotors slowed to a stop. Once the aircraft was silent, she began shouting all of the big words her grandfather had taught her. "Preposterous, gargantuan, magnificent, astronomical, incomprehensible." With those words, Ruth ended the recording session Sully and Salley were desperately trying to continue through the commotion of Salley's husband's arrival. Aggravated, Salley stopped the recorder and kissed her father on the forehead. She then joined Ruth at the tall window to see what was happening.

Riding in a golf cart from his helicopter to the house, Jon, Jr, looked and acted as if he was a king returning to his castle. The house staff was scurrying about, unloading his luggage and trying to please him with their every move. Several of the men of the house staff were running along behind the golf cart, while others blocked the street, so the entourage could cross unimpeded. Watching the hullabaloo from the window, Salley knew her estranged husband's unannounced visit was not likely to be pleasant. Entering the house, the absentee husband walked straight to the sun room and quickly took charge. Without speaking to his wife or greeting anyone, he demanded, "Bring me my son! I want to see him. I want to see what the next owner of Chesterfield International looks like! Where is he?"

Salley, now with her back to the window, stared at her husband with a scowl on her face. She spat her words at him. "You could have called to tell us you were coming!"

"This is my house! I'll come and go as I please and YOU certainly won't tell me when, where or how I will arrive!"

Walking over to the bassinette, Salley picked up their son and begrudgingly walked to her husband. As she got close to the baby's daddy, Jon, Jr. snatched the boy from her arms and swung him up into the air. Immediately, baby Wesley began to scream and cry as if someone had pinched him.

Salley tried to offer the rookie father some advice. "Be gentle, Jon, he's just a little fellow and he's not ready for rough housing."

"Shut up, woman! You're the last person I need giving me advice. He's a Chesterfield and is tough as nails - aren't you, buddy?" The screaming continued and Salley asked her husband to give the baby back to her. He refused and continued to swing him around like a pillow. Salley was now, getting a little perturbed and this time she told him in no uncertain terms to stop scaring Little Wesley and give him back to her. Again, he refused and suddenly Sully's grandson let go of the granddaddy of all upchucks. The little fellow spewed a stream of vomited baby milk over his daddy's face and upper torso. Salley tried to stifle her smile, but her amusement shined through like the sun coming from behind a cloud. That didn't help the situation, whatsoever.

"Damn it! Just damn it, that little piss ant puked all over me! Get me something to get this crap off of me." Reaching for one of Sully's towels, Salley noticed the grin across Sully's face and it was all she could do to keep from laughing out loud.

"What in the hell are you feeding that little animal? It smells like he ate something dead!"

Finally getting Little Wesley back in her arms, Salley took great pleasure in saying, "Relax, Big Daddy, it's just breast milk. It won't hurt you!"

Now this did cause him to flip his lid. "Holy crap! I'm going to shower and get this crap off of me! You keep that little puker away from me from now on!" With that statement, he dashed up to his old room to clean up.

Wiping Wesley's mouth, Salley realized he was clean as a whistle and said, "Well, little fellow, you didn't get a bit on you, but you sure did get your daddy good!"

That was all it took - Wesley's granddaddy, Sully, roared with laughter and proclaimed, "That little man will be remembered prominently in my will! I couldn't have orchestrated that series of events any better if I had planned it myself. That's my boy, Wesley!"

Sully's laughter continued as little Ruth bellowed out, "Stupendous! Stupendous, Papa!"

When he came back downstairs, Jon, Jr. had on one of his father's polo jerseys with a number on it. The jersey was not tucked into his pants and it came down to his mid-thigh. Under the game shirt, he was wearing khaki riding pants with dress socks and his $500 Gucci loafers. He looked like a fool. "Well, that's enough of your crap for me! I'm out of here! I shouldn't have ever come here, anyway, but my mother was having a fit for me to come see that boy. By the way, she wants you to contact her. She's in Hawaii and wants to see the babies. I hope they puke on her, too!"

With those kind words, Wesley's father walked out the door and headed back to the helicopter. Soon, the noisy aircraft rose from the polo field and disappeared into the horizon.

Chapter 12

Salley wondered why Kellah Chesterfield would want
to talk with her. The word about town was that her lawyers had
made sure she got half of her husband's wealth. Salley thought
she would have been glad to never see or speak to the Jon
Chesterfields again. After Salley fed Little Wesley and put him
back down in his bassinet, she called Kellah and had a long
conversation.

Kellah Chesterfield arrived at the Chesterfield mansion
in a black town car driven by a tall, good looking young man.
He opened all doors for her, carried her bags and was always
seen walking just a few steps behind her. Salley was standing
on the front stoop waiting as Kellah Chesterfield arrived. She
had Little Wesley beside her in a stroller and was holding
Ruth's hand. Kellah immediately hugged Salley as she reached
the top of the landing to the front entrance. With both hands on
Salley's shoulders, she admired her from arms distance and told
her motherhood certainly agreed with her. She proclaimed
Salley to be more beautiful than ever. Salley blushed with
modesty, for such compliments were few in her day to day life.
With the responsibility of caring for two kids and her father,
she did not have time to form a circle of friends or have anyone
with whom she could bond.

Within just a few minutes of her arrival, it became
crystal clear why Kellah, as she insisted Salley call her, had
made the long journey to Aiken, South Carolina. It was evident
that the ex-Mrs. Jon Chesterfield, Sr. was determined to have
grandchildren in her world. She played with them in the sun
room while she sent Salley out to have a pedicure and
manicure. She also arranged for Salley to have a facial and her
hair styled. It was the first time in years Salley had taken any
time for herself and she enjoyed every minute of the
pampering. Kellah admiringly said, "You look like a million
bucks - I'd kill to have your body and face, dear. You are
simply beautiful."

While Salley was away, Kellah sat in the chair next to
Sully with Little Wesley in her arms. She had a long
conversation with Sully and they talked about everything. She

asked Sully to tell her the truth about the relationship between her son and his daughter. He was silent at first, but after a bit, he opened up and gave her a complete account of the despicable things her son did to his daughter. He told Kellah if he had been able to get out of the contraption that imprisoned him, he would have, without hesitation, killed her son. Holding her hand to her mouth, tears formed in her eyes, but she held back her emotions. As she held Little Wesley on her lap, she said, "My God, what poor Salley has had to endure." There was a pause in the conversation and only the laughter and squeals of the children were heard. In a quiet voice, Kellah looked at the floor and said, "I wouldn't have blamed you a bit if you had put a bullet through his heart. In fact, if I had been here, I may have done it for you! He's his father's son and though I tried to raise him in a kind and loving manner, his father's evil has taken him over. He's a mother's worst nightmare!"

Sully could see she was upset and he tried to comfort her by saying, "But out of any evil, good can come. Little Wesley has brought me much joy and Salley is thrilled he is in her life. We are thankful he is with us and Salley is determined he not grow up to be like his father. We both love him very much."

Kellah regained her usual formal composure and told Sully, "You, Salley and the kids need to come to Hawaii and live with me a while. I can make all of the arrangements and we can put you, your machine and the family on a plane to paradise in a matter of days.

Sully smiled and softly said, "No, I'm not strong enough for the trip. I have struggled to stay alive this long and I won't risk losing one day of being with my family, even for a trip to paradise. You are very gracious, but it's just not in the cards for me. I hope Salley will visit you one day. She would love it out there."

When Salley returned, Kellah hugged her like she was seeing her for the first time. Looking at Sully, Salley knew immediately he had told her the whole sordid affair. Thinking for a minute she said, "I take it Wesley's father will not be the topic of any of our conversations."

Almost immediately and quite out of character for Kellah, she boldly announced, "HELL NO!" Salley understood everyone's position on Jon Chesterfield, Jr. and that subject was closed.

Kellah stayed in Aiken for two weeks and it was the most wonderful time Salley had had in years. Finally, she could lay out by the pool, go for long rides on Spot and simply lie down in the middle of the day and take a nap. She never realized how much relief a grandparent could provide. Both Kellah and her grandchildren absolutely loved their time together. Thinking to herself, Salley mused, *So that's how normal mothers cope with the stress of home and family. They call in the grandparents!* The only drawback she saw to grandparents was the toy explosion in the house. It was becoming impossible to even walk without having to knock toys out of the way. Kellah saw the joy on both Ruth and Wesley's faces when the delivery man brought toys. She arranged for a huge box full of every toy imaginable to be delivered each morning just after breakfast. Salley just smiled and shook her head. She knew if Sully could, he would do the same thing.

Everyone was sad when Mimi, Ruth's new name for her grandmother, went back to her island in paradise. Ruth begged her not to go and when Wesley heard 'bye-bye' from Mimi, he reached out for her to take him with her. It took a week for the house to return to normal. One day not long after Mimi left, Salley told Ruth it was time for her nap. Ruth immediately pulled her little reading chair up to Sully's machine and climbed up to look Sully in the eye. She stomped her foot and demanded, "Get Mimi!" She loved her Papa very much and even though she knew him as only a head and a machine, he was her go-to guy if Mama wasn't coming through. Holding Wesley on her hip with one arm and Ruth's hand with the other arm, Salley walked them to their rooms while promising both of them she would take them to see Mimi before too long. Sully was smiling when she returned to sit next to him. He realized 'before too long' meant 'after he died' and he was comfortable with that thought. He knew Kellah would be the most wonderful grandparent the kids could have.

With the kids down for a nap, Salley started the recorder and settled back in her chair to listen to Sully's description of the lives of her ancestors. She had become quite engrossed in his epic story. As always, he began exactly where he left off.

***

"The body of Brevet Colonel James Anthony Sullivan, Jr was buried in a Confederate cemetery south of Manassas, Virginia with full military rights by an Honor Guard of Hampton's Legion. The family was informed of his burial site and had received the Confederate Battle Flag used during his funeral. Clara Ruth, however, was heartbroken, for she wanted her beloved husband to be buried beside his father in the Salleys Kitchen church cemetery. Clara Ruth had begged Trip to make the necessary arrangements to bring his father's remains home. But Trip had refused each time she asked, saying the money could be better used to support the farm. Besides his frugality, Trip was not comfortable burying his father in the family plot. Trip's grandfather, the first James Anthony Sullivan, and founding father of the community, hated slavery and fought to keep it out of his community during his entire life. But his son, James Anthony Sullivan, Jr., Trip's father, had ignored the senior Sullivan's wishes and passively allowed his wife, Clara Ruth, to bring slaves onto the family farm. Trip's father had ignored the founding patriarch's warnings and allowed the curse of chattel slavery to destroy the family farm and the community.

"Avoiding the conversation of bringing his father's remains to Salleys Kitchen on many occasions, Trip finally told his mother to stop badgering him. He told her he wanted some time to think about it and if she kept pushing him, he would just say 'no' as his final answer.

"The resentment and hatred of the Sullivan family continued even though Trip and Pastor Poole offered only kindness and help to the people of Salleys Kitchen. Trip's neighbors continued to manufacture lies about the Sullivan family and disseminate them throughout the community. On

312

one occasion, Trip was confronted at the new store that had been opened by one of the scalawags with some ill-gotten money. As Trip looked at the high prices on the items in the new store, a loud-mouth man who had been a member of the Home Guard during the war, confronted Trip. 'Say, you sleeping with that white trash gal you took in? You figure on marrying her or are you just going to keep milking that cow through the fence?'

"Trip turned around and was facing three men known to be disreputable characters. During the war, they were part of a group of men who were paid a bounty for each able-bodied man they could strong-arm and force to join the Confederate Amy. It was said they had dragged a preacher in a nearby community out of his house one night, locked him in a stable and guarded him until the Conscription Officer came to pay them. The unlucky parson soon became cannon fodder on the front lines. Now, after the war, these men were part of the white vigilante groups who controlled the community with their clandestine fear tactics. While Union troops occupied the South, these shady men were considered outlaws by the U.S. Army.
Wearing masks to cover their faces, they attacked those who offered help to the freed Negros under the cover of darkness. They had never messed with Trip, so he just smiled and ignored them. He acted as if he didn't hear them, but their words registered a lingering concern in his mind. He knew they were repeating the community gossip.

"During the war, the Home Guard was made up mostly of men trying to avoid fighting on the battlefields. They were despicable men whom most people tried to avoid and never trusted. Now that the war was over, they had become part of the growing groups of vigilantes who wore sheets and attacked people, mostly Blacks, in the protected shadows of the night. The community's citizens would say nothing ill of this group of thugs, for fear of having their wrath focused on them. Many people looked the other way and tried to avoid knowledge of the dastardly acts perpetrated by these men. The fear they spread across the community only allowed them to grow in power and dominate the frightened citizens of Salleys Kitchen.

"When the Union occupation ended and the Yankee soldiers left, there was no one to hold the hoodlums in check. There was no one to protect the newest citizens of the United States, the newly freed slaves in the South. The night riding louts controlled every aspect of life in the community, especially the voting polls. By seizing control of the election of the state representatives, the white men could write laws that restricted the Black people. With Southern white men running the government, they implemented laws that stripped the Black community of their basic rights as citizens of the United States of America. A white supremist society was now firmly in control and they would not relinquish their grip on society for a century. With despicable and at times murderous acts, they put fear in the minds of the freed Negroes along with any white person who might offer them aid. The icon of this dastardly group of men was a burning cross, which they placed as a warning, in the yards of anyone who didn't yield to their will. Cold-blooded, they ruled by fear, intimidation and lynching. There were many vigilante groups, but the Ku Klux Klan rose to the pinnacle power and included most every white man in the community. Their leadership consisted of white thugs and the fear they generated allowed them to exert an evil supremacy over most of the community. They, however, had found their terrorizing tactics weren't effective with Trip Sullivan. Their illegal methods only intensified Trip's ill feelings toward what he considered to be the trash of the community. He spread the word across Salleys Kitchen reminding everyone that he was a former soldier trained in close order fighting with a bayonet and had won a medal for long distance shooting. He made it plain that he would shoot anyone who came on or about his farm trying to scare or intimidate the people who worked for him.

"To make matters worse, the Ku Klux Klan was bolstered by racist politicians seeking public office. They spouted an ideology of bigotry, prejudice and fear aimed at keeping the poor, ignorant white citizens riled up against the Black community.

"On Sunday morning, Trip found a third burned cross stabbed into the sandy soil in front of the cobblestone columns near the main road. The Ku Klux Klan shenanigans always occurred on Saturday night and Trip decided it was time to find out who was behind the scare tactics. Pulling the cross up, he tossed it in the back of his wagon and drove straight to the house of their leader, the Grand Dragon of the Ku Klux Klan in Salleys Kitchen.

"Everyone knew Shorty Bates was their leader, for even hiding under a white sheet and pointed hood, he was the shortest person in the gang. Pulling the reins of the mules, Trip stopped in front of Shorty's house. Reaching behind the seat, he grabbed the black, charred piece of wood that had been wrapped in a burlap bag and soaked in coal oil. Tossing it end over end, high into the air, it landed with a loud thump in front of Shorty's house. Climbing off of the wagon, he walked into the Grand Dragon's yard and stuck the burned cross in the soft sand, upside down.

"Opening the front door, Shorty's wife yelled, 'What do you mean putting your trash in my yard?'

"Trip answered, 'Because your husband put it in my yard! Why the hell is he hiding behind your skirt tail? Is he afraid to come out and face me man to man and tell me what he thinks?'

"She stepped back inside the house and the little man stuck his head out the door. 'I ain't got no problem telling you how it is, Trip Sullivan! You living with your mama and sister in that big house and shacked up with that young white trash gal - it ain't right. You payin' your niggers too much money and making the other planters pay more. We know your mama don't go along with this here stupidity. You damn lucky we ain't burned your big pretty house down!'

"Trip smiled and returned as good as he got. 'Now Shorty, I've known you all my life and I know you ain't stupid, in fact you're pretty good at inciting a riot, but you're going to stop all these cross burnings in front of my house or I'm going to bring all hell to bear on YOU! You hear me?'

"The patronizing little man said, 'I hear you, Trip, but you wouldn't talk like that if'n the Klan come to visit you one night.'

"'That might be Shorty, but YOU would be the first coward hiding under a white sheet I'd come after. No one else - just you - and you'd pay in a big way. I've had my life threatened by much stronger, smarter and braver men than you and lived through it. Now stop this trash before you make me do something I've been desperately trying to avoid! I'll make everything I'm doing right!'"

***

Salley stopped the recorder after noticing Sully was starting to wheeze a little bit. She asked him if he felt congested and said she wanted to call the doctor to check him. In a whispered, raspy voice he said, "Not now, sweetheart - let's go a little longer with the recording. I'm nearing the end and when I finish I will rest." Against her better judgement, she started the recorder again and put the microphone closer to Sully's mouth.

***

"That night, James Anthony Sullivan, III sat his mother down in the meeting room for a long talk. Starting the conversation by asking if she still wanted her husband's remains brought home to Salleys Kitchen, Trip indicated he was ready to strike a deal with his mother. Quickly she told him, 'Yes, I would do anything to have him home.' At that point, her son told her she would have to agree to a few things she might not like. 'I'll do whatever you want!' she said. 'There's nothing I wouldn't do to have my Lil' Sully home at last.' With that pronouncement, Trip began listing the prerequisites for his arranging to have his father's remains brought home to Salleys Kitchen.

"'First, Mother, you will have to agree to transfer complete and total ownership of the Sullivan farm to Ruth and me. We will provide you with a comfortable home and you may live in the lifestyle to which you have grown accustomed for the rest of your life. But, you will not be allowed to interfere or try to influence any decisions about the farm that

Ruth and I make together.' Trip paused for a few moments and watched her reaction before continuing.

"'Second, Mother, you will reveal to us every source of money you have hidden away and it will be added to the general farm account to be used at Ruth's and my discretion.' Both brother and sister knew of the existence of a hidden bank account, for each time money was desperately needed, it would mysteriously appear. Trip and Ruth knew she had access to a large sum of money and had hidden it, even from her husband. Back during Clara Ruth's father's heyday, there were not many banks and those few that existed were, for the most part, located in port cities. This was because the availability of liquid currency was crucial for the shipping industry. In the early 1800s, British banks had grown rich from charging fees and interest to those who borrowed money to finance their long voyages. Financing the Transatlantic Slave Trade had made fortunes for many banks in England. Clara Ruth's father was very involved in this trade for most of his career on the seas and had made many contacts in the banks of Bristol and Liverpool. The old Captain used the Charleston Bank as well as the English banks to finance his voyages and had large sums of money in every financial institution with which he dealt. Though she had used a great deal of money to build her fine home, Clara Ruth left quite a bit of money in the Charleston Bank. Those funds were wiped out during the War. However, unknown to anyone except her lawyer, she still had access to a significant amount of money in her father's foreign accounts. Knowing that if Trip knew of its existence he would demand it be used to help the community, she never disclosed its location. If she agreed to Trip's terms, her hidden accounts would now be exposed, for putting all of her money into the general farm account was part of his terms.

"'Third, Mother, you will relinquish complete control over the process of having our father's remains reinterred to me and Ruth, including the memorial service, the tombstone and its wording. Again, you will not try to sway our decisions in any way.' Trip knew his mother would make a showy production of his father's funeral. He also knew she would put an even larger and more ostentatious tombstone beside the tombstone she had placed on Lil' Sully's father's grave. Knowing the feeling of the community, Trip knew this would only further infuriate the people of Salleys Kitchen. He was not going to allow her to waste that much money on such a divisive thing.

"'Fourth, and final, Mother, you will donate your books to establish a community library here in Salleys Kitchen to be used by all citizens, white and Black, in their educational pursuits. Furthermore, you will use part of your money to fund the building of a public house to hold and display the book collection. The library you build will also be used for community meetings and events.'

"Stunned by such outrageous demands, Clara Ruth began crying and said, 'My father gave me those books and you read them as a boy. Why would you want me to throw them away?' She cried out loudly and continued to snub. 'You can't take my father's money away from me and you can't make me give up this farm. I made this farm and I'll not let it go.' Trip sat silently and waited for her to speak again. Finally, she threw a last salvo at her son. 'And I will have an appropriately large funeral service for your father. He deserves that honor for fighting to preserve our way of life; I will also purchase as large a monument as I think is needed to mark his memory and service to this community.'

"As she stood to leave, Trip spoke to his mother one last time. She turned to face him with her lace handkerchief at her mouth. In an unyielding voice, Trip looked straight into his mother's eyes and said, 'Mother, the horror, the death and the destruction to which this community has been subjected was caused in large part by you and my father. You knew the man who actually carved this community out of a sand hill pine forest detested slavery and you knew your husband did not want it, yet you still brought slaves to this community and forced them to work on your land. Your greed and lust for money overwhelmed the love my father had for you and the love he had for this community. You pushed the deplorable practice of chattel slavery on my father's back. That act had devastating repercussions for everyone living here and caused them tremendous pain and suffering. Now, the remaining members of the Sullivan family will have to pick up the pieces of my grandfather's beloved community and try to put them back together.'

"Pausing for a moment, Trip continued to stare into his mother's eyes. He then said, 'I believe, Mother, from the depths of my heart, I was spared from certain death on many occasions because it is meant for me to make restitution for the part my family played in bringing such unspeakable horrors upon the people of Salleys Kitchen. This is my ancestral home and I will not leave this world without offering my most earnest effort to amend for the torment you and my father brought to this land. Mother, there will be no further discussion of this matter. Either you accept my wishes now or the subject will be closed permanently. If you refuse my offer, the remains of James Anthony Sullivan, Jr. will never be buried beside his father and they will be left in Virginia.' Trip's eyes stayed locked on his mother's face for a few moments before she turned and abruptly left the meeting room in tears. She hurried into her bedroom, slamming the door.

***

Salley could hear Sully's wheezing getting worse and she stopped the recorder again and asked Sully if he was okay. He whispered, "Yes, it imperative that I continue." After Sully took a few sips of water, Salley wiped her father's mouth and again asked if he was sure he needed to continue with his narration. In his raspy and failing voice, he said, "Absolutely!"

Looking into her father's eyes, Salley thought of the nights her father spent on the couch in his office. As she pictured the mass of papers scattered about, she remembered the bare shelves that covered all of the walls outside his office. Sully's story was making complete sense to her, now. Looking at her father, Salley asked if Trip's ultimatum to his mother was the reason the bookshelves in the Sullivan mansion were empty to this day. He said, "Yes, sweetheart, that's just one of the many facets of the Sullivan mansion that illustrate Trip Sullivan's legacy'. Salley realized Sully's voice was even weaker. She tried again to get him to stop, but to no avail. He was adamant about not ending the recording session, so Salley put the microphone even closer to his mouth and started the recorder again.

***

"There were no more crosses burned in front of the Sullivan mansion. The next Sunday, Trip and Lucinda stood in front of the preacher, just after he finished his sermon. In front of most everyone in the community, they were married. Equally shocking, the newlyweds turned to face the congregation and Ruth Sullivan stood to make an announcement. 'There will be a reception at the Sullivan home this afternoon at three o'clock for everyone to meet the newlyweds and help them celebrate their new beginning in the Sullivan family and our community!'

"As the gossip mongers sat with their mouths gaped, Lucinda walked arm in arm with Trip out to the wagon. Wearing a new white dress, purchased hurriedly in Aiken the day before, Lucinda surprised her new husband by giving him a passionate kiss just before he swung her up onto the wagon seat. Most of the womenfolk standing on the porch of the church gasped at such an open display of an intimate moment. The new couple was grinning from ear to ear as Trip grabbed the reins of the wagon. Whipping the reins across the horses' backs, they came to life, pulling the wedding party out of the churchyard and onto the road home.

"The only folks to attend the reception were the preacher and his wife, along with many Negro friends from the community. There was dancing and singing and clapping and shouting for the joyous occasion, but Clara Ruth stayed in her room and refused to associate with the 'darkies'. That was her church name for Negroes, since Trip forbade her to say 'nigger' in his presence. An embittered woman, she found herself a minority on the Sullivan farm. In vain, she had tried desperately, through the back channels, to change the status quo. She had instigated the burning crosses, thinking Trip would be forced to make Lucinda leave the mansion. But by trying to force what she considered 'white trash' out of her house, the stern old woman had isolated herself from the rest of the family and now the unwanted house guest was her new daughter-in-law.

"Both Trip and Lou, his pet name for his bride, celebrated late into the night and both fell asleep alone. She surrendered to the 'sandman' in the early hours on the fainting couch near Trip's office as she watched him work on the farm's record books. He fastidiously recorded every receipt and charge to the very penny. In his military training, discipline was forced upon him, but now it seemed second nature. He did not like to go to bed without balancing the books, for one was not promised tomorrow and he was not about to let his laziness become a burden to his sister, Ruth. She was the new co-owner of the Sullivan farm. Making sure she was aware of every move he made concerning the farm, Trip also wanted Ruth to know the reasons for his decisions. She often told him, 'Trip, you are my brother and I love you and I may own half of this farm on paper, but I will never understand why you insisted on having me as your partner. As far as I'm concerned, you alone will always be in charge of everything that happens on this sandy land.' Later in life, Grandma Lou would swear that Trip had a record of every penny spent during his time as caretaker of the farm.

"But for all his penny-pinching, the farm did not produce the abundant life style it had in the past. Trip, however, did not hoard his mother's money. A lot of the money was used to fund several black farmers to whom the white controlled banks refused to lend money. He helped them start farming and growing cotton and watched over them for the rest of his life. He kept the unscrupulous scalawags away from them and helped them understand and become part of the cotton economy. The rest of his mother's money was invested in three different agricultural pursuits on the Sullivan farm: producing cotton, raising cattle and growing wheat and corn to be milled into flour. Trip purposefully created a large payroll and it took creative farming to make the land produce an adequate living for all. His unique method of farming did not follow the norm. He planted the large flat area of the farm, known as 'The Griddle', with wheat. This grain crop always seemed to do well in the sandy loam soil of the region and had many uses. While the crop was young, still short and tender green, he periodically grazed the cattle to supplement their diet during the winter calving season. Never overgrazing the immature young wheat, he would stop grazing the crop as the pasture grass came out in early spring. This allowed the young wheat stalks to mature to a golden crop, with seed heads waving in the summer's gentle wind. In early summer or as soon as the grain matured, he and his help cut the wheat and shocked it for threshing later. Immediately after harvesting the wheat, he proceeded at break-neck speed to turn the wheat stubble under and harrow the sandy soil flat, readying it for the cash crop, King Cotton. During lay-by time when all the cotton had to do was grow, a traveling thresher would be hired and the big, noisy machine would separate the wheat from the chaff while engulfed in a cloud of dust. The grain was then drained from its huge hopper, bagged and stored in the warehouse. Over the winter some would be milled for flour, some would be sold and some used for cattle feed. The corn was pulled off by the ear and stored in a corncrib until it was needed.

"By rotating the fields, Trip always had a crop growing, cows grazing and corn or wheat to mill, thereby keeping the workers busy and a positive cash flow for the farm. This method of triple cropping required precise timing and the help of Mother Nature, who didn't always cooperate. During years of drought or flood, he depended on the cattle. Trip weaned the calves each spring. He then sold the heifer calves to other farmers who wanted to start herds of their own. Only the top one or two of the best male calves were kept as bulls for breeding and the rest of the male calves were slaughtered for meat to eat and to be sold to others. Another supply of income came from milling a large portion of the wheat harvested into flour and the corn into cornmeal. This was accomplished by using a new energy source to power the mill.

"Having realized it was impracticable and much too expensive to rebuild the dam of the millpond, Trip turned the old pond into a productive field. This meant finding a new way to power the mill. As he was talking with the owner of the steam powered thresher who visited the farm annually, Trip learned of a thresher operated by a new-fangled power source, a Brayton's Ready Motor. The owner of the traveling thresher went on to tell Trip that the owner of the cutting-edge engine had died and his son was not planning to use it. Instead, the son was getting in the horse-trading business and his father's land would soon be a horse farm. Trip quickly corresponded with the young man who owned the engine and made a lowball offer. The owner of the engine considered it a hunk of junk, but wanted to make enough money from its sale to buy a good stallion. This put Trip Sullivan between a rock and a hard place. He could easily trade his beloved stallion, Two Bears for the engine and save all the money he would have to spend to purchase the power source. But he and Two Bears were inseparable. His beautiful Appaloosa stallion had come into his life just before his arduous journey home after the war. Given to him by the son of the great chief Two Bears of the Nez Prez Indian Tribe, the horse held a large place in Trip's heart. They had traveled across much of the nation together on the long road home from the Dakota territory. How could he trade part of his heart for an engine?

"Trip spent a long night in Two Bears' stall and the two talked until dawn. The next morning, Trip packed his saddlebags, kissed Lou and Ruth and told them he was going to Virginia on business for the farm. He didn't say very much and they knew he was struggling with a hard decision. Ten days later the new power source arrived at the railroad station in Windsor, along with Trip. It was quickly put to work on the farm. The engine was used to power the sawmill and produce lumber. It ran a corn shelling machine that greatly reduced that time-consuming chore. But most of all, it took over the milling job that was so desperately needed in the community of Salleys Kitchen. In the end, Trip could not turn down an opportunity to help feed and bolster the people of Salleys Kitchen. His adored Two Bears was sacrificed for the needs of his beloved community. My Grandma Lou told me, just before she died, that losing Two Bears was the hardest thing with which her husband ever had to cope. He refused to go near the barn for a long time after his return from Virginia and he kept his old army saddle and bridle under the bed until he died.

"The new engine was a kerosene burning, cantankerous, belching, hissing, green and yellow hunk of steel with a flywheel on the side. It was the power source for not only the grain mill and the sawmill, but it was used to cut firewood and to pump water out of the well. Later, it powered a used thresher Trip agonized over, but finally bought. The modern and laborsaving device was the main topic of conversation among the local farmers of the community. Its unique sound could be heard across Salleys Kitchen when it was in operation. As it popped and fired its two cylinders, the sound of the contraption seemed to be a beckoning call to the area farmers. Rumors of how the state-of-the-art machine operated flew through the community, with all wanting to see the unique source of power in action. The flywheel could be turned by hand to start up the mass of metal. After it 'kicked over' and began percolating on its own, the 6-inch flywheel on the opposite side could be engaged to power the machinery. Using a long, wide belt, the engine transferred its power from the flywheel on the motor to the mill or saw or thresher. While running, the engine would spit and knock in quite a peculiar manner and had to be tinkered with often. As the crowd watched it run, they stood with their arms across their chests.

"Getting the grain mill running again was only one of many sacrifices Trip Sullivan made for the people of his community, but they never recognized the good of his actions and he never said much about it. Ruth, Lou and LuDell, however, knew the things he had done and they loved him for his goodness. The sound of the engine running could be heard for miles along the South Edisto River and Grandma Lou always said that sound was the sound of her husband's goodness being spread across the community. That unique sound always signaled to the community that flour was being produced at the Sullivan place and hot buttered biscuits would be on their table soon.

"On cold mornings, though, Trip often said it would have been easier to turn the damn mill by hand than to try and coax that green and yellow devil into running. He claimed it was a female engine - only running when IT wanted to run, but not always when HE wanted it to run.

"Slowly, Trip began to rebuild his family's reputation in the community. The influx of Clara Ruth's hidden money allowed the farm to increase its payroll and invest in new equipment. Any decision to purchase equipment, however, always put a huge amount of pressure and worry upon Trip's shoulders. For months, he would anxiously crunch the numbers as he tried to decide how to use the farm's meager funds. The Sullivan farm was the largest employer in Salleys Kitchen and he felt any purchases the farm made had to eventually help the whole community. With a deep sense of civic duty, Trip always offered to lend any of the equipment to the other farmers of the community. Very few accepted his offer, as the majority of independent farmers did not want to be associated with the Sullivans in any way. Those who did take up Trip's offer never wanted the other farmers to know they had used his equipment. That foolish resentment became ingrained in many of the old timers in the community and gradually it became part of a tradition in Salleys Kitchen.

"One of the most disappointing of Trip's efforts to build goodwill in community was the public library. Mrs. Poole, the preacher's wife, was chosen as the librarian and she dutifully kept the new book depository open and available to anyone who chose to make use of the many volumes it held. As the local schoolmarm, she promoted reading and would teach anyone, white or Black, the skills of reading and writing. Many children of freedmen learned to read at the hands of Mrs. Poole and some few went on to further their education. Staying true to their Christian beliefs and principles throughout the war and reconstruction, the Poole's espoused true Christianity. Because they stuck to their principles, they were always looked upon with disdain by most of the people of the community.

***

When Salley reached to turn off the tape recorder, Sully asked her to leave it running. As she leaned back in her chair, she listened as her father offered his commentary about the churches of the South and their affinity to people of color.

"In telling my family's story, I wanted to explain the reasons for the racial divide and vitriol that had engulfed Salleys Kitchen for more than a century. But I also wanted to explain why the everyday working farmers, who had nothing to gain from slavery, had joined the rich slave-owning planters in their fight to preserve chattel slavery. The small poor farmers did not own slaves and had never benefited from slavery. So why would they join in a fight to the death to help the rich farmers who had always looked down their noses at the small poor farmers?

I have never been one to attend church or become involved in an organized religion because I dislike the proselytizing and holier-than-thou ways of the dominant religion of the south. My distain for religious people stems from studying the actions that so-called Christian leaders took prior to the Civil War. Further, my dislike for churches has been reinforced by the efforts of so-called Christians to deny basic human rights to Black citizens of the Civil Rights Movement. It seems this attitude of hatred towards people of color stems from a long history of arrogant white supremacy in the United States of America. It also appears directly opposed to the teaching of Jesus Christ.

Just after the English colonies gained a footing in the New World, a 'religious awakening' movement began to sweep across the land. It waned somewhat during both the French and Indian War and The Revolutionary War. But as the colonies gained their independence and formed a new nation, that 'religious awakening' movement returned with a renewed vigor and again swept across the land. As the new nation entered the 1800s, this religious fervor began to capture the minds and hearts of the mostly uneducated, new Americans. Reaching a crescendo during the run up to the Civil War, this movement gave the church of the South a prominent role in the lives of the backcountry people. Most small farmers and their families did not get to town often, thus the church was their gathering place, their place of education and the place they learned about the matters of the world. Preachers were very influential leaders in most communities and as their influence grew, often did their arrogance. With a 10% tithe of income demanded at most churches, pastors courted and recruited the wealthy members of the community for their congregations. Most of the South Carolina's wealth before the war was created on the backs of slaves. Religious leaders sought to pad their coffers by catering to the wealthy planter class. The rich planters were slave owners and their continued wealth and success depended on keeping the institution of slavery. If the church wanted to keep these rich people in their churches and receive their 10% tithe, the church had to support slavery. This is why almost every member of the clergy in South Carolina espoused the belief that slavery was ordained by God. As false prophets, the country preachers 'cherry picked' scriptures from the Bible and used them to appease their wealthy members and sway the common men and women to accept their dastardly way of thinking. Railing from the pulpit against those who wanted to end chattel slavery, they accused the people of the North of being atheists for wanting to end the South's inhuman use of the Negro. In this time of so-called 'religious awakening', the preachers in the pulpits of the country churches were the main reason everyday farmers, who had never owned a slave, fought and gave their lives to continue the practice of human bondage.

Through their false doctrines and fabricated interpretations of the Holy Scriptures, they reinforced among the uneducated rural masses of whites, the need to protect the Southern way of life.

"Pastor Poole had come to the community of Salleys Kitchen as a young preacher during the elder years of James Anthony Sullivan, Sr. Pastor Poole was chosen and welcomed by the community's patriarch because he was one of the few preachers who believed slavery to be wrong. Preacher Poole and his wife, Ann, had grown to adulthood serving the people of Salleys Kitchen and had been tireless workers, alongside the community's founder, in building and strengthening the social ties of its citizens. In the later years, as war fever swept through the area, Reverend Poole was removed as pastor because of his anti-slavery beliefs, but he and his wife continued to live and work in the community to which he had been called. After the war, when there was no money to pay a preacher, he became the de facto church leader. His wife was a large part of the effort to rebuild Salleys Kitchen and though never formerly recognized, she was the pioneering educator in the region. Though underused and misunderstood, the library she championed did bring an air of respectability to the community. Many people in the surrounding areas began to think of Salleys Kitchen as an educated group of people. While the reputation was not always valid, it was a much-needed source of pride among the citizens of the community.

"Though forgotten through the years, the little house, filled with Clara Ruth's books, was the first public library established in the newly formed county. Ann Poole was an unsung hero with a heart of gold. Like the first Salley Sullivan, Ann Poole will be forgotten but the influence and impact that both of those women had on the community of Salleys Kitchen can never be measured.

"Along with Trip's struggles among the people of the community, he was also grappling within himself to figure out his new marriage. Foregoing his wedding night for an accounting session, he did not join his new wife in bed. Many nights, as Trip walked past Lou's room, he would pause at her door, as it was always wide open, and watch her sleep. He thought she was more beautiful than the pictures of Venus as she lay uncovered on her bed. It seemed she was always wearing a thin gown that outlined her nubile body. To Trip, she personified beauty and he longed for the feel of her arms embracing him and the sweet smell of her body. But he always felt perverted for lusting for her body. He was such an older man and to take sexual advantage of such a young girl somehow seemed wrong.

"Lou did not feel as Trip did. Knowing he would pass by her door on the way to his room, Lou often tried to poise in erotic ways to catch his attention and lure him to her bed. But her valiant attempts to attract him had never worked. As Trip passed her door and sulked to his bed, Lou's eyes would open to see him gone and tears would trickle down her cheeks.

"When Lucinda became part of the Sullivan home, she was a 12-year-old girl and not the least bit romantically drawn to Trip. Released from the stress of responsibility of caring for her siblings, she experienced, for the first time, the carefree days of childhood. Having never been allowed to run and play and be silly, she reveled in the freedom and took every opportunity to play and frolic in and around the mansion. Having bows in her hair and dolls to dress were exhilarating new experiences that became part of her life for the first time. Ruth was a woman of twenty-two when Lou arrived and soon became the older child trying to recapture some of her adolescence lost during her very adult Abolitionist efforts. With a unique bond, Trip's sister and Lou loved to laugh as they played hide and seek in the huge house, screaming and running to the chagrin of LuDell who often told Ruth she was too grown-up to act such a fool. But it didn't faze Ruth in the least, as breathlessly she spat back at the cook, 'Your words don't bother me, it's fun and I've never done it before! Think what you will of me. I don't care!' Both girls gradually changed as Ruth began to act her age and Lou started asking about boys. Though a decade separated them in age, they were as close as biscuits in a pan, held together by the strands of femininity, friendship and family, all interwoven and tied together with a Gordian knot of love.

"Until the day he died, Trip could not pin down his reasons for marrying 16-year-old Lucinda Mae Plunkett. It was an impulse decision, he first believed, to save her from the gossip and innuendo that had inundated the community. Gossip, however, had never influenced his decision-making process in the past and his marriage was certainly not his mother's desire. Finally, upon reflection, he made himself believe it was necessary for her protection. But even that never completely answered his question of why he had such a lingering attraction for this young girl. Her personality was great, she was very pretty, she was a wonderful helpmate and he enjoyed her being around. *Oh well*, he thought to himself, as she worked beside him pulling weeds away from the young cotton. He even enjoyed her smell and many times while in the cotton fields together, he would make up reasons to move closer to her and breathe in her scent. Suddenly, he realized he was thinking of her constantly, which caused the opposing sides of his conscience to argue. *It's been three years since I married her, why haven't I been her husband instead of her friend?* His pragmatic side forced the opposing answer. *She's just a girl and you're old enough to be her father. You're almost 20 years older than her.* As his argument with himself continued, his passionate side would urge him forward. *But she is so beautiful and she seems to want me!*

"Even those working in the fields with the couple could feel the magnetic attraction and see Trip's foolish resistance. As much as possible, the field help left the two alone in the waist high cotton. But again, Trip's conscience grappled with his thinking. His pragmatic side offered its reasoning. *She's still a teenager; why would she want an older man like me? I would feel like I was forcing myself on her.* His passionate side always replied in opposition. *Now, you are kidding yourself. She has wanted you since she started thinking about boys.* However, practicality would then win the round with a stinging thought. *The last time you gave your heart away ended in disaster. You know she'll want a man her own age one day. You do remember the last time you fell in love, don't you? Do you want that all over again?*

"So, he continued to battle with himself, bringing Lou to the point of total frustration. She may have been able to understand the first year because she was still acting like a silly little girl with Ruth. But in the last couple of years, she had become a woman. Ruth showed her how to dress and act like a mature lady. Lou had put away those silly, little girl ways so he would know she had matured into an adult and he still hadn't taken her fully as his wife. Now, as they approached their 3rd anniversary, her husband was still not sleeping in her bed and she was completely and totally bothered to the point of provocation. During the Christmas season, she gave extra diligence to being as attractive and desirable as possible and set a goal in her mind not to reach another anniversary without him sleeping in her bed.

"On Christmas Eve, as their third anniversary approached, the house was dressed with candles and soft glowing oil lamps. There was a smell of Christmas in the air from the fresh cedar tree decorating the huge foyer and cedar logs were being burned in all of the fireplaces. As she sat on the floral couch next to his office, Lou used every seductive move she could think of and had not even gotten him to glance away from that damn accounting ledger. Frustrated and fuming, she stomped up the main stairway, letting her feet send a loud message of vexation on each riser. Once she heard him climbing the stairs, she made sure the door to her room was open and began to set her seductive trap. Quickly flopping onto the bed, she pretended to be sleeping on her stomach. Pulling up her gown to the point of nearly showing her entire naked backside, she gave her most provocative display of passion. Fully realizing it was a move only a desperate woman would make, she had no scruples at this point, for she was fraught with desire.

"Trip walked slowly by her open door and glanced in as he passed. Though it was a delayed reaction, she did catch his attention with her voluptuous display. Trip had quickly passed by her door with only a fleeting glance in her room. But when he realized what he had witnessed, he stopped and backed up a step or two to view the erotic sight again. Lou's heartbeat soared and she could hardly contain herself as he walked softly over to the side of her bed and stood, staring down at her. She could feel his eyes as they traced her outline, taking full notice of the partial view of her exposed backside. Hearing his shirt rustle, she knew he was reaching to touch her and cold chills ran down her back. But instead of touching her, he lightly pulled her gown down to cover her self-exposed bottom. Afterwards, he turned and walked back into the hallway, then to his room.

"At this point, it is needless to say, Lou was ready to finally consummate their marriage. With nervous determination, she tip-toed, barefooted to the open door of her husband's room. Trip was standing with his back to the door as he removed all his clothes. Standing naked for a second or two, he turned slightly before he pulled his nightshirt over his head. With her heart beating out of her chest, Lou peeped in the door and plainly saw the undeniable evidence that her husband was as ready as she was to become intimate. (Lou and Ruth had talked and giggled about the male anatomy and the signals it could offer.) After staring out the window at the full moon, Trip turned and went sadly to his bed.

"As the glimmer of moonbeams lit up Trip's room, they mingled with the amber light dancing from the flames of the cedar fire. Climbing into bed, Trip tucked the covers under his chin and released the air from his lungs in a long sigh. A dazzling romantic glow had engulfed the room and as he closed his eyes, he could only think of Lou's naked behind. As he lay thinking, a sense of her presence opened his eyes to see her beautiful nude body standing near the window. The light from the moon gilded her body, making her silhouette glow. As his wife moved closer to his bed, the amber firelight danced across her body, immersing the room in a dream-like ambiance. Finally, the planets had aligned and the moon was right as she climbed under the covers and moved her shivering body next to his warmth. As she cuddled beside him, Trip saw his wife as his lover for the first time and he leaned closer to her face as she stared into his eyes. Ever so gently, he kissed her. Unable to hold her yearnings at bay any longer, she threw her arms around him, pulling him on top of her. As their lips met, she smothered him with a long, wet, passionate kiss. With her emotions reaching a fevered pitch, she had no time for him to remove his nightshirt. She ripped it open and pulled his body close to hers. Finally, she felt his chest on her breasts, a feeling for which she had longed for over two years. Tonight, her wait was over. With moonlight shining through the window and the low flames flickering from the fire, she would become his complete wife and he would become her complete husband.

"Afterward, she lay with her head on his chest listening to his rapid heartbeat. It had seemed an eternity waiting for the right moment, but neither could have received a greater Christmas gift on that perfect and unforgettable Christmas Eve. Exhausted and breathless, Lou now felt like a wife and Trip was elated that love had finally given him a second chance. Seldom would they ever sleep apart again, until death took him away.

"The attitude in the big house changed drastically as Lou and Trip began singing a new and happier tune. No one was a bit surprised when soon they heard a little one was on the way. They knew Lou would make a fantastic mother. Never sick, she kept up her chore-filled routine around the mansion until the last few days of her pregnancy. Harri, aka Harriet Louise Sullivan, was born in September and named after LuDell's mother, Louise, who was forcibly separated from her child and sold south by Clara Ruth. No one ever knew of the final destiny of LuDell's mother, but the unfeeling Clara Ruth mentioned her often as her second mother. Hearing of the new child's name, the matriarch gave a harrumph. The coal-black hand-servant cried and snubbed for most of the morning after first hearing of her mama's name being given to the first child. LuDell said it was the greatest honor she had had in her life. Still snubbing, she said, 'I's knowz I's don't deserves hit, but I's shos pre'she'ates y'alls is kindness in 'membering my mama.' Every member of the Sullivan family, except Clara Ruth, knew LuDell, as well as her mama, deserved the recognition most of all. Almost a year to the day, Abbi, aka Abigail Rutledge Sullivan, was born and LuDell had another set of diapers to change. Clara Ruth smiled from her favorite chair when she was told that Rutledge was her new granddaughter's middle name. With her legs and lap covered with a blanket, she sipped her tea and said, 'That's nice.' She declined to hold the new baby and said LuDell should hold her.

"The girls were so much alike, that most people thought they were twins. Harri and Abbi were inseparable through their teens until they were attracted to boys and the loving sisters became fierce competitors.

"Clara Ruth's sleeping quarters, as had been since the mansion was built, were a suite of rooms she and Lil' Sully shared on the first floor in the northeast corner of the house. She occupied that area from the moment she entered the new house until the day she died. As she emerged slowly from her secluded suite on that Christmas morning, she pretended to complain about the early morning noise of the babies. LuDell almost instantly appeared from the kitchen to help Mrs. Clara Ruth into her comfortable chair in the meeting room near the fire. She then darted back to fetch the silver tea service tray ready and waiting in the butler's pantry. Once in her chair and covered with her favorite blanket, she took a sip or two from the tea cup in her hand.

"With a grin painted across her entire face, LuDell placed gently placed a pretty red present tied up with a green bow in her lap. Trip had put LuDell in charge of giving Clara Ruth the gift they all knew would capture her heart. The aged matriarch smiled with anticipation after pulling the knot that held the ribbon around the package. Opening the paper wrapping, she carefully removed a 3" x 6" picture from its soft covering. Overcome with emotion, she sat staring at the picture with tears forming in her eyes. She had immediately recognized Lil' Sully and her heart skipped a beat. This tough, overbearing, strict woman held the picture of her husband to her heart and said, 'Dear God, my husband, my hero, my love.' and started uncontrollably sobbing.

"She was holding a photograph taken at the Battle of 1st Manassas by a photographer working from one of Mathew Brady's rolling darkrooms on the battlefield. He had slipped behind the Rebel lines and had taken only 5 photographs before he was killed. As the Confederate Army began to take the field and the Union troops were retreating, a bullet entered his ear and ended his life. Having set up his camera just before the main conflict, his attention was captured by a majestic Confederate officer, astride his horse with sword in hand. He quickly took a picture of that Colonel and as he started to move his camera, he was killed. The photography wagon and all of his equipment was left on the battle field. Trip did not know it existed until Robert Smith, a photographer and fellow POW at the Johnson Island Prison sent Trip a letter telling of its existence. Having made his own camera from scavenged parts while in prison, Smith was a consummate picture taker. After the war, Smith attended a reunion of former Confederate officers and was approached by the former Confederate officer who had found the camera equipment and carefully hidden it away after the battle. Needing money, as did most ex-Confederates, the officer who found the camera equipment offered to sell everything to Mr. Smith for a Yankee dollar. He quickly bought the camera and equipment and took it home with him. When he started examining the camera, he found an exposed plate that had been left in the camera. Developing the photograph, he immediately recognized the subject as Colonel James Anthony Sullivan, Jr. and knew it would be of immeasurable value to the Sullivan family. Robert Smith wasted no time in contacting Trip Sullivan.

"Upon hearing of his father's picture, Trip had carried on a clandestine letter writing campaign and fee negotiation to obtain the photograph. For an exorbitant amount of money, Mr. Smith agreed to sell the picture and sent it to Trip without Clara Ruth ever knowing. Sitting comfortably by the fire in her favorite chair, with her faithful LuDell waiting at her side, she looked up as Trip and Lou entered the grand room. Both had a baby in their arms. Continuing to hold the picture close to her bosom, she said, 'I made that sash he is wearing in the picture. I will worship this picture of my brave husband until the day I die.' And that she did.

"Never one to seek vengeance, Trip had compelled his mother to accept some things in her life that he felt might shorten her time on earth. Yielding to his demands, she had given up her secret bank account in England and was permitted to have only a small, family gathering at the re-internment of the Colonel's remains. She had also, begrudgingly, agreed to share a modest tombstone that would mark her and her husband's graves with only each one's name, date of birth and date of death. Trip wondered as they stood at the graveside during the reinternment if her tears were for her husband or for the loss of control over what she considered her farm. Trip's misgivings over the extreme changes he had pressed upon his mother were somewhat placated by giving her the photograph and that made it worth the money he had paid for it.

"As a true believer in the Confederate Cause, Clara Ruth Rutledge Sullivan was a stalwart who had stared General Sherman himself in the eye and spat upon his boots. She did everything she could to bolster and perpetuate among the people of Salleys Kitchen a hatred for the North. She prophesied that one day soon, with the help of God, 'the South would rise again and when we did, the Soldiers of the South would rain death and destruction on those who destroyed their way of life!' But even this most staunch believer had to surrender, as time raced on and her battle for reason began to wane. With hatred seething in her soul and reality fleeting, she slowly became less lucid. Like a dying ember, she flamed sane rarely, when the winds of reflection blew gently across the ashes of her yesterdays.

"One blustery November day, Clara Ruth developed a cough and it progressively got worse. After the doctor diagnosed pneumonia, Clara Ruth continued to lose her grip on life. At times, the elderly matriarch would cough to the point of exhaustion. She had a rattling in her chest and as she grew weaker, she became bedridden. Finally, on a cold January day, she passed away with LuDell holding her hand. Both women were mere breaths of the women they were during their heyday.

"Clara Ruth was laid to rest beside her loving husband, Lil' Sully, among the Sullivan family graves. As her son demanded, the couple shared a small tombstone that revealed only their names along with their birth and death dates.

"Within a few days, LuDell died in her sleep. Undoubtedly, she felt her reason for living had ended with the death of her mistress. She unconditionally loved the woman who tore her away from her mother and moved her away from the only home she had ever known. Clara Ruth had owned LuDell like a piece of property that could be disposed of at will. LuDell always replied, when asked about being Clara Ruth's slave, 'Dem dazes his water dats dun passed unner da bri'ge. Wins youz gits free, yous don'ts lookz bak. Mrs. Clara Ruth twas my secon' mama and mos peepels don'ts neber gits buts one. I's still lubs hers wid alls mys hart!'

"LuDell was buried at the foot of Clara Ruth's grave after a private funeral service in the white church she had attended all of her adult life. Though a grown strapping man, Trip held Lou and sobbed unconsolably at LuDell's funeral. He purchased her tombstone and still today its epitaph reads, '*Well done, my good and faithful servant.*'

"Time continued to pass on the Sullivan farm and Lou threw up at the birthday party. Harri was 9 and Abbi was 8 and they were dashing about, excited about the festivities. Birthday parties were a rare occurrence in Salleys Kitchen, even for a family who could afford one. Most adults who had been through the war and Reconstruction weren't about to waste money on such a frivolous thing. Trip, however, said his mother celebrated his and Ruth's birthdays before the war and he wanted to bring that tradition back. Lou was hurrying around trying to get everything set up before Ruth's friend Rebecca, whom she called Becky, arrived.

"Ruth was near forty years old and had never married, but she had a very close relationship with another unmarried lady just about her age, from Camden, SC. She had met her through her friends, the Grimke sisters. They got together as often as possible and seemed sad whenever they had to part. Today's visit, however, was unusual because Ruth's friend was to be an overnight guest and that was a special occasion at the Sullivan mansion. Ruth was determined Becky should have a good time at the girls' party, so everyone was scurrying around making sure things were shipshape. In the hurly-burly, Lou became dizzy and leaned against the coal black slate table in the kitchen. Grabbing her stomach, she dashed for the carved sink and vomited. Ruth looked on and said, 'Uh oh!'

"Still flushed, Lou tried to compose herself and replied, 'Don't be silly. I had my last period…' A silence fell over the huge cookery, then both women screamed, 'OH, LORDY!' in unison. If it were true Lou was 'in the family way' again, this would be the first time during one of her pregnancies she had been sick.

"Ruth ran over and hugged her sister-in-law and put her hand on her stomach. 'It's a boy! I know it's a boy! I've heard boys always make you sick.' Ruth quickly reverted to the little girl ways that she and Lou had shared when they first met. Putting aside her grown-up behavior, Ruth smiled and skipped her way onto the back porch singing in a teasing way, 'I've got a secret and you don't know it.' She knew the birthday girls were playing on the cobblestone area under the arbor and upon hearing the taunt, would demand to know what secret was being kept from them.

"Lou pulled Ruth back into the house and admonished her, 'My Lord! You are a bigger child sometimes than either of the girls! Don't go saying anything until I break the news to your brother. He's sure to take a while to adjust to the possibility of another girl. Let me tell him after I've softened him up a little."

"Ruth grabbed her mouth and let out, 'OOOOOOOu! You sure know what it takes to settle him down. Y'all better not make too much noise tonight!'

"Again, Lou admonished her sister-in-law, 'YOU BETTER HUSH YOUR MOUTH!' Then she smiled and said, 'We're not noisy, anyway.' Laughing and hugging, they suddenly heard the sound of the sugary sand being churned by buggy wheels. As the familiar sound made its way to their ears, they dashed toward the front porch together.

"Becky arrived in Windsor by train and was met by Trip in the family's best buggy. After picking up her trunk, Trip and his sister's visitor traveled back across the South Edisto River to Salleys Kitchen. The excited folks were ready to treat her like an honored guest. Once they pulled up in front of the mansion, Lou and Ruth came clamoring out of the house and hurriedly shuttled down the steps to greet their company. Becky and Trip had talked on the ride home and he found her very amicable, easy to like and just the type person he thought should be Ruth's friend. But she had a masculine way about her. Trip described her 'she looks like a woman but acts much like a man.' But it made no difference to him. If she was Ruth's friend, she would be his friend, also. As she stepped out of the buggy, Ruth enveloped her with a bear hug and kissed her on both cheeks, while everyone else took her hand and added a polite curtsey. When the excited group of women finally moved into the house, Trip led the horse and buggy back to the barn, where he hoped to find someone to help him with the huge trunk. Finding one of the men from the field, Trip shanghaied the unsuspecting worker. Working together, the heavy container was pulled and pushed upstairs to Ruth's room. No sooner than it crossed the threshold of the door, the two friends fell into unloading the treasure chest. The two seemed to be nesting.

Chapter 13

"That evening, after molasses cake and ice tea, the girls were sent up to bed with their presents and their parents retreated to their room for the night. Lou's naked body always set off her husband's passions and it did that night as usual. Trip always told Lou, after a particularly busy session between the sheets, that he was much too old to be trying to satisfy such a younger woman in her prime. With a smile, he said he knew it was going to send him to an early grave one day. This time, as they lay side by side in the fluffy and now tossed old feather bed, the old man, as he called himself, was panting and trying to catch his breath. He was perspiring profusely and panting for air. Wearing a grin from ear to ear, he slid his hand over Lou's naked body. She took his big calloused hand in hers and held it on her bare tummy as she, too, panted. Without having to say a word, 'I love you' was exchanged as each beamed with delight. After the heavy breathing subsided and smooching began, Lou lay back on her pillow and asked Trip the question.

"'Have you ever thought about having another child?'

"Lying on his back beside her, he said, 'I think about it sometimes - having a son, that is. But we're pretty happy, so I've always had the notion that if it was supposed to be, it would happen. I guess it just hasn't happened. He turned his head to face her again and she turned her head to face him. The huge smile painted across her face was a familiar indicator for Trip. He knew she had something to tell him.

"Lou's smile triggered a memory deep in Trip's brain, a recollection of the smile on her face when she told him in church that Abbi was on the way. BINGO! His brain quickly surmised the message and he communicated his understanding with his eyebrows. They shot up on his forehead and his eyes widened to the size of silver dollars.

"'Are you saying what I think you're saying?' She nodded affirmatively and returned a soft, motherly smile to her shocked husband.

"'Your wife is pregnant!' Trip enveloped his wife in a happy hug. He could not believe they had created another little Sullivan. The news made him feel like the luckiest man in the world.

"Having heard the great news, they both lay silent for a while. Lying on his back with his hands behind his head, Trip, as usual, began to crunch the numbers in his head. Reflecting on Lou's announcement, they both looked at the ceiling as the conversation took a long pause. Trip was the first to speak and it was obvious his thoughts included his mortality.

"'I'll be an old man when my son is just becoming a man. I won't get to see him as a mature man with his children.'

"Lou shot back to him, 'That's what you get for waiting so long to take me as your wife!' as she elbowed him and laughed. Then she added, 'Besides - you don't know it's a boy.'

"He quickly shot back, 'It's a boy! I know it's a boy.'

"This pregnancy was to be totally different from the other two. Lou got sick to her stomach often and didn't want to eat very much. Forcing herself to eat created a cycle that always led to regurgitation. Also, with this baby, her back ached and she was unable to get comfortable at night, leaving her sleep pattern altered. Lou was often irritable and this behavior was totally out of character for her. Trip quickly learned to stay busy in the fields. If not in the fields, he hid in blacksmith shop or saddled a horse to ride through the timber on the farm. Ruth and Becky took over most of the house chores and the girls swore they would never have children.

"As it became time for this child to be born, it also became obvious this baby did not want to leave the womb. On pins and needles, the entire farm staff walked carefully as not to raise Lou's hackles and risk facing her wrath. Hence, an odd, dark cloud hung over the farm into the wee hours of Saturday morning. Doctor Worrel was not to be found and the eighty-year-old Doctor Betanbaugh was high as a longleaf pine on Irish whiskey. Trip was forced to choose plan 'C' and stopped by Miner White's house. Miner was the local mid-wife and she hastily grabbed her bag and jumped in the buggy. The buggy ride was an adventure, as Miner held on to buggy with one hand and her little flowered hat with the other. She had taken many buggy rides such as this and was undaunted by the speed. They arrived at the mansion and came to a sudden stop beside the hitching post at the bottom of the steps. As Trip tied the horse up, Miner hurried up the steps and into the huge house.

"Once in the room, the practiced old medicine woman shooed everyone out and counted the contractions. Realizing the intensity and time intervals between each session of pain, she called the daddy into the room and poured a bottle of rubbing alcohol into a waiting dough bowl. Dipping her hands and arms in the cold liquid, she thoroughly coated them and held them up in front of her. She nodded for Trip to do the same. Afterwards, she placed the scissors and two pieces of string into the bowl of disinfectant. Placing a clean, white towel in a waiting pot of boiling water, she let it soak a few seconds, then cautiously pulled the steaming cloth from the scalding water and wrung it dry. Unfolding it, she placed it over her hands and arms, all the while telling Lou how well she was doing and how easy this delivery would be.

"Sweating profusely and writhing in pain, Lou screamed as she wallowed in the bed. As that contraction ended, the veteran baby deliverer told Lou the next contraction would produce her baby. As the next contraction began, Miner placed her towel-covered hands close to Lou's womb and caught the head of the baby as the expectant mother pushed. Carefully inserting her finger, she felt around the neck of the baby and found things to be in order. On the following contraction, the baby's shoulders appeared and Miner said, 'Oh, mama, hit's all downs hill foms hera. Yous dun fine and dis times likely to beez yos lass push. Den yous kin sees yos baby.'

"Right as rain, with the last push, the baby scooted out with the umbilical cord throbbing and attached to the placenta. Swaddling the baby in the warm towel, she placed the newborn on the mommy's now concaved stomach and reached for the string in the bowl. Tying one piece about six inches from where it was attached to the baby and another about six inches further down, she handed Trip the scissors from the bowl of alcohol.

"With an air of finality, Miner told the nervous father just what to do. 'Now cuts dat cawrd and sots dat baby free.' Trip did as he was told and Miner then urged him away from the action and around to Lou's side. As mother and father basked in the glow of the newborn on the mother's abdomen,

Miner continued to her work out of view. After mother was taken care of, she took the baby to a table and carefully un-swaddled him. Checking him from head to toe, she announced, 'Yous twos duns gots y'alls ha fin baby boyz! He look purfet!' She then re-swaddled him in a linen table cloth and handed him back to Trip, saying, 'Gos han shows yo'is wifes you's and her's is new son. She beez ha wait'n to sees dat bo.'

"As the midwife had done hundreds of times before, she tended to Lou while her husband showed the new baby his mama. They counted fingers and toes and checked to see if he really was a boy. Then, ever so gently, the midwife cleaned him up and gave him to mama to suckle. With just a little coaxing he began nursing and Mama and Daddy breathed a sigh of relief. At last, the rest of the family, who had been waiting on pins and needles, was allowed in the room to see the baby and share the excitement with the third-time mom. As Trip was walking Miner back to the buggy, Dr. Worrel came driving hurriedly down the lane and pulled up to a dusty stop. Trip beamed and said, 'Well Doc, you're a day late and a dollar short.'

"The old doc returned the smiled and said, 'You had the most experienced person around to help you. You really didn't need me, but I'll check on her if you want me to.' All three climbed the steps and entered the house. Moving upstairs to Lou's room, the doctor checked on the new mother as Ruth, Becky and the two big sisters stood over the newest member of the family.

"While Miner and Trip waited downstairs for the doctor, they celebrated with a sip of blackberry brandy. When the ole doc returned to the meeting room, a cordial of brandy was placed in his hand. Downing the amber liquid in one gulp, the medicine man said in a loud and boisterous voice, 'Just as I figured, she's in fine shape! She just needs two or three days of rest and things should start returning to normal.' He whispered a few words into Trip's ear and the new father nodded his head in agreement. Promising to return and check on Lou at a later date, the doctor and Miner left the new family in a jubilant mood. The girls were over the moon at having a real live baby to dress and were making plans to spoil him rotten.

"As James Anthony Sullivan, IV, or Jay, as he was dubbed by Becky, grew from baby to boy, it was obvious he was not an outdoors person. The bugs used him for target practice and the sun would turn him red at the drop of a hat. He let it be known early he didn't want to be a farmer. Playing with his toys on the kitchen floor, he never wanted to get dirty. As his age reached double digits, though, Trip had other ideas and put him to work in the fields with the men. He loathed manual labor and dodged it in any way possible. Jay was his mother's only boy and was raised in a houseful of girls. Though both his mother and father tried to introduce him to the great outdoors of the farm, James Anthony Sullivan, IV, liked the finer things in life and usually got them. Petted as a baby, then raised as a coddled toddler, he became the epitome of a spoiled child. Constantly fighting with his sisters and irritating their lives, he was happiest when causing turmoil. Reaching school age, he was picked on often and bullied by the older boys who called him a sissy. It was during his last few years at the one room schoolhouse that he became infatuated with girls. With teenage urgings and hormones raging, Jay Sullivan became an entirely different type of annoying person. Finding the opposite sex quite appealing, he had many adolescent girlfriends, all of whom he led to believe his affections were exclusively theirs. He, however, was never one to limit the pleasure of his company to a single person and the only son of Trip Sullivan greedily enjoyed the benefits of many relationships until the day it all caught up with him. His father and mother continued to work and manage the farm, as Jay worked himself into trouble.

"During the coming decade, many changes would occur as Trip struggled to make a successful living on the farm. He would often have to deal with men of 'unseemly character', those who the locals still referred to as Yankee scum, scalawags, or carpetbaggers. They were the greedy middlemen who took advantage of the downtrodden people of Salleys Kitchen. Using fraud, deception and outright lies, they stole from the good people and always had their unscrupulous and backstabbing hand in the pie. Trip never wanted to associate with the unethical ilk, but out of a necessity to meet his payroll, keep the unreasonable taxes paid and keep food on as many family tables as possible, he was forced to do business with them. Keeping the farm solvent and employing as many members of the community as possible, the liberal-minded planter held his nose and traded with 'the riff-raff.' This infuriated most of the community and caused the old repartee of rumors, lies and innuendo concerning the Sullivan family to resurface. The falsehoods seemed to flow as freely as the water flowing through the huge chasm in the millpond dam.

"Still, Trip continued to help anyone he could and share what he had with his community. Ignoring the abusive words of the reprobates, Trip tried to consider and understand the bitterness brought on by the war and the furthering of that hatred by the Union occupation of the South during Reconstruction. Before he lashed out at those who constantly criticized him, he tried to remember his mother's bitterness and what it had done to her. It did not excuse their hate, but it helped mitigate his loathsome thoughts when their abuse was particularly scathing. Sadly, those who had been taught to revile the Black community and those who exploited and abused the Negro community grew in number. The misguided and ignorant fed on what they had learned from their parents and grandparents. But Trip Sullivan followed his grandfather's footsteps as he struggled to keep the fever of hate as low as possible in Salleys Kitchen. Realistically, he knew it was hopeless to believe that in his lifetime the people of Salleys Kitchen would allow any person of color to have equal status in the community. That was Trip Sullivan's impossible dream and he devoted his life to bringing it to fruition.

"With the farm routine continuing from year to year, the Sullivans gradually created a sustainable life and they lived the lives of average folks in the community. The farm, however, had a large payroll and Trip was always trying to increase the amount he paid his workers in gracious appreciation for what they did in his fields. Growing steadily, the farm was finally solvent and with a regular dependable income, the Sullivan farm became the community's largest employer and a significant part of the economy of the community. There remained, however, a thinly veiled grudge against the Sullivans and the smallest of incidents often fueled new resentment. When Trip began raising hogs, he soaked corn in water and fed them mash. Immediately, rumors began circling that Trip was making moonshine and the local law set upon catching him. They gave up after a couple of months with no leads.

"Trip's goodness kept him at the top of the list of people the vigilantes believed needed to be punished for their actions. Identifying the help and assistance he offered the black community as an effort to mix the races, they tried to vilify him. Well after the turn of the century, the vigilantes stringently enforced the Jim Crow laws with vicious efficiency and continued to spread their fear at night. Groups clad in white robes and armed with shotguns and rifles rained terror on Black owned homes and farms. The dominant white ruling class forced the Black community to yield to their terms and brutally kept them in poverty, uneducated and subservient to their wishes. The bigotry and hatred became traditional as the white people of Salleys Kitchen worshiped in their grand white-only churches and no longer allowed the Blacks to sit in the rear of the sanctuary during services. As the community grew, whites built superior schools and hired well educated white teachers. The Blacks were given the rundown former white schools. Segregating even the waiting rooms at the doctor's offices, the whites assumed complete control and reigned supreme over all elements of Black life.

"As the years became decades, the generation of Southerners that had been knocked to their knees by the brutality of the Civil War and Reconstruction began to die away. The extreme vitriol, however, did not wane as the old-timers spoon-fed their children a legacy of hatred and bigotry. The new generations were taught the ideology of white supremacy as their parents and grandparents proudly taught their children to hate the Black man and those who supported him. Through the years, this ingrained prejudice continued to be passed from one generation to the next until it became the traditional way of Southern life.

"As it has always happened, the grease that helped the wheels of economic growth turn was money. That money came from the North and for that reason, the people of the South were gradually forced to tolerate and coldly interact with the people of the North. The war had preserved the Union and the populations of the South had to accept that fate. Once again, the people of the South sent their representatives to the Union capitol and they began participating in the governing of the nation. Through fear and intimidation, the white ruling class in the South, once again, won political control in the former states of the Confederacy. That ruling white majority arrogantly chose to continue its oppressive reign as they forced the people of color in the South, to live as second-class citizens. This culture of inequality became an integral part of Southern society and Southern politicians quickly recognized that racial hatred was a handy tool. They used the tools of prejudice and bigotry to promote themselves and continue their grip on the reins of power. It became normal for politicians seeking higher office to whip the less-educated Southern whites into a frenzy with race baiting and bigoted rhetoric. In the post war South, the sure-fire way to rally support for your candidacy was to lynch a few Blacks and demand the other Negros humble themselves in the presence of white people. This brutal political tactic was always successful.

"Originally produced from a primal fear of having to compete with the Black community for survival during reconstruction, the hatred of Blacks by lower class Southern whites grew to a fevered pitch. Having lost everything, the people of the post-war South had to fight with animal-like instinct to remain alive. They realized only the strongest would survive and therefore, survival took precedence over education. The resulting ignorance brought on a primordial instinct of brutal dominance. This ideology grew like cotton in bottom land during Reconstruction and that despicable stain was ironed into the fabric of Southern life. In the fertile seedbed of the South, the foundations of hate were fertilized, cultivated and perpetuated.

"Trip knew this way of thinking had to change for his beloved community to grow. His personal campaign against hatred and evil continued, but as the ebb and flow of this generational battle waged, evil began to dominate the battlefield of Salleys Kitchen.

***

Sully looked to his daughter with sad, tired eyes and faintly said, "Please, stop the recorder, sweetheart."

Salley stopped the recorder and moved the table away from the platform that held her father's head. She could hear a lingering rattle in Sully's breathing and she wanted to call Dr. Baughman, but it was after 11 PM and the weather was rumbling in the west. She decided to wait until the morning to call Sully's doctor. After leaving her father for a few minutes to put on her pajamas, she came back to kiss Sully good night. He began to talk to her in a low, strained voice. "Sweetheart, might I impose upon my most beautiful and benevolent daughter for one last favor?"

Sully's daughter smiled as she rubbed her hand across her father's unruly hair. "You may ask for anything, Daddy. You must know by now I love you with all my heart and I will try my best to obtain whatever you desire."

Smiling, Sully said, "I would like to record a few more words before they are lost to the fleeting winds of time. Would you start the recorder for just a few minutes?"

Dutifully, Salley moved the table on which the recorder sat to within inches of Sully's head and pressed the button to start it. Holding the microphone just a few inches from Sully's lips, he began to speak in a labored and weak voice.

***

"On the battlefield of Salleys Kitchen, my grandfather, Trip, fought against wickedness. He valiantly did everything he could to right the wrong his mother and father brought upon his community. No man could have tried harder or sacrificed more, but in the end, he was overwhelmed by evil.

"The Sullivan children my Grandfather Trip and my Grandma Lou produced were raised among that vileness. They chose to run away from the evil and never return. As I am doing for you, my Grandma Lou told me everything about my family. For some unknown reason, I could not run away from the evil that had taken over the community my great-great-grandfather founded. I was determined to take the torch passed to me and make Salleys Kitchen a better place, but my weakness and lack of self-control caused me to fail miserably. I, too, have let evil win the day. Salleys Kitchen has once again fallen into the hands of the evildoers.

"James, grew up in and around those evil people and was trying to get away, but like a fool, I brought you to live in that wicked locale. I should have never allowed you near such a cursed place. But you would have never met James and you would have never known the exhilaration and excitement of first love and we would have never known the love we have for Ruth. In one of his poems, the poet Tennyson once asked, 'Is it better to have loved and lost than to have never loved at all?' You alone will have to answer that question, Sweetheart. I would never pretend to know how much you have sacrificed for me and I could never know the depths of love you have for James. I pray you will forgive me, sweetheart. I was a frail and weak man who knew well the evil that had been growing in Salleys Kitchen for centuries. I did not protect you from that onslaught."

Sobbing, Salley told her father he was wrong. He had done more than any other man in Salleys Kitchen to stop the wickedness, but no man could have stopped such horrible people alone. Through tears she told him, "Daddy, I'm prouder of you than any man in the world. You will always be the hero of Salleys Kitchen to me and I am happy to proclaim to the world that James Anthony Sullivan, V is my father and I love him with all of my heart."

By now both father and daughter were sobbing as Salley gently caressed her father's cheek. After wiping her eyes and Sully's face, she kissed him and told him to sleep well, for the morning would come soon and the people who loved him would want to be with him. He said, "Good night, Salley, I love you more than anything in the world." Salley blew him a kiss as she headed to bed.

Salley found Sully dead the next morning when she came into the sun room. The machine was pumping and hissing and everything seemed fine, but Sully did not tell her good morning as he usually did. This reminded Salley she needed to call Dr. Baughman and get him to come check the rattling in Sully's chest. At first, she thought he was asleep, but when she touched his face, he was cold. In a panic, she called the doctor and he was there in minutes, but it was too late.

Sully had died in his sleep. All the doctor could do was hold Salley and try to comfort her as she began to deal with the trauma of losing her father. The house staff took the children to their rooms and Salley walked out to the barn to be with Spot while they took Sully's body away. She felt as if a cold veil of loneliness had engulfed her entire being. Though she was standing in the sun, she trembled as if she was freezing. Spot seemed to understand as he bowed his head and let Salley hold on to him. Dr. Baughman walked out to the barn and asked if she wanted him to call and let the rest of the family know what had happened. She told her father's friend and doctor she would let the rest of Sully's family know of his death. As an after-thought she asked the good doctor not to tell Jon Chesterfield, Jr. or his father of Sully's death. She told him she would handle telling them. Salley called her mother and brothers that night and they arrived the next day at lunch. As she had assumed, all they wanted to talk about was settling Sully's estate. After the family's trip to the funeral home to choose Sully's coffin and finalize the funeral arrangements, they came back to the Chesterfield estate and Salley took Wesley and Ruth for a long walk. Ending their walk at the fence around Spot's paddock, Salley tried to explain to Ruth that Papa had gone to heaven, but the post-toddler acted as if she didn't hear anything Salley said. In the somber silence, Ruth looked at Salley wearing a huge smile. She said, "Papa gone - Preposterous!".

Salley held both of her children close to her heart and repeated her daughter's words, "Papa gone - Preposterous - indeed!"

Sully was buried in the church cemetery at Salleys Kitchen near three of the other James Anthony Sullivans who had gone before him. Jay Sullivan was not buried with his ancestors. Sully's body was not taken in the church and only graveside rites were offered. The pastor was told not to elaborate or make a long talk and as soon as he stopped talking, Ruth stood up and boldly pronounced each word Sully had taught her. "PREPOSTEROUS! TREMENDOUS! GARGANTUAN! MAGNIFICENT! ASTRONOMICAL! INCONCEIVABLE!"

The family rode back to the Chesterfield mansion in the funeral home limousine. Though Salley had called Kellah and Jon, Jr., none of the Chesterfields had attended Sully's funeral, but when Salley stepped out of the funeral car at the mansion, the first person to greet her was Kellah Chesterfield. She wrapped her arms around Salley and held her for a long time.

When they walked back inside, Kellah stood facing Salley and held her head in her hands. Looking straight into her beautiful blue eyes, she earnestly implored, "Salley, please come back to Hawaii with me! This house is not where you need to be!" Without any thought or a minute's hesitation, Salley hugged her and said she would love to spend some time on her island.

Everything was packed that night and under the protest of her mother and brothers, Salley, Ruth and Little Wesley followed Mimi, as Kellah was now called by Ruth, aboard her private jet and they left the Aiken airport well before lunch. There was a stop in Denver and another in San Francisco for fuel before the last leg to Hawaii. Mimi had to take the kids for ice cream in Denver. Then in San Francisco, as the plane was being readied for its flight over the Pacific, she had pizza, soda and ice cream catered at the airplane hangar. After eating, Mimi found an old soccer ball and began to teach Ruth how to play soccer. Along with some of the employees at the hanger, they played soccer, they screamed and yelled and ran until they were breathless. Completely exhausted, Ruth crawled up into Mimi's lap and they both fell asleep as soon as the wheels were up on the little jet. They landed on a private landing strip where a brightly colored Jeep and a van were waiting to transport them to Mimi's island estate. As they climbed into the Jeep, Salley had to ask, "Where ever, did you find this Jeep?' As she started the engine of the four by four, she said, "I stole it from your husband." Then with a smile she said, "I was hoping you recognized it. I was watching through a window at the house in Aiken the first time you rode in it. I hope it brings back good memories." Salley was speechless as she thought through the years - back to the day she and James took Spot to see the vet. Kellah was right, it did bring back good memories – of James and Spot.

Suddenly Salley remembered Spot. "Oh my God, I didn't make any arrangements for Spot. He'll be crazy without me and there's no telling what Jon, Jr. might do to him. I've got to call Dr. Carr or someone and tell them to go get him until I can get back!

As always, Kellah seemed undaunted and offered Salley the surprise of her life. "Before we left, I made arrangements with a company that moves expensive race horses from place to place around the world. They are professionals and are experts in handling temperamental horses. Spot will be here day after tomorrow and you will be riding him on the beach real soon. I knew you could not leave him so I took the initiative to arrange everything. I hope that's okay with you, Salley. I knew you needed him and I wanted you to have him near you while you were here.

Salley hugged Kellah's neck and said, "You rich people never cease to amaze me. Money might not buy love, but it seems to buy everything else!"

Kellah smiled and said, "It's nothing but paper you have to manage until you spend it – then it turns into something that makes you smile!"

As they entered Kellah's palatial island home, they were informed that Salley had received several urgent calls from her mother and brothers. Holding Little Wesley in her arms, their host just smiled and told Salley not to worry because she knew the exact reason they were calling and there would be plenty of time to get in touch with them later. When Salley asked how she knew what they wanted, Mimi sat Little Wesley down in front of a bunch of brand new toys and put her arm around Salley as she spoke. "When your father and I were talking, we found out we had the same lawyer. He's from Aiken and has handled my legal affairs there for years. I think he went to school with your father - anyway, they had known each other for a long time. I'm sure my lawyer is the one who gave your family my phone number, but I'll forgive him for that little faux pas. While your father and I were talking, as if he wanted me to know for some reason, he told me he had left his wife and sons $100,000 each in his will. He told me the rest of his assets, which he believed were worth a little over $5,000,000, including his stocks and bonds along with his family farm, were, left to you. So, sweetheart, you and I both know what they want to talk about! There will be plenty of time for that later. You relax and think about how much your father loved you and feel blessed to have been his daughter." When she finished talking, she pulled Salley's face close to hers and with the greatest of ease, kissed Sally on her cheek. She then picked up Little Wesley as he held onto a toy truck and walked into the kitchen. Ruth was demanding Mimi fix her a peanut butter and jelly sandwich.

The traveling party had arrived just before sunset and while Mimi was entertaining her grandkids, Salley walked out onto Kellah's magnificent deck overlooking the Pacific Ocean. As the waves crashed on the beach below and the western horizon blazed into a multicolored mosaic, Salley stood in awe, watching the unbelievable scene in front of her. It was at that moment she felt Sully's presence. His familiar aura and warmth engulfed her once again. Then from the kitchen across the house, she heard Ruth describing the sandwich Mimi had made for her, "MAGNIFICENT!" For the first time in days, Salley laughed out loud as she watched the sun ease down and kiss the ocean.

With tears in her eyes, Salley stared at the beautiful sunset as she heard her father roaring with laughter. He was with her and she told him, "Sully, you will never leave my heart, you crazy old fool - I will love you until the end of the world!

James Anthony Sullivan Family Tree

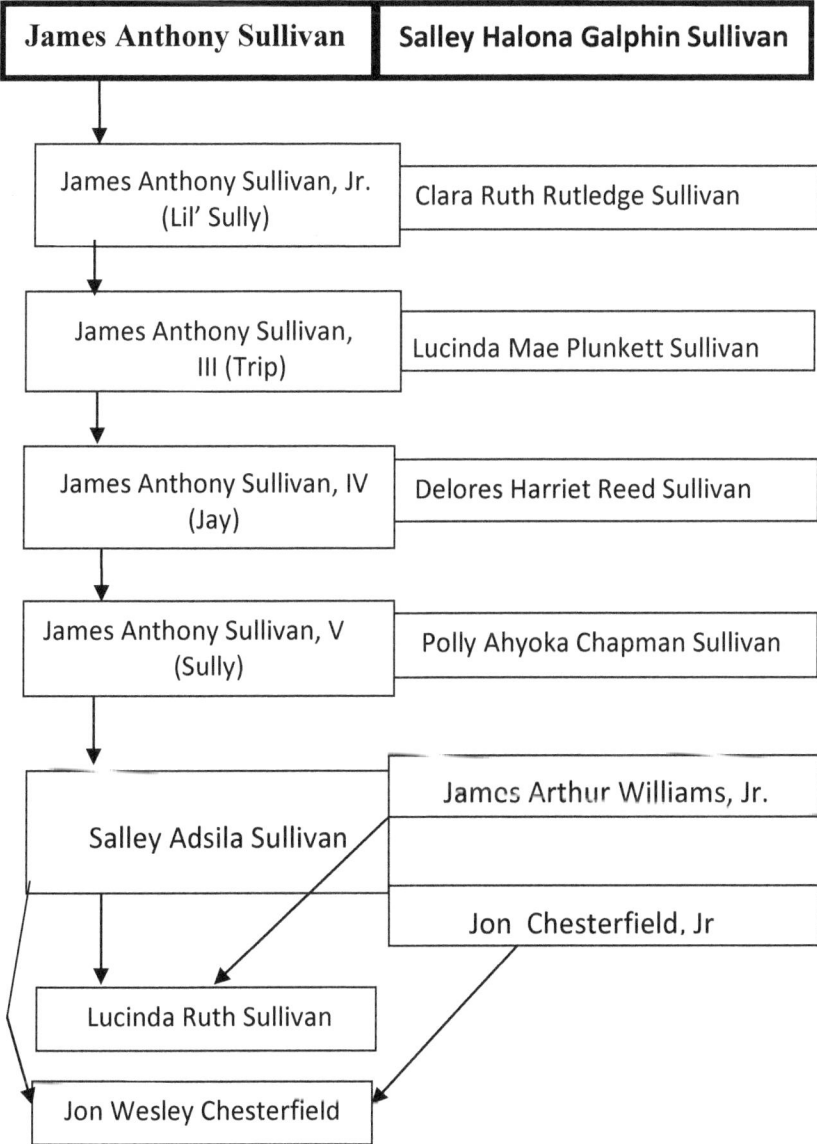

James Anthony Sullivan	Salley Halona Galphin Sullivan

James Anthony Sullivan, Jr. (Lil' Sully)	Clara Ruth Rutledge Sullivan

James Anthony Sullivan, III (Trip)	Lucinda Mae Plunkett Sullivan

James Anthony Sullivan, IV (Jay)	Delores Harriet Reed Sullivan

James Anthony Sullivan, V (Sully)	Polly Ahyoka Chapman Sullivan

Salley Adsila Sullivan	James Arthur Williams, Jr.
	Jon Chesterfield, Jr

Lucinda Ruth Sullivan

Jon Wesley Chesterfield

ABOUT THE AUTHOR

Bruce Weeks was born in 1954, the year of the Supreme Court Decision, Brown vs Board of Education and reared in the sand hills region of western South Carolina. Growing up on his father's cotton farm in the community of Kitchings Mill in eastern Aiken County, he entered the cotton fields at an early age and worked alongside the African Americans that toiled in his father's fields. Attending Salley Elementary School, then Wagener- Salley High School, he left the area in 1972 to attend Clemson University. In 1976, he began working in research for Clemson University. In 1993, he went back to college at age 40 and received a Bachelor of Science Degree in Elementary Education. After 5 years in the elementary classroom, he became certified as 'Highly Qualified' in secondary History and taught in high school and middle school until his retirement in 2012. An avid fan of the Appalachian Trail, he has section hiked the trail from Springer Mountain, Georgia to Damascus, Virginia. He is now working on a hiker rest area near the trail and his cabin in the mountains of Virginia. A resident of Townville, SC, he and his wife, Jan, also a retired school teacher, have lived there for over 40 years. They have two children, four grandchildren and two Boykin Spaniels that they spoil as much as possible. When not writing, Mr. Weeks works on an extended list of honey-dos.

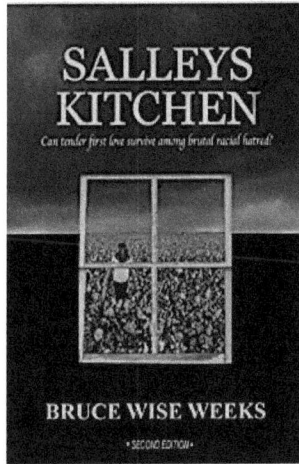

You may purchase a copy of Mr. Weeks' first
novel, Salleys Kitchen,
by going to the website

http://www.salleyskitchen.com

and
you may contact Mr. Weeks by email at

bruceweeks@salleyskitchen.com

www.ingramcontent.com/pod-product-compliance
Lightning Source LLC
Chambersburg PA
CBHW071404090426
42737CB00011B/1349